# AMERICA SET FREE

WORKS OF

## *Count Hermann Keyserling*

---

CREATIVE UNDERSTANDING

THE RECOVERY OF TRUTH

THE TRAVEL DIARY OF A PHILOSOPHER

EUROPE

THE WORLD IN THE MAKING

THE BOOK OF MARRIAGE
(*A Symposium*)

❦

MENSCHEN ALS SINNBILDER
(*Symbolic Figures*)

PHILOSOPHIE ALS KUNST
(*Philosophy as an Art*)

UNSTERBLICHKEIT
(*Immortality*)

DAS GEFUEGE DER WELT
(*The Structure of the Universe*)

POLITIK, WIRTSCHAFT, WEISHEIT
(*Politics, Economics, and Wisdom*)

DAS OKKULTE
(*The Occult*) (*in collaboration with Count Hardenberg and Dr. Happich*)

❦

*A number of the above-mentioned works have been translated into French, Spanish, Hungarian, Swedish, Dutch, and Czech*

*Count Hermann Keyserling*

# AMERICA SET FREE

BY THE AUTHOR OF "THE TRAVEL DIARY OF A PHILOSOPHER," "EUROPE," ETC.

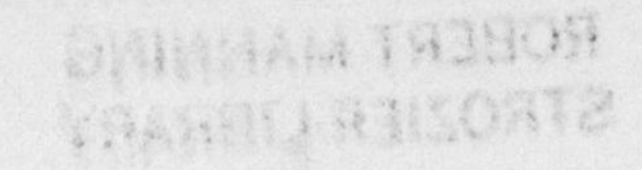

HARPER & BROTHERS PUBLISHERS
NEW YORK AND LONDON
MCMXXIX

*

I-D
*FIRST EDITION*


PRINTED IN THE UNITED STATES OF AMERICA

# Contents



*Part First*

## THE AMERICAN SCENE

*Part Second*

## AMERICAN PROBLEMS

## *Introduction*

WHEREVER there has been a question of essentials, all creative spirits of all times have acted according to the principle of Lao-tse: "Act without quarrelling"—whether, as founders of religions, they demanded faith, or, as statesmen and military leaders, they required obedience or, as poets or sages, they calmly gave utterance to their knowledge untroubled by the opinions and objections of the world. The reason why it had to be thus is today scientifically comprehended: all creative effect is based upon suggestion, and this can work only where the consciousness lays itself completely open to an influence. This is true in exactly the same sense whether it be a question of physical procreation or of the transformation of the soul by words and deeds. Technically speaking, it amounts to the same whether the sage requires of his disciple that he meditate upon a given phrase—that is to say, that he should *not* think about it but let himself be inwardly affected by the phrase until he is possessed by it; or whether a keen judge of human nature casually lets fall the idea which is to him most important because he knows that it thus calls forth the least resistance and is, therefore, most convincing; or whether, on the contrary, the dictator paralyzes all counter-initiative by striking terror into the breasts of his opponents. This, then, is the reason why all creative spirits have been enemies of discussion, or why, if they did consent to use it, they aimed at something entirely different from what their enemies meant—they considered discussion as a safety-valve (parliament and the press as viewed by Bismarck), or as a means to tire out their adversaries and thereby to clear the way for suggestive influence (the method of Buddha). Indeed, no child has ever been engendered by mutual concessions and compromise. And something analogous is the aim of all creation.

Now there is no doubt that the typical aversion of all creative spirits does not solve the problem of discussion, taken in the widest sense of the word, from war down to simple debate. Otherwise, the aversion to the latter would be the rule and not the exception, at any rate, not an exception generally understood and always unfavourably looked upon by the majority. On the contrary, the latter has always held that argument is productive. And in spite of the many cases in which it obviously has had bad results—public opinion clings to the prejudice in favour of it. Therefore, this prejudice must somehow be founded on experience. The fact is—however astonishing this may sound—that there is no fundamental antagonism between public opinion and the statement at the beginning of this introduction. *Discussion is productive to the extent—but only to the extent—that it brings forth the same results as suggestion in the cases we considered first;* that is to say, in so far as *something new* originates from the discussion.

And this, discussion really can effect. Here lies one of the justifications of war, which is the original form of all debate. Superficially considered, it seems difficult to understand how a war which does not end with the literal destruction of one of the adversaries can fulfil its meaning. As a matter of fact, only those wars which remained undecided from the material point of view of the soldier have proved to be productive and, therefore, meaningful; for this reason, too, one of the fundamental laws of all military ethics has been to honour the foe and to spare the vanquished—other practices have gained ground only in unwarlike nations and times [which is the principal reason why the modern war of extermination is so infamous]. The explanation of this is the following: the real aim of war is not the destruction of the enemy, but a change in the balance of powers, which, again, is only possible for a considerable period of time if the souls of peoples have become transformed. Such transformation is the inevitable result of creative influence. And in this sense *mutual* transformation necessarily takes place, wherever there are strained relations of any duration between human beings on the basis of equality of rights, and where this strained situation leads to a solution of some kind. For, whether they wish it or not, and however much they may consciously keep apart—strained relations of any duration mean as such communion. But that being the case, the connexion in question means a reality superior to the two opponents, which must needs work deeper changes in them the more intense the strain and the longer it lasts. Hence the assimilation of husband and wife in marriage; hence the typical spiritual conquest of the conqueror by the conquered on the plane of accomplishments in which the latter excelled the former, from the hellenization of the Romans and the persianization of the Arabs down to the prussianizing of the Entente Powers as a result of the World War. For in this connexion it signifies the same whether a strained situation bears the signs of love or hate. Both are equally creative and they change places, moreover, without difficulty; were it not so, the reconciliation of two enemies after an honest fight would be a rare exception, and not the general rule.

We have herewith reached the core of the problem of discussion in general: it is *not* the arguing as such which makes discussion productive. On the contrary, arguing is of value in the exact degree that it is the expression of *communion*. For then, and then only, is the tension creative and finds its normal solution in the creation of something new.

AT THIS point we determine the sort of discussion which is wrong: namely, every discussion which is not based upon the spirit of a pre-existing communion. A war in which the adversaries do not consider each other as equal in rights is not war, but organized murder. Hence, the almost entirely negative results of the World War: by most nations it was carried on in the spirit of murderers and robbers. In exactly the same sense, every discussion is absolutely evil when any one of the disputants fails to consider the others' point of view or his opponents as worthy of his respect, but rather assumes the incorrectness of an opinion or a position differing from his own. There are, of course, things which are absolutely wrong; obviously Truth should conquer. But this can reasonably be postulated only on the plane of objective logic—and on this plane it is contrary to sense to argue as man with man, because the opponents involuntarily end by being "personal," whereas here the discussion must be based on objective considerations. For this reason I disapprove of personal argument which aims at objective understanding; and for the same reason scientific congresses, if they are to be something more than a special means of publishing the results of scientific research, are, to my mind, of value only to the extent that a noble kind of social intercourse plays a more important part in them than debate. In the same sense it is absurd to debate after a lecture which has offered new illumination or with a person from whom one wishes to learn: in this case creative influence can work only if the one side surrenders in the feminine receptive manner; for the purely defensive attitude in favour of the personal standpoint, or the attitude of claiming to know more or better what has been said, or even the purely reflective attitude, has the effect of a plane-mirror which totally reflects the incident rays. This much is already true in the field of knowledge. But a discussion aiming at the refutation of the opponent is a foolish and nonsensical undertaking where objective truth *cannot*, in the nature of things, be the last resort. And this is the case wherever one life-unit as such opposes another, because here it is obviously impossible for either to give up his point of view, since that would mean his giving up his life. Among the many grotesque circumstances of the World War, this was surely the most preposterous: that one nation should undertake the task of "refuting" the other. This state of mind could not but engender the monstrous demand for absolute destruction, for by this means a refuted error is done away with; and that there should exist a something beyond "error" was inconceivable to the intellectually blinded masses of those days. The conflict which is still raging as to French "*droit*" and German "*Recht*" is the result of a similar error of judgment: in this case it is simply a question of the conflicting (presupposed) life-necessities of two nations, which are projected onto the plane of juristic theory only in the imagination of the two opponents; and neither can ever admit as valid law or right that which implies its own death-warrant. On the plane on which life is opposed to life, there are only two reasonable ways of discussion: war as the communion of hate or war—*in signo Veneris;* that is, as a game of love.

We are now in a position to define exactly and without danger of being misunderstood in which case alone discussion may be productive in the vital sense. It can be productive then only when the one opponent undertakes no more to "refute" the other, as the man tries to "refute" the woman he has intercourse with, and vice versa; when neither expects to convince the other and when, in spite of this, the argument is not carried on in the spirit of indifference. These three principles of every fruitful discussion imaginable certainly are completely foreign to ninety out of a hundred of all those who expect arguments to signify salvation. They are absolutely valid nevertheless. And they mean something entirely different from the principles professed by the promoters of mutual understanding and compromise: for the aim and the result of the observation of these principles are *not* assimilation of the opponents in their *status quo*, but the origin of something new, thanks to their union—whether both are inwardly transformed, and thus do not continue in their original state, or whether a generation with new ideas and emotions originates from them. Therefore, friendly debate bears fruit only when it is the expression of the same attitude as war, but with the opposite sign. And this means when life measures its strength against another life. The objective result can only follow spontaneously; that is to say, it can only be born out of the womb of the unconscious, as the child is the spontaneous result of love.

From here we perceive clearly which are the style and the technique that alone make a discussion productive. Both opponents must observe the same attitude, the one with regard to the other, as that of the creative spirit, and the other that of the passively receptive, if the former wishes to fecundate and the latter to learn. *Each* must be open to the influence of the other without prejudice and without the armour of reserve. In doing this a person does not give up his "being" any more than the woman who yields to the man; and what he imagines himself to be, and is not in fact, had best melt away as soon as possible. Wherever there have been discussions of this kind the results have been good and productive of good. One great example will be more instructive than a hundred thousand minor ones. In Late Antiquity all the cultured nations opened up their spirits and souls to reciprocal influences. What was the consequence? Neither syncretism nor eclecticism, although these did make their appearance at the beginning; but they soon died out from sheer lack of vitality. The result was *all-embracing Christianity*, in which all that had been theoretically irreconcilable, and in the discussion of which legions of spiritual fighters had bled to death, was united in a living synthesis.

WHY have I set down the foregoing general remarks as an introduction to this book? Because in its essence it is not a book *on* America, but *for* Americans; and because the productive effect it may have depends primarily on my readers' adopting the right sort of attitude from the outset. While I was preparing for my lecture tour in the United States I was asked to name "my subjects." My answer was: "I have none; I am not the representative of some particular philosophical theory, I *am* a philosopher, which means that my consciousness is normally centred in understanding; it is centred there as normally as the consciousness of the *grande amoureuse* is centred in love, or as the consciousness of the painter is centred in his visual powers, or that of the business man in the grasping of the right corelation of material values. Therefore, in principle, it is the same to me what subject I have to deal with. I most certainly am not equal to all problems. Far from it. But if a subject presented to me is at all within my range of vision, I can deal with it as a matter of course, within the limits of my capacities. I feel I can do so because philosophical treatment has nothing whatever to do with the subject-matter: a treatment is philosophical or non-philosophical according to whether the particular angle of vision is that of the philosopher or not. Now I am an improviser by nature; moreover, the only object I have in view when lecturing is to help others. Unless I feel a vital need calling for my assistance—a vital emergency to which I have to rise—I have nothing to say; from my own personal point of view I would much rather remain silent. Therefore, let those who wish to hear me find out for themselves what subject *they* wish me to deal with for their benefit, and let them write to me about it in a suggestive way: then, and then only, shall I be able to give my best—whatever this best may be worth in itself."

Things came to pass as I had anticipated. The most understanding and intelligent questions were put to me. In almost every case I felt a direct contact with the concrete audience I had to address; and accordingly I do not think that I have ever really delivered the same lecture twice over, however frequently the subjects printed in the papers may have been the same. But above all, this way of proceeding brought me into direct touch with the very depth of the American unconscious. Thus it gave to me whatever I was able to receive. And from my own point of view I have certainly received very much more than I have given. I have come face to face with life-problems entirely new to me. I have come to ask questions I should never have asked on my own account. Even while travelling in the United States, I felt that a process of gestation was going on within me. And no sooner was I back in Europe, than I knew that I should presently be able to state in a permanent form what I believe I can give to the Americans in return for the wealth of suggestions they have given me. So I set to work at once. The spiritual children, in the form of chapters which saw the light that way, were all surprises to me: in the subconscious new elaborations had taken place.

The views and conclusions I have come to are, in the first instance, personal and subjective conclusions. The introductory paragraph of the first part of this book will show my readers how few illusions I cherish personally as to my infallibility. But then all the value a man of my kind can have for others resides precisely in his subjectivity and in his uncompromising truthfulness. In the chapter "Universal Tension and World Ascendency" of *The Recovery of Truth* I wrote, with respect to the type of man the School of Wisdom tries to form: "he must produce the effect of eccentricity; for he represents, from the viewpoint of the actual state of things, an element of disturbance. He will annoy continually the majorities, *precisely in so far as he is wise.* The Chinese, who know more about wisdom than any other race, designate the wise by a combination of the ideographs for wind and lightning; wise, with them, is not the serene old man bereft of all his illusions, but he who, like the wind, rushes headlong and irresistibly on his way and cannot be stopped nor laid hold of in any station of his career; who purifies the air in the manner of lightning and strikes, whenever there is need for it." This also explains part of my partiality for provocative expression. It is obviously the first duty of any man who believes he knows better in some respects that he should not conform to the prejudices of others; he would rather be the most hated man in the world than popular. But the chief reason for my stating what I think true without disguising the subjectivity of my convictions is given by the first part of this introduction. I want to contribute my part to America's progress. For that purpose I must do all I can to endow my words with the qualities of what the Greeks called *Logos spermatikos.* I am fundamentally indifferent to the question whether I am correct in all my statements of facts. Most probably on many occasions I am not. And this not only because my information is limited, but chiefly because, in order to act creatively, I had to simplify, to exaggerate, to caricature even, as the case may be; what may appear to many as a lack of information, is very often an intentional artistic form. Nor do I want to convince intellectually: what I aim at in all cases is to start a process of "creative understanding" in my readers. Whether the way to this goal lies through approval or violent attack makes no difference to me. In order to explain my true intention, I may perhaps say something of the effect my book *Europe* has produced on the continent it deals with. Most people are of the opinion that I have treated Switzerland worst of all countries I have considered; and since I know that country very well, I can see myself that many of the judgments passed are one-sided. But my one object was to induce a change. And precisely in this I have succeeded. Nowhere has this book been read so much, comparatively, as in Switzerland; it has provoked no end of discussions and debates. And the result is that within six months after the publication of the book a fairly clean severance seems to have taken effect between those Swiss who stand for a better future and those who are satisfied with everything as it is. I never hoped for anything better. Nor did I ever mind the misunderstandings and the attacks I was exposed to. In order to make finally clear what I mean to an audience a fair proportion of which in all likelihood is not accustomed to consider the possession of enemies as an asset, it is probably best if I give one more quotation from another book of mine. In the preface to the French edition of my *Travel Diary* I wrote: *J'ai souvent répondu à ceux de mes amis que chagrinaient les malentendus dont j'étais l'objet: "Le malentendu est, selon moi, la première incarnation légitime de toute vérité." Il me semble vraiment ridicule, qu'un novateur—si modeste qu'il soit comme tel—se plaigne de n'être pas compris: l'âme étant un organisme vivant, elle ne peut assimiler que ce qui lui convient. Et si un élément étranger est introduit dans son système, il produit des troubles dont l'intensité est directement proportionelle à sa force propre. Dans ce sens, j'ai toujours été reconnaissant envers ceux qui ont bien voulu m'honorer de leurs attaques. Jamais je n'ai cru nécessaire de me défendre: ou bien la drogue que je représente agit, ou bien elle n'agit pas.*

Accordingly, *America Set Free* is anything rather than a book of criticism: it is intended to act creatively. It is primarily not a book *on* America, but *for* Americans. I want to help them to see themselves and their own problems with greater exactness and clarity than they seem to have done so far. To that end I have gone out of my way many a time to restate in a popular form —although I hate repeating myself—recognitions contained in a less easily intelligible setting in other books, in order to make absolutely clear what I think the true American problems are [or should be, as the case may be] precisely from the American standpoint. And for this very reason I have even had the courage to write in English; only a very few passages have been originally written in German and translated into English by the translator of *Creative Understanding*, Frau Theresa Duerr. I am well aware that I do not master that language as a man of letters should. But on the other hand, I *think* in English not only when addressing English-speaking audiences, but even when thinking of them and their problems. And as thoughts cannot really be translated from one language into another, because each nation *thinks* different thoughts, I found it impossible to write *in* German and *for* Americans. I hope my readers will forgive the defects of my style on these grounds.

And now the time has come to link up finally the general remarks at the beginning with the explanatory introduction I had to give my readers about the peculiar character of *America Set Free*. *If* my readers wish to derive real profit from this book—then let them think that they and I are arguing together in the only creative sense outlined in what has been said above. I have entitled the book *America Set Free.* It has in reality turned out to be a kind of psycho-analysis of the United States. I have tried to disentangle America's truth from the untruth, both objective and imagined, and then to show the direction of that possible development which would lead forward and upward in the absolute sense. Accordingly, there really should be no real question as to whether I am objectively right or not; no psycho-analytical interpretation ever was right in this sense: it was true to the extent it endows the analysed subject with new powers. Now, since my one object is to contribute to the creation of a better state of things, and since the only reasonable object my readers can have when paying attention to me should be to derive as much profit as possible from a—possibly undesirable—alien, why should they not conform to my wishes? Let them begin by assuming the receptive and passive attitude, and see what happens. Should the undesired or undesirable happen after all, there will be ample time later on to criticize and eventually to do away with me. But again, why should they not give me a fair chance? It certainly would not be in the American spirit to deny me that.

In conclusion, I wish to tell my readers how I should like this book to be read. For the first time, at any rate, it should be read from beginning to end in the original sequence. It was written thus; only when read this way, can it be fully understood, for every later chapter presupposes the foregoing; only then will the reader find this book productive in the sense it was intended. I begin with the description of the American Scene at large; all particular problems of America are marked and surveyed in what seems to me their true correlation. The second part then takes up these problems one by one, proceeding from the basis, and ending with the highest possibilities of a spiritual life on American soil, as I see them.

*Part First*

# *THE AMERICAN SCENE*

## *The American Scene*

IT WAS not so difficult to discover America for the first time. Successes of the kind Columbus achieved are commonly overrated. The ideas of discovering a new continent, or of devising a new way to reach a known one, are rather obvious ones. Men of adventurous spirit always abound; and, notwithstanding the respect due to a great man, I personally doubt whether Columbus ever had the opportunity, during his whole career, of showing as much pluck as that shown by many an obscure photographer who took a motion picture of a tiger just about to attack him. But it is not this side of the question I intend to examine here. It should have been comparatively easy for Columbus to discover America in the true sense—that is to see it really, to understand it—because he had few prejudices which could obscure his vision; as far as my knowledge goes, he started with only one single prejudice of any moment—that America would prove to be India. And since it was this very prejudice which led him to the discovery of the New World, one cannot fairly pretend that it did him harm. For everyone who subsequently started out to discover America the task became more difficult—and every individual has to re-make for himself all the discoveries ever made, just as every individual starts life anew—for there were always thicker and thicker strata of prejudices, both within the soul of the newcomer and in the souls of the people he visited which had to be pierced through, as it were, in order to get at the real truth. A French thinker who is little known, Jules de Gaultier, has worked out a whole system of philosophy (called *Le Bovarisme,* after Gustave Flaubert's famous novel) on the basis of the idea that it is man's chief characteristic to imagine himself different from what he is; Beaumarchais said: *boire sans soif, et faire l'amour de tout temps, voilà ce qui distingue l'homme de la bête.* Dostoievsky wrote that Man was the one animal which could get accustomed to positively everything. There is truth in all these sayings. But undoubtedly Gaultier has hit the mark. Man *is* the one animal capable of error; he is the one animal endowed with free imagination. The result is that, more often than not, what a man sees is not what stands before him but what he expects to see. And since this applies as much to his own being as to that of others, and to others as much as to himself, what people see and think of one another very often does not correspond with the truth.

It follows that it was obviously easier to discover America for the first time than it has ever been since. The strata of prejudices grow thicker and thicker with every generation. With every generation, more of them sink down into the unconscious, where they are beyond reach of possible correction. Eventually it is the most piercing glance only—only the man endowed with mental X-rays, as it were—who is able to discern the truth in spite of so much accumulated experience. For, speaking generally, information is desirable only *after* you know—never before; understanding alone means true knowledge; and understanding can never be derived from information; which problem I shall treat at length in a later chapter. Mere information is of no value as a means towards understanding not only because no statistics ever account for the single case and because only the knowledge of absolutely all the facts, not only present but also past and future, would reflect a situation as it is, but chiefly because only the right interpretation of facts makes them true. Take a recent example —Katherine Mayo's *Mother India.* This is one of the most unfair books ever written. Yet I personally am convinced not only that most, if not all, of the information it contains is correct, but that even much more information could be collected to support her thesis. The trouble is that that worthy lady did not understand the first word of the underlying meaning of the facts she wrote about. She had looked at India from her own middle-class American prejudices and it is impossible to understand India until one has discarded these.

All this I knew, of course, before setting out for my own discovery of America. I took great care, accordingly, to read as little as possible about that continent before I went. During my travels about the country, I guarded myself with almost old-maidish precaution against information. I looked at none of the obvious sights if I could help it; I asked few questions. I succeeded in meeting none of those men who are called great because they happen to be, as they say in America, on the map. I went out little; I read hardly any papers; I did everything in my power to keep my conscience clear from accidental impressions. I persevered as much as possible in that same purely receptive and inward-bent attitude which in times past resulted in the creation of the *Travel Diary;* I kept in contact almost exclusively with the subconscious side of American life. And as far as I was mentally active, I used exclusively the faculty of intuition—the one faculty which establishes an immediate contact with the wholeness of life. But all the same I am far from sure that I have hit the truth all the time. First of all, I stayed in the United States too long—fully four months. Intuition works instantaneously, and a protracted experience does not improve its processes. The best chapter of *Europe* is, I think, that on Spain, of which country I knew least when I visited it and in which I spent only about a week. What I seem to have understood of China and India, was the result of a still shorter time. So much for this side of the question. But there is that other side to it, that one can never know beforehand whether an insight intuitively gained is true or false. Later experience alone can prove its worth.

Since this book is a book of almost pure intuition, as far as it concerns things seen and not ideas created from within, it is perhaps as well if I outline, along with the advantages, some of the dangers of an intuitive turn of mind; and I cannot do better than dash off a summary sketch of the way in which the American mind works. No nation gives the impression of sounder intelligence than the American nation wherever social or economic issues are concerned—all the more so as her sons and daughters are by both nature and education good psychologists. The American way of life develops, within the frame of normal American activities, a practical knowledge of men as probably no other has done, since the Ottoman Empire passed away; for in ancient Turkey, too, the right men were usually called to responsible positions, and there, too, not on the basis of proved professional ability, but of general human quality. The

American technique of advertising alone, so very superior to the European technique not only in quantity and success but also in subtlety, provides the proof of the high psychological quality of the workings of the American mind. But, on the other hand, one may say—which in another sense is true of the English—that the Americans are not a thinking nation at all; and this quite apart from that lack of essential interest in purely theoretical and abstract issues which is the common characteristic of all primarily practical nations. Whether this be due to the predominantly social quality of American life, or to its leaning on the future rather than on the past, or to its speed, or to all these causes taken together—the leading function of the American mind is not thought but intuition. Indeed, human beings can be judged as living wholes only intuitively. Intuition alone, not reflection, can foresee the future; lack of time also renders reflection futile for practical purposes. This, then, leads to the remarkable result that the average American thinks, if he does think, in headlines; in fact, the technique of headlines, so extraordinarily developed in the American newspaper business, seems to me not a particular phenomenon but an expression among others of the general fact that the American mind works with a kind of mental shorthand. Headlines are crystallizations of intuitions, not of thoughts; to that extent they are sufficient unto themselves and need no development or explanation. They belong on the same plane as Chinese ideograms: but with the difference that the latter are concentrated expressions of a sage's mind, while the former reflect the intuitive quality of the Man in the Street. Now the intuitive faculty leads quickest to the perception of truth, in case it is keen enough to find it. On the other hand, if it misses the truth, there is very little possibility of correction. For intuition acts instantaneously, both in its active and passive moods; and its result appears primarily true or untrue, not according to logical but to psychological standards; for which reason proof or refutation on the plane of reflective thinking is of little value. No proof or denial can annul the vital effect of a good headline. Since the American is always vitally concerned if he is concerned at all, this means that an effect, on whatever line or plane, means a great deal to him. If we apply this general truth to the Man in the Street and remember his education by newspapers (not always of the finest quality), then we come to the conclusion that with this type effect must often mean more than truth; and this state of things must needs develop into some sort of sensationalism. The other conclusion is that this type of man must think in catchwords to an extraordinary degree. Catchwords are always abstractions and hasty generalizations. Accordingly, the man who delights in such cannot help missing as often as not the real purport of a concrete situation, the instantaneous mastery of which is the chief advantage of intuitiveness. Finally, with this type of man any development of thought must become shallow and mechanical.

From these simple considerations it follows that the working of the average American mind has certain inherent defects; and these can be noted in all its typical expressions. The average American does certainly not care as much as most Europeans do about the truth of what he reads, or, if news-writing be his profession, even of what he writes. He has very many prejudices—for catchwords as cheap generalizations always amount to prejudices, and he is exceedingly tenacious of these prejudices; for a headline, if it is a good one, sticks. Finally, his consecutive thinking is seldom interesting. The fact is that the expression of an idea really congenial to him is the headline; there is nothing beyond this short expression; the possible developments do not concern him vitally. This state of things alone explains how American editors can decide, as a matter of course, how many words the treatment of a certain subject may contain and order articles, as it were, by the yard; this would be altogether impossible if the development of the contents of a headline were not to the average American a matter of mere mechanical technique, to be taught and learned mechanically. To any one to whom development of thought is a natural occupation and vital concern this way of article-writing seems nonsensical, an impossibility or a monstrosity. Thus, a mental life almost totally based on intuition has, indeed, its limits, as has every life based on a single faculty. I may mention one more shortcoming due to the same state of things. Thinking in headlines stands the pragmatic test when readers or listeners are of a similar psychological texture. Individual intuition is the most adaptable faculty in the world. But intuition incarnated in the small change of a few types of catchwords cannot be transferred. This is the reason why the American finds it more difficult than the members of most other peoples to change his business methods to suit new national environments; he is always a missionary, no matter whether as a preacher, a salesman, or a headlining newspaper-writer. For this reason he so often fails to understand ways of living or thinking different from his own. This is one of the most interesting phenomena I have ever come across: a nation essentially intuitive appears, at the same time, intrinsically unadaptable.

Being essentially intuitive myself, I am undoubtedly prone to sin to some extent in the American manner. In particular, I undoubtedly have a bent for sweeping generalizations. I guard as best I can against the defects of the workings of my mind inherent in its intuitive quality; but I think it wise to guard my readers too. Not because of so-called humility (I have no inclination for conscious lying of any kind) but because of the following reason: if my readers do *not* read me in a blindly believing mood, but simply use my mind as a magnifying glass, as it were, which may undoubtedly at times distort the right perspectives—then they will benefit by my observations in any case, whether I be right or wrong; they will then start thinking for themselves. My readers will then perhaps find out *why* I made certain mistakes, and the cause of Truth will triumph in spite of my errors. This result is almost certain to be achieved if they keep in mind during the time they honour me with their attention the chief argument of the introduction to this book, *viz.*, that a man or woman can derive profit from the thoughts of another only if he or she does not listen or read as a mere preliminary to discussion or debate, but in the attitude of receptivity towards a stimulant which may prove creative.

This much should suffice as a prelude to this chapter. I am now simply going to state what I have seen and felt. I will develop my personal vision of the American

Scene—whatever may have been seen and thought about it by others.

FIRST of all—what is the American Scene? It is not the landscape. It is not what educationalists glibly talk about as "surroundings." The scene presented by any inhabited continent is the result of the interaction between nature and man.

This result bears more or less clearly the stamp either of man, or of nature, as the case may be. In Japan and in Holland man is the decisive factor; but for him, even the physical landscape, as it presents itself today, would not exist. Holland is essentially a land claimed by man for his own purposes. As to Japan, the understanding of nature of its inhabitants is so inordinately great, that they have subjugated their surroundings æsthetically; in the same way as a single patch of colour can determine and change the meaning of a picture, the Japanese, by deliberately inserting his particular existence into surrounding nature has transferred the keynote of the latter completely into himself. As opposed to this, inanimate nature predominates in Switzerland; it has, in the long run, created a type of man unto its own stony image. The same applies, *mutatis mutandis,* to most types of fishermen and seafarers all over the world; indeed, the man or nation has yet to be born the spirit and soul of which would be powerful enough to put its stamp upon the sea. And the same applies in the highest degree to Africa. It is not because Africa is, on the whole, a desert-country; it is not because there our earth appears more like a star among other stars, revolving in the cosmic void, without life's playing any appreciable part in it, that in Africa the emphasis in the picture is placed on nature and not on man; it is because human life *has* played the predominant part there on the planes of spirit and soul for thousands of years; only it has become participant of the austere grandeur of the stellar character of the African landscape, a fact to which the great religious men born on African soil bear witness. The resulting equilibrium between man and nature depends in principle on the balance of the forces in play. If nature is all-too-powerful, then man can play no conspicuous part in it. On the other hand, the more man is gifted or developed, the more he must predominate. Hence it should follow that all countries long enough inhabited by modern technical man should be essentially man's domain; the more nature is conquered, the more the atmosphere should breathe man's spirit; and this implies, that of all continents the North American should appear as the most humanized. But this is not the case. When travelling in the Yosemite Valley in 1912 I wrote: "I find it excessively difficult to lead a mental existence; I succeed only with an enormous effort in concentrating my mind upon the problems of Eternity; the magnificence of Nature round about me hardly finds an echo in my soul." I experienced exactly the same thing in 1928, throughout the territory of the United States, whenever I opened the gates of my soul and mind to influences of environment. And when I then recalled my African experiences, I knew the reason: America does not impress one as humanized, not only because the primeval forces of nature are overpowering—were it only for them, America might be a second Africa. America really impresses one as the greatest possible contrast to Africa. *And this is so, because it has as yet no soul,* which the latter possesses to so high a degree. No gods have as yet been born out of its marriage with man. There was, of course, Manitou, and his ghost still hovers, here and there, over the prairie; but because of the weakness of the Indians, as compared with the land they inhabited, he was never strong enough to become the soul of the continent, as Osiris and Allah and Jahve did on theirs. Externally, man does predominate in America, which he does not in Africa. But he predominates only as a physical being. He has not conquered nature psychically—whether in the sense of the Japanese, as described above, or in the sense of the Hindus, in whose eyes nature is but a veil covering spiritual essence much in the same way as women use veils in order to look all the more alluring, or in the sense of the Greeks, to whom nature was the adequate expression of their inward world of myths.

This seems to me the primary outstanding fact of the American Scene. Now one may say the psychic atmospheres of India, Greece and Japan, as we know them today, surely were not in existence in those early days when the respective countries had just been invaded by their present rulers; the human soul needs time to conquer matter. This certainly is so. But then we have to deal with present-day America. And for the present, America presents a spectacle which is truly extraordinary in these days of planetary maturity, namely that man predominates exclusively as a physical being, very much as the Saurians did in their day. This, then, makes one realize all at once the fundamental significance of that mysterious entity called psychic atmosphere which is experienced in the same general sense by all who possess the organs necessary for its perception. I shall state the facts here as they are, without further explanations, which may be found in other books of mine. Man is, in the first place, a psychic being; his direct experiences are of a psychic, not of a physical nature. Moreover, the subconscious of all men is interconnected, independently of all conscious realization of the fact, so that the background of the thoughts and emotions of each individual is simultaneously the background of those living around him; this accounts for at least forty per cent of the likeness between parents and children, usually attributed to heredity, as it certainly accounts for ninety per cent of all national like-mindedness or of the similarity of contemporaries belonging to the same sphere of civilization, independent of nationality. Under these circumstances, this background belonging to the collective unconscious must grow in importance, as a force among other forces, in proportion to the quantity and quality of the psychic forces in play on the one hand, and, on the other, the length of time these forces act. This explains why the atmosphere of Europe is essentially intellectual and stimulating to thought, whereas that of Northern Africa is spiritual in spite of nature's predominance. As opposed to this, the psychic atmosphere of America bears a likeness to that of Russia and Northern Asia. The reason is that in all three cases the background of thoughts and emotions which stands out behind the individual native of the country is a very small item as compared with the physical forces in play. This explains why both in Russia and in America, as opposed to cultured Europe, alcohol is used not to stimulate, but to numb: only a few have original thoughts or even emotions; and to become unconscious seems indeed the simplest device to overcome a feeling of inward emptiness. This also explains why both in Russia and in

America, as well as in Central Asia, every original psychic activity produces the impression of not only reckless but inordinate energy: it is working in a vacuum, as it were, which must needs create the feeling of *horror vacui.* The psychology of a Genghis Khan, who swept over the world like a tornado, of a Peter the Great, or a Lenin, who dictated their personal will to millions of men, or of an American Trust magnate who thinks "godless" any nation which does not buy its oil from him or who deems it the only possible thing from all points of view—the moral point of view in particular—that everybody should use only the type of motor car manufactured by him, is in this respect essentially the same. But the same considerations also go far to explain that "soullessness" of which practically all foreigners complain as being characteristic of the American. At first sight this seems strange, for the first settlers were probably no less endowed emotionally than any representatives of the European stocks they sprang from and the same applies to most of the later immigrants. But only a few moments of clear thinking on the basis of a sound knowledge of human nature make one understand that it cannot be otherwise: what one may call American "soullessness" is due, in the first instance, to the fact that America is as yet a *colony,* and that a really native civilization has up to now not been developed.

We have reached herewith a very important point. What may be said of present-day Americans might no doubt have been said of all colonials of all times and all places, as long as they remained colonials in their psychological adjustment. Here I can speak from a point of vantage, because I myself belong to an originally colonial stock. The Balts, a German-speaking race, the founders of which settled in the territories today called Esthonia and Latvia in the period dating from 1200-1500, remained colonials at heart because they saw their essence in their Germanism and refused to form a new nation with the other inhabitants of the country. They have, of course, become natives all the same, and are today—as I have shown in the chapter of *Europe* which deals with them—more akin in many respects to the Esthonians and Latvians than to the Germans of Germany; in many respects they are superior to the latter. But they are lacking in soul, as compared with these, in exactly the same sense, though to a minor degree, as the Americans seem when compared with Europeans. That is, they lack fine and differentiated emotions. What they appraise as such, is usually nothing more than sentimentalism; and sentimentalism always denotes a crude and undeveloped state of the emotional sphere. The explanation is to be found in what follows. Whatever the precise reasons may be—we are not yet sufficiently advanced in psychology to account for it with satisfactory exactitude—experience proves that when a people changes its abode, it takes along with it, roughly speaking, its body, but not its soul; the only exceptions we know are provided by the colonies of the ancient Greek type, which broke away from their mother-cities very much as swarming bees leave their hive; that is to say, they settled in foreign lands as fully organized bodies, taking with them everything, beginning with their gods. The Jews likewise essentially belong to this type. In the case of all other emigrants it appears that tradition, in the sense of a vital background represented by a continuous collective Unconscious, falls away after a few generations; it may continue in the Conscious or in some secluded layer of the Unconscious in the form of what psycho-analysts call complexes and repressions—but if it lives only there and thus, it has no creative power in the constructive sense; all really vital psychic forces emanate from an unbroken and well-organized Unconscious. On the other hand, whenever a new vital tradition sprang up, it was a local tradition. Now as far as I can see, these facts allow of only one rational interpretation: *that the sphere of the emotions and feelings*—I speak here, *nota bene*, of the emotions belonging to the empirical as distinguished from the metaphysical plane of spiritual experience—*is closely linked to the earth.* From this recognition it follows *a priori*, that whoever emigrates for good from his native country, by that very fact renounces racially, not individually speaking, his soul. And this can only lead, as time goes on, to complete soullessness, just as long as a new soul has not been born from a new communion with Mother Earth. This is what we witness today in the United States; but it could no doubt be observed everywhere, wherever a colonial soul has long survived as such. The Teutonic invaders of Italy and Gaul certainly were soulless for a long period during the interval between the time of the dwindling of their original tribal memories and the time when the real spirits of Italy and Gaul pervaded them; if the antique world saw in the "Nordics" of those days pure barbarians—whilst, on the other hand, Tacitus, that most Roman of Roman writers, wrote his eulogy of native Germanic life—it certainly was because they had as much reason to call them soulless as Europeans have when applying that epithet to Americans. And here I may enter at once upon one aspect of the negro Problem. Why is it that the coloured man seems to wield such a disproportionately enormous influence in the United States in the field of emotional life? It is due to the fact that the coloured man alone of all settlers surrendered himself immediately to the spirit of the New Earth. He was not in the material position merely to exploit it, as the white settlers were; nor could he live an intellectual life independent of the earth, because of his lack of mental endowment; thus he came to be the one peasant-type among the settlers. Owing to this fact, the negro was able to develop an authentic soul and, being very highly gifted emotionally, he was even able to develop a very powerful soul. In the similar region of the white American's subconscious there was and still is a comparative void. The black soul accordingly invaded and continues to invade it, as a gas pours into a vacuum with tremendous force.

THE aforesaid should suffice to account for the comparative lack of a psychic atmosphere in the American Scene. And the same should explain why the North American continent—of all continents the one most subdued by man—does not appear humanized in spite of this fact; its atmosphere is still very much the same in kind as that of Siberia. The fact is that humanization depends entirely on the force of the psychic atmosphere and this, again, depends not on intellect but on the undifferentiated basic subconscious, which is linked to the earth by the emotions. Now this leads us to the paradoxical result that, in spite of the fact that American Man has conquered the earth in the material sense more than any other representative of the human race, *the American Scene is to a greater extent determined by the Earth as such, than by man.* This, then, accounts for its primeval quality. In spite of all external civilization, America impresses the sensitive observer as an extremely young country from the point of view of human evolution, but at the same time as an extremely old country from the point of view of nature. Here I refer my readers to what I have said in my *Travel Diary* on the primordial forces still alive on the American continent; it is not without significance that such a thing as the Mariposa grove exists only in that part of our planet. These primordial forces are extraordinarily powerful. If the American woman of American descent is, on the whole, the longest-lived human being on earth, this is obviously due to them. The amazing single-mindedness and tenacity Americans show in the pursuit of what in a later chapter I shall call "The animal ideal" is another proof of the same. The same accounts to a considerable extent for that rejuvenation the European stocks experience in the New World. Last but not least: its primordial forces do create a new human species. As we are witnessing only the first beginnings of a process requiring a very long time for its accomplishment, there can obviously in this case be no question of a mature type. But if one remembers that the earliest settlers, both white and black, came across the ocean only little more than three hundred years ago, and that the process of immigration is still continuing, allowing only slight opportunity for national consolidation, then one simply stands *amazed* at the formative powers of Mother Earth. There can indeed be no doubting the fact that the so-called melting-pot, if it is given a chance, does produce a unified type. Even today everybody who has eyes to see can distinguish at first sight the typical North American from every other human type; he is a man of a distinctly American physique and American soul, however numerous the varieties in which he may present himself. Many citizens of the United States do not, of course, belong to this type. When I said above: "if Earth is given the chance," I meant to imply that the forces of the earth must not find too great a resistance in forces belonging to other planes. The closer to nature a generation of man has been living, the less question there can have been of such resistance. Accordingly, the authentic American type is most frequent among descendants of the old farmer—or cowboy—stocks, and among those families of indifferent descent which did not mount the ladder of material success too rapidly; it is least pronounced in the wealthy families of city-dwellers. Attention has often been drawn to the alleged fact that there is a convergence between the physiques of the white and the red American, which grows more marked the longer the former has resided in the country. However, to my mind, one ought not to stress this point too strongly; if it were as important as many pretend, the physique of the American negro, the American closest to the earth, should also converge with that of the red Indian—a thing of which, as far as I know, we find no trace. On the other hand, the researches of Hermann Wirth (see his epochal book *Der Aufgang der Menschheit*) have made it almost certain that the purest types of red Indians are the closest kinsmen of the European Nordics. It appears that the forebears of both originated in what is today the Arctic zone, whence America was settled before Europe; accordingly, the convergence of the white American with the Indian may easily be due to that "decivilization of the European" many writers have claimed to be the essence of americanization; that is, to the reversion of the European to a more ancient type. But there really is no need, for our purposes, to insist on the Aryan-Indian convergence: the fact is that the new continent *does* irresistibly develop a new type of man—I say "irresistibly," because that type develops in spite of the fact that the immigration from without into the American continent has continued for centuries, whereas in all other similar cases we know of the influx practically ceased after one single wave, or at the utmost a few waves, had swept the land. *And this, in its turn, must lead and is actually leading to the birth and development of a new kind of soul.* What one may fairly call soullessness can continue as a national characteristic only for as long as men remain nomads; nomadism implies a minimum of earth-influence. And a large proportion of the present-day Americans are still nomads. But they, too, will settle down some day, as all nomads capable of civilization have done. We may, therefore, affirm even at this early stage of our investigations, that the soullessness of the American type is not the fated characteristic so many European writers take it for. Here, then, two chains of causes make a safe prediction possible with regard to the future: the one refers to the European heredity, the other to the extraordinary formative power of the American earth.

BUT ere we proceed further, we must try to arrive at a somewhat clearer conception of what the word "environment" stands for even in scientific circles. Everybody talks of the influence of climate. But it is by no means evident in what sense climate can affect man, apart from making for a greater or smaller degree of good health or a greater or smaller share of physical vitality. Although I am no specialist on the subject, I dare assert that environment acts creatively in one way—and in this one way only: in changing in the long run the correlation of the endocrines and similar organs. I have been experimenting a good deal with hormones in my own body, in addition to observing others, and I have found that in accordance with the relative predominance of one or several hormones—I mean "relative" in the sense of deviations from what one may take as a norm—the constitutional type actually does change. And then I have found that there is a striking parallelism between pathological cases and some of the most marked national types; a parallelism in the sense that the former present caricatures of the latter. I cannot enter into details here, but one example, the example of the respective effects of an exaggerated plus or an exaggerated minus in the secretions of the pituitary gland should suffice: in the one case, we have a caricature of the Anglo-Saxon type with his lean, lithe body, his narrow head and prominent chin; in the other, we have a caricature of the Russian, with the seal-like distribution of fat over his whole body. I have passed on my suggestions to several specialists and I hope before long we shall have more detailed information on this subject, although full knowledge cannot be expected before centuries have passed, because in this case it is a question of nations, not of individual men. But even on the basis of the scanty information at hand today, I feel satisfied personally that there is a real physiology of nations underlying all psychology; that the type of each depends chiefly on the correlation of the endocrines, and that this correlation is, in its turn, conditioned to a very high degree by the material surroundings—indeed, to a higher degree than by heredity. I cannot see why, were it otherwise, the descendants of those who emigrated to Russia look much more Russian than anything else, and why the same applies, more or less, to all countries. Certainly all climes are not equally creative; this explains why in some countries "heredity" seems to mean more than "environment." If it is a question of endocrines, the possibility of such differences is a matter of course. But environment always has a marked influence. In some countries it seems to predominate. Switzerland is one of them—the extent to which in this case, it is a question of endocrines seems proved by the frequency of what the French call *goitre* (bronchode) and idiocy in the Alpine lands; America is another.

From my own point of view this is, indeed, one of the most important intuitions which have come to me with the force of a revelation of obvious truth as a result of the opening of my soul to the influences of the American atmosphere. The truly native-born American is *not*—what everybody believes him to be—the man least dependent on Mother Earth; on the contrary, he belongs to a type of man which owes its main characteristics to the latter. In the course of this book I shall give all the illustrations and proofs of this thesis that have come to my notice. But since it is of the utmost importance to be as exact and as clear as possible in this rather obscure connexion, I wish to enlarge a little on another aspect of the same problem before finally concentrating on the particular subject of the American type. We said that there is no doubt that the so-called melting-pot does produce, if given the chance, a unified type; and we added that by "given the chance" we meant that the forces of the earth must not encounter too much resistance from forces belonging to other planes. This resistance, again, decreases in proportion to the closeness to nature in which a stock has been living for generations. How about this closeness to nature? It can hardly be a question of physical nearness or distance; in this sense, there is no escaping her. It is a question of psychological closeness.

The town-dweller is psychologically distant from nature in that particular sense that he takes no direct notice of her; the same applies to the "intellectual," wherever and however he may live. Now if Oswald Spengler is right in anything, he is so in his assertion that, as far back as history's records go, these types have never played any permanent part from the point of view of biology. Urban and intellectual civilizations there have been long before the days of Babylon, but these civilizations have always depended for their continuance on a constant influx of country-dwellers; in all great civilizations the towns have been the brains of the national body and no more; and the more vital the brain in question was, the more this was due to the richly developed lower organs which, in this case, means a rich and developed provincial life close to nature. In modern Europe France, of all countries, seems to depend most on its capital; intellectually and culturally, the French province hardly counts. But then the vast majority of noted Parisians were born in the province, and there is no more earthbound type in the world than the French provincial. If the life of the French nation depended on Parisian heredity, it would have died out long ago. Thus, it was not accident which founded the first great city, in the American sense, that we know of in history—

Babylon, in the fertile valley of Mesopotamia, and the same applies to the great cities of Egypt; here, the peasant has not changed for at least five thousand years and it was always he who safeguarded the continuance of Egypt's history through all its vicissitudes. The races of unadulterated town-dwellers and intellectuals have invariably degenerated or died out in the course of three or four generations. And what has been true of the past is certain to remain true for the future, for here it is a question of elementary forces. It is nothing short of ridiculous to expect that that type of the American which has lived for many generations in Boston or New York, or even Chicago, will provide the exemplar for future American civilization. An urban tradition can indeed provide the *frame* for a national tradition, but it must derive its life-blood from without, by a constant process of metabolism, as best illustrated by Paris. Without contact with the vitalizing powers of the earth, man must lose his vitality, and this has already been proved by America's own history, however short it be. The descendants of those types who have lived as mere exploiters of the earth all the time of their existence on American soil—whether as pioneering nomads or industrial prospectors—are all of them strangely lacking in vitality. After leaving America, I went first to England. From the biological point of view the main characteristic of the English nation is its love for the homeland, understood in the wide sense of England's Nature. The Englishman does not exploit his land; he rather leaves it wild and uncultivated and enjoys its beauty; even the most hard-working Englishman is in the habit of opening his soul to the spirit of his land. Now what struck me first after coming to England from the United States was that every Englishman is a much more vital personality than the seemingly most vital of those Americans who are representative of their present-day urban civilization.

In this connexion, therefore, we need give no heed to the town-dweller, taken as an organic type; in him there are no forces which could oppose the workings of nature's processes. Still, the aforesaid does not exhaust the problem. It is true that without close inner contact with the earth there is no question of man's prospering on its surface for any length of time. Yet man need not be moulded exclusively by the earth. If a human type appears purely earthbound, this is so because he has nothing in him that makes him superior to the close-to-nature-type. Man is not only a son of nature, but also of the spirit. Man is even more spirit than nature [1]—and spirit, too, can vitalize. Only it must be a question of vital spirit, not of mere intellect, the most superficial expression of the former; it must be the spirit of which the best-known expression is great religious faith. If there are spiritual forces in existence the root of which grows in those deep regions, then they can counteract or counterpoise the forces of nature. We may witness this fact throughout history in the domains of sex, morality, and religion. But we can witness it also occasionally in the sense of a preservation of the original character of a race which emigrated into a foreign land. The greatest example of this is provided by the Jews. They have had no really native country for thousands of years; they have spread all over the earth, settling down in almost all countries; having become a fundamentally

[1] The reader will find a full exposition of the problem of spiritual reality in the last chapter of this book.

parasitic nation (compare my thorough examination of the Jewish problem in *Europe*), they have lived in closer touch with "environment" than most autochthonous races. And yet they have always remained, even as a physical type, what they originally were. This is due to two causes. Firstly, to the unequalled understanding the Jews possess of the laws of the blood. But if it were a case of this only, a change of type would certainly have taken place in every country in which they settled. The preservation of the original Jewish type is due to the second of the causes in question: to its spirituality. For the Jew the law of his religion always represents his closest "environment." He had to practise it with the utmost strictness, consistency, and severity; his life was everywhere spiritually determined. Owing to this, he has proved stronger than nature; he has continued in his original type in spite of her varying influences. But on the other hand—*if* the Jew ever becomes unfaithful to his law the result is truly disastrous; this has been avoided only where he has immediately succeeded in becoming part of a new national body, as in Spain and to a certain extent in Italy. But so consolidated a type as the Jew cannot easily become part of a new nation. And since his type is essentially spirit-born and has no support in the forces of the earth the process of denationalization with the Jew only too often leads to nothing less than moral putrefaction.

So much for the Jew. But what has been said of the creation of his type applies to those nations as well which have developed a caste-system. The prototype of these inhabits India. Nothing could be more foreign and uncongenial to the physiology of the early Aryan invaders (they were not exactly "Nordics," but they had retained, in what is today Persia and Afghanistan, such fundamental traits of the Nordic race as could survive in hotter climes) than the brooding heat of India. Besides, the natural forces which are active on this peninsula wield truly tremendous power. Instinctively, the invaders built up a system of spiritual rules capable of counteracting these influences. And it did counteract them. In spite of this system, the spirit of the Indian peninsula soon took hold of the deeps of the Aryan soul; had it been otherwise, the essentially non-mystic conquerors (there is very little mysticism to be found even in the Rigveda) would not so soon have become the greatest of all mystic philosophers; had it been otherwise, India, racially much more Drawidian than Aryan today, would not still be essentially the same nation of thinkers and seers it always was. But the spirit of India took hold of the deeps of the Aryan soul within a pre-existing spiritual framework; and this framework is more akin to European intellectuality than to the irrational maze of Drawidian intuitions and emotions. Thanks to this circumstance, even the original physical type has continued within the higher castes to an extraordinary degree.—The same applies, in principle, to all caste-systems which have ever existed. It applies to all European aristocracies. They were all the descendants of original invaders, and during many centuries the knights felt much more akin to members of their own class who lived in other countries and spoke another language than to the other inhabitants of their own country. They had a code of honour and conduct of their own which stood for exactly the same thing the Law stood for with the Jews, and caste-tradition with the Hindus; accordingly, they resembled one another much more than they resembled the lower classes of their own land. *But the same also applies to American Puritanism.*

It is quite true that Puritanism was invented in Europe and that America was not exclusively colonized by Puritans; there were, from the very first, the independent types of the pioneer and the business man; moreover, many other religious types apart from the Puritan and possibly even outnumbering the latter, have lived in America long enough to conquer it spiritually. But why has Puritanism in Europe not played anything like the part it has in America, and why does everybody instinctively use the word Puritanism and no other when talking of the spiritual influences which have moulded the New World? Why can there be no question even today as to the fact that whatever civilization there is in America is of Puritan origin? The extraordinary rôle Puritanism has played, and is still playing in the United States, is really not a matter of religious faith: it was, and is, a matter of caste, as in the case of the Aryan invaders of India and in that of the Jews; and as far as the qualifications of this caste are concerned, the extraordinary power of Puritanism is the result of the fact that this spiritual force alone was strong enough to counteract the influence of the American soil and thus to make for the preservation of the ancestral type. Puritanism alone could achieve this because no other spiritual force at hand was equally deeply rooted, well defined, and strong. There was, of course, the Cavalier-type of the Virginian, the spirit of which competed for a considerable period with the Puritan. But the latter completely defeated it. The reason was, first, that the Puritan was a much more spiritual type; one should always remember that Puritanism means a reincarnation of the spirit of the Old, as opposed to the New Testament, and that the spirit of the former, as the spirit of the most one-sided Ethos the world has ever seen, has from the very first proved to be the most potent influence on earth; the entire conquest of the material world is, in the last analysis, an effect of the spirit of the Old Testament; the spirits of Brahminism and Confucianism have never achieved anything even approaching the effects of the spirit of the Old Testament. Apart from this, Puritanism as opposed to Cavalierism had a much better chance, because America developed into an industrial democracy. Here I may quote what Harvey O'Higgins and Edward H. Reed have to say on the subject in their book *The American Mind in Action* (Harper & Brothers), one of the few really good books I know on the subject of the American soul:

> Unremitting toil and keen dealing and untiring application put the Puritan into positions of conspicuous success where even his least admirable qualities aroused the instinct of imitation in others. Puritan ideals of godly toil and blessed prosperity became the dominant ideals of the land. And no life has ever lent itself to the formation of a national ideal with greater facility. There was no caste system to divide the social mass into varying class aspirations. The canal boy became the President, the errand boy the banker, the clerk the head of the trading corporation, the laborer the captain of industry. The ideal of the highest class could be followed by a member of the lowest as a guiding star to his ambition, and a particular class-purpose in life could become as general and popular as a classy fad in clothes. Such an ideal, once formed, could be held up to all children by all parents, taught to youth by educators, fed to the people in the popular reading, and diligently realized by energetic young ambition with sufficient success to establish it in the habits and customs and traditions of the nation.

Thus the spirit of America is essentially Puritan in so far as it continues the traditions of the first three hundred years of its history.

The Puritan outlook has predominated much in the same way as the Brahmin outlook always predominated in India, although the Brahmin caste represented but a small minority: through the prestige it commanded—a prestige always born anew owing to the superior type of man it continued to create. We can observe the essential parallel in spite of all diverging appearance. And now we can likewise understand why the Puritan rule has always been so severe. A caste-rule, which means a safeguard against the spirit of a foreign soil, is always most akin to military rule, in particular to the rule of an occupation-army. The Brahmin rule was and is severe enough in this sense; but it applied, and still applies, only to the spheres of religion and social life. The settlers in America were, like all Europeans, essentially world-bent; they also were essentially aggressive. This has caused a much greater severity and exclusiveness of caste-rule than ever existed in India. In the beginning of the colonization period this was not so obvious, because America was supposed to be the Land of Freedom and a refuge for all; therefore the principle of tolerance counteracted the genuine spirit of Puritanism fairly successfully for a considerable time. But the spirit of tolerance is no match for a spirit of aggression, whatever it be. Besides, the more democratic a country is, the more the existing laws must be strict in their essence, and the greater must be the severity with which they are enforced. This is so first, because an organized mass can be ruled only by severe laws (this is exemplified by every army); second, because the acknowledgment of laws by a great mass gives them a tremendous authority. Accordingly, we see that America has become—and still is growing—ever less tolerant in spirit as time goes on. There is nothing less tolerant on earth than the spirit not only of the Ku Klux Klan and of Fundamentalism, but even of the Moralism of the small Middle-Western town; this is amply proved by prohibition and, more generally, by the amazingly slight degree to which freedom of thought appeals to what in Europe we still call the Land of Freedom. Indeed, a vital spirit manifests its true character ever more clearly and more forcibly as time goes on; it can even prove strongest when the people have ceased to adhere to it consciously; for if it is really a vital spirit, the centre of gravity lies in the unconscious. This growth of strength of an original spirit can and does take place in the United States to an unusual degree, because the spirits of the two types of strong men who made the country—the Puritan and the Pioneer—soon merged into one. Apart from all religion, the Puritan spirit soon became the very backbone of the American business man. This explains why the necessity of work in pioneer days developed into the present-day religion of work and enterprise. Eventually, the fact that Puritanism means in its essence the caste-rule of a conquering race on foreign soil may even assert itself in the traditional military and political sense. What America unconsciously aims at is the spiritual americanization of the whole world. And though it is true that when her sons penetrate new countries their bullets are made not of lead but of silver, it should be borne in mind that this style of conquest merely bespeaks an industrial age. At this point we may note a further curious connexion between the spirit of the Puritan and the spirit of the Pioneer. It was an article of faith with the first colonists that material success is the immediate proof of divine election; the roots of American aggressiveness lay in a religious impulse. But centuries have elapsed since the first Puritan era. Today the majority of the population constitutes what under the Indian system would have formed the lower castes. The spirit of the conquering race still rules, but the race has changed. The optimism of the modern American was unknown to the Pilgrim Fathers; emotions and enthusiasms were foreign to them; they did not envisage a prosperous world as being an end in itself. Still, whatever in the United States continues the early tradition, appears, from the European point of view, even more Puritan in spirit than American life seemed in its early days, because since then that spirit, from being an exclusive manifestation of religion, has become the very backbone of the whole of traditional American life. The reason is that the Puritan spirit alone as a caste-spirit is strong enough to counteract the influences of the New Continent. The Cavalier-spirit was not strong enough for that, nor was that of any class with a less narrow religious, philosophic, or moral outlook.

ALL this is true. But on the other hand there is no question as to the fact that today America is traversing the first great crisis in her history and that the chief characteristic of this crisis is that it saps the foundations of Puritanism. Unquestionably the latter is today fighting for its life as a ruling power, and in all probability it will be defeated. What does this mean?—The answer to this question leads us back to our argument, that in America the spirit of the earth, as opposed to the spirit of man, seems to predominate. If under the banner of the Revolt of Modern Youth a new type of American has come into predominance, this means fundamentally that the same process which took place in India thousands of years ago, when the Drawidian soul got the upper hand with the Hindu to the detriment of the Aryan, is now at work in the territory of the United States. We shall deal at length in the next chapter with the general rejuvenation which is the first consequence of the process under review. But in order to make my readers realize at once, and with a shock as it were, what a tremendous change is going on under their eyes, I shall quote here a passage of the lecture which the great Swiss psychologist Dr. C. G. Jung gave at the 1927 Session of my School of Wisdom; in the general context of the problem of the extent to which man's soul is conditioned by the earth, this lecture dealt with the problem of the transformation the American type is undergoing just now (the lecture has been printed as part of the VIIIth year-book of the School of Wisdom, *Der Leuchter, 1927*). I do not identify myself, *nota bene*, with all of Jung's views, but I do think that they contain a good deal of truth; this is why I restate them here, although I have already quoted them in *Europe*.

> The first thing that attracted my attention among the Americans was the profound influence of the negro, a psychological influence, of course, without admixture of blood. The expression of the emotions in the American, his laughter above everything else, may best be studied in the society columns of the American newspapers; that inimitable Rooseveltian laughter is found in its primal form among the American negroes. That peculiar walk, loose-limbed, those swaying hips, observed so frequently among American women, are of negro origin. American music draws its chief inspiration from the negro; the dance is the negro dance. The expressions of

the religious emotions, the revival meetings, the Holy Rollers and other abnormalities, are strongly influenced by the negro—and the famous naïveté of the American, in its charming as well as in its more unpleasant forms, can be easily compared with the childlikeness of the negro. The extraordinarily lively temperament of the average American, which shows itself not only at baseball games, but more particularly in an astonishing passion for verbosity (the most instructive example is the boundless and interminable torrent of words in the American newspapers) can hardly be traced back to a Germanic ancestry; it resembles much more the "chattering" of the negro village. The almost total absence of intimacy and the overwhelming mass-sociability of the Americans reminds one of the primitive life of the open huts and the complete identification of the individual with all his tribal relatives. I had the feeling that in all American houses all the doors are always open, just as in the American country-towns the gardens are without hedges. Everything seems to be part of the street. . . . In the hero fantasies of the American the Indian character plays a leading rôle. The American concept of sport goes far beyond the good nature of the European. Only the Indian initiation ceremonies can compete, for brutality and cruelty, with the rigorous athletic training of the American. The mass achievement of American sport is for that reason astonishing. In everything that involves the American will, the Indian comes to the fore; in his extraordinary concentration on a given goal, in the obstinacy of his persistence, in his unfaltering endurance of the severest difficulties, all the legendary virtues of the Indian come into play. . . . I have observed that among my American patients the hero-figure also has the Indian religious aspect. The most important figure in the Indian religious ritual is the shaman, the doctor and exorciser of spirits. The first American discovery in this field—one which has also become important for Europe—was spiritualism; the second was Christian Science and other forms of mental healing. Christian Science is an exorcistic ritual; the demons of sickness are denied to be existent, the proper formulas are chanted over the rebellious body, and the Christian religion, which represents a high cultural level, is used for magic cures. The poverty of spiritual content is appalling, but Christian Science is alive; it possesses a thoroughly earth-rooted power and has worked those wonders which we would look for in vain in the official churches. Thus the American presents a curious picture: a European with the manners of a negro and the soul of an Indian. He is sharing the destiny of all usurpers of an alien soil; certain Australian aborigines assert that it is impossible to conquer an alien soil, for alien ancestral spirits live in that alien soil, and thus the new-born children of the conqueror will incarnate alien ancestral spirits. This contains a great psychological truth. The conquered alien country assimilates the conquerer. Unlike the Latin conquerors of Central and South America, the North Americans have maintained the European level with the sternest Puritanism; but this could not prevent the soul of their Indian foes from becoming their own. It is everywhere within the power of virgin earth to bring down at least the unconscious of the conqueror to the level of the autochthonous inhabitants.

The negro influence cannot, of course, be accounted for by the spirit of the American continent. We have already found one other reason for this: it is a matter of the emotional vacuum within the soul of the colonial which must inevitably be filled from without. Another reason lies in the rejuvenation of America, its relapse, or rather lapse, into primitivity with which the next chapter will deal at length; as a primitive, the coloured man is naturally superior to his white brother; his expressions are more authentic, more genuine, which superiority is enhanced by the negro's great emotional endowment and his equally great gift of artistic expression. Perfection of expression makes even those who themselves are lacking in them share his feelings and emotions.[1] But the chief reason is the fact that hitherto the black native of America has been, from the point of view of Mother Earth, a more authentic American than the white native, even though no alien blood has been

[1] I have developed this trend of thought in the chapter "Meaning and Expression in Art Life" in *Creative Understanding* and "Invention and Form" in *The Recovery of Truth*, Harper & Brothers.

admixed with that bred in America since the days of the *Mayflower*. I know that my American readers will not like this assertion, but there is no evading the truth. The American negro is a purely American type and much more convincing as such than any living white type. I do not in any way beg the question: his convincing power has asserted itself all over the earth; nothing America has created so far can bear the comparison with the convincing power of negro dancing and music, possibly with the one exception of Christian Science.

But is the type of the American negro really native-born? Of course it is. There has never been anything like the American negro in Africa, nor is there anything like him in the West Indies or in South America. The negro dance, jazz, those songs which sweep every American audience, are self-expressions of the *emancipated* negro, of what the black man has developed into on American soil since the Civil War. He is, accordingly, as American as opposed to his forebears, as any Middle Westerner of old Pioneer stock can claim to be. And since the black American happens to have native-born feelings and emotions, true to the American soil, which the white man has not as yet developed, he really supplements the latter. This, in my opinion, is the chief reason for the fact that almost all expressions of American emotionalism seem to be of negro origin. They really are of *American* origin. But since the white man's soul has not yet grown in this respect beyond the stage of receptivity and imitation, it must needs express itself in the black man's way, in order to live out its own life.

It is perhaps as well if in this connexion I say as much of the very delicate negro-problem as the context allows. The coloured man is as true an American as his white brother. The American Constitution does not allow any kind of persecution of its citizens and, owing to the extreme conservatism of the American temperament, there is little likelihood that the Constitution will soon, if ever be changed. There will possibly continue to be a certain amount of lynching, as a sort of safety-valve, for a considerable time to come, but I cannot imagine that a consistent anti-negro policy will ever be carried through. The social question is already solved, as far as a solution is possible under the circumstances. In the South, at any rate, a tacitly acknowledged caste-system is in existence, and nothing wiser could have been invented. There is equality before the law, but the white and the black lead separate lives. Such a state of things is always possible; not only do the various species of animals live closely together without mixing, the same has been the case in most countries inhabited by various races, such as India for instance. But the American Constitution takes care that the superiority of one caste does not involve oppression of the others. Thus the negroes need not feel humiliated, they can develop, *as Americans*, a racial pride of their own. And they will perhaps even build up a culture of their own, and this culture may even be acknowledged, by the non-American world, as America's most authentic culture. The fact is that the soul only has direct attractive power, not intellect nor technical achievement, for only the soul is really "man." If America had nothing more to show than technical invention, then there could be no question of a lasting American influence on the world; the printing-press was invented in Germany, so was gunpowder—but the world has not become German on that account; had Germany produced nothing else, its very existence would soon have been forgotten. Technical inventions are soulless and can be appropriated by everybody; they belong eventually to him who gives them a soul. There is nothing paradoxical, therefore, in my anticipation that America's greatest cultural achievements may easily be due to her black sons. This is still less improbable since the white man's prejudice counts everyone with even a drop of negro blood in his veins among the black. If only the really black were thought of and treated as negroes, then the superiority of the white man would continue in all fields for centuries to come. But there is an immense percentage of really white people in the negro-caste. Under these circumstances it is not in the least unlikely that the first original geniuses of the New World will belong to the black; let us remember that the grandfathers of both Poushkin, Russia's greatest poet, and of Alexandre Dumas were coloured men. And not only from the point of view of culture, from that of biology as well, the black native of the United States has great chances. On the whole, the white American of today seldom gives the impression of genuine vitality. This is sometimes due to degeneration: the pioneers or the other first generations of immigrants often were obliged to work so hard that their descendants have to pay for it. It may be due also, in part, to the earth in this respect that this continent breeds a comparatively unvital type of man; in this connection the red Indians are closely akin to the white Americans I am considering. But the chief reason should be the same which accounts for American soullessness. Mother Earth was there before man; she will outlive him. Physical life has its source in the earth—and this means more than that man requires food and shelter. If a race becomes almost entirely a race of town-dwellers, to whom nature means nothing but raw material, its prospects cannot possibly be hopeful. As far as we can look back in history, towns, from the point of view of biology, were places of spending, and not of earning or saving. It is true that industrial civilization has created new conditions; but this civilization will become stable only when a new state of balance has been arrived at between Man the Son of the Earth and Man the Exploiter of the Earth. At the present turning-point there is a very real danger that the whole North American continent—with the exception of a few mountain ranges—will become something like one single town, and a town of vampire-like quality at that. It is not easy even today to determine where New York ends and Boston begins; owing to the fact that all modern town-planning and building has been carried out under the assumption that everybody owns a motor car, there is no limit to the extension of suburbs. Chicago even today covers a territory which would have sufficed to form a handsome kingdom thirty years ago. The standardization of American life makes it ever so much easier and cheaper to live in town than in the country, all the more so, since—or if—farming does not pay; nor is there any probability of a tradition-bound farmer-type developing in the near future; for the only solution of the farmer problem which the Department of Agriculture at Washington seems to visualize is the creation of an exceptionally intelligent and scientifically trained farmer-type—and all human history goes to prove that active intellects have never found lasting happiness conforming to the always slow processes of nature. All these circumstances co-operate in producing a general town-dweller psychology. The love of crowds and the extraordinary docility of all Americans in following the suggestions of advertising agents help to complete the picture. Yes, the territory of the United States may actually some day become one single town; and then, of course, it will stand out some day as one single ruin. I spent several weeks at that truly wonderful place in the Californian Desert which bears the name of Palm Springs. It counted hardly a couple of hundred permanent residents, but there were no less than sixty-three real estate agents. One radiant morning I went up a hill. From the summit of it I saw the whole desert already plotted out with street names and the rest. And then I realized with horror that the whole of the Californian Desert may soon grow to be one single town and that this town may even soon merge into the ever-spreading Chicago. . . .

But all jesting apart, the problem is really very serious. For if the white American continues on his present line of development, then America may end by becoming the black continent of post-modern times. We know today that from palæolithic days onward there have been at least three great civilizations in Africa, the original representatives of which were not black. In those early days the negro seems to have played a part similar to that of the gorilla today. But the ruling races eventually lost their vitality; they lived too much aloof from Mother Earth. So the negro, although inferior, had the last word.

LET us now turn back to the general argument that in America the earth, and not man, seems to be the ultimately predominating force. I do, of course, not really believe that America will end as the Black Continent of the future, but I thought it wise to over-stress at this point the dangers of urban civilization, because as yet Americans do not seem to be at all aware of them. Now I may say that the true earth-rooted American type *is* developing in spite of all that has been said above. But let us first consider the course events did *not* take in the United States, although they might have taken them, and which types of men do *not* count for the future. The New Englanders never became a really native type because they were the principal representatives of the unmitigated Puritan spirit, that is, of the spirit of a caste-rule intended to preserve the original racial characteristics against the impact of the influences of the New World. Had they developed into a caste of warriors or statesmen, they might have continued at best as a specialized ruler-type, as the Jesuits did in some parts of South America. But on the tree—artificial from the point of view of the American earth—were grafted from the very beginning cultural aspirations of a very unworldly kind; this could not help resulting in a form of cultured life of an almost ethereal quality. I know of no less vital, no more fastidious, no more prejudiced type than the Bostonian; and to it belonged even men like Henry Adams and Emerson. But the restless pioneers, too, whose essence was the love of adventure and enterprise, never really became natives of the earth; from her point of view they were essentially nomads. If they remained nomads, they could develop authentically only in the form of a very specialized and narrow type, such as the cowboy; they could not take root in the soil and, accordingly, developed no culture. In theory, the same general development might have taken place as did in Europe as the result of the Wandering of the

Nations (of which the American rush to the West represents the last stage): the conquerors might have developed into something equivalent to the feudal landlords of the Old World and might thus have become linked to the earth on a higher plane. The first tradition of the pioneers was, indeed, aristocratic in almost the same sense as was that of the Teutonic invaders of Europe; the latter, too, all felt equal among themselves; and the former, too, were intensely individualistic and heroic. Accordingly, the Far West, the last region where this type of man has prevailed, feels consciously aristocratic even today, and its open contempt of the Middle West is exactly of the same quality as that of the nobleman for the burgher. But an aristocratic order presupposes the acknowledged existence of inequalities. This could not become the foundation of a country which was colonized by men whose one desire was to escape from inequality of any kind; nor could it develop where the colonists were originally poor and humble in spirit and lacked the self-assurance which characterizes the warrior-races. Nevertheless, theoretically speaking, the taking-root of the immigrants in the New World might have assumed the form of landlordship; all the more so as there exists a certain likeness between the settling of America and that of India. It is true that America was practically an uninhabited continent when the white man invaded it, but the variety of the races that followed one another across the Atlantic soon led to a diversity similar to that which characterizes India. Had this colonization taken place some thousands of years ago, a caste-system similar to that prevailing in India would undoubtedly have been the final result. However, since the colonization began under the influence of the idea (or, better, the religion) of democracy—the counter-religion of caste-ruled Europe—the existing differences in the population never became explicit nor even quite conscious; it is, in fact, a religious principle that racial and social origins did not count—as of course they did not at the beginning of the process, since the pioneers and Puritans were really of the same stock, and they alone were "the Americans." But this state of affairs in America changed with every wave of immigration from new countries. Today a mild caste-system is unquestionably in existence, of which more will be said in the chapter "Democracy." However, the outstanding fact is that America actually has *not* developed an aristocratic system. Neither did the earliest settlers find a native race they could rule for their own benefit, nor did they secure privileges for themselves giving them a superior status as against the later comers. All the same, to what extent an aristocratic America would, in principle, have been a reasonable development is proved by those parts of it which were colonized by Cavaliers and where labourers were supplied in the form of imported slaves. In the Southern States the immigrant took root in the new earth in a form equivalent to that of the feudal landlord; he accordingly does not resemble the Swiss. He is as deeply rooted in the soil as the latter, but he retains his aristocratic character. Still, the Southern Gentleman is not "the" American of today who has taken root in the American soil. "The" American belongs to the Swiss type.

What does this mean? And what is the reason for this state of things? It means that the principle of earth-boundness as opposed to spirit predominates, and accordingly, matter and inertia as opposed to creativeness and freedom. In the chapter of *Europe* dealing with Switzerland I have insisted exclusively—as the purport of that book compelled me to do—on the negative side of what one may call Swissdom. But there is, of course, another side to it, and I take pleasure in qualifying my previous statements on the basis of a criticism of them which Dr. C. G. Jung published in the June issue, 1928, of *Die Neue Schweizer Rundschau*. Doctor Jung there explains that there are two opposite types of men, which cannot help cordially disliking each other, but which, considered from a cosmic point of view, appear equally necessary for the continuance of human life on this planet: the types of the man of the spirit and of the man of the earth. These two types correspond, says Jung (it is not really so, but in the connexion in question the often so misinterpreted Chinese terms will do, be cause they do not distort the facts), to the two basic principles of Chinese philosophy, Yang and Yin. The man of predominating spirit is Yang, whose life is ruled by spiritual ideals; the man of the earth is Yin, who is characterized by a primary adjustment to the earth. These two are enemies from eternity, and yet they need each other. Earth-bound man, too, lives according to a basic principle; to that extent he, too, partakes of the great and of the noble. "All the good and all the bad qualities of the Swiss are results of his essential earth-boundness: his rootedness in the soil, his narrowness, his lack of intellectuality and spirituality, his love of saving, his solidity, his obstinacy, his dislike of foreigners, his distrust of others, his dialect, and his indifference to what is going on outside his own circle. Should it be true (as Keyserling says) that we Swiss are the most backward, conservative, obstinate, self-righteous, and porcupine-like nation of Europe, this would mean that European man is really and thoroughly at home in his geographical centre, rooted in the soil, indifferent to what others think, self-assured, conservative, and backward; and this again means that here he is still intimately linked to his past, that by his very nature he occupies a neutral position between the fluctuating and contradictory aspirations and opinions of the other nations." I think that every intelligent American who reads this characterization of the Swiss will see at once that it applies to an astounding degree to the Middle-Western type as well; only that the same basic type which manifests itself in Switzerland as a petty bourgeois, does so in a new wide-flung country—where saving would be absurd—in the shape of the enterprising George F. Babbitt. This is highly interesting and very important. Babbitt is essentially a rooted type; he is a native product of one kind of soil and of no other. And let us survey with our mind's eye the thousands of native-born Americans whom we have all seen in Pullman cars, hotel lobbies, and who, if we happened to make their acquaintance, appeared all so much alike as types, in spite of distinct local differences. Are they not really all Swiss in the best sense? Their love of their native town, however young it be, is fanatical; all customs and conventions are sacrosanct; America is the best place for Americans to live in, as a matter of course—but within America, everything distant and different from home is considered inferior. Everything unusual, to say nothing of what may be interpreted as revolutionary, is suspect; pure intellect is of no value whatsoever; the "feelings of the people" are considered as the last intellectual resort. The value attributed to traditional emotions is all the higher; and most of these refer to the soil. Let no one be misled here by the counter-example of the American who still lives in the nomadic stage—a type which must needs be very numerous in a young country flooded by newcomers year in year out: the point is that, *in spite* of this, the Middle-Western type is already so predominant that most Americans will tell the foreign visitor that real America begins in the Mississippi Valley. Nor should anyone raise the objection that the American localist cannot really be a genuine type since even he rarely spends his whole life in the same place: the salient point is that the longing for rootedness is so vehement in the American's soul that he can transfer it at once almost to any place, as a spinster transfers her maternal feelings from one lapdog to another. Also let no one be misled by George F. Babbitt's love of progress: "progressing" in his sense is precisely the traditional American way of living; this kind of progressiveness is the very expression of conservatism on American soil. A stag is no less conservative in his habits than a tortoise because he runs faster. That this is so should become clear to anybody who has the slightest idea of psychology if he will only consider that speed and variability in this one respect are not only compensated, but even over-compensated, in this type of man by an extraordinary slowness in all other respects. He walks more slowly than the European; he speaks slowly; his mental processes are all slow, with the one exception of those which command his immediate interest; but in this case every animal is quick. This type of American is as impermeable to new ideas as a Swiss, except, again, on the one line of material progress. When I say impermeable, I mean in the sense of assimilation. Even Babbitt reads inordinately; as far as this kind of absorption of mental food goes, he is superior to the greatest genius ever produced by any country. While in California, I once counted in the rough the words contained in the Sunday edition of the Los Angeles *Times* which everybody seemed to read over there from beginning to end, and I found that it seemed to contain more words than my *Travel Diary*. . . . But Babbitt's reading, very fortunately for him, resembles a liquid passing through a sieve.

In order to gauge the full importance of these facts we should realize that the Middle-Westerner is the prototype of the hundred-per-cent-American all over the United States and that he is usually a descendant of adventurous pioneers. This proves that he really is a nomad turned agriculturist. How is it possible that he of all men should converge with the Swiss type, considering that Switzerland is small and America so very vast? The explanation is obvious. Every autochthonous culture in the world began as a local culture. Culture is always a daughter of spirit, married to earth. A man who is not yet the native son of a soil can conquer matter spiritually only on a small scale. We observe the same phenomenon at all new beginnings of history. When, accordingly, M. P. Follett (compare her book *The New State*) considers the next step in the development of Democracy to be the establishment of "Leagues of Neighbourhood" she is wrong when thinking in terms of progress, but quite right as to the facts of American life: a really native American life can develop only out of small and narrow beginnings. It is true that there is a striking contradiction between the wide-flung life of the American nomad, who actually rules the country today, and the extreme localism of the Babbitt-type; but this contradiction really amounts to a counterpoint—relationship. And the particular quality of this seems to be due to the co-operation of the following causes. First of all, the spirit of the American earth is so powerful that in the beginning, at any rate, man can only dominate it in the sense of amalgamation on a very small scale. The reason next in importance for the narrowness of the type in question is to be found in the soullessness of the colonial. This soullessness is more pronounced in the case of the American than in any other colonial, because in his case the inevitable loss of qualities belonging to the emotional sphere coincided with an extreme development of such powers of the lower intellect as are necessary for success on technical lines; intellectualization without an equivalent soul-development always makes for barbarization and the barbarian is always a restricted type of man. Puritanism made for soullessness in its turn, and on the other hand, the soulless felt a natural bent for Puritanism; for the Puritan system having no place for cultural values and, more generally speaking, for the values of a richly expanded life, the colonial felt the impoverishment of his nature which inevitably followed his transplantation in foreign soil less the more of a genuine Puritan he was. Now in America this soulless kind of man found a tremendously wide field of activity. All the more did he crave for compensatory narrowness; the typical sentimentalism of the American always from the very first applied to the nearest and closest in the case of the small man. Thus, when the nomad became ready to settle down, his under-developed and unspent emotional energies found their natural object and outlook in the strictly local.—The third reason which plays a part in this connexion co-operates to the same end. Most Americans are the descendants of poor people, belonging to the lower classes; as far as heredity goes—and it does go a long way—a narrow frame of life should be their natural surroundings. All this taken together should suffice to explain what bewilders most foreign visitors and what even most Americans apparently fail to understand: I mean how it is that the normal outlook of the typical American should be a decidedly provincial one. He is not only entirely indifferent to what happens outside of America—he really cares only for the events of his neighbourhood. And this tendency is increasing from year to year. I have met with very wealthy people in the West and in the South who had never been to New York and who told me that they never meant to go there.

The Babbitt-type is, of course, the lowest type of the native-born American. But in a democracy of the American pattern he had to develop and to give the tone first; it is only in aristocratic communities that development can begin with high culture. In the United States, the higher types will develop later on by a process of differentiation, and that will take time. But then, the Americanization of the American has only just begun; it must be a very slow process because, on the one hand, of the continual influx of alien blood, and on the other, because of the still widespread ideal conception of America as a refuge for all, as a land of complete freedom, unfettered by prejudice of any kind. These ruling ideals of liberty make the resulting narrow type of man cling all the more vehemently to his narrowness. It is impossible to understand the Ku Klux Klan, Fundamentalism, hundred-per-cent-Americanism, and more generally American self-righteous provincialism, unless one realizes that a feeling of antagonism against existing conditions plays a great part in their psychological structure. But then, again, America's history is really only beginning. No race which emigrated from other countries has ever become truly native in its new home within the short space of a few hundred years. And the present-day reversion to a narrow type of man and to localism really signifies the best possible promise for the future. Very many, not only in Europe, but also in America, complain of the equalization, standardization, and levelling down supposed to be the fate of all types of men who submit for a sufficient length of time to the influence of American life. The complaint is only too justified. The standardization of all means and ways of life inevitably reacts on soul and mind. And if a standardized life were all there were in the United States, their expectation of a possible culture would indeed be hopeless. But precisely because of the modern processes of narrowing down and increasing provincialism—which processes are going on at right angles to that development of American life which is visible to the blindest eye—there *is* hope that a true culture will grow out of the soil of the United States in days to come. Localism alone can produce in America a thoroughly authentic type of man; this type alone can be the germ-cell of an authentic American nation. Again, localism alone can lead to culture, for culture, too, must start as a singular and single and, therefore, small thing. It will grow and spread as time proceeds. The only really cultural atmosphere one finds today in the United States is that of Virginia. The cultured men who were born in its field of influence are responsible for most of what is of cultural value within the entire territory of the great Federation. But how different Virginia is from all other states! Its culture is a singular one; it is not merely a question of age, but of kind as well.

LET us now consider, in the form of a short sketch, the localisms and provincialisms and regionalisms which already stand out within the United States. Here, I am, of course, restricted to the narrow range of my personal experiences; but since it is here a question more of type and symbol than of facts, I think that the following will suffice for that purpose of general orientation which can be the sole aim of a book hoping to make its readers think and see for themselves. I will say no more of Virginia or of the South in general; we will revert to it soon for a more thorough investigation. My lecture-tour of 1928 took me to practically all parts of the United States. Everywhere it was not only my chief, but my only, concern to get into touch with the *genius loci* of the place I was visiting; for all the success of my lecturing—I mean all the success I care for, that is my being successful in giving vital impulses—depended on that contact. When I started on my tour I naturally expected to come across that uniformity everybody talks of. But to my surprise I found that, in spite of the short time which had elapsed since the foundation of most towns and in spite of the mixed and nomadic character of a considerable percentage of their inhabitants, each of them had a distinctly individual atmosphere; the uniformity is all on the surface. First of all, America seems to be subdivided even now into large provinces of a comparatively unified character, provinces out of which there would undoubtedly have grown, in earlier days and under different conditions, separate cultures. There is New England, the East, the North, the Middle West, the South bordering the Middle West, the South in the real geographical sense, and the Far West. But within these provinces almost each town has a spirit of its own, so that, while travelling, I came to think constantly of the dawn of European civilization, when the Teutonic nomads were just beginning to settle down around centres such as Cologne, Worms, Nürnberg, Paris, Carcassonne. Take, for instance, Dallas, Texas. This part of America may be called the youngest part, because it began to thrive on this side, so to speak, of the discovery of the value of oil. It began to thrive after the crazes for skyscrapers, apartment houses, mere speed, etc., had blown over, at any rate, after their original force had been spent. On the other hand, there was still lingering in the air the romance of the cowboy and the prairie, and near by was the ancient culture of Mexico. This co-operation of different causes and traditions might easily have created a *mixtum compositum* of the most distasteful kind. As a matter of fact, there is even today at Dallas a perfectly delightful *genius loci*. On the material plane, the oil interest of course predominates. But private life has already developed a charm quite in harmony with the lovely country. One notices in the souls of the residents something of the wide sweep of the prairie, the beginnings of an innate taste regarding things visible such as one meets with, as a matter of course, in every Italian, and a vital exuberance attributable in equal parts, I should say, to the generosity of the southern sun and to the prospects of prosperity due to the co-operation of man and of the earth. I should be greatly surprised if, after a few centuries, Texas did not develop a very delightful original culture—all the more so, as this state includes the wonders of the desert, wooded hill-lands, and the prairie, and all this beneath the spell of Mexico's ancient cultural spirit.

Now, as opposed to Texas, let us just cast a glance at Minnesota. It seems a providential thing that this state has been colonized to such a large extent by Swedes; for the landscape is essentially Swedish. Thus, the Swede will take root most easily in this soil. The atmosphere of Minneapolis is thoroughly authentic. It is Swedish at bottom and yet thoroughly American. This may lead to a very promising development. One should not forget that Sweden and Finland are, in Europe, in many respects the most modern countries in the American sense, and yet cultured.

And now let us pass over hundreds of miles and give our attention, without transition, to Missouri. This state represents a borderland between the Middle West and the South. But this general description misses the main point. The Missourian is first of all a Missourian, which does not only mean, as popular saying has it, that he wants to see a thing before he believes in it, that he is suspicious and close-fisted—he is essentially rooted in the Missourian soil; he is the one white American I met of peasant-like qualities. Missouri is not only one of the most prosperous, but one of the most beautiful states of the Union; in the fall its scenery must be of an entrancing charm. Accordingly, the psychic atmosphere of Missourian cities is even today one of harmony, which makes one think of France as opposed to Germany. To this, the peculiar gaiety of St. Louis owes its singular attractive power.

New England's great and very original charm is, alas,

that of a dying culture. There is little likelihood that it will survive even for a century; all the less so as it represents an artificial civilization from the earthly point of view. It was almost purely spirit-born; only a certain ethereal lyricism seems to harmonize with the peculiar hazy beauty of the land. In centuries to come, America will probably see New England's main, because most lasting, achievement in the fact that its sons are chiefly responsible for the colonization of the South and the Middle West. The lines of development American historians are in the habit of drawing between New England's past cultural achievements and the present and future state of America are all, in my opinion, practically untrue. New England's culture was an exclusive thing in itself, beautiful but essentially sterile; and even today what is vital in America derives little more from Boston than it does from Athens; what seems to be of New England origin is really of generally Puritan or even simply European-cultural origin. I should not wonder if New England would end as an essentially Irish country; less because of the growing percentage of residents of Irish extraction, than because of a pre-established harmony between the Irish temperament and the New England landscape.

Now let us fly across the continent to the Far West. California is so young that it should be impossible, one would think, to foretell anything of its future. Its present chief characteristics—for instance, that it has the largest output in the world not only of oranges and tomatoes but also of world-saviours—cannot fairly be expected to last. At present the population, to an extraordinary degree, shows signs of a hysterical temperament; and this can only mean—since the climate in itself is excellent—that the present inhabitants are to a considerable extent not yet adapted to their surroundings. This state of transition could probably have been avoided only if the land had been colonized by members or descendants of the southern races of Europe. But it is not possible that under this bright, exhilarating sky, in this unique electric atmosphere, there should not develop, sooner or later, a corresponding type of man. And this means a type of man very different from the native of any other part of the United States. I wonder whether it will ever be a cultural type; perhaps no culture would ever have developed in the radiant atmosphere of the Greek isles and seas if the Classic Age had been an age which conquered nature when life was easy for all, and of Democracy at that; the latter conditions would rather have made for a type akin to the Hawaiian. But very few peoples have ever developed real cultures and many have been great peoples without it. What I could sense in the psychic atmosphere of California was that it is inhabited by a primitive sort of man; there is more of the frontier alive in him than in any other American. But on the other hand, he has an innate sense of beauty; beauty *means* a great deal to him. And there is something of champagne in his blood which may, some day, mature into a vintage entirely different from anything else that grows in the United States and will certainly act most beneficiently as a counterpart and counterpoint to the bourgeois quality of Eastern, Northern, and Middle-Western life.

San Francisco is, of course, a thing in itself. Its atmosphere represents a delightful blend between the Far West and the Far East; it is the most attractive international seaport I know, and in centuries to come, when America will have developed its own culture, it may play a part corresponding to that of Alexandria in Roman days—the Egyptian quality of Greek Alexandria being represented in San Francisco by the Chinese and Japanese, which foreign element forms an integral part of the atmosphere around the Golden Gate. It has been from the outset a city of ease, if not of luxury. The grim Puritan has never played a prominent part in it. This was due, in the beginning, to the dominant rôle played by the representatives of the races to whom life is first and foremost a joyful thing, the Latin peoples. The different races soon began to blend, and the result is a general atmosphere of ease, of light-heartedness, of frivolous levity, which is the exact opposite to the atmosphere of Boston; all the more so, as San Francisco, too, is essentially American.

This, then, leads me to a short description of those towns, the *genius loci* of which is less American in the sense of truth to type, but which, for that very reason, act like leaven or spices within the whole of the American atmosphere—whether it be only as a sort of tabasco, the fire of which is undoubtedly banished from Hell because of its excessive heat. Since we are still lingering in the Far West, let us begin with Los Angeles. This city, as it presents itself today (it was quite different when I visited it in 1912, and may become different again) possesses the most unreal atmosphere I have ever inhaled; it is probably for the purpose of redemption that Hollywood was established just there: according to the mathematical law that the multiplication of two negative quantities results in a positive one, the frankly avowed will-to-be-unreal of the film-city alone can give a reality to what is essentially phantasmagoric. Los

Angeles is the most weirdly unreal city I know, because its psychic atmosphere is chiefly constituted from the emanations of the most unreal, the most ghostlike type of man in the world: the type of the—retired American. A modern American who retires cannot settle down and live in a kind of pseudo-Riviera, if he has any sincerity. There is as yet no leisured class on this continent; leisure is not yet recognized as a possible life-form; above all, those cultured interests which are found among representatives of any race and can make a place of rest both meaningful and delightful anywhere, provided they form an integral and essential part of the atmosphere, are completely lacking in the class which is most prevalent among those who retire to Los Angeles. The vast majority belong to the Babbitt-type. They have decided to have a good time as retired gentlemen and they think they are having it—but in reality they are most of them bored to death. They have no idea what to do with their leisure.—But perhaps this extravagantly comic element is very necessary and wholesome as part of the general texture of American life. American life is on the whole too serious in the sense that most Americans take themselves too much in dead earnest. It would do them good if they were to make up their minds as a nation to regard Los Angeles as a place to be kindly laughed at. This will perhaps help them also to develop a real sense of humour. For in this, whatever they may think themselves, the Americans are singularly lacking. One may, of course, use the word in many ways, but if "humour" is to mean in any way what it has always meant in all the worlds of culture, then, what Americans call a sense of humour is only a love of cracking jokes and enjoying jokes; and these jokes more often than not lack what the French call *pointe*. He only has humour in the real sense who knows how to give expression to a profound, and even tragic, opposition from the vantage of a benevolent and serene mind. His is the quality of divine laughter of the man inwardly superior to those things ordinary people take with such fearsome seriousness. Accordingly, there can be no high quality of humour unless intellectual understanding acts as the keynote. This is why ancient Chinese humour must be appraised as the highest yet produced by mankind. This is why real humour is not merely a sense of proportion as such, as the English would have it—it is a sense of proportion ruled from within by a keen appreciation of spiritual and intellectual values. Now there is not the faintest trace of this kind of understanding to be found in what Americans call humour. In their case it usually signifies nothing more than a device for refusing to notice the real conflicts of life, as the criminal about to be hanged often uses the last moments of his earthly existence to play the part of the man who does not care; or else it is an outlet for repressions or for a feeling of inferiority. Here again I may quote the book *The American Mind in Action* (pp. 33-35):

> American humor is what science calls a "folkway." It is an outlet for repressed emotions in disguise. At its crudest it relieves a suppressed hatred—as, for instance, in the practical joke, which does its victim an injury but compels him to join in the laugh at his own discomfiture, if he wishes to be considered "a good sport." The joke disguised your vengeful purpose, but that purpose is the unconscious motive of your joke, and the victim shows that he recognizes your hidden motive when he responds to it with the anger and animosity which he suppresses. The American cartoon represents this sort of cruel humor. In drama and in the moving-

picture it takes the form of slap-stick comedy. The cruelty of the popular moving-picture comedy is almost savage. And in the dressing tent at the circus you will hear the battered clown complain, "If I was to fall down and break my neck, these rubes would laugh themselves to death." They seem almost to hate him, and their laughter at his mishaps sounds cruel, because in that laughter they are draining off suppressed hatreds which the civilized conventions of morality have reservoired. The greater the repressions, the louder the laughter. Humor is a conspicuous quality of American life because in that life repressions are so general. Mark Twain tapped a well of hatred and revolt in the subconscious minds of his generation, and it paid him like an oil gusher. . . . His sense of inferiority made him conceal his satire in buffoonery—that is to say, when he wished to satirize his reader, he satirized himself, and the reader laughed at his own absurdities put forward as Mark Twain's. It is this sense of inferiority which makes his humor seem "kindly." The laugher is playing a sort of practical joke on himself and enjoys his own discomfiture. By laughing at his shortcomings, he feels superior to them and escapes his own condemnation of them. Here is the quality in American humor which Rudyard Kipling struck at, in his lines about the American's "cynic devil in his blood . . . that gilds the slough of his despond but dims the goal of his desire." The reformer attacks the slough, to drain it instead of laughing at it; and the typical American always complains of his reformers that they have no sense of humor. If they had, of course, it is not likely that they would be reformers.

And now to New Orleans. Nowhere did the absolute superiority of real culture strike me so forcibly as there. The percentage of Frenchmen who live in that city today is infinitesimal. Yet it is imbued with the tradition of the eighteenth century; it still owes all its charm and all its value to the leaven of Old France. New Orleans is the one place in America where cooking is considered an art; and I thoroughly agree with Mr. Langdon Mitchell when he says that bad cooking and the way people put up with it are gigantic obstacles to an American culture. Personally, I consider an original aptitude for cooking—or else a training towards the appreciation of its value more important, culturally, than any "education" in the usual sense. For since hunger and thirst are the most elementary impulses of animal man, an association of these with æsthetic values means more for spiritualization in general than any intellectual and moral training. There can be no doubt that a high culture in terms of a simple life is possible; but this is the most difficult kind of culture to attain; the case is analogous to that of the simplicity of classic art. The example provided by drink is perhaps more illuminating even than that provided by food. It is certainly not impossible to be at the same time a cultured person and a water-drinker; on a foundation of abstinence even a very high culture can be developed. But then all that sense of quality and discrimination which the connoisseur applies to vintages must find its application in the distinction between different kinds of water. This is one of the wonders we must admire in the greatest representatives of Islamic culture: they discriminate between waters and wells as Europeans do between vintages. But whoever merely drinks ice-water and thinks himself superior for this reason to the wine-drinker errs most lamentably; he stands, as far as soul-development goes, far, far below any man of the Falstaff type, provided the latter is primarily a lover of quality and not of quantity. I must take this opportunity to make quite clear to what a terrifying extent public opinion in America appears misguided in these fundamental respects. "Cleanliness" and "purity" seem to the American the alpha and omega of quality. Obviously food and drink should be wholesome. But this has nothing to do, in principle, with the extermination of microbes. The symbiosis, not the conflict between microbe and man, is the primary phenomenon; most of these tiny creatures are not only harmless but necessary for a sound metabolism; they become the causes of diseases only when irritated. Further, no organism catches a definite disease unless it is predisposed to it. Now a great deal of what makes for good taste is due to the collaboration of microbes; only think of the various processes of fermentation. What, then, can be expected as a general result if food is sterilized? Probably loss of nutritive value—all animals live on raw food—but most certainly loss of taste. In California they are now growing dates on trees which descend from those acknowledged as the best of African, Arabian, Syrian, and Mesopotamian growth. But those American dates which one can buy in the shops are almost entirely devoid of taste; that is, they have been so well sterilized that the microbes which are responsible for the taste have been exterminated before they could perform their duty, or else their work has been destroyed by chemical processes. The effect is much the same as that of the cleansing of precious old vessels covered with patina.

But let us return to New Orleans. This one place in America with a tradition of good cooking is being kept up by the French element. But the latter's beneficial influence does not stop here: owing to it even Americanism acquires a halo of beauty in New Orleans. I spent a night walking through those docks and market-places where vegetables and fruits are loaded and unloaded and sold at wholesale and retail in overwhelming, truly American quantities. But the exquisite sense of beauty of the French has conquered and now rules even this extravagant accumulation of material. The millions of radishes, beans, bananas, oranges, and so forth, in their arrangement look like so many artistic bunches of flowers; a walk through the market-halls of New Orleans at night is probably the most remarkable sight of culture-born beauty one can find in the United States. The French are the most tenacious of all races. This beautifying of American market-places proves that the French sense of quality, challenged also by American quantity-production, seems more than ever determined to live. Now is it not wonderful that America should contain a great city of such innate culture? It will be purely American before long, though, of course, of a peculiar southern, even tropical variety. But the French sense of quality will continue to act, not only as a leaven, but as the determinant formative influence. A time may come—and I hope it will come—when New Orleans will wield more attractive power in the eyes of the Americans than New York. Should it come to this, then Americans would prefer the former in the same sense as every cultured German thinks more of Munich, not to mention Vienna, than of Berlin.

And now we are ready to face Chicago, that most uncanny city in the world. If ever there was a "thing in itself," Chicago is one. It is *not* America; it is just Chicago. But on the other hand, if it goes on spreading as it does with as much intelligently directed energy, it may some day swallow up the whole of the United States. The atmosphere of the city is not pleasing; that which I wrote in 1912, under the impression of what I experienced during only two days spent in that city without talking to a single soul, is true; even more true today than it was then. And here the *genius loci* is unquestionably due to man and not to the surroundings, which are as beautiful as they can possibly be; Lake Shore Drive could compete, for beauty, with the coastline of Naples. As far as I can make out, the atmosphere of Chicago is made up chiefly of the following elements: First, the parasitic growth of a "thing in itself" almost independent of all American tradition, that does not belong to the sphere of technical expansion. This again is due—we have herewith come to the second element—to the crowding together of a population alien in its majority; which is—thirdly—of German extraction in all its most efficient members. This results in a curious convergence of Chicago with modern Berlin; the typical modern Berliners are, as a matter of fact, more akin to German Americans than to the Germans of traditional culture. There is, in Chicago, no trace of Anglo-Saxonism. The quality of efficiency is German in spirit; so is a certain impression of unreality its results produce: it resembles a city of the year 3000 A.D. as anticipated by motion pictures made in Germany. Unreality of spirit is, as I have shown in *Europe*, one of the foremost characteristics of the German, while the exact opposite is true of the Anglo Saxon. Here lies the *raison d'être* of that phantom-like quality one cannot help sensing in the atmosphere of Chicago; there is something phantom-like even in the technicized mass-slaughter of the stockyards. One feels—if Hell does exist, such mechanized operating with the mystery of death would be an impossibility there and would certainly be judged as an abomination. Therefore, there is also something unreal about the Chicagoan type of man; he, too, would appear more natural in a motion picture than he does as a being of flesh and blood. On the other hand, the phantasmagoric quality of Chicagoan crime agrees well with the general atmosphere of a film-city. I remember a dinner party where a gentleman suddenly asked to be excused for a few hours. We asked him, what was the matter? He replied: "A few days ago a gang of gunmen came into my city office" (he was a banker) "at ten o'clock in the morning and took away all they could find. It was, of course, no use applying to the police. But today I was sent word to the effect that if I should put in an appearance at a certain spot at ten o'clock this evening, we might reach a gentleman's agreement." I think the criminal life of Chicago, which is more adventurous than anything one finds in books of adventure, is due much more to the general atmosphere of unreality than to the number of Italians who live there; certainly in a way Chicago resembles pre-Mussolinian Naples and Palermo; but there are many Italians in other cities as well, and yet there this does not lead to anything like what it does in Chicago. If one wants to find general reasons of any sort, one should rather look for them in the fact that, man being a living being in spite of all mechanizations and a human being at that—not an ant or a bee—he *must* have some safety valve when his life becomes mechanized beyond a certain limit; for this reason, I rather expect an increase than a decrease of crime in the United States as "civilization" progresses. But however this may be—the apparent mixture of such incongruous elements as Berlin and Naples is well in accordance with the general atmosphere of unreality characteristic of Chicago. Whatever there is absolutely real, is, generally speaking, decidedly unpleasant; personally, I had only agreeable experiences with those I got to know better; but I must admit that the Americans of other parts of the Union I met, who all seemed to dislike Chicago, are right as far as the general atmosphere goes. It is the one place in the United States where one senses at all the presence of ungenerosity, malice, and ill-will. All this is so. Yet Chicago is an amazing thing. And being "Berlinese"—which means that it is more thorough and more apt than any other city to grow immeasurably without breaking—it has undoubtedly a very great future. I hope Chicago will not absorb the whole of the United States, which is quite within the range of possibility. But if it remains what it is, an immensely powerful "thing in itself" which, incidentally, also accomplishes a good deal of work of national importance, its contrast with the rest of the Union, as it grows, will of necessity lead to fruitful tensions and polarizations. All the more so as Chicago happens to be—again a weird, unreal thing—the most important city and the industrial capital of precisely—the Middle West.

And now to New York! Every intelligent American will tell every intelligent European he meets that New York is not America. It is indeed no longer representative as it undoubtedly was as long as technical development was the one thing the Americans thought of, and before the real native had come to conscious life. Yet New York belongs to America, as a part of the planet, as necessarily as any other city. It is America's clearing-house. There is no doubt that it harbours today more foreigners than native-born. Also, it possesses no unified atmosphere. Then, life is feverish there; this typical quality of every business-centre of the Wall Street type is enhanced by the truly horrible climate of New York. The climate is not stimulating in the least, it is merely unsteady, oscillating from one extreme to the other; it is electric and damp, relaxing and bracing at the same time. But whatever New York's drawbacks may be, it means to America exactly what St. Petersburg used to mean to Russia, and Vienna to the near East: it is America's window opening onto Europe. Here American and European influences meet; here one of the great brains of mankind is developing. And accordingly, the best brains of America crowd together in New York and will continue to do so for a long time to come. The relationship of New York to America is very curious; it is not comparable to that of Paris with respect to France. Nothing of national importance has happened there; New York rather stands for the continuance of that not-national American life which all who are purely business men and all recent immigrants naturally like best. But precisely because the real America is narrowing down and will inevitably do so to an ever-increasing degree, the existence of a powerful New York with its world-wide interests is even more of a necessity for America than any metropolis has ever been for any country. But for a powerful New York, George Babbitt and what he stands for might easily become predominant even in foreign politics, which, considering the tremendous power the United States wields today, would be dangerous.

To conclude this short survey of America's manifoldness and diversity, let me add a few words about Washington. To my surprise this city also struck me as unreal. I soon found out the reason: a political centre in an essentially unpolitical country (I will develop and prove what I hint at here in the chapter entitled "Privatism") must needs give an impression of unreality. Besides, the members of the Diplomatic Corps give the tone to a certain extent in social life. This fact makes for an apparent survival of the colonial days, when great gentlemen continued the typical eighteenth-century life in a new world. If a man like Mr. Coolidge happens to reside at the White House, this only qualifies the general impression of the paradox which Thomas Jefferson incarnated. This man who, as far as my knowledge goes, invented most of the slogans concerning equality, was himself an eighteenth-century *grand seigneur,* if there ever was one. He advocated, as a statesman, the equal rights of all. But this did not prevent him from building tunnels for the invisible passage of his slaves, a device which would have delighted a Trimalchio or even a Nero.

YES, America is at bottom a new land of budding localisms, much as Europe was at the end of the Migration of the Peoples. I have been able to sketch a very few of these localisms, but I imagine that they will suffice to draw the attention of my readers to this very essential aspect of the American Scene which now each of them may follow up according to his own knowledge. As far as I am concerned, I must now strike a new keynote. For at this precise point the possibilities of a comparison between America and Europe are at an end. The fact is *that the localisms I have described will never—because they cannot essentially—grow strong enough to disrupt the unity of the United States.* In order to realize this, we must now give our attention to another and still more important aspect of the American Scene, the relationship of which to what has already been described is that of a logical contradiction.

We have shown in *Europe* that the continent with

which this book deals finds its prototype in the Balkan peninsula. All that is good—not only all that is bad—in Europe depends on its multiplicity, on the fundamental differences between the European peoples and their mutual antagonisms. For they create those tensions which are the vital roots of all creativeness; they are responsible for all the richness and variety of European life. As opposed to this, America is essentially a unified continent. It might, of course, have become a country of many languages, races, and states; there are geographical boundary lines which would have made as "natural" frontiers as any statesman or general could wish for. And, as a matter of fact, there is one boundary line in existence on the North American continent which is very marked, although that one is no "natural" frontier at all: I mean the line separating the United States from Canada. Here the fact that the neighbours belong to different systems of culture perpetuates a difference of type which persists in spite of all continuous intercourse and all similarity in the mode of life; a circumstance which proves the tremendous power of cultural tradition. Yet I do not think it an accident that the territory of the United States has become one unified country: its very spirit is one of width and vastness. This spirit of width and vastness is similar to that of Russia and Central Asia, and entirely different from that of Europe.

These things cannot as yet be satisfactorily explained. But a sensitive traveller feels it obvious that America must needs be a unified whole, as it actually is. It could very well have been split up into politically autonomous parts, as has happened to both China and Russia. But the essential unity—I mean a unity as natural as variety is natural in Europe—would have persisted all the same and reasserted itself time and again, one way or another, on the plane of appearance, as it has always reasserted itself in China and Russia; of this the spiritual insignificance of the individual States of the Union, however autonomous, provides the decisive proof. This country embracing provinces with arctic, tropical, northern, temperate, and southern climates, seashores and deserts, woodland, mountain-ranges, and prairies manifestly cannot help being one. Even the first settlers with their scanty material means of expansion felt themselves as the virtual possessors of the whole. And the rush to the West against all odds would not have been so imperative but for this feeling that America is and must be essentially vast and yet one. Here, then, the Spirit of the Earth asserts itself in another and more imposing manner than in that we have already considered before. We have seen that in America as in Switzerland the factor "nature" in the synthesis of nature and man, which we have called the "scene," appears as the greater power; this explains how, given the soullessness of the colonial, so small a kind of earth-bound type as that of the Middle-Westerner could develop. But the rush for expansion on the material plane is in itself also a result of earth-influence: were it otherwise, the European immigrants would not have been animated with so much more kinetic energy here than at home. American nomadism is the first primitive expression of an inward wideness; such it has remained with the Central Asiatic to this day. Both phenomena are equivalents of the purely bodily movements by which an imbecile baby expresses feelings which find utterance by means of mental symptoms in the insane adult. The Russian who lives in an equally vast country is not a nomad; nor is the Chinese. But then the majority of the Russians belong to a passive type whose way of approaching the wide and infinite is not external conquest, but inner experience; Russia's ruling class, which was responsible for its political greatness, always belonged to the Central-Asiatic type. And the Chinese are an essentially cultured nation, to whom their feeling of cultural supremacy makes even the narrowest conditions appear spacious.

I had first to stress—and as I may now confess: in an exaggerated way—the point of American narrowness as a result of the creative influence of the earth because it seems to me the point least noticed and least understood —a misunderstanding which in its turn has a detrimental influence on the narrow type on which the future of the American race chiefly depends. But the essential effect of the influence of the American earth is no doubt that it widens and broadens. The narrowing effect is due simply to the laws which govern in general the process of taking root in the soil by a race not belonging to the ruler-type. I once said jestingly to reporters that America looks to me less like a gigantic Switzerland than like a gigantic Canton Appenzell. But the emphasis should be laid on the adjective "gigantic." Physical vastness and width do make for corresponding broadness. A giant, however narrow-minded, who inhabits a whole continent is, as a matter of course, something bigger than the European localist. Now this quality of vastness inherent in the continent, and by its influence impressed on man, stands out so strikingly as the fundamental characteristic that one may safely prophesy that, however much localisms may develop, they will always remain a secondary aspect of American life; and the developing differences will never amount to more than the differences between Northern and Southern Russia and Northern and Southern China. The uniformity of America, accordingly, means something more essential than a mere effect of standardization. It would probably be more true to fact to say that the latter could only go as far as it has gone because of the unifying and broadening American atmosphere. If the unity were chiefly due to standardization, then it would be entirely of the surface; and this is actually true of that psychological equality the achievement of which within the shortest possible time seems to be the one aim of those schools, to the influence of which foreign-born children of poor immigrants are first submitted as a matter of principle. Real like-mindedness is based on common feelings and emotions and not on common slogans—the so-called common thoughts rarely amount to more—and feelings develop slowly because they can only grow as children grow in the mother's womb; herein lies the root of the typical dislike of the scion of old native American stock for all aliens who pretend to be Americans. Now the American who can legitimately claim to be an original son of the American soil belongs to the same type of man, in whatever part of the continent he may have been born. This, then, leads us to the realization of a new and highly important truth. *One can compare America to China; one can compare America to Russia. But it is entirely wrong and entirely unfair to compare America to Europe in any respect.*

That this truth has escaped the notice of most is easy to explain. All white Americans are of European stock; the forebears of more than half of all living Americans crossed over only within the last hundred years; immigration from Europe still continues. Intellectually and spiritually the whole Western World seems to be one, and all its creative influences still emanate from the Old World. In addition to these objective facts there is a subjective corollary, *viz.*, that the majority of both Europeans and Americans of the educated class are, at any rate unconsciously, of the opinion that the Americans *ought* to be Europeans. But if the power of America's Earth-Spirit asserts itself anywhere, then it certainly is here. In spite of all the above-mentioned facts, the American is even today more akin to the Russian and the Chinese than to the European. Like them, he is essentially a child of width and vastness.

This, then, leads us to a modification of American narrowness, which, in its turn, implies a limitation of our argument that the Middle-Westerner belongs to the same type as the Swiss. There are very narrow types in Russia, too; one need only think of its sectarians; nor can the Chinese peasant or small merchant justly be called broad-minded. But both belong to an essentially broad and wide-flung type of man, as parts belong to a whole; in the same sense, the British provincial whose conscious horizon does not extend beyond private and local interests forms an integral part of an essentially empire-building nation. That the American, too, belongs to an essentially broad and wide-flung type, even if he be a Babbitt in all essential respects, can be best realized in his narrowest representatives. The manner in which the ordinary business man earns and spends money and always visualizes the shortest way to reach his end, disregarding all petty considerations, his capacity of co operating with others in spite of all minor differences and even clashes of interests, his readiness to break at a moment's notice with his past—these characteristics alone denote an originally wide-flung type of man. For the rest, there must be individual or class-types which are narrow within every national whole; the greatest genius must have the ordinary kind of feet to walk on. Now Chinese philosophy has given a very good theory—expressed, of course, in the language of mythical imagery—of the true connexion; and I think it wise to give its chief outlines here because the full understanding of the case is of the utmost importance. According to the Chinese conception, Heaven and Earth, the events of the world and the lives of men, morality and the normal course of nature, form one single interconnected whole. Heaven comes first, then the Emperor; he is the tie uniting Heaven and Earth. But the peasant represents the link which joins the earth to man. Man—with the one exception of the Emperor, who is to that extent more than man—"has the earth for image." The peasant is the man most strictly subjected to the earth. But for this very reason he is the foundation of the whole. If he does not rigidly perform his duties, then the State as well as Heaven begins to totter.[1] In the language of modern psychology, the meaning of the ancient sages of China would amount to this that in every man two elements of different origin co-operate: spirit and matter. These two elements may unite in any kind of ratio. There are men of predominating spirit—they are the born leaders. But no nation can be considered as soundly organized if its foundations are not built up by a class of an essentially earthbound character exceeding all the others in number. In the

[1] Compare the chapters "Tsi-Nan-Fu" and "Peking" of my *Travel Diary*.

United States, owing to peculiar circumstances, there is—at least for the present—no peasant class. But what the peasant stands for in the scheme of things is represented in the New World by that narrow type we compared to the Swiss; indeed, give to a peasant of any country a liberal surface education and create such conditions that he has to refer to it in whatever he does and says, and he will inevitably take on the appearance of a perfect Babbitt; Babbitt represents the exact equivalent of that which made such a convincing type of Molière's *Bourgeois Gentilhomme*, in the days before the *tiers-état* was of any account.

The earthbound, narrow type of the American, then, corresponds to what the peasant represents all over the world. No wonder, therefore, that most men who were successful in New York in later life were born in the Middle West. There is no greater contradiction between the narrowness of George F. Babbitt and the wide-scheming and world-embracing type of American than between the peasant and the ruler in China and Russia; they really belong to each other, supplement each other, and constantly revert to each other. From this follows one thing that seems to me important for Americans to realize. *They should not be ashamed of Babbitt.* He is today the soundest and safest type of the whole continent. What they should really wish for and aim at is that the earthbound type should cease to play as a matter of course a part which is the American equivalent of the rôle the *Bourgeois Gentilhomme* played in seventeenth-century France; that he should become class-conscious and, accordingly, take less interest in matters he is physiologically unable to understand; for the earthbound type *is* physiologically unable to understand things spiritual. Moreover, the Americans who do not belong to his type should cease to see in him "the American," whether as glorification or as disparagement; they should leave him alone—and he really asks no more. Finally, they should do everything in their power to further the development of a superior earthbound type, a type corresponding to that of the landed nobility in the Old World. The nobleman is the type in which the elements of spirit and of earth counterpoise each other; this is the reason why in all history he was the born leader. He has proved the born leader in America as well, for the fact that an overwhelming majority of important Americans were sons of the South, and in particular of Virginia, really amounts to this.

One may, therefore, compare the American to the Russian and the Chinese and the Central Asiatic, but not to the European. This stands out most clearly when one realizes that not only the Swiss-like but also the wide-flung variety of the American is essentially confined and exclusive, both inwardly and spatially. This has been the case with all peoples the majority of which live in what one calls continental as opposed to oceanic climes. Seafaring nations are as a rule an awakened class; this explains why all far-reaching and transplantable and colonizing civilizations have originated by the sea. But the Chinese never looked beyond China; China was to them not only the Middle Kingdom, but all that counted in the world. In exactly the same sense the Russian, vast as his soul is, always looked upon the non-Russian as not sincere; when he spoke of man in general, he really always meant the Russian; this applies even to Dostoievsky. As to the inhabitants of Central Asia

—they were often world-conquerors, but their manner of conquest and subsequent rule illustrates that inner exclusiveness which is characteristic of all inhabitants of continental climes. The case of the American is analogous. His genuine native-born type instinctively looks upon everything non-American as inferior or uncomprehending, or even as a moral abomination. Herein lies one of the roots of that missionary spirit which is the very soul of every American salesman, and, generally speaking, of American advertising; only in America could advertising "as such" become an independent business. The slogan "America is the right place for Americans to live in" rings true and means something different in kind from the Englishman's love for his home-country. But the same explains why the American is essentially unadaptable in spite of his versatility. He cannot colonize: he could only conquer and absorb. However much he may honestly believe in the equal rights of all peoples, his involuntary attitude towards neighbours such as Mexicans and Central-Americans is that of an old-fashioned teacher who wants to improve the character of a bad boy. He cannot see that what he calls "Democracy" may be only a life-form among others, well suited to Americans, but perhaps entirely unsuited to other peoples; in his opinion his own peculiar ways *must* be absolutely the best in the abstract. This is exactly the way ancient China always felt and the way Russia is feeling even today; the real soul of the Bolshevik world-propaganda is to be found in this attitude and not in Socialistic theory. Here we also find the explanation of the fact, why the so-called land of freedom cares so very little for liberty of thought. The American is essentially dogmatic. One may, of course, say all sorts of things as long as it does not seem to matter. But let a real spiritual influence come to power which does not harmonize with original American tendencies—and the Ku Klux Klan spirit will at once arise in some form or other. It struck me from the beginning as a remarkable fact that American radicals—the word taken in its European sense—do not seem to feel responsible; neither do they seem to take their criticism very seriously, nor even themselves. The reason is that their position in life is very much the same as that of the court jester in the Middle Ages. The significance of the court jester was not that he was a fool—usually he was even the wisest man at the court—but that his wisdom was without any power or influence. To complete the picture of American limitation and exclusiveness, we should remember two other facts. There seem to be no bounds to the possibilities of standardization and mass-suggestion on American soil. But on the other hand, their influence does not reach beyond the geographical and political borders of the United States; it does not even reach beyond the Canadian frontier. This means that the soul of American standardization is the belief which every American instinctively cherishes, that what is good for one must necessarily be good for all. This is again a modernized expression of the same spirit which animates Russian nationalism and Chinese exclusiveness. This alone suffices to explain why things American are essentially not transferable and transplantable. There can be no question of an americanization of the world. Certainly very many technical inventions and business methods, and even particular ways of life which originated in America, will be taken over by most countries as far as they are of practical use. But if the word americanization meant no more than that, this would imply that America has no soul. Either a nation is a soul or it is non-existent. We shall see later on what the exact meaning of the term "soul" is in this connexion. But we can realize even now that the American soul is essentially an exclusive soul; accordingly, America is essentially a closed system. This is why the Monroe Doctrine appeals so strongly to all Americans; this also partly explains (we shall find more reasons for it in later chapters) that conservatism which appears as a more determinant element in this young country than it ever did in pre-revolutionary China: a closed system must needs be essentially conservative. Its basis must be immutable. China never dreamt of changing the Confucian code; Russia's Christianity (up to the last revolution Russia's real unity was of a religious nature) did not admit the mere possibility of an evolution. In the same sense, America clings not only to its Constitution, but also to certain institutions which all thinking American individuals admit are antiquated, inefficient, or even contrary to the very spirit of civilization.

Thus we see that the differences between Europe and America are not mere differences of age and culture or differences in particularities, but that they express a fundamental dissimilarity. Owing to the continuing influx of Europeans, this fact cannot yet stand out with perfect clarity; but it stands out even today clearly enough to prevent any misconception in regard to the basic situation. And it stands out thus not only for the foreign observer; the same is true from the point of view of the American's inner experience. Here we have reached the point at which we can appraise the truly tremendous importance of the World War for the United

States; it has undoubtedly meant more in their history than in that of Europe. Not so much because from being a nation of borrowers, America has of a sudden become a nation of lenders; not because it represents today, the richest country in the world; not even because of the enormous political and moral influence it has acquired. All these acquirements may, after all, be nothing but temporary acquirements—and, in many respects the present state of things certainly seems far from secure. The World War means the most important event in the history of the United States up to now, *because owing to the shock and clash it produced, America as a whole has for the first time become conscious of her individual soul.* Before the War, America still essentially considered herself a colony of Europe, or at least one of the many parts of a unified Western World; she could do this without difficulty because there was a continuous coming and going from and to Europe, and because the ruling idea was not that America was a nation, but simply the Land of Freedom. The shock of the World War made the native-born American conscious for the first time of his Americanism, that he possesses an exclusive national soul. And this awakening has been so powerful that even the young generations whose parents were foreign-born feel American today and nothing else; which means in most cases: they feel American as opposed to European. Since this new soul has only just awakened to consciousness, it cannot express itself in the form of perfection; the superior type of the American has yet to be born. But if the Babbitt-type stands out today with the convincing power of a mythological figure, this is due first and foremost to the fact that the narrow type of American could first feel American and nothing else.

And he could reach a prominence very few sons of older civilizations seem to understand, because to be American at all means at the beginnings of the making of the American, as of every other nation, *the* primal value. He has actually come to prominence today in all spheres of life, which would have been impossible before the War. Now this means so much that one can safely say that America's real history has begun only with this crisis; what happened before was European colonial history or, as it would seem to the American in whom the past is alive within him, America's mythical period, as the Homeric age was to the later Greeks. This one fact goes far to explain America's post-war attitude: its repudiation of Wilsonism, its retreat from the League of Nations, its debt-policy, its laws to restrict immigration. Even Prohibition possibly comes in here. The more I think of it, the more the Eighteenth Amendment seems to me to correspond to something profound and fundamental in the American temperament, no matter whether or not the law will remain what it is today. The red Indians, too, are not only an ascetic, but a joyless kind of people. One should not object here that Prohibition is not really enforced: the law-breaking instinct, too, is a fundamental American trait. What seems to me so characteristic is that the range covered by law should include Prohibition. We shall see later that law does not in any way mean the same thing to Americans that it means to Europeans.

The World War, then, means the birth-moment of real America. That it was precisely this war which called to life American consciousness chiefly accounts for the suddenness and extravagance of certain phenomena. This applies in particular to the sometimes exaggerated way in which that rejuvenation, with which our next chapter will deal—a rejuvenation due in itself to causes which have been operating ever since the continent began to be settled—is manifesting itself. As the consciousness of being American as opposed to European awoke only yesterday in the form of a sudden shock, the young generation feels very much what Adam and Eve must have felt. Its spirit is essentially that of a first generation. Nothing that was before them counts; as far as they are concerned, there has been no past. All the great traditions are being laughingly discarded. Yes, the boys and girls of today really seem to feel like the first human beings at the time when they had their memorable transaction with the Tree of Knowledge; only that they seem sure that they will find a better solution than Adam and Eve did. They do not mean to be chased from what they think is Paradise.

WE HAVE now traced a sufficient number of co-ordinates, all pointing in the same direction, to allow us to determine the essence of the American Scene. Let us recall our definition at the beginning of this chapter: the Scene presented by an inhabited continent is the result of the interaction between Nature and Man. We found that in the case of America the stress should be laid on Nature. This is so firstly—I am recapitulating the fundamental causes only—because of the extraordinary formative power of this particular continent; then, because of the short time it has been inhabited by white man; lastly, because this man, in exhausting all his energies in external work, has retrogressed in his soul-development, which fact—since soul only creates a psychic and spiritual atmosphere—gave to the physical atmosphere an additional chance of influence. On the basis of our last observations we may add one more factor which makes for the same result. Owing to the fact that up to the World War America continued to be thought of consciously, even by native-born Americans, as the Land of Freedom, the asylum for all, or the melting-pot inevitably changing everything for the better in some abstract sense, American *thought* was to an extraordinary degree unconnected with reality, and, therefore, could exert no creative influence. Even today America's abstract thought is something more abstract than that of any other race; it thinks in terms of purely abstract values, whether of Democracy or Morality, or Liberty or Idealism, or what not. It is true that, in opposition to this, there soon developed on American soil a more matter-of-fact way of appraising things and values than has existed anywhere else; the general denominator of the multiple tendencies in question is best described by the term pragmatism, although what I mean to express by the word covers a much wider range than really belongs to that particular school of thought. The decisive idea is that the value of everything mental or spiritual should be gauged by the so-called pragmatic test, which is usually even conceived in terms of success. This very extremeness of American matter-of-factness proves that fundamentally it means an ideology of contrast: because American thinking had a traditional tendency toward pure abstraction, it consciously tended all the more emphatically towards the tangible. But how much do these abstractions mean even today? America is even today the most idealistic nation in the sense of abstract idealism; it is as severe and radical and uncompromising in its idealism as schoolboys are. And this idealism is constantly being reinforced by the ideologies of the newcomers, who must insist, from pure self-interest, on America's not being a country like other countries and the Americans not being a nation like other nations; in their eyes, America is just the promised land of realized ideals. Nevertheless, abstract ideals have very little power in themselves. Any one who might have doubted this before the World War should know better now. President Wilson's Fourteen Points have really wrecked Europe and imperilled the position of the whole white race. They are the spiritual parents of Bolshevism, because but for the idea of the self-determination of nations and Wilson's utter disregard of historical connexions, the Bolshevists would never have succeeded in revolutionizing the whole East and never even dreamt of attempting the same in Europe. As a matter of fact, the temporary rule of purely abstract ideals without any connexion with reality only gave a chance unheard of in modern history to the irrational powers of the subconscious. The same applies to America itself. If the idealism of the cultured classes were not of so abstract a quality, the spirit of the earth would have had no chance of asserting itself so powerfully in the primordial figure of Babbitt. The best illustration of the truth that the rule of purely abstract ideals means devitalization is provided by New England: its traditional type would be less anæmic, and Boston would not so soon have become apparently even more remote than the atmosphere of Mount Athos in the Christian world, if it were not for this lack of connexion between mental and non-mental life. For since the focus of modern man's consciousness lies in mind,[1] such a lack of connexion implies that the whole man loses his connexion with the elementary vital powers.

So far, so good. Still, there is another side to the question. Religions whose dogmas had no connexion whatever with the ruling vital impulses have ruled the earth; of this, Christianity provides the best example. And these religions have exerted a tremendous influence all the same. It seems certain that no typical Westerner ever resembled in the slightest the type which the immediate followers of Jesus expected the Christian of the future to be. And yet the Christian ideals have helped to shape our world. It would probably have made little difference if the Eastern races with their metaphysical and passive disposition had been converted to Christianity. But the aggressive, acquisitive, and essentially worldly Westerner would unquestionably have become a worse type of man than he actually is, if it were not for the fact that for long centuries he has believed in Christian ideals. Now religion is a thing very different from abstract idealism. But the fact is that the attitude of the typical American towards what would mean abstractions to a European is a religious attitude; he is not intellectually convinced of their truth, he believes in them quite irrationally; this applies in particular to Democracy, Morality, and Liberty. Now belief is a very vital thing. It is true that believing in a thing does not make it more real on the material plane than it actually is; but it reacts on and shapes believing man. Thus, we have found a definition of the polar opposite to American earth-boundness. Life always is a polar

[1] Compare, for the development of this trend of thought, the chapter "The New Union between Mind and Soul" in *Creative Understanding*.

phenomenon; whoever posits one thing inevitably posits its opposite at the same time. For that reason earth-bound man as a type is always a religious man as well. The more primitive a race, the more does it believe in spiritual connexions and correlations. In its case these usually are entirely unreal from the point of view of fact; but they are symbols of the real. And as an earth-bound type develops, its religiousness develops into a higher kind. India is the land of religion *par excellence* because the extraordinary power of the Indian soil has effected in the highly gifted race that inhabited it, as a compensatory process, a correspondingly powerful and clear realization of the spiritual. One should remember that the Nordic races as such are not religious, but idealistic; their ruling principle is not Pathos but Ethos; [1] the model of their type is to be found neither in the Earth nor in God, but in Icarus and Lucifer. In one respect the Jews are more earth-bound than any race on earth; to no other race of comparable importance did and do "blood" and "seed" mean so much. The Chinese cannot properly be called religious because their type represents a perfect state of balance between the two principles of Spirit and Earth, Yang and Yin. Nor can the Europeans, because they are essentially idealists; here the principle of Yang predominates. As opposed to this, the Russians are a deeply religious race. Devoid of all idealism in the European sense, as earth-bound as the Hindus, only with respect to another less exuberant earth, they are conscious of the reality of spirit in the ratio of polar correspondence. Now the native-born Americans, too, are a distinctly religious race; in

[1] I must here refer my readers to the chapters "The Ethical Problem" and "The Religious Problem" in the *Recovery of Truth*.

this consists one of their fundamental differences from the Europeans. And they are religious or, to use a more general term, they are spiritual for the same fundamental reasons and in the same general sense as the Russians. That their spirituality today appears to be, as a rule, of a primitive kind (one should call to mind the quotation of Doctor Jung) is only natural. If earth-bound America is primitive, so must spiritual America be. From this vantage-point one can even anticipate, as a matter of necessity, the peculiarities of American religiosity. Since American life is bent on the conquest and rule of matter as no life ever has been before, it is a logical necessity that America's really native and original religion should be Christian Science or something akin to it; for Christian Science denies matter altogether. And since the established churches are developing more and more toward the type of successful business-enterprises, it is also a logical necessity that the most savagely primitive ideas of official Christianity should find successful promoters. Here I am thinking first of the Rev. Billy Sunday (a man I greatly admire and to whom I am personally grateful, because he did me the great honour to fulminate against me in one of his mammoth-meetings as against Satan incarnate) who provides as complete information about Hell as did ever any primitive painter, and who is alleged to have given to the newspapers, shortly before I left America, a statement to the effect that the Devil should not hope to find peace after his death, since he had ordered in his will that a drum should be made out of his skin, the beating of which would annoy the Evil One for ages to come.

We seem to have drifted far away from the problem of American earth-boundness. As a matter of fact, only this apparent "drifting away" has led us to its complete definition. Man is a synthesis between spirit and earth; he is spirit as really, concretely, as he is matter (we shall deal in detail with the problem of the reality of spirit in the concluding chapter). And the more man is earthbound, on the one hand, the more he is physiologically predisposed, on the other, to realize the reality of spirit. And original religiousness thus also belongs to the essential characteristics of the American Scene. It follows by implication that there is little prospect of America's ever becoming a land of predominating intellect or of any intermediate stage between pure materialism and pure spiritualism. By this I do not mean to imply that the Americans are not or will not remain intelligent; they are even a decidedly intelligent nation. But intellectual problems as such do not mean much to them today and will probably mean even less as the nation becomes more "native" in quality. And it is this circumstance, not intelligence as such, which decides the question of the intellectuality or non-intellectuality of a race; one should remember here what I have explained in *Europe*, as to why, even in Europe, only two nations can be called intellectual, the Germans and the French. There is also little prospect of America as a whole ever developing a culture in the Chinese or Greek or French sense; for in this case, too, it is a question of a predominating intermediary stage between spiritualism and materialism. Here again one should think of Russia. Russia is physiologically anti-cultural; its most representative spirits were, for a considerable time, the nihilists: they called themselves by that name because they saw no value in culture and strove to annihilate everything that was not pure spirituality on the one side, and pure utility on the other. The Americans belong to a similar type, only that they are less spiritual-minded as a race and utilitarian to a much higher degree; quite naturally so, because extraversion and an active modality of life preclude, physiologically, many possibilities of inner experience. When the Russians speak of the socially good as the supreme value, they still mean by implication that spiritual values form its background; they believe in poverty and not in riches; to that extent even the Bolsheviks belong to the early Christian type. A really utilitarian life-conception must logically consider comfort as the supreme value. This is what most Americans do. Now comfort as an accepted ideal can never become a vehicle of cultural values. Culture develops only where Beauty as such stands foremost, and not utility, Truth as such, and its pragmatic value. To that extent the prospects of American civilization point in the direction of the Roman as opposed to the Greek ideal. Here, then, we see finally why America cannot be compared to Europe, and why the two continents and civilizations must inevitably drift ever farther apart, as time goes on. Europe, the small Balkan-like peninsula, subdivided into many different fields of forces, which will never come to a compromise and will never fuse, a scene of both tremendous and most minutely varied tensions, is for that very reason the predestined homeland of intellectuality and culture in the modern world. Intellectuality and culture both presuppose differentiation and an original feeling for differences and values. It is true that China in its great days developed a wonderful culture in spite of its uniformity. But then it was not uniform in the beginning; it was almost as multiform as mediæval Europe. Moreover, the Chinese race is endowed with an innate gift for the visible form which the Nordics lack; finally, the Chinese Scene was always different from the American and the Russian, in so far as it incarnated a perfect state of balance between Spirit and Earth. In this connexion, then, America can be compared only to Russia. In Russia there never was a culture in the European or the Chinese sense, nor will there ever be. But it has a great and wonderful soul nevertheless, deeply religious, deeply philosophical, profoundly musical and full of love.

WE HAVE now reached a point from which it should not be impossible to arrive at a vision of what may evolve out of the American Scene, when the spirits of Man and of the Earth will have finally united and when the nation will have reached maturity. Up to now no such union and no kind of maturity has been achieved. What we saw during our survey corresponded throughout to a preliminary stage, to first beginnings even; and indeed, all actual and pressing and immediate problems of America are problems of embryonic life. With these I will deal one by one in the second part of this book. In the present context I will only say this much about this particular subject, namely that for some time to come America is not likely to advance in the absolute sense, but rather to become more primitive. Let us, then, leaving alone all intermediary stages, try to trace the general outlines of what the future American nation and culture is likely to be after having reached maturity. Only, before we enter upon this, I must make four more preliminary remarks in order to clear the way. There is, alas, the possibility that owing to bad heredity, of which there is far too much in the United States by reason of the quality of those who immigrated during the last century and the greater fecundity of the newcomers, the nation will *not* develop according to its best potentialities; this possibility I will simply discard, for should it become a fact, it would mean one of those decrees of destiny which lead to an absolute and inevitable end. Then there is that other possibility that America may never become a nation, that it may remain that unsuccessful melting-pot many thoughtful observers think it is today. This possibility I will likewise disregard; for should this alternative become true, then America's future would be entirely devoid of interest. A third possibility is that all hopes for America's future may ultimately have to be confined to technical and financial progress; this seems to be the view held by most American and European prophets. But I shall not deal with this possibility either. We have already pointed out that inventions and institutions as such never make a stand for national values; the printing-press was invented in Germany and the world has not become German for that. We pointed this out also in order to refute the current idea of an imminent americanization of the world. But all possible wealth of inventions and institutional improvements would not even make for an americanization of America. All these externals are essentially like money: they have no intrinsic substance; anybody may take them over and handle them. Even if some day America became the paragon of all imaginable progress, it need not for all that become a nation and, still less, a civilization: it would then be something essentially artificial like a model farm or a model factory; it would above all be intrinsically lifeless, for only "things" can be perfected to such a degree; it is impossible where living beings are concerned. Americans should face, once and for all, a truth which at first sight will strike them as paradoxical in the highest degree, namely, that most of those men public opinion calls great in national significance really are entirely devoid of any significance; if America has a cultural future, then a hundred years hence professionals will remember only names like those of Rockefeller and Henry Ford.

I shall, therefore, discard also the possibility that America's future can be defined completely in terms of technical and financial progress. And I shall do so not only because then America's future would be devoid of interest—in that case it would amount to an entirely impersonal factory where things rule men—but because personally I think that such a hopeless future does not even lie within the range of the probable. For one thing, a real soul-life has already begun. But, above all, the more one faculty of mind or soul seems over-stressed, the more certainly will evolution, sooner or later, experience a solution of continuity; and such a solution almost always leads to a new development on different lines from the previous one. Let my readers remember what has been said in the chapter "Wisdom Ancient and Modern" of *Creative Understanding* about the true meaning of the contrasting orientation of Christianity as compared with the Pagan world: the former stressed exclusively the emotions with concomitant contempt of all intellectual values, because the antique world had believed in the latter only and because it had exhausted all possibilities of the intellectual development then existing—while, on the other hand, the quality of love within man's nature had remained under-developed. In America life is undoubtedly over-rationalized; standardization goes so far there that all those tendencies of human nature which stand for the differentiated, the exclusive, and the non-rational find no food. This will inevitably lead to a banking up of the unspent energies which will, sooner or later, break forth and dig their own channels. Even today, the American strikes me as fundamentally more irrational than the European. All that has to do with his emotionalism, his quick changes of mood, and his sensationalism, not to mention his sentimentalism, is an expression of this quality. When American provincials begin to talk of their feelings as decisive factors, then the most intelligent listener who sticks to reason must lay down his arms. American love of superlatives cannot be explained in the case of so businesslike a nation by any reasoned appreciation of quantity, nor even by a tendency to use quantity as a symbol: it means, on the contrary, a compensatory escape from the exactitude business demands; it is an escape on the plane of imagination. I have often concentrated on the subconscious minds of such men as indulged in the wildest exaggerations: they never really meant them, but on the other hand they had to utter them. In the same way, the American faculty for enthusiasm, delightful as it is, never means anything fundamental; fundamentally, the nation is serious and calculating. It simply means the necessary compensation for a life too full of calculation. And the same applies to the typical American religious revivals in which reason seems to play no part and, last, but not least, to the equally typical American waves or tides of criminality. A reporter once asked me why there should be so many crimes in America and particularly in Chicago? My answer was: because you want them for your front pages. This was a joke, of course, but I was serious at bottom. On this plane also there seems to be a kind of pre-established harmony between those who do the things and those who like to hear about them. Most serious-minded modern men, myself included, love reading detective stories; the reading of them gives a chance to the adventure-loving part in man to live itself out within a too well-ordered scheme of life—in the case of the fighting soldier, the reading of sentimental love-stories best meets an analogous demand. American life being over-rationalized, over-mechanized, and over-standardized, there must be a compensatory amount of lawbreaking, wild adventure, and bloodshed. Now what is true in the dimension of simultaneity is equally true in the dimension of succession. Human nature is incapable of an indefinite one-sided development. In Europe the era of continuous progress resulted in the World War, the most irrational and barbaric event the world ever saw. In the same sense, I am convinced that the present line of American development will not go on very much longer. Soon the law of *Enantiodromia*, of the reversion to the opposite, will set in. This does not mean that I am expecting an annulment of the results of previous developments, but that on the basis of these, evolution will start on a new line which will not be a continuation of the development America chiefly stands for today, in its own eyes as well as in those of the world.—I think I have now removed the principal obstacles which stand in the way of a correct estimation of American possibilities. I shall now finally try to materialize my vision of what may evolve out of the American Scene, when man and the earth will have united and when the nation will have reached maturity.

One cannot predict America's future on the basis of its institutions as such. In the chapter "The Animal Ideal" I will show in detail what a dangerous fallacy is the idea that everything can be explained by "environment"—which in this particular case would mean that the way in which the human material will probably respond to institutions might make it possible to predict the future of American Man. On the whole, it is never safe to "explain" vital phenomena by external causes. One of the joys of my life is to read American statistics: they never prove a single vital thing, because in the domain of life significance creates the facts and, therefore, the deductions at which American scientists arrive are as often as not as irrational and as thrilling as the conclusions of fairy tales. If history has ever proved any axiom true, it has proved that one first stated by Gustave Le Bon: *les peuples ne sont pas gouvernés par leurs institutions, mais par leur caractère.* This means that if institutions happen to be the exact expression of a nation's character, then they are representative and to that extent sure to last; if there is no such harmony between character and expression, then the best of institutions are futile. Now the present institutions of the United States may correspond to the inner state of the nation; but they also may not. They may not for the good reason that the nation is as yet in the making, that the original Constitution was drawn up by and adapted to a majority very different from that of today, and that by the time the nation reaches maturity it may have changed entirely; by that time an entirely different proportion between Anglo Saxon and other blood may prevail, and the distribution of power and importance among the different elements may have changed completely. And the present institutions of America may not correspond to a final inner state for an even more vital reason: they hardly take any account of man as he is really and inwardly; their creative basis is either an abstract ideal of inner man, which he has never reached and never will reach, or else a purely external ideal like that of efficiency, standard of living, or productiveness; and a day may come when the Americans will realize that such an ideal does not ultimately express what they mean and that they do not even care for it. The Russians very much prefer starving to a life of comfort conditioned by American hustle and bustle. I do not wish to express any definite opinion on this question, for in fact I have none; but I do want to caution my readers. The fact that most Americans believe their institutions to be absolutely the best is only one more proof of Babbitt's provincialism; as I have shown in the chapter "Italy" in *Europe*, there are no such things as institutions which are absolutely the best in themselves. Under these conditions, if one wants to forecast the national and cultural future of the United States, their institutions can be taken into account only to the extent that they directly and immediately express America's soul. Now what is the soul of a nation? And—since we said that a nation is essentially a soul if it is a nation at all—what makes a nation?—It is neither race nor environment nor even history as such. A *collectivity is or is not a nation according to whether or not it represents a unity of style.*[1] Seen as a whole, the

[1] The reader will find more elaborate development of the trends of thought that follow in *Europe*, p. 358, the chapter "Spiritual Parent-

biological material has always been the same. The nations and the cultures which emerged from it depended solely on whether a spirit—and what kind of spirit—animated it from time to time. It is exactly the same with the art of the painter. Colours and forms and the laws that govern them are accessible to every man; but a Rembrandt creates something *unique* by means of them. A significant national being stands and falls by the same character of uniqueness. Thousands and thousands of peoples, all of them built up of the same or a similar primal material, have wandered over the earth; but few of them have acquired real form, and among these only the smallest number has asserted itself permanently. These last were, in every case, peoples which bore the same relation to others as the work of a Rembrandt bears to that of an inferior painter. The changes and wanderings of the nations which have been predominating forces on earth are, therefore, in reality, the changes and the wanderings of styles, not of races. Since the time of Adam the latter have reproduced themselves as the primal raw material; they take their form from the spirit which rules for the time being. There can be no doubt that the latter is, in its manifestations, more or less bound to a specific blood. The Nordics, for instance, from times immemorial have showed the same fundamental instincts which are characteristic of the pure Anglo Saxons today. Nevertheless, it is quite incorrect to lay the main stress on this bond; it is not the primary instincts which make a nation—though they may define a race—but what a definite spirit makes of them,

---

hood" in *The Recovery of Truth*, and the essay "*Jesus der Magier*" contained in *Menschen als Sinnbilder* (French edition: *Figures Symboliques*, Paris, Librairie Stock).

and how he uses them; it is precisely America which presents the most striking proof of this. The European type from which the typical American—of however pure Anglo-Saxon stock—differs most psychologically is—the Englishman. The difference between these two is so marked that one may fairly call it a freak of nature that they both speak the same language. Think of the extreme lack of reserve of the American and the supreme cultivation of it in England; the extreme publicity there, the supreme sense of privacy here; the highly developed political sense in the Englishman and the almost complete lack of it in the American; the fundamental individualism of England and the equally fundamental social outlook of the American; the prevailing sense for hierarchy and caste and quality in general in England, as opposed to which America is democratic in the sense of believing in equality, like-mindedness, and standardization as supreme values; the Englishman's love of little things and the typical incapacity of the American to realize that value does not depend on quantity and size. The differences between a Norwegian and a Neapolitan certainly amount to less. This line of thought should, incidentally, convince of their error all those who believe that in the domain of life anything can be really explained in terms of external causation. Practically, all Americans of old native stock—and these are really the fathers of the country—are children of the British Isles by blood and tradition and culture, and even as far as their fundamental institutions are concerned; and yet . . . By means of these general considerations we have already approached the true understanding of what the American nation can develop into. *To talk of the diversity of races inhabiting the American soil as an ob-*

*stacle towards national unity is to miss the point altogether.* All great nations were the results of blood-mixtures; these are indispensable for the all-important reason that spirit can manifest itself on earth only by means of material tensions, precisely as tightened strings only can produce musical sounds.[1] Most decidedly there are originally superior and originally inferior races. But then there are no pure races left on earth and, moreover, all higher culture has always blossomed forth when the determination by blood-heredity had become the lesser force as compared with spirit. It is also true that there are races which at *a given period* unmistakably represent a bad blend. But no one can foretell whether something good may not develop out of the bad later on. The present-day Eurasian type leads one to think that the first products of the cross between Aryan and aboriginal blood in India must have been of a decidedly inferior type; so probably were the first blends between the Nordic invaders of Greece and the Pelasgians and between the non-African invaders of Egypt in the dawn of Egyptian history and the native stock. Yet from these very crosses originated the great civilizations of India, Greece, and Egypt. Now cultures as such are primarily expressions of *spirit;* so are nations. Their one exponent is style, as in the case of art. And the nature of the style can never be surmised from the material used.

The question of America's national and cultural future is, therefore, exclusively a question as to whether

[1] Compare the considerations on the advantage of blood admixture in the closing chapter of *Europe* and, concerning the general question of the relationship between spirit and its earthly means of manifestations the chapter "Life and Death" in *The Recovery of Truth.*

or not an original style will animate and co-ordinate some day the given material and express it in a new original form. But does style then come down directly from Heaven? Figuratively speaking, it does. This is why masterpieces are always explained by the co-operation of such mysterious qualities as "genius" or "inspiration." It is perhaps best to begin the explanation of a state of things essentially inexplicable by a statement of its least intelligible expression. Oswald Spengler has advanced a theory according to which the various cultures have souls of their own, dependent on the landscape, but almost entirely independent of both racial material and individual spiritual endowment; according to this author, any racial material should, in principle, be able to give expression to any soul; again, the great individual should not be the initiator but merely the executive of ideas preconceived by that super-racial and super-individual entity he calls Culture-soul. This sounds rather mystical in the worst sense; I have found no difficulty in refuting the theory as Spengler frames it, in the chapter "*Spengler der Tatsachenmensch*" of *Menschen als Sinnbilder*. Yet there is truth underlying Spengler's errors. And this truth has been grasped and expressed to a certain extent satisfactorily by Leo Frobenius in his booklet *Paideuma*. It appears that among primitive races, with their collective consciousness, a culture really represents an *a priori* with respect to the individual; it is an independent entity, as sharply separated from others and as incapable of fusing with others as a plant, because of its essentially non-rational quality. With the growth of the transferable quality in man's psychological structure, in particular, with the growth of the intellect, this similarity to a plant dwindles proportionally. Yet it remains true that a culture is a thing in itself, a "Beyond" from the point of view of both the individual and the race. The general reason is that on all planes of life the whole is pre-existent to its parts, if not in the sense of material fact, then always in the same sense that the whole of a melody is conceived prior to the sounds that compose it. Collective life temporally precedes individual life; the fully self-conscious individual finally emerges from the group, as the flower grows out of the stem. In the same sense, there is a collective unconscious which forms the vital background of all individual consciousness. Now the law of this whole, invisible in itself, always predetermines from within all visible events. Save in exceptional cases, a man never dies of a particular disease, but he succumbs to any, even the most contemptible bacillus which happens to be at hand when the melody of his life approaches its natural end. At certain turning-points in the history of the earth, as recorded by geology, certain types of creatures suddenly died out, producing the effect of a general catastrophe; there may have been hundreds of accidental causes at work from case to case, but the real reason always lay in the essential finiteness of every single form of life. In the same way, the duration of the life of a shoot depends on the age of the tree from which it was cut. The case of nations and cultures is identical. A nation that only yesterday seemed full of vitality, and is physically vital even today, may tomorrow suddenly appear—historically speaking—dead. Even so every culture has a life-cycle, temporally limited from within, and it is impossible for it to continue to exist after it has completed this cycle, however much one may try to galvanize the corpse. This is why Julian the Apostate did not succeed in revitalizing paganism, and why there is no possible going back, psychologically, anywhere on earth to states prior to the World War. Looked at from this angle, the phenomena of nature and culture belong to the same plane.

These last trends of thought will lead us most quickly to an understanding of what "style" means in the case of nations and cultures. With the individual, style is the result of the complete embodiment of his spirit in matter according to its laws—spirit remaining, however, the ruler; in this case it is a question of a purely individual spirit. Yet even here it is not certain whether the individual actually represents the ultimate terminus: most geniuses, whose works were results of inspiration, have believed in spiritual powers beyond and outside themselves of which they were only the mouthpieces. On the other hand, all great art which was, or is, thought representative of a nation or of mankind is of super-individual origin not only in the dimension of super-terrestrial spirit, but in that of the race, likewise. There is a collective memory as there is a collective unconscious which forms the background of every individual. Accordingly, the latter has a collective background not only in the sense of physical but also of spiritual parentage. Those races which embodied a high unity of style live on as *genes* in the human heritage; they continue to live personally exactly as a *gene* does in the new life-unity of the single cell; this is why we learn the ancient languages in order to measure up to modern life: the study of these languages serves to vitalize our *own* living heritage. At this point, then, we can grasp the true relationship between the collective, the individual, and the unique. Actual life is always individual; hence the essential uniqueness of every true style. But just as the individual quality of all actual life always stands out against a collective background, the essential uniqueness of spiritual man always expresses itself by means of forms derived from the collective unconscious. This being so, the fact that all cultures have been founded by great individuals and that, nevertheless, each culture is a thing in itself ceases to be mysterious. Even the collective can be adequately expressed only by the individual. But this is not all. The spiritual is something different in kind from the collective; in principle, every spirit should be able to express itself by means of any collective unconscious, exactly as the believers in reincarnation will have it; in any case, we are here in the presence of an element which cannot be forecast—if no great men are born, a nation can never find its complete expression. Still, even if a God is incarnated on earth, he resembles his parents; he will teach his Eternal Wisdom in the language and in the terms intelligible to his group. Moreover, on his line there always were forerunners, not only in relation to the collective unconscious, but also to the spirit; thus the possibility and the necessity of a figure like Christ was foretold by the earliest Hebrew prophets. *Accordingly, that essentially intangible thing, the Soul of a Nation, can be anticipated in its general outlines, although it may not yet be born or may even never come to life.*

Let us now look into the particulars of the problem of a national style. The most individual style has also its generic or typical aspects. There is, first, the style inherent in the language employed; there is the general style of the race and of the age in question; there is, last but not least, what one may call the immediate hereditary style. Even the greatest creators of language, as the body of a national soul, like Homer or Goethe or Poushkin or, in our days, Rabindranath Tagore, have shown family characteristics in their style; and the parents were in most cases not proficient in the field of letters. From this it follows that the style of a nation as it may develop some day can be defined with considerable certainty even before it has become articulate. Perfection is reached only when great geniuses are born; before they have done their work it is always possible that a nation may not develop to its full height. But for the determination of the soul of a nation even minor styles count, provided they can be considered as types. And the great outlines are predetermined by the comparatively constant factors of the earth and the collective Unconscious. It is a similar relationship to that between marble or bronze or colours or sounds on the one hand, and human genius on the other. Certain masterpieces can be created only in marble, others only in bronze; others, again, are conceivable only as paintings, and others as symphonies. Each material presents specific inherent limitations. From the point of view of Spirit in the highest sense, nations, even conceived as souls, represent only a material. Every truly great genius is essentially super-national. On the other hand, it is possible to speak of the soul of a nation which finds its expression in an individual style independently of all maturity and perfection attained.

WHAT are the essential qualities of the American nation, and what is its culture likely to be, if it develops? Let us begin by transposing what we recognized as the American characteristics as conditioned by the American continent, on to the plane of a possible style.

The American Scene is, in its great outlines, closely related to that of Asia and Russia. One should remember that it is not so very long ago that the American continent separated from the Asiatic; the red Indians themselves are partly of Mongoloid origin. Were it only for this reason, the native type of the future is bound to become a broad and wide-flung type like the Russian, and totally different from the European. On the other hand, it must become singularly earth-bound owing to the influence of two causes: the one is inherent in the extraordinary power of the American earth, the other in that pure extraversion of American interests for several centuries which necessarily entailed a corresponding backward development and an emptying of the soul, owing to which the primordial spirit of the earth had a chance, unique in modern times, to play the prominent part in the creation of the psychical atmosphere. Now history is an irreversible process. Just as for the individual the way he was brought up makes a psychological difference ineradicable and not to be repaired by any kind of later self-education; just as a glorious or an abject historical past decisively influences the character of a nation one way or the other—even so the effects of the quality of American life during the first three hundred years of its existence will naturally remain embodied in permanent characteristics. This is one more reason why there is no likelihood that America will develop such differentiations as are essential for the European spirit. America may even easily become more "Nordic" in the original sense than the Old World is today, owing to the fact that the pioneer life, together with the general simplification, recalls to pre-eminence many a trait which was characteristic of the first inhabitants of the Arctic Zone, from which, as we now know, both the present-day Nordics and the pure-bred red Indians originally sprang; but then these remote ancestors of ours were entirely unlike intellectualized Europeans. For the same reason, however, there is every hope that America will achieve great things on lines predominantly conditioned by man's earthly nature. All the extraordinary mechanical and institutional accomplishments of America belong to this line. But America's deep-rooted social instinct belongs to it as well. We shall be able to explain in the last chapter only exactly what kind of reality the word Spirit ultimately stands for. But this much can be stated even at this point: there is no greater fallacy than to attribute spiritual value to social accomplishments: social and spiritual development take place in different dimensions. The teachings of Jesus Christ provide the proof of this. Standing exclusively for Spirit, he was anti-social to the extent of saying to his mother, "Woman, what have I to do with thee?" and of ordering his disciples to forsake family and friends. Nor did he ever countenance "philanthropy" when extolling the value of love. When, in the Sermon on the Mount, he opposed to the Hebrew law his own ("but I say unto you") he did not mean mankind at large but those who belonged to his type, the children of the Spirit; the emphasis lies on the "unto *you*," his immediate followers.[1] Thus, Calvinism was true to the original Christian spirit when differenti-

[1] To understand this truth fully, one should read Johannes Müller's book *Die Bergpredigt* (Verlag C. H. Beck, München).

ating between those who were chosen and those who were not. There can be a spiritual development only of the unique, and, accordingly, the category of quantity never applies to problems spiritual. But it does indeed apply to social problems and their solution. Only these are problems not of spiritual, but of earthly man. Therefore, a high development of social tendencies always presupposes a high degree of earth-boundness. It always presupposes a lack of individuality and a lack of understanding of the value of the unique. So primitive tribes seem nearer to perfection in this respect than the most highly civilized communities. And for the same reason, the social talent of a race is always proportional to its earth-boundness. There are, of course, cases of an almost perfect balance between the individual and the social principles; England presents an instance of this. Ancient China provides an example of a state of equilibrium in which the social element predominates, but in which the unique is still a sufficiently potent factor in the psychological structure to render possible a great artistic culture. But the case of America seems to be similar to that of Switzerland, on the one hand, and Russia, on the other. The Swiss democracy is as coherent and tenacious a thing as a beehive. In Russia, again, social values have always been considered as the ultimate values, although the curious structure of that nation makes it impossible for it to realize the ideals of democracy. (The reader will find this argument developed in the chapter entitled "Socialism.") In both Switzerland and Russia the individual as such is of little account; since they fail to recognize the truth that all spiritual values have their earthly exponent in the unique, both nations think more of the ordinary than the extraordinary man. This is again due to the predominance of the earth-principle. Average man is obviously closer to the earth than the man of genius. There can be no doubt that America is evolving in a similar direction. It started doing so even in those days when nothing of modern "socialism" was as yet noticeable on the surface: this explains how men like Emerson and William James could develop in their days ideologies which are as obviously ideologies of contrast, as Jesus' teaching was with respect to the orthodox Jews; I am thinking of Emerson's doctrine that man's value is bound up with the fact that he does *not* conform, and William James's idea that mankind is composed of exclusive "Eaches." All the aforesaid can be translated without difficulty into the current terms of American life. To mention but one instance: the "man in the street" in the United States exactly corresponds psychologically to the Russian "workman" and the Swiss "burgher."

We have herewith determined the chief earth-born components of that style-unity which will be the essence of the future American nation, as it has been the essence of every nation. The intellectual, moral, and spiritual components are more easy to determine. Foremost stand the ideals of the eighteenth century which underlie all mature American customs and institutions. The traditions of the Bill of Rights and of the Common Law also belong to the spirit of that century. Then there is the moralism of the eighteenth century. But this, in its turn, embodies spiritual forces which it never embodied in Europe and which give to American moralism an entirely individual note. Eighteenth-century moralism is, in America, the vehicle of Puritanism; it has, accordingly, a religious foundation and a very deep-rooted one at that, while European moralism was at bottom irreligious; the latter was rather the reincarnation of the spirit of the Stoa, as represented by Seneca (I do not mean stoicism in the current sense, but that particular kind of hedonism developed in Rome on the basis of the belief that the man who is unmoved by external events and always does the right thing, must inevitably be happy). Accordingly, the Americans are fundamentally, not merely incidentally (as even the French have been at times) a moral nation. Again, this American moralism has been enhanced by that exclusive bent towards earthly success which is the child of the original pioneer-spirit. A life ruled by the business spirit must have an essentially moralistic outlook; for all permanent success in business depends on reliability and good faith of some kind. All trade began as an instrinsically dishonest profession; but the more it grew and spread, the more honesty proved profitable. Trade began likewise as an endeavor to "put over" on others as much as possible; but the modern possibilities of mass-sale (because of mass-consumption) have made all intelligent salesmen realize that huge profits are obtainable only where the idea of "service" rules. Here we are faced by another curious and yet specifically American fusion between two originally independent spirits and traditions. American Protestantism soon began to develop along the line of Calvinism—Calvin himself probably never intended it to exist in the form in which it developed later—a line which could become the main line only, because the three different spirits which animated the first settlers blended into one: I mean the spirits of the Pioneer, of the Puritan, and of the Man of Enterprise. All the important, though otherwise so varied forms of American Christianity agree in this one thing that they regard material success upon earth as a fairly sure evidence of the Grace of God. The man who is pleasing to God must grow rich. On the other hand, the man who does not want to be rich, who does not put his talent to the exchanger or does not seriously labour for the honour of God; he who is content with what he has is regarded as lukewarm. To what extent such a view must have stimulated religious souls, such as the first Anglo Saxons mostly were, is obvious, all the more so as the ideal stimulus was given a very real background by the banks; they were all re-insured, as it were, by religious professions; and they gauged the amount of credit which they gave by the sects to which their clients belonged, and by their religious zeal. All these spiritual, moral, and intellectual elements, taken together, constitute a very strong tradition.

That this tradition is really very powerful, and will form a highly important and practically immortal part of any national style which may develop on American soil, is proved by the rapid americanization of most immigrants so far as their conscious goes. Here there can be no question of earth-influence. Nor can there be any question of purely abstract ideals. Abstractions are always quite powerless. Two things only can give them power: the vital belief in them—in which case it is clear that not the abstract ideals as such are the decisive elements, but what they mean vitally to the mass or race in question; or else a vital tradition of which they are the exponents. Now only a vital tradition can absorb a newcomer—the most fanatical belief does not change his nature unless he belonged inwardly, as a type, to the new nation before he became part of it—because a vital tradition only is a "soul," an organized synthesis of thoughts, feelings, emotions, desires, and involuntary impulses which as such can directly invade and assimilate a less articulated individual soul in a relatively short time. There is, then, a very potent tradition in America. But it must hold its own against two other forces. The first of these is the traditional ideal of what America is and stands for, as it figured in the imagination of most immigrants when they made up their minds to leave their native countries. These ideas have, moreover, always been endorsed by the representative public men of America, up to Woodrow Wilson and Calvin Coolidge; even John Dewey has said: "The peculiarity of our nationalism is its internationalism." There is little use in saying, as the hundred-per-centers are in the habit of saying, that this or that phenomenon is "un-American" if that very phenomenon stands for America as an ideal, recognized in words by the leaders of the country, and recognized in the most serious sense by the foreign-born, when we consider that these foreign-born, or the sons of only half-americanized immigrants, happen to constitute at least half of the population. In my introduction to *Europe* I wrote: "There is a fundamental distinction between that which a person means to himself, to others, and before eternity. Here we may already perceive the significance of one of the most tragic aspects of the 'I-and-you'-relationship: no man is ever really loved or honoured for his own sake—and he can never be, for it is impossible for the 'I' to see the 'You' otherwise than in relation to itself. The significance of historic personalities lies altogether outside of their intrinsic character: their personality serves only as the exponent and representative; and frequently the distortion between the personality as such and its significance 'for others' goes so far that the living individual sees all the importance attached to something which to him mattered least of all. That which holds for inter-personal relations holds also for international relations. The question, too, what a nation means to itself and to other nations, calls for three fundamentally different answers which can never be reduced to a common denominator." This is true of all nations. But the case of America is unique in this sense that it is inhabited in approximately equal numbers by two sets of people who look at it in a fundamentally different way and to each of whom America stands for something totally different. No trouble looms ahead for America because many of its citizens remain faithful to the traditions of their native countries: this has been particularly true with the Anglo-Saxon settlers, out of which the hundred-per-cent-American tradition has developed, to an even greater extent than with any German or Irish newcomer. But trouble might come from the fact that there is a very powerful tradition of what America means to the newcomers *as opposed* to the natives of ancient stock. The mere nomination of Al Smith meant, I should think, a more vital issue in the inner life of the American nation than any issue since Abraham Lincoln's days. All those Americans who have not been long in the new country have a common denominator in an ideal which is foreign to the hundred-per-centers. And this ideal is all the more powerful because it finds a very appropriate body in that tendency for equalization and for thinking in terms of quantitative as opposed to qualitative differences only, which is inherent in America's industrial, financial, and social development.[1]

We must then reckon with the idea the newcomer cherishes of America as with a very powerful counter-tradition to that of the hundred-per-center. It is an indubitable fact that the memories of the Civil War, not to mention the War of Independence, mean nothing to about half the American population simply because those memories form no part of their unconscious. On the other hand, in the heart of this half very strong American ideals are alive which are derived from the opposition of American Liberty not to a lack of liberty in the past, but to the narrow conditions of modern Europe. And this foreign-born idealism is, moreover, strange as this may sound, more in harmony with both the wide-flung spirit of the Continent and America's new rôle as a world-power, than the old idealism. The native-born American is narrowing down, as a type, for the time being; this is a natural process which cannot be checked. But it cannot help giving, for a while, an extra chance to the foreign-born or the native of only a few generations, if he is capable of living up, in practise, to his ideal of American life. Moreover, the latter's idea of America is more in harmony with the spirit of the age. We shall, therefore, hardly be refuted by later developments if we take it for granted that the future "style" of America will be built up to a considerable

[1] Is it not probable that the Republican and Democratic parties, the members of which until recently (the contest between Hoover and Smith really was the first presidential campaign based on vital principles, although this fact did not express itself in any official program) stood for almost the same aims and ideals, will ultimately become the means of expression of the two different fundamental types of Americans outlined above?

extent by the ideas and ideals prevailing among the comparative newcomers.

Still, the native-born American should not despair; in the end, he will win the race. Why? For the simple reason that in the long run all immigrants will become natives of the soil and that the resulting native type, being to a very great extent the product of the earth, will obviously be more like the present-day native type, whatever the blood may be, than like the European forefathers in question. Only it is quite possible that the oldest native stock will never again predominate. But, however this may be, in any case it is preposterous that the descendants of the early settlers alone should today believe themselves to be "the" Americans. A constant influx of immigrants up to the year 1923 is a *fact*, whatever it may be worth. Accordingly, the conditions of the beginning actually continued until then. The nation is still in the making, and it is quite possible, in principle, that the earliest historic tradition may have to die for the benefit of a more recent one.

It may seem strange that, when listening to the complaints of highly cultured Americans of ancient native lineage, I was almost reminded of my own fate as a Balt (compare the chapter "The Baltic States" in *Europe*, where I have described that strange fate at length). For seven hundred years, we Balts, who really were the first settlers as compared with the Latvians, but who on Esthonian soil were likewise the only natives playing an active part (as opposed to objects) in the shaping of history, thought ourselves the only real Balts; the others were simply aliens in our eyes because they did not share our traditions. Up to the World War none but the most far-sighted among us ever doubted that we represented the only true natives for all ages to come; and we sneered at the desire for equality of the others in exactly the same way that hundred-per-cent Americans sneer at the aliens And yet we Balts had to go—not in all cases in the sense of reality, but all the more in that of significance, we were outnumbered. And what is more important: the Latvians and Esthonians proved to be more in touch with the spirit of the age; they were, as a matter of fact, less provincial than we were. And then happened that most astounding thing from the point of view of the Baltic hundred-per-center: although they discarded him, the Esthonians and Latvians actually continued his very traditions. Today they are the real up-to-date Balts, while our traditional type is the representative of a dead past. . . . If the most ancient type of the American continues to cling to the belief that he alone is "the" American, that Anglo-Saxonism, as such, is an American issue; if he continues narrowing down and developing provincial traits, then his fate in the future is bound to be similar to that of the Balt.

Yet, again, the native-born Americans should not despair. And not only because the future natives will eventually be more like them than like the foreign-born of these days: some of the former are sure to predominate in the future even more than they do now. Only this will not be true of the Babbitt-type, but of the aristocratic type bred in America; it will be true of the best Southern type. When wandering through the United States I was struck from the very first by the extraordinary superiority of the best type of the Virginian individual, as compared with any other American, in particular the native of the North and of the East. Later I found out that an overwhelming percentage of all Americans who have played, and still are playing a really important part in the country in the sense of human superiority, were and are sons of Virginia and the adjacent states. Then I visited these states myself, and I found Virginia not only one of the most beautiful and delightful countries in the world: it is the one region of America which has a general cultural atmosphere in a broad sense. There is a cultural atmosphere in New England, too, but quite apart from the fact that it is vanishing, this culture is much too narrow; it is, moreover, too bloodless; in the chapter entitled "Morality" we shall see why it is impossible, in principle, that on the sole foundation of Puritanism a culture should ever develop in the sense in which the word has always been used in the world's history. But there is true and high culture in the atmosphere of Virginia. There, the Cavalier tradition still survives. This is an aristocratic tradition; and this means that the emphasis in man lies on his uniqueness. Now, since man's essence is actually his uniqueness, only an inner adjustment of the aristocratic type is capable, in principle, of leading to the development of complete souls. That this is true independently of the political and social status, and more still, of the name it happens to bear—in our days everything good is usually called "democratic"—this is not only proved by the whole of history; it is proved, in particular, precisely by that of the United States, where Democracy itself, ever and ever again, has made born aristocrats its chosen representatives. The superiority of the Virginian is due also to the superior stock which forms its backbone; unfortunately, the immigration of the later centuries presented the New World with no heredity of a quality equal to that of the first immigration. Still, this superiority is to a greater extent a result of the tradition which is still living; this is so powerful that even newcomers are quickly absorbed by it. Under these conditions, time inevitably works for the American of the Virginian type. All inhabitants of the United States will sooner or later be true natives; but it is a law of life that the original equality must increasingly make room for a state of differentiation; and once this is recognized, the standard of quality will inevitably predominate over that of quantity. And again, once quality has been recognized as the decisive factor, this will in its turn inevitably lead to the predominance of the superior *human* type. And such a superior native type is to be found only in the South today.

But how can the South possibly mean so much for America's future since it is "backward," and civilization seems certain to continue on the lines of rationalization and industrialization? In Virginia, in particular, the wounds of the Civil War have not yet healed. The country is poor; it is comparatively little industrialized; and the Southerners are supposed to be slow by nature—however astonishing this may sound, it is precisely this that makes me anticipate a future predominance of the South.

As a matter of fact, it is out of the question, for mere logical considerations, that the Northern type should always predominate. And the mere fact of the glorification of the "Nordic" proves to everyone who knows the A B C of psychology that there must be something wrong about it. The American of the Northeastern type is one-sidedly dynamic; he is essentially a nomad; he is not rooted in the earth. Stop his movement, and as a type he is done for. And his *raison d'être* will cease to exist even sooner than was the case with earlier nomadic tribes because of the Northerner's religion of work and success. He believes that if he only goes on working, every successive year must be better than the preceding; his progress, he believes, is guaranteed by the moral order of the world. But this cannot be. There will always be good and bad years, periods of advance and regression, both depending on planetary conditions which man cannot control. Therefore, it is as certain as a mathematical truth that the Northerner's world-philosophy will *not* stand the pragmatic test for any length of time. And since all Americans believe in the pragmatic test, this result is bound to lead, sooner or later, to a break-up of that whole philosophy. This is one of those future events which I anticipated when saying that I felt certain that America's development would soon pass through a solution of continuity. But in this connexion it suffices to consider the more general causes. Mother Earth was there for millions of years before man started becoming a nuisance on it from her point of view. Even today, she is stronger than he is, and man has in the first instance remained her child, even though he rules her. This is true in any case in that sense that there is no lasting happiness for man unless he is in harmony with her rhythm. And this means that the only state which can endure is a comparatively static state. It certainly is man's privilege to live by the initiative of his spirit; this privilege embodies also man's highest dignity.[1] But there is a difference between an assertion of man's freedom as such, and one-sided

[1] I have developed the trend of thought concerning man's relation to the earth and the relationship of man's Freedom to destiny and natural necessity in *The Recovery of Truth.*

dynamism. If man is rightly adjusted within the Universe, then he balances his dynamic and his static poles. If his life is purely static, then he does not progress; he continues, more or less, on the animal level. But at least he does not die out because of that. On the contrary, wherever it is a case of one-sided dynamism, there is no equilibrium between man and nature, and premature death is the inevitable result. This applies not only to tragic heroes like Alexander the Great and Napoleon; it applies as well to purely dynamic nations. The Huns died out in no time. The Normans, in the course of a few centuries, overran and sacked the whole of Europe; they even founded kingdoms. Yet their type did not live long. In most cases, they died out altogether. In some, they blended with static types, and then great cultures were the result; *vide* England, France, and Sicily. But the all-important point in the present context is that the Normans did not last as such and that it would have been against the laws of nature had they lasted; in an essentially stable, and to that extent static world, pure and one-sided mobility can never fill more than a short interval. Now the case of the present-day American, of the quick, sharp, hustling and bustling type, presents the nearest approach I know to the case of the Normans. These Americans are invading and conquering and exploiting in exactly the same sense as the former did. And they are equally devoid of any quality that makes for permanence. They will certainly conquer the whole of America; they are already conquering the South. But the latter will not become Northern for that. The Northern type will organize and industrialize and commercialize and socialize the whole of the territory of the United States as far as reason and the nature of things permit. But then it will disappear exactly as the Normans disappeared. That is, a change of type will take place among those who survive, making for a better state of equilibrium within the Universe. And since Nature is cruel at heart, she is certain to inflict the death-penalty on all those who went too far in their denial of earth as their mother. Even today the descendants of those Northerners and Easterners, who appeared most energetic in times past, show a singular lack of vitality; on the whole, there is little true vitality to be found in the modern North; speed, there, is as a rule not an expression of strength, but merely of neurotic restlessness. The more one moves southward—of course, not passing beyond a certain latitude, where the climate becomes too hot for the white man—the more full-blooded in the sense of a complete man the American appears. The Northerner will, no doubt, continue to exist, but in days to come he will be recognized as the poorest, the least superior type; he will mean to America at large what the most narrow type of Prussian means within the German nation. The Middle West will in all likelihood continue to represent America's national foundation. But if ever a culture develops, and the stress is laid on culture, then the hegemony will inevitably pass over to the South. There alone at any rate can there be a question of a lasting culture. The reason is the same as that which makes French culture both more perfect and more tenacious than German—only that the same relationship appears more accentuated in America, because here the Teutonic and Nordic element has no cultural bent whatsoever; its highest ideal is civilization in the Roman, as opposed to the Greek sense. When first I met that lovely type of woman called "The Southern Girl" I was struck at once by the fact that she bears relationship to her Northern sister similar to that which the French woman bears to the German. While the latter has little sense of proportion and, for that reason, little true inward strength, the French woman by nature sees everything in the right proportion; her adjustment within the general scheme of life, too, is based upon an inherent sense of the true mutual relationship of all its sides and potentialities. Hence her sense of beauty, her taste, but also her moral strength, her *tenue*, and her innate feeling for the order of nature. No woman in the world knows better than she what family means. She has the quite undeserved reputation of being immoral, simply because she knows that an occasional adultery is a venial sin as compared with the legally most justified divorce which breaks up a home and harms the souls of children. She knows how to discriminate between what is passing and what is permanent; she knows the difference between infatuation and true love. In our days nothing, of course, that was ever written in French novels can compete with what happens in real life among the best classes of Nordics, in both Europe and America. But in principle it was always so. Sexually speaking, the German, the English, and in particular the Scandinavian women have always been much more immoral, if they only had the chance, than the French, not to speak of the Italian and the Spanish women. (In my young days several Italians came to live in the same Berlin pension where I lived. I asked them why they had come. To make love, of course, was their reply. There is no chance to do so in Italy. In Spain, matters are very much worse still from the point of view of the libertine.) The fact is that the

French woman knows the exact relationship between the laws of the spirit and the earth and is instinctively inclined to observe them. This is the true reason why the French race is so extraordinarily tenacious and vital, both in the physical and in the moral sense, and why there are fewer signs of degeneracy there than in Northern Europe.—Exactly the same is true, in principle, of the Southern girl. This explains, among other things, her exceeding beauty.

But to the brilliant future prospects of the South the law of historic counterpoint, as explained in *Creative Understanding*, contributes in its turn. Just *because* America has been so one-sidedly dynamic for some centuries, it is certain to settle down later, if it survives, into an all the more static condition. That this will be so is already foreshadowed by several present-day characteristics: for instance, by the fact that the American is fundamentally slow and essentially conservative. At this point, then, the Anglo-Saxon blood comes in as an inalienable advantage: no other race is equally conservative in the best sense, and not one among the Nordics has a better sense of proportion. If no degeneration takes place and no catastrophe in the sense of mexicanization or a complete loss of soul, then the type of American which will be determinant in the future will be very different from the representative type of today. The present-day hustle and bustle will cease; in any case it will no longer be a matter of pride. No one will think of skyscrapers and speed and business methods as being essential American characteristics. Men like Rockefeller and Ford and Carnegie will no longer be thought of as representative. What America stands for today in the eyes of the world, may cease to exist at all—partly because it will really cease to be, partly because these things American will have become acquisitions of mankind at large.

WE HAVE now said enough of the details of the problems in question, as far as they can be recognized and anticipated without prejudice, to justify, in conclusion, the attempt to unite them in a general synthesis. What is the style of the American civilization when it reaches maturity likely to be? Style is not an abstraction, but a very concrete thing. There is no use, therefore, if one wishes to anticipate the facts, to look for representative ideas or theories as such. It is only living types that count. And, as every past civilization had its forerunners in a few individuals, it is certain *a priori* that there must be Americans in existence who incarnate even today the nation's future style.

For a long time I looked for them in vain. I soon saw, of course, that none of the Americans whom the public at large considers as representative, really are so. Men like Rockefeller, or even Henry Ford, might, in principle, belong to any nation. What they have developed into is due to the external opportunities America offers. This is probably true even in the one respect in which some of them seem to be American and nothing else; I mean the tendency for social service: in their case precisely I do not feel at all sure of the primal quality of that tendency. The great New England types certainly are no longer representative. The same obviously applies to types like those of Franklin, Washington, and even Jefferson; every European aristocrat is more akin to their type than the average American. There are, of course, millions of citizens of the United States thoroughly representative of the American business man or the social worker or the clubwoman or the flapper as a type—but in all these cases, there is no question of deeper tendencies. What makes a nation is its *soul*, and the above-mentioned types are merely types of external expression which, in principle, might embody any kind of soul; those Americans whose essence expresses itself in these types are essentially soulless and, therefore, they do not count. For a long time I actually thought that America's real soul was black, since the coloured man alone has so far developed a convincing style of his own which is yet essentially American. But then it occurred to me that because of the very loudness, publicity, and superficiality of the surface of American life, its depths should, by compensation, be correspondingly inconspicuous and even hidden. I had by that time already discovered that the American is at bottom a very shy and sensitive and reticent and modest kind of human being. So I began to give all my attention to such phenomena as seemed to mean most to the best, the aspiring, the idealistic classes of the American population. After some time, then, I found out what at the moment was a real surprise to me: that the most representative, the most important American living is—Dr. John Dewey.

Wherever I succeeded in penetrating the creative part of the American unconscious, I found John Dewey playing the part of a primary symbol. This was one of the most significant experiences of my life. I had met Doctor Dewey several times: he had made practically no impression on me. Nor did his philosophy mean anything to me; it has never meant anything to Europeans, nor is it likely ever to mean anything to them in the future. But at the same time I realized Doctor Dewey's importance for America, I heard, by a fortunate coincidence, that he is reverenced also by modern China, the educational system of which has been outlined by him, as possibly no sage has been reverenced since the days of Mencius; that he likewise enjoys a very great prestige in Bolshevik Russia, and that he of all men was asked to reorganize the educational system of Russia and subsequently of Mexico. Thanks to these examples of far-reaching influence, I began to understand. America evidently belongs on all planes to the same new world to which Russia, China, and Turkey belong. Accordingly, it belongs to an entirely different order from that of Europe. It is true that Dewey is not representative in the same sense as Goethe was of Germany, or Tolstoy of Russia; one of the most significant facts about him is that he has no style. But then there can be no question of representative men in the sense of classic examples with nations still in the making; least of all in the case of a nation which started as a democracy and did not begin, therefore, by developing a higher type, different from the rest, which might serve as a model. Doctor Dewey most decidedly does not play the part of America's head, else he would be more conspicuous. But he is undoubtedly its most important endocrine. He is representative of the inner aspirations and possibilities of the nation. Thus, one has every reason to believe that he, who understands the type of Dr. John Dewey, understands "the" American as far as he differs, as a general type, from other nations.

One has every reason to believe so, because at bottom Doctor Dewey belongs to the genus of the Babbitts. He is the Anti-Babbitt, to be sure, but this qualification is only possible on the plane of Babbittry. And Babbitt does stand, as we saw, for the most native and rooted American type. Now what characterizes Doctor Dewey? It is, in four words, *psychology bent on education.* Doctor Dewey does not believe in metaphysics; he is essentially earth-bound in all his tendencies. But he does believe in the possibility of indefinite improvement of the individual as a member of the group. He is essentially social-minded. He believes in democracy understood as a form of life which does not admit of original differences in the quality of being, but only of ability; and he sees the ideal in an organization providing equal chances for all. All this makes him essentially congenial to both the Chinese and the Russians, for they, too, are positivists and social-minded and democratic, but they do not believe in equality in that nonsensical sense according to which incompetence and weakness should be treated on equal terms with competence and ability. Doctor Dewey believes in practical issues and tests only; he even seems to be the inventor of the word pragmatism. This again makes him very congenial to the Russian and the Chinese. The Russian *intelligentsia* never believed in intellectual values apart from their social utility, and the Chinese have always been practical in their outlook; they, too, have always established a kind of equation between conformity to sense (understood as my philosophy defines it) and success. Finally, Doctor Dewey is essentially a moralist. He is not so explicitly nor does he countenance any current system of morals, but morality is his very essence. In this respect, he does not resemble the Russians, but more than ever the Chinese. When I realized all that I left the field of abstractions and saw in the form of a concrete image what Doctor

Dewey really stands for in America. He is the equivalent to what the *censors* were in ancient China. There, even the Emperor had to listen to the criticisms of some humble and poor sage recognized by public opinion as a guardian of the Truth, and to obey him whenever he was manifestly in the wrong; the censors were, so to speak, the materialized conscience of China. Something like that may be said of John Dewey with respect to America. But the same was true of Doctor Eliot of Harvard and, more or less, of all men who have meant most to American consciousness, such as George Washington and Abraham Lincoln. This, then, leads us beyond the plane of mere Anti-Babbittry and shows us in what sense John Dewey is representative of the most ideal American tendencies and in what sense they are unique—incomparable not only with anything European, but also with anything Russian and Chinese. There never was so practical a general outlook as that of America; for even though the Jews and the Chinese and the Russians and even the English, too, are centred in this life, they do not, for all that, believe in success as the one thing needful, and success never stands with them as a symbol of spiritual value. Again, never before in history has a practical outlook coexisted with an equal amount and degree of kinetic energy. Further, nowhere was there ever so great and general a passion for education. We shall see later on that in most individual cases this passion stands for something very superficial. But if one meditates on what it means in the case of John Dewey, one realizes that it can be very deeply rooted. We said before that the formula comprising the essentials of what Doctor Dewey stands for is *psychology bent on education.* Here psychology plays the same part as metaphysics do in India and Germany, and education means the same as "seed" does with the Jews, and culture with the Chinese. This is something absolutely novel. I have shown in my *Travel Diary* that, though the Chinese do not think as profoundly as the Hindus, their actual life is an expression of equal depth; also, that patriotism in the Japanese sense, which cannot stand for ultimate depth in the case of Europeans, actually expresses it in the case of the ancient type of Japanese. Even so, if John Dewey's philosophy as representative of America seems shallow when gauged by European standards, it is not so in reality. It is possible that true profundity may express itself in a non-reflective, practical, simple, and direct way on the lines of social organization and education on the basis of psychological insight.

But there are other unique features which one can already perceive in the American style. American moralism is something very different from Chinese moralism. It is an essentially Protestant moralism, which means that not the whole of life should be ordered according to moral standards, but that morality is an independent essence on a particular plane of its own. The facts of what has just been said, visualized in the form of a concrete image, show the figure of a very definite type of man. His fundamental characteristics are the same as those of Babbitt; only that Babbitt represents its lowest expression and its negative aspect. In order to understand that the same fundamental adjustment can also find a very high expression, one should remember that to Plato the idea of the Good, understood in a practical sense, ranked above those of Beauty and Truth. The Americans are no ancient Greeks; indeed they are anything but intellectualists. But the analogy may help us to understand how moralism of the Protestant kind plus Pragmatism may eventually lead even to a state of culture or, at any rate, need not be an obstacle to its birth. It is only a question of the general denominator. What was understood superficially in the early days of the nation may be understood profoundly when it has reached maturity. If the one-sidedness of moralism perishes, outshone by the light of understanding; if the religion of mere success has once led itself *ad absurdum*, as it is sure to do in the near future, then it is quite possible that the same kind of man, of which hitherto Babbitt was a true representative, will build up a true social and moral culture. One should remember here again the unequalled lack of jealousy, envy, resentment, and ill-will in America's psychical atmosphere: such a beginning certainly promises well for the future. For the present one meets most frequently Babbitts and Anti-Babbitts, the latter type corresponding to the positive aspect of the same figure. If the type of a man could be compared to an atom and each nation to a particular chemical compound, then the John Dewey-type would stand for the most important atom in the future American nation.

But there is more than one kind of atom within the latter; these atoms unite to molecules and new quantitative arrangements result in new qualities. Thus, all sorts of more complex types are conceivable within the general scheme of American civilization; all the more so as the fundamental type is never the only characteristic type. In Russia three essential types stand out. We have mentioned two of them so far and compared the one to a big piece of butter, the other to a small but sharp knife. But there is a third national type, the saint; the man of pure spirituality. In China, too, there are at least three essential types: the man of practical life ranging from the peasant to the merchant, the artist, and the sage. The American type seems to be more unified than that of any other country. But for that very reason his direct opposite can be representative as well. The purely practical type is counterpoised by the pure idealist; the democrat, who finds his ideal in the man in the street, by the most exclusive aristocrat. The moralist finds his compensatory opposite in the most fanatic believer in liberty the world has ever seen. Last but not least, the average type, which believes in facts and things, is compensated by a type of man who believes in spirit only, denying to matter all reality.

This must make, as the nation matures, for an exceedingly interesting synthesis. The stress of importance will, of course, lie on different types in the different parts of the country. New England will probably continue to be essentially moralistic, the Middle West social-minded, the Far West representative of America's width of soul, and the South of America's culture. The more the means of communication improve, the more chance there is that localisms will survive and the more they will mean. For great facility and frequency of intercourse counteract mutual influence, nor is like-mindedness any longer the necessary premise for friendly intercourse. I have shown in *Europe* and in *The World in the Making* that humanity's new scheme of life means a synthesis between the two principles of the universal and what is local and untransferable. But now let us survey at a glance the natural gifts typical of the American, as they seem to develop as a matter of general rule on the whole territory of the United States. I will not attempt any explanations here, nor enter into details; this will be done in the second part of this book. I will only give the most outstanding facts. The Americans are highly gifted psychologically, more gifted in this respect than the Europeans. Their intuitive powers are unusually well developed, whereas they are not, properly speaking, thinkers. Their social tendencies are both strong and differentiated, but not their individual impulses. They are highly efficient in all practical ways of life, but not in the field of disinterested understanding. They are intelligent as a type, but hardly ever intellectual; their proficiency in the field of science, generally speaking, is entirely confined to statistics, to facts as opposed to significance. Their ethical faculties are very marked, but those qualities which belong to the realm of pathos are singularly lacking. On the other hand, the American is originally spiritual, more so than the European; this, again, brings him close to the Russian; he is fundamentally religious. His moral sense is highly developed, as it is in the Chinese. But, as opposed to the latter, he seems to be singularly lacking in artistic endowment and interest. I repeat that I take and give these qualities as facts pure and simple, without attempting to explain them. As far as they are a question of natural endowments not inherent in the European heredity, they cannot even be explained on the basis of our present state of knowledge.

What type, what style of civilization can be expected to develop out of this material? It cannot in any case bear the slightest resemblance to that of modern Europe. On the one hand, it may become akin to that of Russia; only that the tremendous tension between the animal and the Child of God in man—this chief characteristic of the Russian—is lacking in the American. It may also develop a certain likeness to the civilization of ancient China. But this likeness, too, cannot be very strong, because there is very little prospect of an artistic civilization in America and because morality means something very different to the Americans from what it does to the Chinese. Also, the Americans have no original feeling for the universal connexion of things. In spite of their differing so much from the Europeans, they are the most typical of Westerners in the dynamic sense and instinctive desire for world-power. They are, in fact, owing to the rejuvenation effected by a New World and the peculiarly energetic type of man that first settled in it, more like the early Nordic forebears of the Europeans than are the latter. We saw that in all probability the American civilization will finally settle down in the form of a static civilization. But its statism cannot possibly ever become like that of China. *Now all this only goes to show that American civilization will turn out to be something perfectly original.* And this is the best that could be said of it. What the world wants is the creation of new values. Repetition, even of the best, is contrary to the law of life, the essence of which is uniqueness both in the sense of singularity and "once and never again."

And yet, even the new will bear some resemblance to things that have been. Therefore, *pour fixer les idées,* I will give in conclusion two very different co-ordinates which will help the imaginative among my readers to anticipate what cannot be actually foreseen. The Americans, being of European stock, will obviously retain some European characteristics, just as the Hindus have retained some traits of their Nordic forefathers. And here the traits which are likely to persist are most akin to the fundamental characteristics of the ancient Romans —*except* for the latter's political sense and love of war. The Americans will in all probability always remain an essentially earth-bent and practical race; and of no previous race can the same be said to an equal degree except of the Romans.—The other co-ordinate I can give—and this is probably the more important and finally decisive one—finds its only model on American soil. This is the civilization of the Incas. Theirs also was an essentially social civilization. There, too, the citizens were essentially hard-working people, and content to do their work. The Incas, too, were practical on the one hand and religious on the other. They, too, cared little for freedom. For freedom in the true individual sense is, as we shall see later, something the American cares less for than does any other type of man.

This much can be foretold with a great degree of probability. But many developments lie within the range of the possible which would seem accidental when judged from the point of view of the nation's essence, and yet would considerably change the picture which resulted. If the South really becomes predominant, America will develop a true culture, in spite of its Roman as opposed to Greek tendencies. If it does not, or to a slight degree only, and if the cultural type continues to be valued as little as it is today, then the emphasis will never lie on the cultural. If the irrational part of the American soul we spoke of breaks forth soon, this may lead to creative tensions mitigating the general uniformity by greater variety. Should there be many wars with other continents, then the Americans, in spite of their innate peaceableness, may become a nation of warriors and conquerors, and this again would considerably change their national type. For nations are much more the children of their victories and defeats than they are their parents. Much also depends on the eventual state of balance between the different heredities. An America fundamentally Irish and German, with some Slavic and Jewish admixture, would probably be less social-minded than the America of today, but it would be more productive of individual talent on other than business lines. Very much also depends on the way the American soul will react upon the influences of the conflicts with the non-American world. America being essentially a closed system, its existence within a world of unheard-of inner and external vastness will inevitably lead to more tensions than any closed system in history ever had to hold out against. This will lead, in the first instance, to two things: a withdrawal into an increasingly exclusive Americanism on the one hand, which would make for the unification of the nation in the same sense as the Shogun-period (during which no citizen was allowed to leave the country) did in the history of Japan. But on the other hand, this exclusiveness will not be able to maintain itself as it would prefer in our modern, so widely and universally interconnected world. This again must needs lead, by reaction, to a deepening and developing of the American soul. For the more a man is exposed to foreign influences, the more deeply conscious does he become of his own exclusive essence. And this, again, would make for culture. Indeed, only if the nation is forced to lay emphasis on its depths, is there any chance for the growth of an inner organization which would give prominence to the really best within a nation which so far has been occupied as no other has been with external expansion. Again, only if such an inner organization does take place, will America become equal to her possible great mission in the world. The provincial type of man cannot intelligently meet emergencies of world-wide importance. Babbitt is no acceptable *arbiter mundi*. Nor is a narrow cultural type; of this, President Wilson has provided the symbol for all times. There are great gentlemen in America even today. They should come to the fore and be valued more highly, if only because of the American belief in efficiency; for it is only their type which can cope with world-wide issues. Indeed, the international difficulties and disillusions which are bound to follow—for even in the case of material victory all pet illusions of American provincials will be defeated in the first clash with a wider world—will probably mean the shortest way to put Babbitt into his right place and to open the national eye to values of human superiority. I do not think that the general factors of America's future style, as I sketched them here, will ever be refuted by the facts. Nations are the children of continents and collective psychological forces. Accordingly, accidents and individual variations mean little. No defeat has ever changed the destiny of a nation inwardly strong if it was not annihilated. Nor has any victory which was not founded on intellectual and moral superiority ever lasted. There is, of course, the possibility of the American nation not being basically strong. Many intelligent observers doubt the vitality of the American continent—and undoubtedly the present-day type of American is not vital, less vital in any case than the European. But my own personal opinion is that this is due only to false adjustment. As far as I can see, there are, on the contrary, more primeval and, therefore, vitalizing forces at work on the North American continent than on any other. It is for man's initiative to make the right use of them—not merely in the sense of material exploitation, but for the benefit of the growth of his soul.

*Part Second*

# *AMERICAN PROBLEMS*

## *Youthfulness*

AMERICA has not always appeared young. Everybody has, independently of his actual age, an essential age. The "self" of the man or woman which self-consciousness reflects is in each case timeless in itself; if there were no surrounding world (to which the body also belongs) to teach him or her the truth, no one would realize that he or she was aging. But it is precisely this timeless entity which appears young, or middle-aged or old, as the case may be. Just as there are gods which everybody involuntarily pictures as patriarchs and others as adolescents, even so does every human individual present itself to the inner eye as a type of a certain essential age, independently of the number of years he has actually existed on earth. This type is, of course, a symbol. But it is none the less real; the symbol, on the plane of subjective experience, is as adequate an expression of the reality of life as the body is on the plane of external facts; only it expresses a more fundamental part of this reality. He who pictures Alexander the Great as a youth, and Goethe as a patriarch and Shakespeare as a man of about thirty-five, shows deeper understanding than he who insists on the facts of their development in time.

What is true of individuals is all the more true of nations. The symbolic image which incarnates for others their essence presents the very clue to their true character. Now who in the past was America's most representative symbol? It was Uncle Sam; an elderly gentleman. And if now we turn from the plane of symbols to that of fact, we find the truth of the symbol confirmed in all representative cases. One cannot honestly picture a Pilgrim Father under fifty, nor an authentic Puritan under forty-five. The peculiar detachedness of New England's best cultural type distinctly suggests the mood of a man who has retired from active life. Daniel Boone, the prototype of Cooper's Leatherstocking, appears unreal when pictured under the age of seventy; and what is true of him, and was true also of most American intellectuals of the nineteenth century, seems to repeat itself of late in the case of the great industrial pioneers. Thomas Edison has been to me a wizard hundreds of years old as long as I can remember him; John D. Rockefeller has the essential age of at least eighty; and as to Henry Ford, when looking at his parchmentlike complexion, I am startled at times when I realize that he is not actually as yet a patriarch. Then: why is it that representative Americans so often grow unusually old? Is it not because their essential age demands it? In any case there is more evidence in support of the theory that the American continent as such creates a type of man of an advanced essential age than in support of the popular theory that it makes for youth. The essential age of the red Indian is seldom under forty-five, and if today the faces of many elderly Americans look infantile, one should never lose sight of the fact that life is a polar phenomenon, for which reason infantilism and senility always go together. One should really cease to speak of America's youth. Primitiveness in the cultural or historic sense and essential youthfulness are two very different things. There are aborigines, in many parts of the world, not only older from the point of view of time than any civilized nation, but also old in the sense of essential age. The hard life he had to face in America brought the immigrant from Europe back to the aboriginal state; it did not make him younger.

But the new generations of Americans *are* young. The symbol of Uncle Sam, when applied to them, appears thoroughly unconvincing. This is proved by the significant fact that the most responsible posts in big business have been only in exceptional cases occupied of late by men over forty-five; above all, in present America youth gives the tone to a degree unparalleled in history. Here, again, symbols teach more than facts. In pre-revolutionary China, if you remarked to a charming young lady, "You look sixty," you were paying her a compliment; to be at least forty was the unconscious ideal of all youths in the days of New England supremacy; in those days only the men and women of forty really counted, as it was (and is) the case with all mature civilizations. But today everybody wants to be young and everybody strives at any rate to look so, by all means, both good and bad; today youth holds almost the same position in America as old age held in the last period of ancient China. The quality of reverence is altogether lacking in the intercourse of the young with their elders. On the contrary, the latter try to justify their existence by giving all their attention to the former's welfare; there lies one of the roots of American educationalism. How are we to understand this change, a change so great and so abrupt as almost to amount to a solution of continuity? . . . In order to solve this particular American problem, we must envisage it first as an expression of a far more general one.

THOSE who believe in uninterrupted and, as it were, inevitable progress forget, among other important facts, that every concrete expression of life is essentially finite; it is a melody with a beginning and an end.[1] The best symbol of its initial stage is a young green shoot, flexible and pliant, capable of almost indefinite growth and change and regeneration; the best symbol of its final stage is an old tree with a hard bark, incapable of any further growth or change. This applies to ideas and civilizations as much as to individuals. In the case of the former, one is apt to be led to misjudge the situation by considerations of value; but the eternal truth underlying an idea, as well as the eternal value incarnated in a particular civilization, does not, unfortunately, interfere with the laws of Life and Death which rule its manifestations on the plane of space and time. Every concrete expression of life is, without exception, primarily an organism, the existence of which follows the typical rhythm of all organisms; the eternal soul it may incarnate has no power to change the fact that it was born as a definite and limited being, as the bearer of a definite heredity, and that it cannot develop beyond a certain climax which means its specific perfection; having passed this, it must needs decay and die. Its eternal soul can continue manifesting itself only by means of reincarnation, and reincarnation always implies a change of individuality. Let me give a single instance: Within a few centuries of amazingly rapid growth

[1] See the full development of this idea in the chapter "Life and Death" in my book *The Recovery of Truth* (Harper & Brothers).

Greek culture had reached its stage of perfection. After that it grew more and more rigid; routine took the place of original creativeness. Eventually it died as an individual life-form. But not only its eternal essence survived—its offspring, too, survived: the Christian Church, half at least of the doctrine of which is of Greek origin and bears exactly the same relationship to antique culture as a son does to his father.

Here, then, we have the key to that phenomenon of rejuvenation of which the rejuvenation of America provides but one particular instance. If each concrete life-form represents a finite melody, a greater melody, in relation to which the former represents only a single bar, flows through it. And it does so on all planes by means of the device that a young life continues the old in exactly the same sense that a son continues his father's life. He is not identical with the latter; only a part, his unspent, his germinal part survives. Nor can one say that the son begins where the father left off; because he begins exactly as the first man began: as a helpless babe. But *by means* of this retreat to first beginnings life at each recommencement makes a fresh start. In periods of continuous development this law of nature manifests itself only in the obvious form of fresh individuals pursuing with slight deviations the road traced by their forebears. But when the solution of continuity, which characterizes the relationship between two generations, happens to coincide with solutions of continuity on other lines and planes, I mean when definite religious or philosophical or political lines of development simultaneously reach their natural life-term—then centuries seem to separate fathers and sons. The normal process of rejuvenation then takes the form of what De

Vries has called "mutation": an entirely new form of life comes to light. And this form, being entirely new, its youthfulness must assert itself in an exaggerated manner, too; for there are no traditional ways of behaviour, in conforming to which youth might lose in appearance its essential quality of barbarism. Thus it was at the beginning of our own era. The outlook of the early Christian was different in kind from that of his pagan parents. And as he had to make an entirely fresh start, he soon became primitive in all fundamental respects, however sophisticated his predecessors may have been—only think of the archaic quality of early Christian art. The reason is that the new generation did not only physically, but also culturally, start as a new-born babe. It is, of course, not easy to understand how it happens that on the cultural plane things are the same as on the physical; but then one should remember that the physical phenomena of birth and death and rebirth are just as inexplicable. They must be accepted as ultimate facts. Only this much can be said to mitigate the essential incomprehensibility of the phenomena on the cultural plane. As a psychical being, man is essentially malleable and changeable; almost as changeable as dream-figures are which change from one shape into another and fuse and differentiate again as though by magic. Then, on the psychical plane, the child never grows up nor does it ever die; it produces out of itself differentiations, yet the aboriginal being is always there in the depths. Accordingly, a reversion to childhood is not only possible at any time, it is the normal process wherever some differentiated life-form has reached its natural life-term before the life-force itself is spent. On the other hand, every new vital impulse which has penetrated deeply enough into the unconscious starts a process of regeneration. Psycho-analysis has proved that in the sphere of dreams the creative essence of the images visualized is their meaning; it is "meaning" which expresses itself in the form of pictures. In the same sense does significance create the facts in the whole domain of life. When a new idea germinates, it calls out all the creative forces of childhood. But the first beginnings of life are always ugly and barbaric.

The very same phenomena which characterized the age in which infantile Christianity superseded antiquity can be witnessed today all over the world. I have not to deal with the general problem here, having done so at full length in *The World in the Making*. In Europe the fundamental cause of the manifest rejuvenation is this, that the ideas of the eighteenth century—the last truly original ideas which shaped Western life—have reached their normal end. There is, for instance, no vital force left in Europe in the idea of Democracy, because it has conquered; if a movement achieves its end it ceases to exist for that very reason. The idea of the rights of the majority as opposed to the privileges of minorities is no longer an idea working for good, since there are no more privileged minorities, while on the other hand the triumphant numbers threaten to exterminate all quality and so on. I will dwell on this particular aspect of the question in a later chapter. What I want to point out here is the general possibility of a rejuvenation as we are witnessing it, and its general significance.

But before turning our attention to the particular problem of the United States, it is necessary to give some further thought to the general issue which confronts us. Rejuvenation never means progress in the usual sense of the word—from the point of view of a cultured father a new-born babe is anything but progressive. Least of all can it mean progress at the present time, because it is precisely the age of progress that is passing away. Let us not be misled by a prejudice in favor of abstractions: what everybody means by "progress" is a very definite idea and this became a life-force, for the first time in the world's history, in the seventeenth century. Before that time nobody believed in anything of the kind. Why not? Because before that time the emphasis of life was placed on religious development or philosophical insight or artistic or moral or cultural perfection—and applied to those lines the idea of progress has no meaning. It has a meaning only when applied to the lines of *intellectual* development, to science and its applications. Here only can there be a question of general acquirements, of boundless generalizations, of values transferable to the extent that each following worker can begin where his predecessor left off. As opposed to this, the case of every God-seeker or Truth-seeker, every artist, every man who strives after moral or cultural perfection, is essentially unique. Take art as an example: it is sheer nonsense to draw a line of "progress" from Bach to Beethoven and, farther on, to Strawinsky. For an age to attribute the highest value to progress presupposes that all the emphasis within the soul rests on the intellect. Today this premise (I have explained the case at length in *The World in the Making*) no longer acts as a vital force. This is proved by the over-mechanized character of that part of Western life which still continues the traditions of the seventeenth century. We pointed out that a civilization which has grown old can be compared to a tree with a hard bark, as opposed to a pliant shoot. In the same sense, mechanism, understood as a pure routine-life, is the general symptom of old age. Life is essentially creative and free; as long as it dominates, the laws of matter, which are all laws of routine, play no greater part in its expression than do the laws of harmony and counterpoint in the creative efforts of a Bach. But when the vital impulses grow weak, then the laws of matter get the upper hand; then life becomes mechanical, whatever its particular character may be—Chinese mandarinism or Byzantine bureaucracy or Catholic scholasticism of Prussian militarism are just as mechanical as any one of the most machine-dominated expressions of modern life. But today it is the mechanical character of life, as understood by children of the machine, which reveals old age; there was no question of life's being over-mechanized while the era of progress was still young.

This era is aging fast; as a vital force it is practically already dead. We shall see in the next chapter in what sense this does *not* imply the end of the technical age. Within the context of this one, however, we have first to focus the following problem: *if* the age of progress is past and an extreme rejuvenation is taking place, then the only reasonable expectation for the nearest future of the human race cannot be the expectation of farther advance, but rather of a new Dark Age.

WE HAVE indeed to face this truth, whether we like it or not. We stand today on the threshold of a new Dark Age—an age like that which followed the era of Roman splendour. This does not mean that a period of decline is about to succeed the age of progress, but that an age different in quality and significance from the era lying between the Renaissance and the World War is at hand; an age not of realization, but of preparation. Every young life matures in the dark; from the dark it issues into the light. It does so through chaos and ugliness. This is true of the human embryo; it is equally true of civilizations. Dark ages mean periods of gestation. Accordingly, the ages of light are not, as most believe, the only true and significant ones—they are simply the ages of maturity and perfection. Thus, as long as humanity lives, ages of darkness will alternate with ages of light. And as a matter of fact, in past history they have been not the exception but rather the rule. Very rarely as yet have whole peoples attained states of perfection. The fact is that the whole human race is as yet groping for the light. In the next chapter we shall see that the real history of mankind is only just beginning. The state of most human communities existing up to now has really been an embryonic state. One does not call the respective ages Dark Ages simply because there has been no light to contrast them with. Americans stand aghast at the present state of Russia or of modern China: very likely nine-tenths of all the periods of human history have been more like these than like those of pre-war Europe. And if, from time to time, there has been an Age of Light, it has been something like the old saying:

*Parturiunt montes*
*nascetur ridiculus mus.*

Quantitatively speaking, the truly cultured ages, gauged both by the time they lasted and by the proportion of people who had a share in them, have been nothing but episodes and accidents. In the first chapter we saw that it is unity of style which makes a nation; the same applies to culture. How many grand styles have there been on earth? There have been many approaches to style, but most of them ended in failure. And if a style ever came into existence, sooner or later it invariably ended in congelation. And then a new period of gestation set in.

In this sense the symptoms of the new Dark Age which is at hand are obvious. Today, as at the beginning of the Middle Ages, the new generation is completely indifferent to the ideals and aims of its fathers. Cultural traditions, however beautiful, no longer carry their old convictions, whether religious, social, political, or artistic. What I have called the chauffeur-type in *The World in the Making*—man become primitive again, but in command of all the mechanical devices of our civilization—is everywhere becoming the model and the ideal. Whatever doubts have existed in this respect should have been removed in Europe by the World War. The significance of an event must not be judged by those professed intentions that accompanied it, but by its results; for these alone correspond to subconscious desire. The real result of the World War was not, by any means, the triumph of the ideals of the Allies, but the liquidation of the old order. And I do not allude so much to changes in the political alignment of the world, as to changes in its psychological structure. It is not in Russia alone that a new type dominates: The same is true of Germany, of England; it is more true of the United States than of any other country. This new type, whose highest symbol and exponent is the chauffeur, is not cultural. It is primitive, violent, full of the vitality and arrogance of youth. It is, of course, impossible to foretell the facts of the future, unless one be a prophet, which I am not. When one of the last of the Russian saints was asked what he thought would be the characteristics of the new religious era, he tapped his interlocutor on the shoulder and said, with an indulgent smile: "One can know when a child is to be born; one knows all about its parents and one may guess what heritage it will carry; but no one knows what it will look like." Still one can point out the general course of events. And here an example from the past will serve best, when used as an image for meditation, for understanding both the trend and the significance of the present. I will, therefore, before dealing with the problem of the United States devote a little space to the analysis of the period in which the power of the Roman spirit came to an end.

The age of darkness that followed the splendour of Antiquity lasted for almost a thousand years. That darkness persisted even when the barbarians did their utmost, on their own initiative, to romanize themselves; even when, as under Theodoric the Great, they put forth their best efforts to continue the Roman tradition. The reason why they did not succeed is this: you may learn, take over from others whatever you like, you will never be like them, *unless you are at one with their spirit.* Let a Chinese learn the English language to perfection: he will never become English. To all outward appearance many a Goth lived the life of a Roman—inwardly the very fact of his Roman education only deepened the absyss between the Gothic and the Roman soul. Arminius, the Cheruscian who liberated Germany from the Roman yoke, was to a very high degree a Roman gentleman; it was this that made it possible for him to conceive a Germanic State—something altogether inconceivable to most Germans of his day. But what, in their heart of hearts, could the ancient Romans think of these barbarians who lived like them and yet were not like them? They certainly considered them poor imitators, thoroughly incapable of ever becoming their equals in any respect. Indeed, the Germanic tribes which had learnt to defeat the Roman legions by means of Roman tactics and to administer provinces by means of Roman laws stood in much the same relation to the Roman nation as that in which the westernized Malays or negroes stand to the cultured Frenchman or Englishman of today. And yet these Germanic tribes came to be the heirs of the Romans and the rulers of the world. They created a new culture, one utterly unintelligible to the fundamental mind of Antiquity.

This simple parallel, conscientiously examined, should suffice to make clear how absurd it is to think of all evolution in terms of progress. The Goths and the Vandals did not become Romans. Even if Arminius made the impression of an almost perfect Roman gentleman, and Theodoric the Great could perhaps deal on terms of equality with the best Northern Italians of ancient stock, this Roman character steadily faded out from generation to generation. The example of France is particularly instructive in this respect. France was thoroughly romanized at the time of the Frankish conquest; nor did the invaders, comparatively few in number as they were, destroy much of the ancient order. But the *soul* of France changed irresistibly after the conquest. By 1000 A.D. France had become thoroughly Germanic, and it is only within the last few centuries that the Latin character of the French civilization has regained the upper hand. This is because French culture is aging, so that modern France resembles the declining Roman Empire much more than did the France of the centuries immediately following the reign of Augustus. These brief observations should suffice to prove that the decisive factor is not "race" and less still "education," but the vital spirit which from within rules both blood and conscious tradition. This vital spirit bears the same relationship to external facts as the meaning of a sentence does to the words and letters of which it is composed. The vital spirit of Egypt cannot be deduced from the technique of pyramid building: the exact contrary is the case. The Greek spirit meant a new point of view from which the Mediterranean races looked at the world. The same is true of the Christian spirit as compared with the spirit of Pagan Antiquity. Life never is a mechanical process. However much heredity and education may mean otherwise—what sort of spirit the highest racial type will express, what purpose the finest education will serve, can be foretold with some certainty only as long as a given cultural spirit is alive. Once it is dead, "progress" means nothing if not the birth of a new soul with all its unpredictable qualities. The underlying reality of history, too, is not material, but psychological, and there is nothing more mystical about this than about the existence of the individual human soul. In the first chapter we have seen to what extent man belongs to the earth, on the one hand, and on the other to the domain of unearthly spirit. The spiritual side has a causality of its own. Here, too, from nothing, nothing comes. Individual man, whose essence is his uniqueness, comes from on high. But the collective Unconscious which forms the soul of a nation or a civilization belongs to a plane which we know and understand best in its expression as memory. Memory also fades as time goes on; it survives only as part of new imaginative combinations, and the more time elapses, the more does this part belong to the plane of the implicit as opposed to the explicit. At a certain point there is a complete solution of continuity. This corresponds to the physical phenomenon that no individual lives for ever, and that from a certain point life is continued by means of a child with a new soul. This child, again, never begins its existence as a mature being, but as a germ-cell, first, then as an embryo, and eventually, when it is brought forth, as a very primitive creature.

There have been in the world's history many changes in culture and in spirit. But we know of only one change in our Western history that justifies the use of the adjective "dark": the so-called Middle Ages. Now on what grounds do I foresee and foretell a new Dark Age —this time embracing the whole world? On the grounds that the change which is now taking place all over the world is as radical as was the change of two thousand years ago; and because in both cases the dark age followed a true age of light, so that a definition by contrast is the best way to make its true quality understood. Radical means "at the root." There was an absolute break in continuity between the ancient and the mediæval world, because what survived of the former and entered into the latter served to incarnate a new soul—a soul as new in quality as it was young in years. No child takes up the work of the father where the latter has left it off, and no child takes it up all at once; there must be a long period of incubation, of gestation, of preparation. There must be a period of purely animal growth, a sowing of wild oats; this explains how the extraordinarily refined civilization of Antiquity could be followed by such an age of barbarism as prevailed between the fourth and eleventh centuries. And it was not only actually, but intentionally barbaric: it is the natural reaction of the savage who has seen a civilization he cannot emulate to lay all the more stress on his barbarism conceived as a positive quality; here, too, an inferiority complex finds its normal expression in arrogance. The same is true at this turning point in history. It alone explains how Bolshevism—the term understood in the widest possible sense—and not Democracy could become the general result of the World War: a craving not for peace, but for violence; not respect for the old rights, but the institution of new rights. To the extent that the United States still continue the line of development which began in the seventeenth century, they represent an island sundered from the rest of the world.

This, then, brings us back to the particular problem of America's rejuvenation. I had to state the preceding in order to give the problem its right setting. This can be said to have been achieved only if it appears clear from the outset in what sense the problem we are about to discuss is *not* unique. It is not unique in so far as the rhythm of American life coincides with that of general Western life. If we wish to be mathematically correct we must, of course, admit that there is no real coincidence between the life-rhythm of any two nations. Russia's particular destiny is partly to be explained by the fact that it knew no Middle Ages and no Renaissance, so that the modern era, judged from the Middle-European standpoint, followed almost without an intermediate stage on that of Early Christianity, and that the outlook of the peasant class has not changed since the fifteenth century. Spain did not go though the experiences which the rest of Europe underwent in the sixteenth and seventeenth centuries until the nineteenth. Germany lost almost two hundred years owing to the after-effects of the Thirty Years War, which partly accounts for its convergence with America.[1] In exactly the same way, America's rhythm is not only partly, but fundamentally unique. Its historical start was different. During the crisis of the World War the American nation alone among the Western nations was able to preserve and consolidate the results of previous developments. This consideration alone suffices to show that, contrary to universal opinion, the world was never less prepared and never less likely to become americanized than it is today. Science and technique, desire for prosperity, and a social order based on equality of opportunity are universal characteristics of our age. What matters is not the material facts but the spirit that permeates these facts and uses them as means of expression. Thus in Russia modern science and technique appear as the predestined embodiment of the Bolshevist impulse. The situation is similar in China and India. In the United States both the European heritage and their own original achievements, however transferable they may seem, are steadily becoming the means of expression for an entirely new and untransferable spirit.

But it is not this aspect of the problem we have to deal with here. I mentioned it only incidentally in order to clear the way to the true understanding of the case of American rejuvenation and to remove any prejudices connected with this subject. There can be no

[1] I have dwelt on this convergence at length in my article "America and Germany" in the *Forum* of April, 1929.

doubt, in spite of all the facts above mentioned, that the rhythm of American life *does* to a great extent coincide with that of the West as a whole. And to that extent American rejuvenation is only a partial expression of the rejuvenation of the West as a whole. On both sides of the Atlantic this is due to the fact that the creative ideas of the eighteenth century—to mention only the last of the creative ideas which shaped the Western World—have reached their life-term. But precisely when we envisage the particular problem of the United States as a special aspect of the general Western problem, its singularity stands out with particular clearness. It stands out with singular clearness in the sense on which I laid the main stress in the *Travel Diary*, namely, that the Americans are the most typical of Westerners. Indeed, nowhere else does the solution of continuity which separates the old from the new generation appear so extreme. This is due to the fact that nowhere else could the ideas of the eighteenth century assert themselves in their purity so long. As far as inner experience goes, there has practically been no nineteenth century in America. Whomsoever I listened to among the old generation, I found the spirit of John Locke still determining, and next to him that of all the other leaders of eighteenth-century thought. The peculiar optimism of America has its roots in the outlook of the eighteenth century; if it only asserted itself practically much later, this was due to the fact that there were still a great many seventeenth-century ideas to work out before those of the eighteenth could really get their chance. (That the former are not yet fully exhausted even today, is proved by Fundamentalism.) America's disbelief in any sort of distinction, with its corollary, an overrating of the values of good-fellowship (think of the scale of values invented by the pioneers of the French Revolution, according to which to be *un honnête homme* is the highest goal a man can attain) also belongs to the eighteenth century. So does its moralism, and to a great extent its educationalism and institutionalism. There is nothing in the latter which an average progressive eighteenth-century mind would not delight in. For it was the eighteenth century which discarded the idea that men can be different from the point of view of "being"; it was the eighteenth century which advocated that only "ability" should count; it was the eighteenth century which first proclaimed the belief that education and institution can achieve everything. In this respect, then, the typical progressive American of the older generation belongs not to an advanced but to an ancient type; a much older type, in fact, than any European aristocrat. For the latter, while retaining many traditions, ideals, and characteristics which are much older than those of the eighteenth century, has developed since in accordance with the new experiences of the nineteenth century, which made him correct many of his eighteenth-century notions. In the United States, owing to their unique position, such a correction was not inevitable. And not only that: the ideas of the eighteenth century could go on spreading and growing there, in a vacuum, as it were, thus leading to gigantic formations.

Here, not in modernity of any kind, do we find the real root of the routine- and machine-quality of American life; it is here that we find its psychological roots—and these are always foremost in importance. True, without the inventions made in the nineteenth century and later, most of what makes modern American life would not exist. But the spirit which uses them belongs to the eighteenth century; it is an old, not a young, spirit. Institutions could not prove stronger than living men, the ideal of Henry Ford which transforms men into cogs in machines could not live, were it not for the survival of the ideals of the eighteenth century. In their own day their positive aspect was more in evidence than their negative aspect, simply because they were young at that time and because in those days there was no way of translating them on a large scale into terms of machinery. Do we not here find the most striking example possible of the truth that mechanization to the extent that the machine predominates, *always* denotes senility? And now let us throw a swift glance at the pre-war type of the men who are in entire sympathy with this machine-world. I have seldom met one who did not look centuries old; the kind of parchment-face I mean is the face of a mummy. And what does this type of man talk about? Never a new idea—a perpetual rehearsal of slogans which have their roots in the eighteenth century; a chewing the cud of higher standards of living, better institutions, a sound community-life, and so forth and so on. If such talk is not a sign of senility, I have never seen one. Here lies one of the roots of the American marriage-crisis: a considerable number of American men of the older type are senile because the mainspring of their lives lies full two centuries back. Man as an essentially mental creature ages in every respect when he keeps to old ideas and he appears young only when he is young in mind. An American of the type I mean is old in mind, whereas women have always changed with the times. Besides, in the Twintary of the United States the women alone had the necessary leisure to notice that something had happened in the world of inner experience since the eighteenth century.

AT THE beginning of the preceding paragraph I said that nowhere in the West is the solution of continuity separating the old from the new generation as evident as in the United States because nowhere else could the ideas of the eighteenth century hold their own as long. Is it not obvious for this very reason that the revolt of American youth simply *had* to be much more extreme than it was and is in Europe? Here we find one of the reasons why the youngest American and Russian generations are so similar in type and outlook. The Russian revolutionists called themselves nihilists (since Turgenjeff invented the term) because the existing political and social order meant nothing to their self-consciousness and they simply wanted to annihilate it; reconstruction might take care of itself. The flaming youth of America is almost equally irresponsible. Its revolt is directed against the moral order, but here the revolt is as extreme as any revolt ever was in Russia. And if it revolts precisely against the moral order, this means a wholesale revolt against the traditional spirit of America because the latter consisted essentially in a definite *moral* outlook; this was due to the curious blending of the religious feeling of the Puritans and the specific moralism of the revolutionary eighteenth-century philosophers. But in reality, youth is simply revolting against the rule of old age.

And here we find a further similarity between Bolshevik and American youth. What remains after the traditional order has been destroyed as a frame of life within the soul is in both cases *primitive*. The national consciousness of Russia shifted back, in a single wave, from the plane of the twentieth to that of the fifteenth century; as I have shown at length in *The World in the Making*, this is the real reason of the triumph of Bolshevism. Bolshevism corresponds fundamentally to a very ancient state; its socialistic setting means no more in this connexion than a new fashion in the feminine world. Now most people hold that the Americans have all the backgrounds Europeans possess. They have not. As was shown in the first portion of this book, one can transplant physical but not psychological heredity. The subconscious history of the American nation begins with the seventeenth century, not earlier. This explains why the American revolt against Protestant morality is so extreme, and why there is no point of comparison in this respect between European and American conditions, however dissolute Europe may appear at times. The truth about the Americans is, that they never were pagans; they began as Christians, and Puritans at that. So their developing of a freer outlook in sex questions finds no framework in the subconscious which could make for order and direction. The result is that after repudiating the inhibitions of Puritanism they became, without further notice, utterly primitive. I do not believe that among any known so-called savage tribe, a girl with respectable parents could be found who would carry contraceptives in her vanity-case for all emergencies (I am quoting from one of Judge Lindsey's books), or a set of young people (I am quoting the same author) who would go and buy contraceptives together, and then make use of them in a general hour of joy: not because contraceptives are not known among savages, but because all savages we know of believe in some kind of moral order and feel some kind of restraint in sexual matters, realizing that they belong to the core of the mystery of life. And before an essential mystery, not a matter of fact, but a reverential attitude alone is, even scientifically speaking, suitable.

I began with the most extreme expression of the revolt of modern youth; and I am well aware that it is not safe to generalize too much on the basis of Judge Lindsey's disclosures. But the fact remains that the sexual outlook of a high percentage of modern American youth is, at least in theory, exactly the same as that of Bolshevik youth. And this means that it belongs to an entirely primitive order. What kind of primitive soul is now being born or reawakened in the youngest generation? The question is not easy to answer. We know what psychological reality underlay the superstructure of Russian upper-class civilization. But who is the "American" when stripped of his Puritan heredity? He is an unknown entity. And I do not think it safe to anticipate more of his future type than has been done in the first part of this book. But whosoever he be: essentially the American is an *American*. He is a new type of man. And as such he is as far removed from the Pilgrim Fathers as the European social democrat is from the mediæval knight. For in Europe, too, the race question, which is of such importance in the United States, plays its part. The knights were the descendants of the early conquerors, while most modern Europeans belong to the conquered races.

SO MUCH for this aspect of the problem in the present context. What I wanted to convey with all possible force is the impression of the primitiveness of the new American type. If the type which still continues the traditions of the eighteenth century is essentially senile, the new one is as young as it can be. It is practically without a cultural background.

But we said that youth actually rules present-day American life; and this seems supremely civilized. How about this? The external side of the problem, which is indeed in that respect an entirely new one, will be dealt with in the next chapter. But this external side of the problem is of little importance: one may be primitive or advanced, barbaric or cultured, in almost any external setting. What matters is the psychological significance of the facts in question. If now we survey from this point of view the ruling ideas and ideals of present-day American life, as far as they are not expressions of the surviving eighteenth-century spirit, we shall find that *all of them, without one single exception, are expressions or symptoms not of an advanced but of a primitive state.*

The highest possible expression of human life is the full-grown individuality, conscious of its uniqueness and the intrinsic value of this uniqueness. I do not mean this only in the sense of Jesus Christ, who spoke of the infinite value of each human soul in the eyes of God, and thought nothing of majorities, but in the more general sense that all human value as opposed to mere animal value lies in its uniqueness.[1] There would be no reason not to kill and eat men, as long as killing and eating animals is thought permissible, were it not for the unique value of each individual. But on the other hand, individualized man is not born as such. As a person he develops from the child, the offspring of two parents; the primary consciousness of the child is a kind of dim group-consciousness. In the same way, socially, too, every individualized stage evolves from a stage of prevailing group-consciousness. Thus, whenever group-consciousness predominates, this indicates an early stage. Now this is just what we observe in present-day America. The Pilgrim Fathers, the New Englanders, all the great types of the nineteenth century were individualized enough (I know of nothing so individual as the home of Thomas Jefferson near Charlottesville). *They* did not speak of the group being more than the individual. But that is exactly what Young America believes in. Here also lies the root of the ideal of social service which is supposed to be all-inclusive (it must be generally believed in as all-inclusive, else all those shrewd business men would not successfully "put over" their most obviously personal interests as means of social service). The relationship to others—as such, fundamentally an abstraction—could not possibly be thought more valuable than the uniqueness of personality were it not that primitive group-consciousness predominated once again. Here we find America and Bolshevik Russia once more fundamentally alike: "collective" man, the ideal of the communist party, man who is nothing but a social organ, differs from the American social worker only so far that

[1] This problem can be dealt with exhaustively only in the last three chapters.

the same idea is being expressed in a different language. I have nothing to say against the positive achievements which the ideal of social service has brought about, but they do not alter the fact that the ideal is entirely primitive; it is the exponent of primitive group-consciousness.

The ideals of "normalcy" and "like-mindedness" are likewise essentially primitive ideals. Whenever man has attained cultural maturity, the feeling for differences and their value predominates; it is indeed logically impossible even to imagine a cultural state based on likeness—with only one kind of instruments or all instruments playing one and the same tune, no music of a higher order is possible. There have no doubt existed real cultures on the basis of an unindividualized general state; this was the case in Egypt, India, and China. But then individual consciousness in the modern sense was not yet born, therefore the spiritual could express itself by means of collective impulses—while in America like-mindedness and normalcy mean relapses from a higher to a lower stage. And yet even in the cultures of the past which were based on an unindividualized general state, the ideal always was incarnated in the great man—that he was generally thought of as a god, and not as a man, makes no difference psychologically. Whilst those who in America give preference to the normal do so out of dislike of superiority. The same interpretation applies to present-day discarding of home-life and the general trend to lead an uprooted existence. This is not an advanced stage, not a state beyond the stage of settledness; it is simply the early nomadic stage re-incarnated; it makes no difference, psychologically, whether a nomad uses a camel or an automobile, or whether a man removes his luxurious villa by the most advanced technical devices from one spot to another or sets and breaks up his tent anew each day. Here, too, it is not a question of a state superior to that of settledness, but of a relapse from a higher into a lower state. One should call to mind what was said in the first chapter about the singularly earth-bound nature of the Middle-Westerner: he, a distinctly primitive type himself, represents the first stage beyond nomadism. It is out of the question, that a higher state should evolve from the American nomads without a prior return to Mother Earth. And the same applies also to a good deal of what forms an integral part of the crisis in American sex-life. I am persuaded that one of the foremost reasons for the dissatisfaction of married American women is that in sexual matters, too, American husbands indulge in that simple direct way which is so charming in many other respects. This is, of course, intolerable to a woman of any refinement. But in this respect the men of higher quality often have as much reason to complain of the girls they love. Man being little differentiated by nature as a sensual and emotional being, he stands in vital need of woman's refinement. He wants her to be beautiful on all planes for the same reason of physiological compensation, as woman values foremost man's strength—whether physical, mental, or financial—thinking little of his looks (except in periods of a reversal of rôles, as we are witnessing one today in many sets). Now if woman becomes simple and direct and even aggressive and brutal, then man remains without what he thinks is best in her (whatever *she* may think). Among present-day American men there certainly is as much "disgruntled prosperity" on the psychological, as on the material plane—I say prosperity, because never was sexual satisfaction easier to be obtained. Now the woman of the new pattern described is not in the least a phenomenon of decadence —she represents a reversion to the type of those early days when neither sex was psychologically differentiated. The same is true of latter-day promiscuity—no matter whether it manifests itself in the form of pre-marital liberty or perpetual divorcing—and also of that most recent ideal of "companionate marriage." It is no use trying to veil the true psychological significance of this idea (as Judge Lindsey himself has tried to do of late) by making it mean no more than the legalizing of the use of contraceptives and the divorce by mutual consent. Nobody really minds "bootlegging"—it is part of the fun of American life—and those who want to separate without being guilty of anything or without finding fault with their partners, have long since invented devices for the obtainment of a divorce by mutual consent. What makes the idea of companionate marriage so suggestive and so appealing, is that it corresponds to a primitive state. There has been companionate marriage, exactly as Judge Lindsey describes it, for thousands of years and it exists today among many primitive tribes and among many of the European peasantries which have preserved the customs of early days. It is one of the features of primitive life that boys and girls live together, not exactly for trial—the tribes in question would object to this motivation as much as Lindsey does—but just as companions enjoying sexual intercourse; and exactly as the modern ideal will have it, and in spite of the fact that the use of contraceptives is unknown, there are as a rule no children for a long time. But when a child promises to be born—then life becomes earnest, divorce becomes difficult, if not impossible.

There are many other expressions of the same primitiveness; before I forget, I may mention the fact that an American wants to see and touch a thing before he believes in it or feels a real contact with it. This applies as well to the tendencies of American men to flirt more with their hands than with their eyes as to that extraordinary institution of dummy copies commonly used in the book trade: the publishers must *show* the booksellers the palpable appearance of the book they are to sell, in the shape of bound paper with a few pages of the future text—else they would not buy. I shall deal with more of these expressions of primitivity in the next chapter, because they will appear more significant in another setting. But as a matter of fact, most of those phenomena of American life which call forth the criticism of the sophisticated Americans (not to mention foreigners) belong to the same category. The atmosphere of rejuvenation is so strong on the American continent today that even middle-aged and old Americans, who individually are thoroughly differentiated adult personalities, are permeated with it, just as everybody loses his best self when part of an excited crowd. I have heard white-haired Americans of true merit and even well-deserved world-fame praising one another in after-dinner speeches in a style fit for children of five: everybody likes Mr. So-and-so, he has splendid boys—and these boys had then to stand up, so that everybody might have a look at them—he is nice to his parents, and so forth.

Most of what is delightful in the social life of America, but also most of what is difficult to put up with for a representative of an older civilization, is due to this nursery-atmosphere. There are comparatively more people pleasant to associate with in the United States than anywhere else in the world, and whoever keeps to the rules of the game will find social intercourse easier there than elsewhere. But, on the other hand, nowhere is there so little appreciation of unusual ways of life. In all mature and, therefore, differentiated civilizations, it is taken as a matter of course that men of extraordinary gifts are "eccentric" from the point of view of the average; being above the average in some respects, they have to be different from it in all; they require specialized conditions of life and, owing to the law of compensation, there usually is a *revers de la médaille* to all these qualities; one who is supersensitive in the positive sense of greater impressionability or deeper understanding must needs be so also in his personal intercourse. Children cannot see this; a boy or a girl is either good or bad. A lady once complained to me about the personal defects of a really extraordinary clairvoyant who honestly declared that he associated with angels—a man I also happened to know. "I have lost all faith in him," she said, "because he had five suits and there always was a meticulous harmony between the color of his tie, his suit, and his socks." I hope I saved the situation for the unfortunate seer by replying: "Have you met many angels?" "No," was her perplexed answer. "Well," I proceeded, "as far as my information goes, angels are very fastidious indeed." I have heard complaints about the behaviour even of such essentially simple-hearted and unobtrusive men as Albert Einstein.

This inherent childishness also explains the fact that one rarely hears of any other standard of value but of that of quantitative achievement. The quantitative standard is the aboriginal standard. And the American tendency to call everybody and everything that happens to be admired at the moment the "greatest in the world" is another characteristic of the aboriginal mentality: the combination of exclusiveness plus exaggeration is one of the foremost characteristics of the primitive mind. The whole American manner of thinking in terms of quantity is in fact a sign of primitiveness (one completely misunderstands it who considers the hunt after the dollar its essence). In a later chapter I shall even provide the proof that no nation cares less about money than the American. The American nation thinks chiefly in terms of quantity because to it that is the symbol of quality; it is not yet developed enough, as a whole, to distinguish quality as such, except in a few specific lines. In the same way the primitive artist expresses all that he thinks superior in the form of bigger size. American playfulness equally belongs to an early stage and so does the specific quality of the American gambling instinct, the extraordinary vital significance of the notions of good and bad luck ("the breaks"), and the peculiar American variety of depression, so well described by the word "the blues." And does the same not also account for the emotional waves and the extraordinary inconsistency and fickleness of American public opinion? As yet there exists no determining order of values within the American soul capable of providing a neutral instance beyond the mood of the moment. The surest standard by which to gauge the state of culture of a nation or a class is that of its consistency and reliability. One can trust an Englishman more than any other European, because his soul is completely organized on the lines of self-control; momentary impulses will never run away with him.

The Frenchman is almost equally reliable, only in a different way. He is the most faithful of friends, *provided he is a friend;* the organization of his psyche, which is still partly antique, makes him differentiate in an often un-Christian way between friends and strangers; on the other hand, he is exemplary on the field he calls *probité intellectuelle;* he will never allow fashion or moods to interfere with clear judgment once it has pronounced its verdict. The Germans, being a younger nation, are less reliable; the friend of today may easily betray you tomorrow out of what he calls "inner necessity"—the point is that with the truly cultured such "necessities" never arise. The Russians have as yet no national character-basis at all to rely upon. In the American psyche the moods of the moment play a much greater part than in that of any other white people I know of. And of course these moods have to be reckoned with, when one happens to live in the United States. Still one would do the country the most cruel injustice if one ever were to take them seriously in the sense of their being meant as expressions of real judgments of value. They are nothing of the sort, they are just moods.

There is a wonderful index for all this: the American press. The latter, being a business undertaking pure and simple, has to reflect public opinion in all its shades and curves of change if it is to prosper. These curves and shades correspond everywhere to the typical workings of a primitive mind. So does, in particular, its fundamental quality of curiosity. What many Europeans object to so vehemently and judge so severely—the American press-man's point of view that "news is news," that there should be no limit to publicity, that there is nothing sacred in private life, that any letters the press can get hold of may be published provided they make a good story—is no more objectionable than the curiosity of the aboriginal tribesman, with which it is psychologically identical. Of course such a press may do harm, but it very seldom really means harm. In the worst of cases it acts like the babe who tears off the head of his beloved canary in order to look inside. A charming young lady reporter once played me a rather nasty trick by publishing an interview distorting my utterances beyond what I was accustomed to under a headline that was bound to give offence. Soon after she walked into my room nothing daunted and asked me with a radiant smile, whether I had received many insulting telephone calls (as she had received with respect to me). I reassured her, and we parted on the most friendly terms. I do not see how anybody who has the slightest understanding of the human soul can mind the naughtinesses of the American newspapers. Personally, I have been blessed with more than the usual share of them, but though I am hot-tempered enough, I never once got angry. And putting aside the background of primitivity, there is another reason why even the worst of American press-attacks appear essentially harmless. If the leading idea is that "news is news," then the quality of novelty, of sensation as such, decides; what particular fact causes the sensation does not matter. To a reporter who could not understand why I seemed to delight in the press-attacks instead of minding them, I once replied: "If tomorrow you were to publish that I had eaten my own father and then was so abominably heartless as to have dared to observe afterwards that I had found him unpalatable—the day after scores of strangers would come and shake hands with me and say: 'Mighty glad to meet you, sir; I saw your name in the paper.' "

Of course, the inordinate love of publicity of the American public, without which the press could not behave as it does, cannot be judged as mildly. For here it is not a case of natural curiosity or sound business—the motive is self-advertising at any cost. On this line, I have heard of things done which would have irretrievably discredited those who did them in any older country; for instance: of cases where purely private letters—which could never have been written, had it not been taken for granted that they would remain private—were quite naturally given over to the press by the addressee, by which proceeding he or she certainly gained nation-wide publicity, though at the expense of the writer. But even such *faux pas,* although they cannot be excused, can be judged fairly only if considered as expressions of primitive psychology. Exhibitionism, the aboriginal impulse to "show off," is at the root even of the loftiest ambition; the latter develops out of the former. And its first visible embodiment is frankly ugly: it is a tendency to exhibit what is felt to be improper. The impropriety which one cannot help feeling as an essential characteristic in many cases of American self-advertising means exactly the same, psychologically, as infantile exhibitionism. And of course the nation certainly will soon grow out of it, as every baby soon learns to behave. There is no need to worry about it.

I will add one last word to this aspect of the American problem. It concerns the influence of the negro. I think the first chapter proved that the native-born black man is as true an American as the native-born white man. It also made us understand why the coloured American predominates in the field of art. But we can now say this further: the negro could not possibly be so representative of modern America as he actually is if the modern Americans were not essentially a primitive people. The negro, being not only more, but originally primitive, naturally expresses primitive characteristics better than a race grown primitive only of late.

ONCE one realizes the psychological background of all the above-mentioned manifestations of Americanism and of many others with which I have not dealt here, one cannot possibly judge them harshly. If my stay in the United States was on the whole a great holiday to me, it was just because of American youthfulness. This then leads me to the other side of the question. Is it not simply *wonderful* that a great, prosperous, powerful nation, with all the latest achievements of science and applied science at its command, should appear so young? In this fact alone lies the promise of a great future. Let us recall the considerations at the beginning of this chapter. *Every* new life, on whatever plane, begins like a baby. This is the law of nature; there is no other way of rejuvenation than what from the cultural perfection point of view appears as a barbarization. Here we may refute another popular prejudice: that the Americans are the most materialistic of human beings. At the beginning I made clear, that mechanization typically characterizes old age; it is always a sign of decay when routine proves stronger than creative freedom. I might have added then, because it amounts to the same, that materialism, too, denotes old age. But what I explained on that occasion is not the whole truth. Life is a polar phenomenon; as senility and infantilism always go together, there is also always a point where the opposites meet. In this sense, not only old age, but babyhood too is materialistic. There has never been a baby one could in fairness accuse of having the slightest intellectual and spiritual interests; a decent baby thinks of nothing but milk. We thus find that "materialism" as such is no issue in itself in any way. It either denotes decay, or else first beginnings. In the United States both aspects are to be found. Part of American materialism is due to the senility of the over-aged eighteenth-century type; but the other part is due to extreme youth. Now, youth always conquers. And it never remains materialistic. In fact, it appears materialistic only in early childhood; later an extreme and radical idealism is the normal attitude. And is not such radical idealism much more characteristic of the American mind than materialism of whatever sort? I, for my part, think so. The old men who personally belong to the dying eighteenth century would not so often act from idealistic motives (no matter whether these really are their own motives or whether they conform to the desiderata of public opinion) if these were not very potent factors in the nation's life. And in the case of idealism, too, the ambivalence of life asserts itself, exactly as in the case of materialism. Woodrow Wilson was personally an eighteenth-century moralist, with no understanding whatever of the New World in the Making. But his ideas happened to be high explosives, fitted as no other could be to destroy the old order (there is no doubt that in this respect Wilson, and no other, is the originator of Bolshevism, Fascism, etc., quite setting aside the upheaval of the whole of the non-Western world, the starting-point of which was the ideal and the proclaimed right of self-determination for all nations). This is the reason why young America temporarily took to them: youth felt, subconsciously, that for once the idealism of two centuries back would further its own ideals.

I HOPE my readers feel that I have not only not meant anything disparaging when explaining the primitive character of present-day America, but that there really is nothing disparaging in what I have written. That the primitivity in question can manifest itself in such gigantic dimensions and with such exaggerations is simply the result of the fact that America is on the other hand the modern nation with the highest technical development and with a particular genius for publicity and advertising; and that thus intuitiveness, as shown at the beginning of the first chapter, leads the Americans to think in headlines and slogans. This must needs exaggerate those traits of mass-psychology which are common to all very young peoples. There is an overwhelming and truly terrific amount of mass-suggestion at work in the United States day and night, which, in its turn, must needs contribute to make the quality of life primitive, thus enhancing the primitiveness already in existence. It must be so, because the American advertiser, true again to his primitive state, hardly ever tries to *create* a demand by educating the public to something higher than it is used to, but tries to adapt himself to the general trend of life. This certainly is the best way to obtain a colossal amount of turnover. But since suggestion always acts creatively, adaptation to the man in the street on the one hand keeps the latter on his present level, while, on the other, it lowers the quality of the salesman and thus makes progress almost impossible. I have seen highly intelligent men who after a few years of advertising simply could not grasp the idea that there is a higher standard than the demand of the public as it exists. Another instance: American friends, if they belong to the comparatively leisured class, as is the case with a high percentage of women, are not only constantly meeting in country clubs, etc., they telephone to one another constantly in the intervals of separation, and this makes—not for a kind of communist family life on an immense scale, but for something like one single enormous kindergarten. This also accounts partly for what Europeans and Asiatics criticize as American "soullessness." There can be no real soul-life before the uniqueness-quality predominates within each person; where group-consciousness rules there can be no question of a dominant soul. And a gregarious life, enhanced by overpowering mass-suggestion, must needs transform even highly individualized personalities into herd-creatures, if they submit at all to such a life.

But again, what possibilities for the future! If the Americans were to remain what they are today, their case would of course have to be considered as very serious indeed. But there can be no question of the present state as more than a passing stage. If it were otherwise, most Americans with brains would not be so highly suspicious of its value. I take it, therefore, that the state I have described in this chapter really means just a passing state. Let us remember the general healthiness of American life, the general good-will, the lack of jealousy, envy, and resentment: is it not, in a way, an ideal kindergarten? All the more so as the behaviourist attitude of American educators, of which I shall say more later on, makes them ideally fit to educate small children. . . . And now let us resume the thread of our considerations at the beginning of this chapter, the essence of which was, that the symbolic image in which a nation appears to others than itself, always is a truer expression of its innermost reality than any demonstrable fact. The symbol of the old type of American was Uncle Sam. The foreigner has not yet found an image for the new type; indeed, he generally quite fails to notice the existence of the latter. But Young America has already decided for itself, who is representative of its innermost being and aspirations: it is *Charles Lindbergh.* There can be no way of accounting for the boundless admiration this man excites by facts. He has excellent qualities; he is a splendid flyer; he is one of nature's gentlemen. But if a majority of the students of a great university decided the other day that Lindbergh is greater than Mussolini, and if other young people see in him something of a Christ, this cannot be explained by an understanding or an interpretation of any kind of Lindbergh's personality as it is; Lindbergh is simply the *symbol* of Young America; he represents what the new generation wants to be; he is the national hero. If we now consider the facts of Lindbergh's nature and achievements from this angle, we can grasp the full significance and purport of the symbol. Lindbergh, too, is a distinctly primitive type. He bears a great resemblance to the heroes of the Germanic saga, Siegfried for instance. As a modern European, he would be impossible as a symbol because he represents a reality which was vital before his history began. He is a prehistoric figure. But this very prehistoric figure may well stand for the dawn of a new historic period. We now know that the primeval Nordic race which developed in what is today the Arctic region, settled in America long before it invaded Europe. There must be some kind of significance in the rebirth of the ancient Nordic ideal, which Lindbergh incarnates to such a high degree, and the world-wide appeal it has. May not the heroic task of the forthcoming new age be prepared in some parts of the globe, by a rebirth of ancestral virtues —a rebirth perfectly possible owing to Mendelism?— However this be, Lindbergh *is* possible as a national symbol for a nation just in the process of being born. And taken as such, he is the most promising symbol I can imagine: a clean, pure boy, clean and pure in body, soul, and mind—a truly wonderful starting-point.

WHAT I wanted to achieve in this chapter was to set free the American soul and mind in a particular respect and direction. I wanted to show America the true significance of certain facts. Throughout this book, I am attempting a national psycho-analysis. If I have succeeded in my undertaking, then the wrong and detrimental formations due to a false understanding of the case will vanish of their own accord within all those who are capable of understanding and willing. And those are the only people that count. There is no doubt that most of what America has so far considered as an advanced state, a state superior to that of traditional European civilization, is in reality a primitive state; and primitive states must not be perpetuated; they have to be outgrown. Should they last beyond their normal lifeterm, the result would be, æsthetically speaking, a caricature, and morally and culturally a catastrophe. There can be no question, therefore, of taking the ideals of the present American generation as examples and models. As far as they are true ideals, the true exponents of vital tendencies, they are the ideals becoming to a particular youthful state. But by this I do not mean to say that they will have to be discarded: America constitutes something entirely new and original. Thus out of the ruling ideals of today there will grow—so I hope—in a later stage of development mature and lasting and possibly exemplary ideals. As the ideals of children and adolescents pretend to be ideals of general validity, they ought never to be taken seriously, and that for a very obvious reason: *the idealism of youth is essentially an idealism without an object.* Man being able to see only things that stand before him, he necessarily tries to condense the inward urge he feels into an exteriorized image. This is the *raison d'être* of all exteriorized ideals, for they are all either exponents of inward forces or else they are mere abstractions, that is to say nothing vital. A mature person sooner or later creates an adequate image of the urge within him. But a very young one cannot possibly create an adequate image, because what he strives after has not yet taken definite shape. Therefore, he identifies his aspirations with anything he happens to admire for one reason or another, abandoning it later. Thus, Nietzsche first visualized the anticipated image of his own future being in Schopenhauer and Wagner, which alone explains why he had to turn away from both at a later period; that he did so with such violence was only partly due to his own diseased state: it was chiefly due to the fact he had loved them too well. Thus, every young person identifies himself for a time with some revered and idealized teacher. This "idealism without an object" characteristic of all youth, sometimes manifests itself in the most amusing forms. For a while, the German *Jugendbewegung*, in the hectic days of the immediate post-war period, considered the age of seventeen as such—without any further qualification—to be the all-human ideal: obviously it was given up the moment the boys and girls in question had reached the age of eighteen. The younger and truly significant part of modern America is, from the point of view of essential age, far from seventeen today. Therefore, it is not safe to take anything it stands for as final. To compare European and American ideals is to be thoroughly unfair to both.

And now let us link up the foregoing considerations with some of those of the first part of this book. I tried to show there that America's real history is only just beginning, that America is only just emerging from its golden age. The facts we have so far surveyed should suffice to explain why it is that Europe is coming to feel increasingly different and distant from America, and why the americanization of the whole world, in the sense generally accepted, is an increasingly remote possibility. Every consecutive year in which we meet Americans, we Europeans feel comparatively older. What is taking place at present in the United States is the exact equivalent of what took place in India at the time when the Aryan invaders were becoming indianized. But it is for this very reason that I do believe in a great American Future. India's great culture was the result of the blend of Nordic idealism, energy, and courage with India's mystic spirit. There is no doubt that the culture of America will differ greatly from the cultures of Europe. It will be the child of European culture, of course, but a very original and in some respects a very perplexing child. Only one eventuality could arrest this process: if the Europeans among the Americans—I mean Europeans in the cultural sense—who are still very numerous, were to become a ruling caste. But this possibility is precluded because of the dominating ideal of democracy, and then because of the gradual dying out of this type. America's history until now has in reality been nothing more than European colonial history. What I have called the new chauffeur-world could begin sooner in America than in Europe because in spite of all the unconscious ties of tradition every immigrant began a new life and the spirit of this life was opposed to that of the country he left in his thirst for freedom. The American nation is indeed not yet formed—far from it. A time will probably come when America will look back to the days of New England domination as Russia already looks back at its Czarist days. When that time comes, even Emerson may bear the aspect of a European colonial, just as Greek philosophers who lived in Sicily were regarded as Greek colonials. And Walt Whitman may then be judged as a John the Baptist of a new dispensation which, like most dispensations, never became a historic reality.

## *The Animal Ideal*

IN THE preceding chapter we made a sharp distinction between a life which has become mechanical and a "technicized" life—that is a life which has developed technical civilization of some kind—without, however, going deeper into the matter; the context was that only the mechanical, and not the technical, quality of life denotes senility. Our next step should be to make this point quite clear. For there is no civilization more technical in character than that of the United States.

In order to realize the full importance and significance of modern technical civilization, it is necessary to rise above the usual human point of vantage which surveys only the history of mankind and to look at the latter from the standpoint of the geologist, that is, the man to whom it means no more than a chapter or an episode within the history of the earth. Life has passed through many forms, phases, and metamorphoses since it first made its appearance on our cooling planet. These different phases, in each of which the whole of life took on a general character distinctly differing from any that prevailed earlier or later, can be considered as part of a system in which they appear as subdivisions of a smaller number of so-called geological formations, the most important of which, up to more recent times, are the archaic, silurian, devonian, carboniferous, permian, jurassic, and cretacean; and these again can be subsumed under the three common denominators of the palæozoic, the mesozoic, and the cenozoic ages. Each age and each formation is characterized by what palæontology calls "leading fossils"—the predominance of certain types of animals and planets in each period is such that their presence in some stratum serves to fix it chronologically with absolute certainty. There are characteristic leading fossils for each phase of life's evolutions on earth. But if one surveys the latter from the highest possible point of view, from which only the most general outlines are visible to the eye, then one is led to say that there has been a predominance on earth in the order given here: of the cartilaginous fish, the amphibian, the reptile, the marsupial, and eventually the mammal.

What I have summarized here is the current teaching of palæontology. But is it really true that the age of the mammal is the last of which wc know? Let us apply the time-honoured notions of geological formations and leading fossils to our modern age. Then we cannot help admitting that we no longer live in the geological period of the predominance of the mammal in general, but in the geological period of *man*. If ever there has existed a creature which showed all the qualifications of a "leading fossil," it is modern man. No giant saurian ever put its stamp upon its age to anything like the same degree which modern man does, who changes the course of rivers, drives tunnels through mountain-chains, not to mention his subjugation of all other living beings. But on the other hand, this is true of *modern* man only.[1] If the statement of the Bible is correct, man was already proclaimed the Lord of Creation in the Garden of Eden; as a matter of fact, he was nothing of the sort even two

[1] See the full development of this trend of thought in the chapter "Man and the Earth" of *The Recovery of Truth.*

short centuries ago. Indeed, judged from nature's point of view, he was just one creature among others, always superior in intellect, but so weak in other respects and, above all, so deficient in numbers, especially in his most gifted varieties, that only blind conceit could make him believe that he actually ruled the earth. And as a matter of fact those religious and philosophical leaders whose ideas gave the basic note to all pre-modern life never thought much of man as an earthly power. Within the Hindu system, natural man was just an animal among others, and his soul could easily transmigrate from a human to an animal body. Within the Chinese system the cultural history of man stood out on the same plane as the succession of the seasons. And the truly Christian Age (it is past today) did not look on man in the light of an essentially powerful, but of an essentially weak creature, entirely dependent on Divine Grace for his prosperity. Today, however, man *has* won the position assigned to him in Eden. Today he is the Lord of Creation. This accounts chiefly for the reason why those religions and philosophies in the basic conceptions of which man was allowed no predominance above the rest of creation are irresistibly losing their holds on the minds and souls of men.

We are, then, no longer living in the Age of the Mammal in general, but in the Age of Man. Once we have realized this, we perceive the exact significance of this technical age: it is not only a phase in human evolution, it means much more: *It means, geologically speaking, that from the pre-human stage man has reached the human stage proper;* there is the same solution of continuity between the pre-technical age and the technical age, as between any two geological epochs. For it is science and applied science and nothing else which has made of man in the course of the last centuries the Lord of Creation in the natural or terrestrial sense of the word. But on the other hand, it was precisely the possibility of the development which he has now actually reached which always distinguished man as an animal from other animals; this is why prophetic spirits could visualize him as the Lord of Creation even in pre-Babylonian days; man has really come into his own with the technical age. This, then, explains why the age of so-called progress has been characterized by such an unparalleled vitalization of those who participated in it as pioneers: they felt that it was their privilege personally to reach the goal for which the whole of mankind had been groping for millions of years. This explains also why the age of progress was an age of unparalleled speed: man felt himself like a rider at the end of a race; after having gone more or less evenly for a long time, so as not to exhaust the resources of his horse too soon, he now saw the winning-post before him and rode full-speed to reach it.

But it explains many more things. It explains why technical civilization irresistibly conquers our whole planet. Mortal man is an animal among others; this is the meaning of the current saying that human nature never changes (as indeed it does not). The elementary instincts which call for expansion and power and lust rule man's conduct as primarily as they rule every beast; if there is nothing to check them, they run wild. And there was nothing to check them on the plane of technical development; for no religion or philosophy of the prehuman days (I am again using the word in the geological sense) foresaw its possibility. Thus, technicized man started to conquer the earth as ruthlessly as did any saurian; and as ruthlessly as any gigantic saurian trod down his minor cousins which stood in his way, did technicized man conquer and enslave or else exterminate such human races as had not attained his own degree of technical development. However, this was only the first phase of the process. Soon all races, black, yellow, brown, and white, realized that technical civilization really was the heritage of man as man; much more so than political freedom, since the latter was obviously of little use when not allied to power. This, then, explains the tremendous rush for "technicization" we are witnessing since the Great War (which, by weakening the European nations, gave the others their first great chance) all over the world. For, as I have explained in *The World in the Making,* the real soul of Bolshevism is not a particular form of government but the promise to give to all and sundry of the oppressed races the benefits of technical civilization without making them the slaves of foreign capital. The same applies, *mutatis mutandis,* to the emancipation movements in the entire East. It is also the real motive power of all radical social programs, whatever the country in question be. To that extent these movements are *irresistible*: man as such will not be kept out of his own as the leading fossil of the geological Age of Man. There is, therefore, no question of stopping or checking technical progress, as so many idealists hope for. Should a form of civilization, even the most beautiful, stand in the way of the animal aspirations in question, it will be destroyed, as indeed the Chinese, the Turks, and the Russians have already destroyed their own old traditions; the animal impulses are always the stronger the more primitive the race. And now we can also understand why precisely the primitive races take so passionately to technical progress: the latter means fundamentally a stage within *animal* development; primitive man is, accordingly, in a position of advantage. If now we call to mind the fact that up to now, the majority of human beings were in the position of the oppressed, we can fully realize what the mere possibility of technical progress must mean to mankind at large. It must stimulate them to make for what on the surface appears as a political revolution. But it really means much more than that: it means that *all* men want to enter into their own as the Lords of Creation, as the leading fossils of the geological Age of Man. The issue is a much more fundamental one than that of "Democracy," in which the many reactionary minds of our day still believe as in a progressive ideal: for fundamentally the age of democracy was also an age of privileged castes. It was the age of the privileged white man in general, and of the Anglo Saxon in particular. From now on, the whole of mankind wants to live its life to the full. It wants to have done with all privilege.

All this accounts for the tremendous release and development of energy we are witnessing all over the earth today. But this accounts also for the extraordinary degree of rejuvenation which the stimulus of technical possibilities has called forth. Every new idea which gives a new meaning to life or promises the attainment of a new and desirable goal, rejuvenates. Mankind as such does not age; only every single line of development is finite; let the most ancient type, as long as he is personally capable of change, start on a new line—and he will show all the signs of youth. But what if the idea happens to be an essentially animal idea? This coincidence must make for a truly tremendous increase of earthly vitality. And now let us once more focus our attention on the fact that the age of progress fundamentally means not only a new phase in human development, but that it has inaugurated a new geological epoch. This must needs mean that today man, having attained a new plane or basis of natural existence, is in a state similar to that of any new leading fossil after it has assumed its position as such; that is to say, *it starts on a new animal career*. This, then, accounts finally for the barbaric character of the new world in the making. Similar to a natural catastrophe such as a volcanic eruption, the destruction of all the achievements of previous cultural states marks the advent of the new geological epoch.

It should be quite clear by now in what sense the technical age, although outwardly more mechanical than any previous age, must be understood as an era not of senility, but of extreme youth; there are still many senile elements surviving, but they are dying out fast and, besides, the future belongs to the young anyhow. Let us now turn from generalizations to particulars. Obviously, the new geological epoch must assert itself most clearly in all respects where man made a quite fresh start at the beginning of that epoch or soon after it had set in. Here lies the explanation of the most important difference between America and Europe. But this explains also why Bolshevik Russia and America are so much alike. Russia has violently shaken off all the fetters of its past traditions and, although the Russian soul is entirely different from the American, the fact of a new animal ideal—the ideal of a new adjustment of man consistent with his position of the Lord of Creation within the whole of nature—having become the chief impelling force, has suddenly drawn Russia quite close to the United States. And the same will be the case with all those rejuvenated races which have thought it necessary to shake off their past in order to begin a new life. In a very short time all of these will gravitate either toward the centre the symbol of which is America, or toward Russia; we shall see later what is to be the exact relationship between these two poles of future historic life.

BUT it is high time now to explain clearly why I call the American ideal an animal ideal. Is it not an essentially human ideal? Does it not make for better living, for what Americans mean by the word democracy, for higher civilization? Of course it does. But it makes for all that only for man conceived as an animal, and not as a spiritual being.

America's most essential and most representative ideal is that of a high standard of living. It is no use quarrelling about words or giving new and even ostensibly better definitions where problems of national psychology are concerned; the common use of words and the meaning popularly attributed to them are only important here. And there can be no doubt that the ideal of a higher standard of living is at present the very soul of Americanism. Now nothing whatever can be said against this ideal as such. And apart from the fact that so-called materialism presents no real issue, it is obviously better to live comfortably than uncomfortably. This is finally and conclusively proved by the mere fact of the general good-will, the lack of jealousy, envy, and resentment in the United States, as opposed to what we see in all poverty-stricken countries, in which poverty really does mean privation of what makes up the joy of life (which it does not in the tropics, for instance). But pray tell me—what animal, if it could think, would not enlist under the banner of the highest possible standard of living? "Standard of Living," conceived as an ideal, means fundamentally this and nothing else: that an organism should have the surroundings and a position within these surroundings which give full scope to its inner potentialities. Each kind of organism must accordingly possess a different standard of living. And as long as it has not realized this standard in the facts of its life, the natural equilibrium between it and the world has not been established; there is dissatisfaction, unrest, in extreme cases war or the equivalent of war. Now man has always striven to be comfortable, as every other organism does. But only in very rare cases has he succeeded in being as comfortable as he wished and then usually so at the expense of others, which proves that there could be no question of a really sound equilibrium having been established. In the case of uncomfortable man there was indeed a fundamental discrepancy between the imagined ideal and the realization within reach, a discrepancy the like of which is not to be found among the lowest beasts. Most of these might be called poor, but their poverty does not appear as a problem because in any case a final adjustment between the inward and the outward is within the range of reasonable possibilities for them. For man, however, poverty *does* mean a problem. And it could not be solved in the pre-technical age. Why not? *Because only technicized man as an animal has reached the plane on which every other animal moves from the outset;* it is true of technicized man only that he can obtain the surroundings, and the position within these surroundings, which give full scope to all his inward powers. Now the geological epoch of man has only just begun; man must still conquer his new position within the whole of nature. Is it not natural, then, that an appropriate standard of living should be his chief ideal? It must be, it ought to be for the time being; it ought to be until man has attained the same equilibrium between his inner nature and the surrounding world which is characteristic of other beings. The difficulty inherent in the aspiring nature of man which makes a final adjustment impossible does not concern us here. Our present intention was to make it clear that a higher standard of living is an entirely legitimate but, on the other hand, a purely animal ideal.

We now see in what respect it is absurd to charge Americans with being materialistic. The fact is that America has an animal ideal. This ideal can, of course, be taken in the sense of pure materialism. Russia takes it thus. But the fact that America understands and also reverences Dr. John Dewey, who is not a materialist, is a proof to my mind that neither Russia's materialistic nor America's pragmatical or behaviouristic outlook is a fundamental fact, but that both mean different interpretations of a fundamentally identical elementary situation and attitude.

By this time some of my readers will probably think to themselves: this may be all very true, but why stress the point so much that the ideal of a higher standard of living is an animal ideal? I had my very good reasons for stressing it. For almost all the typical manifestations of present-day American life are not only expressions of the ideal of a higher standard of living—*they really start from the assumption that man is nothing else than an animal* and must be dealt with accordingly.

Which again goes far to explain the likeness between America and Bolshevik Russia.

In order to make quite clear, at the outset, what I mean and what I am driving at, I must insert a few general remarks on the difference between man and the other animals. I cannot, however, enlarge on this subject here; I shall demonstrate the fundamental premise of what I am going to say now, *viz.*, the reality of the spirit, in the concluding chapter only. Whoever is not satisfied with what he finds here (and I hope many will not be), will find full details in my books *Creative Understanding* and *The Recovery of Truth.* Every organism is, on the one hand, an essentially responsive being; its life evolves in response to stimuli and is to that extent conditioned by the external world. And on the other hand, every organism is a being which lives in its own right as the expression of a qualified autonomous life-force. It is impossible to explain any phenomenon of life without recurring to both of these two factors, which are essentially independent of each other.[1] But the autonomous life-force of all plants and animals is, roughly speaking, a constant factor; it manifests no more initiative than does heredity with man. The latter's problem is different. In man the life-force, which is autonomous everywhere, becomes (or can become) focussed in the conscious endowed with free imagination. And although what I said of the animal organism holds true also of man, namely, that the direction of his life is determined by the stimuli it responds to,

[1] At the beginning of the second chapter of *The World in the Making* I have given a full exposition of how life can never be defined by less than two co-ordinates, and how a third comes into play in the case of man.

yet personal initiative plays the decisive part. It does not play a decisive part along the lines of his animal life —but wherever specifically human problems arise, wherever the meaning of facts seems more important (as it does in the case of all properly human issues) than the facts themselves, the initiative of the spirit and not the pressure of the surrounding world is finally decisive. And the higher man rises as a man, the more important does this meaning-giving quality become. The sage is almost independent of outward events; to him they mean exactly what he makes of them, not only in the subjective but also in the objective sense, as is exemplified by the lives of all truly great men who have met with and conquered adversity.

It is characteristic of the American point of view, that it almost entirely overlooks the exclusively human side of man. There are, of course, many exceptions to the rule; there is even more than that: there are very powerful counter-phenomena. But the very exaggeration with which the autonomy of the spirit is asserted there—I am thinking of course of Christian Science, New Thought, and all that is akin to them—goes to prove the strength of the prevalent point of view. Naturally, it takes a long time before an original outlook becomes fully conscious of its own true meaning; for a long time it seeks expression in some intellectual structure based upon a compromise with traditional ideas. Here we find the vital roots of pragmatism, the fathers and promoters of which never succeeded in freeing themselves from the traditions of European philosophy which subconsciously influenced them. But today we can say that the typical American outlook has found its adequate expression on the plane of theory. It is the outlook called *Behaviour-*

*ism.* Every representative American of today (except, of course, the opposition already mentioned) is a behaviourist at heart, whether he knows and acknowledges it or not. John Dewey is also essentially a behaviourist, only he knows too much about the soul to be a behaviourist pure and simple. In John B. Watson the typical American attitude has become fully self-conscious and it has expressed itself with all the exclusiveness and one-sidedness required both by style and by successful action. I do not doubt that one day John B. Watson will be considered as one of the foremost representatives of what the United States stood for in the twentieth century.

WHAT is the essence of Behaviourism? That man is an animal like any other. That spiritual initiative and free will play practically no part in his make-up and conduct. That concrete "habit" stands for the whole of man's vital activity—there is no "beyond it" in the direction and sense of a possible metaphysical or otherwise spiritual reality. And that habit can be explained, determined, ruled, and changed entirely from without and by external influences.

The most interesting part of a theory is hardly ever to be found in its intrinsic truth—most theories are lamentably one-sided or short-sighted—but in its psychological significance. In this sense the most interesting aspects of Behaviourism are its mere possibility and its representative quality. That there could be anything like Behaviourism and that it should be such a success, that practically all living representative Americans are Behaviourists, proves that Americans *do* look upon themselves in the light of animals; they find nothing within themselves that should necessitate any other theory. And what I am saying here is not a sweeping assertion: its truth is proved by all the important facts of American life. Behaviourism holds that any phenomenon of life can be explained and brought about from without, by external influences, and that spiritual autonomy plays no part. There are hundreds of thousands of Americans and hundreds of institutions which officially proclaim the contrary belief. But all the facts combine to prove that the *real*, and in any case the national, point of view is that of the Behaviourist.

During my stay in the United States I had to consult a doctor because of a few alarming symptoms possibly due to overwork. He said to me, "You needn't stop doing mental work; just go ahead. Your brain is used to that. Mine is as good as yours, but it has never formed the habit of thinking." This sounds rather crude. But if one were to render what John Dewey has to say about education, about the forming of the right kind of habits beyond which he, too, does not recognize any metaphysical reality—his last premise is society—in the phraseology of the average American, used to thinking in headlines and slogans, I doubt whether one could find a set of phrases more expressive of the real situation than the above quotation. Man is not different, in principle, from any other animal. Partly for that reason Democracy, as the doctrine which teaches that all human beings are originally equal, carries conviction to most Americans. Man has no unique soul, for doubtless no animal owns one; all differences depend on surroundings, wherein training is included. The last resort is the "community," the highest values they know of are social values. My readers will note that here again Americanism converges with Bolshevism. That

Bolshevism is a distinctly materialistic creed and that Behaviourism is not makes no difference as to the essence of the matter.

The convergence, as far as it concerns us here, is primarily due to the fact that both modern Russia and America made an entirely new start on the new basis of the geological epoch of man; though they did so at different stages of their respective developments; and that both are, accordingly, dominated by the animal impulse to work out a new adjustment within the surrounding world which, since a new animal situation is to be developed, can only mean that all the emphasis should be laid on surroundings and externals. At this point, however, let us once more turn to the positive aspect of the problem. Two things are beyond all doubt. First, that the animal nature of man *can* best be improved by means of influences from without; in the long run, appropriate stimuli inevitably call out corresponding responses. Secondly, that it is very much easier to arrive at satisfactory results when starting from the plane of nature than from that of the spirit. Spirit is essentially free; it acts of its own free will or it does not act at all. Accordingly, improvements originating from the spirit can be brought about only when the freedom of the latter has attained a high degree of development and when both the mental and the moral powers of a man seem sufficiently strong to enable him to understand clearly the importance of the issue in question and to overcome the inertia of animal nature. This is the reason why the level of human existence was never generally raised prior to the scientific age. Science first made it possible for man to regulate outward conditions in so exact a way that the responding mechanism came into play in the direction desired. Before the scientific age, only rare individuals gifted with exceptional mental and moral endowments succeeded in getting much beyond their original state; it is absolute fraud to pretend that the practise, for instance, of Yoga, the most scientific technique as yet devised to change man by means of the spirit, has ever been of assistance to any except those who would probably have achieved the desired results without systematic training. On the other hand, in the past the higher classes always owed their typical higher standard of existence to the fact that in each of their members, from its very infancy, better surroundings developed and bred the responses characteristic of the type; so that the breeding of aristocracies was, in principle, always effected on behaviourist lines. We should not forget that the idea of a higher class as such demands that the higher standard of the individual should be independent of exceptional individual gifts. In accordance with this fact the higher classes alone, in the past, were scientifically educated, and there is nothing new in principle in the idea underlying mass-education in the widest sense. But on the other hand, there is something entirely novel in mass-education as it is practised in the United States and Russia. This novelty consists in the fact that man is *consciously* treated as an animal. From the idea of appropriate surroundings, whatever belonged to the concept of traditions—and traditions formed the bulk of pre-scientific educational environment—is excluded. Man is supposed originally to be just an animal; what he develops into is thought to be entirely a matter of natural stimulation in about the same sense as the frog in the laboratory inevitably responds to specific stimuli in a specific way. Education is to "build in" satisfactory habits and to "unbuild" unsatisfactory ones, exactly as chemical compounds can be synthesized and broken up.

To a man in whom ancient traditions are alive, this idea of turning out the desirable type of man by mechanical processes sounds absurd, as indeed it would be a preposterous presumption to imagine that *his* type could be created by such methods. But things are very different in the case of types without a cultural past. At a party given by the Prussian Minister of Public Instruction, I once met his Russian colleague, Comrade Lunatcharsky, and asked him how the Bolsheviks managed to find and collect such an extraordinary amount of highly gifted men to carry on their propaganda work in the East. His answer was highly instructive. He said, "But there is no question of men of exceptional ability. *Somehow, the instruction on Marxist lines seems to make even Eastern dullards intelligent.*" To make quite sure that I had got the point, I asked him whether he agreed with me in this that Marxism did not improve the intellectual quality of Europeans; he heartily assented. Then I knew how matters stood. The purely animal ideal of Marxism necessarily stimulates whatever powers primitive Easterners possess exactly as every mother becomes intelligent when the life of her child seems threatened. For in their traditional half-starved condition and used, as they are, moreover, to oppression and exploitation, economic emancipation must mean almost as much to them as eternal salvation meant to the Early Christian. Its gospel seems to imply that it is possible to create material values out of nothing. And since this gospel is presented to them by Marxism (as popularized for propaganda-purposes) in a form which can be grasped by even the simplest mind, the vitalization it effects must be tremendous.—Let us examine one more example taken from Russian conditions before reverting to the problem of the United States. Before the Revolution Russia was unquestionably backward in the scientific field, in spite of many individual savants of high standing. Today, in spite of its poverty and the impossibility of endowing the laboratories in the way they ought to be, Russia plays a leading part in several fields of science and applied science; of physiology, for instance, and several departments of medicine and radiology; and this time it is obviously a matter of a national achievement. How can this be? It is again due to the fact that the purely scientific outlook, unburdened by traditions of any kind, sets new energies free.

The case of America is the same in principle as that of Russia and the awakening East. It is the question of a whole nation beginning its historic life on the new plane of existence of the Geological Age of Man. In all these cases it means that primitiveness and scientific and technical proficiency go together. This is the entirely new, the unheard-of state of things. Before the Geological Epoch of Man increased knowledge always meant higher development along the lines of a tradition begun before the Age of Man proper; since the latter epoch has set in scientific development has become the starting-point of a new phase in the existence of *animal* man. And since it is this animal quality that actually predominates, it is only logical that in all respects man should see himself in the light of an animal. And as a matter of fact he does so, whether he interpret his attitude in terms of materialism or Behaviourism or even the most spiritual form of Pragmatism.

But now let us proceed further in the investigation

of the positive side of this phase. We saw that in the past the higher classes as types were in reality bred according to behaviourist premises (though unconscious and unacknowledged). The general level of being can unquestionably only be raised by bringing the appropriate set of stimuli to bear upon a majority for a sufficient length of time and within the right sort of special surroundings. This is the very thing that modern education as understood in the United States and Russia and indeed in all essentially young countries aims at. And at this point we can understand better than seemed possible in the context of the first chapter, why John Dewey, of all men, should appeal, as an educational instructor, as much to China, Turkey, Russia, and Mexico as to America, while meaning nothing to Europe. There can be no doubt whatsoever that this new way of envisaging man purely as an animal is the way of preparing the road toward a higher level of existence—mankind at large on the new basis of the Geological Epoch of Man. Traditional education no longer calls out vital forces except in the case of exceptionally creative individuals. It cannot, because as a matter of fact there has been a solution of continuity; the natural basis has changed. Henceforth all the cultural and spiritual problems must be restated and reset in the right relationship to the new basis. Man can no longer understand himself when thinking of himself in terms of the pre-human period (I repeat that I always use this term in the geological sense). There can be no doubt that the higher spiritual values still are incarnated in traditional culture; there are no spiritual values directly at work in the new education; only social values are acknowledged as such, and it is only logical that it should be so, for from the animal's point of view there is no metaphysical reality. But mankind *has* returned to the animal stage for a while. It must first get settled in its quality of a leading fossil. And in the meanwhile it can really do no better than evolve with the utmost energy the animal nature on animal lines, by methods suited to animals. We know today that most bad habits in the widest behaviourist sense are due to pernicious external influences; we know also that most psycho-analytical complexes which develop in later life may be prevented from developing in youth by the right kind of education. We know, moreover, that a vast amount of the desires and actions man imagines to be the result of purely inward necessity, are in reality the results of a combination of social opportunity and necessity. Therefore, we should take every possible advantage of the opportunities offered to influence life from the outside and scientific method. It is only with the advent of the technical age that man has come to be the Lord of Creation, as he was called in Eden. To take every advantage of his *animal* proficiency is part of his new position. For man must learn individually even where primitive responses are in question; that which animals know, thanks to inherited instincts, he must acquire by conscious effort. And here, again, we see why it is that young countries like America and Russia must be the leaders in this line: those in which the traditional culture is still alive cannot see man in the light of the animal only; they know too much of his spiritual nature to do that; they cannot make up their minds to that one-sidedness which alone leads to success. Not that they are by any means done for—far from it; as we shall see later, their task is even more important henceforth than it was before.

But it remains true, nevertheless, that in the new adjustment of animal nature which has become necessary the young nations play the leading part.

SO FAR, so good. The wonderful progress and expansion of the United States not only in business and along the lines of material and technical development, but also in those of education and scientific research, are primarily due to the primitiveness of the American. He could shut his eyes to the other side of the problem, the one belonging to the spirit, because in the process of rejuvenation he could no longer visualize its reality. This circumstance enabled him to go ahead as an animal with a self-assurance no man of spiritual consciousness could afford. Of course, the American has spiritual needs; but these he satisfies, in accordance with his true state, by primitive forms of religion and philosophy. Christian Science, from the scientific point of view, is a form of Shamanist religion; Fundamentalism, one of the crudest expressions of Tabooism I know of; and the Reverend Billy Sunday plays upon the instrument of the fear-mechanism of the savage tribesman with the most consummate skill. I mention these forms of religion because I have an impression that the more normal churches really no longer play a part worth mentioning in spiritual life: they have become too much of a success for that and are developing too much along the general lines of big business. As to their members—most Americans undoubtedly belong to their churches in no other sense than they belong to their golf clubs, or their luncheon clubs or their Rotary clubs.

There is, then, progressiveness in the absolute sense in most of what America achieves in categories, the psychological background of which is behaviourism of some kind. But, as is always the case, here too complete success breeds danger. The more primitive a man, the more he is inclined to generalize; here lies the root of all superstitions. And if he can solve so many problems to his satisfaction by considering man in the light of a mere animal, he is naturally inclined to believe that all problems can be solved in the same way. This, then, is the vital root of that institutionalism and educationalism which are more characteristic of America in its present state than anything else. I say "the vital root," for there are others going back to the eighteenth century which are still alive but have grown senile. The soul of American institutionalism and educationalism, and today indeed the active soul of practically the whole nation, is the belief that everything can be changed and perfected from without; that environment means everything; that the autonomy of life and the free initiative of the creative spirit can be completely discarded. In many high-class magazines I found a splendid piece of good advertising, the idea of which was the following: Husband and wife drive home from dinner. "You were most wonderful," he said. "You were so witty, so brilliant, every idea was original." "But you too, my darling, may be original," she answered. "Just get that book for two dollars" (I forget the title): "it contains as many original ideas as you can want." . . . Belief varies as to whether such things as freedom and spirit and a metaphysical reality exist, but the practice amounts to the same in all representative cases. Here again America converges with Russia: every Bolshevik will agree that the type a man develops into is entirely dependent on surroundings. That is the reason why, next to America, Russia is the most educationalist of countries.

But in order to arrive at a really accurate definition of American institutionalism, it will be advisable to compare it not only with its Russian, but also with its German equivalent. This will be all the more enlightening as much of what may be called system in America has been taken over from Germany. The Germans, too, as opposed to the English, believe in institutions and organizations. Why is it, under these circumstances, that German and American institutionalisms appear so different in kind, whereas American and Russian institutionalisms seem to belong to the same order? We shall find the reason when considering that the Americans, as opposed to the Germans, do not believe in systems and abstractions. The *raison d'être* of the German spirit of system is that the Germans, a nation of thinking introverts, are not capable of handling any particular thing before they have succeeded in looking at it as the particular expression of a general or, better still, a universal situation or principle. To them, therefore, the abstract is the symbol of inward reality. The most extreme expression of this point of view was the doctrine of Hegel, according to which the Will of the State is the fulfilment of all the particular wills of its subjects. It follows that German institutionalism can never be understood on the premises of behaviourism of any kind, for German organizations and institutions are not supposed to be a milieu calling forth vital responses; they are supposed to be direct expressions of an inward principle. This they cannot really be; and that accounts for the lifelessness and lack of originality characterizing so many expressions of the German spirit of system. But on the other hand, the significance of the latter is never that "environment" should mean everything but the exact opposite; that the spirit within, conceived as an abstract spirit, is a force independent of and superior to all surroundings.

Now with the help of an amusing simile we shall find it easy to understand the specific quality of American institutionalism. The Abbé Mugnier, one of the rare Frenchmen I have known who still embody the finest spirit of the eighteenth century, was once asked by a *dévoté* whose life, I am afraid, had not been altogether blameless, whether he was sure that there existed such a thing as Hell. His answer was: "*Ma chère enfant, évidemment il y a un enfer puisque notre très-sainte Eglise l'enseigne, mais la miséricorde de Dieu étant infinie, je suis à peu près sûr qu'il n'y a personne dedans.*" When present-day Americans think of making their nation musical, they believe that they have done everything that is required when they have built a beautiful institute and endowed it with millions. That the existence of music depends entirely on the talent of a few personalities, that institutionalism entirely misses the point where spiritual values are concerned, rarely ever occurs to them. For this reason a large number of American educational and even scientific institutions resemble Mugnier's Hell. All the more so as very few American Mæcenases realize that to pay men of science and art less liberally than railway presidents, in a country where a high standard of living is a national ideal, inevitably makes for mediocrity in the scientific and artistic field. The same applies to capacity for statesmanship and government; this, too, is shockingly underpaid in the United States, which circumstance largely accounts for the lack of talented men in the political field. In Europe a talented statesman, scientist, or artist could and can be underpaid, because he always was—and still is—considered so immeasurably superior in quality to any man who is merely able to make money, that inferiority in material means really only compensates overwhelming advantages. There is no equivalent to this point of view in American public opinion. The latter simply does not believe in the intrinsic value of genius and talent. It does not really believe in it even in the domain of business, although exceptional talent is recognized and paid here as it is nowhere else. Exceptional salaries are paid simply because such salaries are proved to be profitable and remunerative to those who pay them; no employer knows or would admit that talent is of value in itself.

The soul of American institutionalism, then, is the belief that institutions as such are everything and the creative soul of man means nothing. Man always becomes what his environment makes of him. Under these circumstances it is, of course, perfectly logical to give everybody what is considered to be the best education and to expect that thereupon the general level will inevitably rise in every respect. But as far as my observations go, all thinking Americans realize that the general level has not risen. We have given the reason: American institutionalism looks upon man in the light of an animal. And this must needs make of him as much of an animal as he is capable of *becoming*.

WE ARE now prepared to consider from another angle the wonderful organization of American life. One of the worst fallacies of the idea of progress as applied to biology was the belief that the more an organism progresses along lines of what man instinctively calls progressive, the better is it adapted to the surrounding world. This is entirely wrong. Progress on spiritual lines has no exponent on the plane of material success. I shall explain this fully in the last chapter; for the present it is enough to remember that most spiritually great men have been signal failures from the point of view of sound business, either from lack of talent or because of a lack of interest in success. The law of the material universe is routine. From the first day of Creation to the last the atoms and the stars have revolved and will revolve in the same order round their respective centres of gravitation. The more, therefore, the life of an organism is a routine-work, adapted once and for all to the ever-recurrent side of the world's process, the more successful it is. In this sense, our bodily processes of which the foregoing is true, are unquestionably a greater success than are all the achievements of spirit, mind, and soul; for death as such belongs to the normal rhythm of nature; disease as such is the normal threshold of death, and within these boundaries the body has held its own wonderfully well against all odds, not only since science has assisted it, but even under the worst conditions. The reason is that its processes are essentially routine-work following a rhythm which once and for all conforms to the general rhythm of nature. Our body belongs to the animal world. We now understand why all animals are better adapted to the universe than man, who is again and again being led into trouble, judged by nature's standard, by the freaks of his free imagination. The higher man rises as man, the more privileges he requires in order to exist. And whoever requires these, instead of being able to exist under all conditions, is obviously less well adapted to nature than he of whom the latter is true. Here we find the biological reason of the fact that so far there has never been a culture which was not a culture of privileged classes. Now, whatever material advantages were the privilege of the few in previous ages, technical progress has made accessible, in principle, to each and all. But on the other hand this raising of the general standard of living means that a new *animal*, not a new or higher cultural stage, has been reached. This animal quality asserts itself everywhere; the higher standard of living does not serve, as with the privileged classes of the past, as a basis for a higher spiritual culture, the exponent of which is a higher degree of creative freedom; it expresses itself in a new kind of pure routine. The case is similar to that of the ants and bees and termites, which have possibly reached an even higher degree of civilization in the technical sense than we have. The termites, in particular, certainly have achieved more than we, because they have done almost as much as we should have, if we could live on after the sun had lost its present warmth, or if we could develop any desirable type of man together with the necessary technical outfit by qualified endocrine-treatment. The whole life of these insects follows a plan laid out once and for all. The key to the problem of the amazing success of Americanism is exactly the same. American civilization is the most uniform civilization which has ever existed; whatever surprises it may offer (apart from mere sensations which pass away in a few hours and serve only as harmless safety-valves for an organism which after all belongs to a species endowed with free imagination) lie along the line of further animal development and can, therefore, without difficulty be included in the existing routine-system.

We have already seen that this progress along the lines of animal development is an absolute advantage if it is considered only as a new natural *basis* of life; and later we shall see how it can be made to signify nothing more than that. But for the present the mistaken belief that this new animal development should mean a higher stage of culture leads to disastrous results. Man is essentially a creative spirit. Therefore, what he believes in expresses itself as a reality in one form or another. The *rationale* of this truth has been best understood and made use of by Christian Science. But its actual side is best shown, and with a clarity that leaves nothing to be desired, by the American advertising-technique. The publicity manager himself often believes that he is merely offering to his clients what they want: as a matter of fact, he is *creating* demands even where they pre-existed; if it were not so, there would be no need of expensive advertising. If the director of a motor-car factory can say to his sales manager (as he frequently does): "Next year you will sell two hundred thousand *more* motor cars, or I will fire you," and the two hundred thousand additional cars *are* sold the next year in consequence, this proves the tremendous creative power which is exerted by suggestion. But if this is so, then the belief that man *can* be directed and shaped entirely from without, must also exert creative power. The mass of men must become ever more passive, ever more open to suggestion; again, as those who give the suggestions do not believe that they create demands but simply meet them, they believe ever less in true initiative. Today the latter rarely achieves more in the United States than the invention of what may best meet existing demands. There is no question of developing man into something higher than he is. This then creates a purely static general condition, as far as man's spiritual side is concerned. And the result accordingly is the progressive animalization of American man. That this statement is true is finally proved by the fact that no civilization in the world thinks less highly of creative freedom.

How is it possible that these characteristics do not breed general discontent or even hatred among foreigners? They do sometimes, but in the majority of cases they rather awaken a desire to become American. . . . The reason is that the problem of animal life on the new plane of the geological epoch of man has been better solved in America than anywhere else in the world. This is proved when we consider that in this country it really seems possible, in principle, that everybody should be comfortable, which is impossible not only in fact but in principle anywhere else. Several Hindus and other Orientals called on me during my stay in the United States. They had been living there for years. I asked them why they had lingered, since they pretended to loathe American materialism. They replied that they did not know, it had just happened thus; they had come for a few lectures, and then they had stayed. Of course, the reason was the same which Mencken is alleged to have given when asked why he continued residing in America, which he criticizes so severely: "It is so damned comfortable!" It is indeed. *If* a man conforms to the rhythm of American life, he is taken care of by a whole civilization, very much in the same sense that every animal is taken care of by Mother Nature. The uniformity and routine-quality, together with the general progressive trend of the rhythm of American life, inevitably make for the satisfaction of every individual who conforms to them completely, just as every organism living in its natural surroundings and following its instincts is contented. This also explains the general optimism of Americans as far as it goes. But above all this explains why in America every progressive movement along the lines of success, when compared with its possible European equivalent, gives the impression of a geometrical, as opposed to an arithmetical, progression. The general requirements alone, not those individually desired, count. The demand for the former can easily be created by such as know the laws of mass-psychology. This, in its turn, creates a tremendous mass-suggestion from which even the most individualized man escapes with difficulty. Again, the ready acceptance of a suggestion given makes for dis-individualization. The final result is a uniform spirit the like of which never existed in any army, and not even among the Jesuits. Most Americans *want* to obey as no soldiers ever have done. This alone explains the manner of travelling of American caravans (what a wonderfully symbolic name), at which Europeans stand aghast. Individual eccentricity is practically eliminated. To each suggestion received American humanity responds like one single co-operative organization. But since it is not a case of coercion but of suggestion voluntarily accepted, which results in dis-individualization, there are practically no limits to intelligent suggestion. Here, then, the influence of a belief kept up day and night by suggestion sets in: the belief that everybody can advance materially and socially if he only wants to. It is in itself an entirely irrational belief. But it works wonders. It suffices to proclaim in the rigid way that some kind of "progress" makes for precisely this general advance, and each and all will help toward its success. Only think of the incredible success of Listerine—to my mind one of the worst and one of the most disagreeable disinfectants I have ever come across—I have been told that in its day it was boomed by an advertisement explaining that most boys and girls who did not marry were condemned to singleness because their breath was not as it should be and that the use of Listerine would inevitably improve it. Thus a circle is created which one would have to call "vicious" were it not for the fact that an overwhelming majority profits by it. It is really true that not only for mass sales but also for the unheard-of number of individuals profiting by these mass sales, America is a land of unlimited possibilities. And since the immense majority of men live by or on trade, the majority really do profit. It is quite true that sound business in America, *as it is*, means social service. Only, again, there can be no rise of level under such conditions. One more example completing that of Listerine. The motor-car business was wonderfully profitable for a while owing to the simple slogan that everybody must own a car. But eventually everybody had one. The sales decreased. The sales managers of all companies held council. All sorts of intelligent proposals were made inducing the public to go on buying. Suddenly a simple sort of a fellow got up and said, "Let us give nation-wide publicity to the sentence: 'Everybody must have *two* motor cars.' His advice was followed. And since then business has prospered. For there are many American citizens who do not yet own two motor cars. . . .

I WISH to repeat once more that I consider it an unequivocally good thing that animal man should be able to attain to such all-round satisfaction. And the fact of there being so exceptionally little ill-will, resentment, envy, jealousy, and pettiness in American life proves conclusively, in my opinion, that it is a good thing not only from the point of view of the body, but also of the soul. In this sense there is nothing to be said against uniformity and standardization. If all men are to live comfortably, then a large amount of uniformity and standardization of material life is inevitable—you can make millions equally comfortable only if their requirements are to a large extent alike—and the disadvantages of that necessity are doubtless smaller than its advantages. But the negative aspect begins to predominate when what is animal is not actually looked upon as animal and when the spiritual requirements, too, are taken care of by methods appropriate to animals only. This, then, shows the fundamental vice of American civilization: its *topsy-turviness.* Lafcadio Hearn and Basil Hall Chamberlain have described the Japanese solution of the problem of life as being topsy-turvy from the European point of view. Yet the Japanese topsy-turviness is nothing as compared with the American. The latter's topsy-turviness consists in this, *that it attacks almost every problem of life at the wrong end.*

If marriage is to be a success, one should obviously begin by marrying the right person. The Americans apparently do not think so; they try to cure bad marriage by better divorce. It seems desirable that a sense for the beauties of nature be developed: the Americans then create what they call beautiful surroundings, entirely ignoring the fact that there is no beauty except when man sees his idea of beauty into the things; nature seemed beautiful to an earlier civilization because nature's objects were thought of as incarnated gods.—The American nation is to become musical: the finest institutions in the world are being created—never mind whether there will be anybody to live in them. After my first lectures I was again and again perplexed by the experience of having people ask me, "Wasn't the audience wonderful?" In Europe it would be an insult to talk to a speaker who gave his best—whatever this best may have been—about the merits of his listeners. But soon I understood. The idea was simply this: *if* this man could attract a large audience and *if* this audience remained attentive for an hour, then he must be a good speaker. In the same way a best seller must be a good book; or—as an American Mæcenas recently put it—one can prove the value of great art in dollars and cents. From this there is only one step to the conception that a book which is not expensive or a best seller, or a man who doesn't make much money, can be no good, and that money provides the right standard on all planes and lines. This has nothing to do with dollar-madness; it is simply an illustration of that topsy-turviness which is the most salient characteristic of present-day Americanism. The American nation has been so consistently educated to believe that spirit can in no wise be the cause, but that it is an effect in the sense that it only responds to stimuli and can do nothing without them—that it involuntarily thinks and acts *as though* the effect were the cause, even where it knows better. Here lies the real root of that national belief which most Americans simply explain by the word "Democracy," *viz.*, that the judgment of the man in the street provides the absolutely right standard. This belief really means that there is no such thing as an autonomous spirit which has claims in its own right, and that there is no standard of value which might be considered valid independently of its standing the "pragmatic test" of material success. If the public does not like a thing or a man—why, then it or he is bad or wrong or useless. On the other hand, if the public likes it or him, then there "is money in it or him." This, again, adds to the prestige of the idea that money worth provides the real standard. Moreover, money always makes for comfort. And if money is made under the assumption that the taste of the man in the street counts first, the making of it by one or a few really is of profit to all. If we now remember that the American ideal is originally an animal ideal, we are ready to understand that the topsy-turviness in question must be exceedingly difficult to cure. It *does* stand the pragmatic test so well! And its disadvantages are detrimental only to the few, not to the many. And even to the few they are not materially detrimental; for with the help of good advertising the highest qualities can have a higher market value in the United States than anywhere in the world and to that extent the spirit finds more support there than anywhere else. This is quite true. But it is equally true that this topsy-turviness, just *because* it leads to good results along all sorts of lines, blinds the organ for spiritual reality and its intrinsic laws. A typical American cannot understand why a spiritually conscious man would rather be hated by all and sundry than conform to the prejudices of the masses. He cannot see why "being liked" by others—or even why working for the happiness of others cannot be for the former an aim worth aspiring to.

Yet, if the spirit is really powerful in a man, he can succeed in America in spite of the above objections because of the exceeding suggestibility of the American nation. But there are very few who have sufficient suggestive power. And worse still: human nature being weak, most creative spirits unfortunately give up their best for the sake of their family or whatever the pretext may be, when they are successful. In any case, with every successful year the *nation* develops more and more along the lines of spiritual blindness. The salesman's point of view prevails more and more. Many Americans told me, when I talked to them about that extraordinary book in which Christ is represented as the model of a good salesman, that it meant nothing and that the writer was just a fool. I do not think so. America at large really does think that way. What should be understood as effect is being taken to be the primary cause. The idea of the book in question is that Jesus Christ did not succeed in christianizing the world because He had a great and true message to deliver, which later on inevitably resulted in "good publicity"; but that from the outset He thought only of the latter. All my personal experience makes me believe that it is the real, because the involuntary, general American point of view. Were it otherwise—would newspapers and publishing houses think almost exclusively of what the public wants? Would they think that the pure business point of view is the legitimate one for a man who is demonstrably capable of commanding and directing public opinion? Were it otherwise, would the sales manager play a more important part in American business than the inventive spirit? The latter has to meet the requirement of the mass; that is the central idea. His position is a truly "ancillary" one, as was that of philosophy with respect to theology in the Middle Ages. From the point of view of the spirit as the creative essence of life, such a life-view is topsy-turvy in the absolute sense. Yet it would be the normal view if man were an animal. This, then, brings us back to the central argument of this chapter. America would not be topsy-turvy if man actually were an animal. But unconsciously he is viewed in that light. And the aforesaid topsy-turviness in its turn helps towards the materialization of this belief. It makes for the progressive animalization of the American.

My readers will now see clearly in which sense American institutionalism is also an expression of the animal ideal in general, and of the topsy-turviness of the workings of the American mind in particular. Were it not for that topsy-turviness, institutions would not be expected to achieve that which rests with creative spirit alone. On the other hand, the American really becomes a product of the existing institutions. He does so because he believes in their unlimited power. This is why Americans become more "like-minded" and "normal" with every succeeding year. And with that like-mindedness the tendency to conform to existing institutions in its turn inevitably increases. There is, of course, an external reason belonging to another order which accounts for this tendency to conform to what is essentially lifeless: there being no unity of blood, of traditions, and emotions in the United States, their inhabitants instinctively try to build up a unity on existing foundations. As Benjamin Franklin put it: "They have to hang together, or else they would hang separately." Another reason is the democratic prejudice—since all men are supposed to be equal (which every intelligent person knows they are not), all *should* become equal; the idea of "should" or duty invariably comes in wherever a man subconsciously knows that the truth he pretends to believe in is not really true. But the fundamental reason of American uniformity and standardization is the conforming to a standardized order of life on the accepted premise that externals account for everything. If the belief in them is strong enough, they do indeed. Here lies the chief reason of American suggestibility. The Americans would not be more suggestible than other people, and advertising would not be so immeasurably more successful there than anywhere else, were it not for the behaviourist belief that man's life is nothing but "habit" and that every habit is the outcome of given external influences. In this connexion, the life of the United States presents the image of one single gigantic vicious circle.

NOW let us proceed a step further. If "environment" is believed to account for everything; if, accordingly, it achieves as much as the laws of nature permit; if, on the other hand, standardization is a fact and uniformity an ideal, then man's life must become very much like that of ants and bees. It has often been said that ants and bees are the most "human" of animals. The reverse, too, is true: if civilized man reverts to an animal-type, then he does not become an ape or a dog, but an ant or a bee. For these insects are the most social and, at the same time, the most hard-working of animals; they are, moreover, the animals most bent on specialization and the most rigid in their routine. They do not in the least resemble primitive or savage or even cultured man—these have their animal counterpart in the lion or the fox or the racehorse, as the case may be. But they do resemble technicized man. It is the distinctive quality of the latter that routine-work plays the principal part in his life. Now the routine of the ant and, in particular, that of the termite is wonderfully adapted to the rhythm of the universe. The termite has so far held its own as no other creature has and it will probably continue thus to the end of our world. The same may happen to technicized man. Only if it does, it will be at the expense of all free initiative. It is a fact well worth meditating, that most Utopias written of late, which were based on American conditions, foresee a future state of utter serfdom; free will would practically count no more. This will indeed be the case if the Lifeless is to give the law to the whole of Life. This will be all the more so the more perfect the antlike co-operation grows. If human life becomes essentially a routine, the rhythm of which fits into that of the world at large, then a state of tremendous stability must follow. For such a life inevitably stands the pragmatic test. It cannot help being a complete success. It must become more successful with every step on the way to standardization. Everything will prosper—except man's spirit. The latter must decay. I say, it must, for this also is inevitable. Spirit lives only in the dimension of free initiative. And this must needs diminish in extent and power as American life develops along its present lines. The animal side must needs grow to ever greater bulk and power. "Facts" as such must more and more become the one thing that matters. Herewith, then, we have found the supreme expression of America's topsy-turviness. When I came to the United States my first inquiry was: which are America's most current superstitions? I always inquire into the superstitions first when I wish to understand a nation, because they are much more representative of the unconscious, which is a very non-rational thing, than anything reasonable. Then I found to my amazement that Americans believe in—facts; everywhere and in every possible connexion. I never have come across so quaint a superstition. In the domain of life, facts never are primary things; significance creates them on the one hand, and on the other, they derive all their value from the significance they embody. And significance is never inherent in the facts themselves. Every institution originated from an invention which was not a fact in the beginning. The power of a government is based upon the authority it has—and that, too, is not a fact; it depends on belief. And so does the value of the most objective value on earth—gold; if people did not believe in it its "facts" would mean nothing. Exactly in the same sense does the fact-side of "Democracy" depend on what it means to men. Whether physical love is a beautiful or an ugly process, depends on the meaning attached to it. And so on. The belief in facts is, from the point of view of man conceived as a spiritual being, really the quaintest and at the same time the grossest of superstitions. It can be explained only by the topsy-turviness of American thinking. But since in reality significance creates the facts, and not vice versa, the topsy-turvy belief actually does create a world in its image. And this again means that the animal side in man, as opposed to the human side proper, grows stronger; the significance of the facts, which really makes them human, grows ever less important. The final result is that man must become a higher animal pure and simple.

Are we not alarmingly near such a state? Love is already being considered as a purely biological function; health is the supreme ideal. The American is progressively losing sight of the fact that what distinguishes man from the beast is precisely his lack of equilibrium, for that alone enables him to keep on striving beyond himself.[1] Health is a purely animal ideal. It was one of the deepest truths taught by Christianity that ill-health is a more normal state for spiritual man than health. The latter means a stable equilibrium. But an equilibrium can be stable only if there is no change. If man progresses inwardly, a destruction of the equilibrium previously existing inevitably follows. The more spirit, which is movement eternal, predominates in man, the more unstable must his state of balance be. This is the reason why from the point of view of the man in the street every spiritual man has always been less "good" or "nice" than any fool. Besides spirit acts on earth only by means of tensions (as opposed to harmonious relationship). In this respect health is really an anti-spiritual ideal. The ideal of health, then, contributes in its turn to the animalization of the American. But the same is true of education, as it is generally understood. It is becoming more and more a form of training such as animals can be submitted to. The ideal of a high standard of living will eventually end—if the process should reach its natural goal—by becoming the general denominator of all ideals. Herewith man would retire from the adventure of human life proper and revert to

[1] Compare the full elaboration of this trend of thought in the cycle "Birth and Death" of *The Recovery of Truth.*

simple and safe and secure animality. For "standard of living" is the highest possible *animal* ideal; it is in no wise a human ideal. Viewed from this angle, the American habit of appraising everything in terms of the dollar seems very dangerous. For it simply means that the ultimate significance of all human ideals and values should be to make an animal feel comfortable. And this again would imply that the charming human qualities of the American, his directness, kindness, and simplicity, would have to be attributed not to higher human development but to a prehuman stage; there are no vicious or pretentious or malicious beasts. . . .

This is the great danger which threatens the United States. Russian philosophers of the immigration, true to the doctrine of Early Christianity which they all unconsciously profess, have raised their voices several times to warn mankind against the American ideal; their idea is that there are two kinds of Satanism. The one expresses itself in terror and cruelty, the other in comfort. And the latter is by far the more dangerous. No doubt, inertia is the law of matter as opposed to spirit. Wherever routine predominates, spirit dies. And very likely the routine of comfort is the most stable of all routines. The condition of America is no doubt more critical, from the point of view of spiritual progress, than that of Bolshevik Russia, because the terrible material condition of the latter country must needs keep the spirit awake. Russia can be reborn at any time. A tremendous effort will be required if the same is to happen in the United States. . . .

But now let me add at once: *if* spirit should conquer there, this victory would mean more for the general progress of mankind than any previous spiritual conquest.

For then spirit would for the first time find itself secure upon the basis of accepted material comfort, which it never was before. But no more of this. We shall deal with these grand possibilities at the conclusion of this book.

BEFORE I conclude I want to draw the attention of my readers to some other dangers. Man developed into the Lord of Creation is the most dangerous animal that ever lived. Not only for others, but also for his own welfare. He conquers and destroys everything he cannot use. To him nature is nothing but a raw material. Of this, again, present-day America provides the best illustration. In America there is no sense of beauty as a motive power of any national importance. But such a state of things is highly dangerous. Beauty is the result as well as the expression of right proportions. If there is ugliness, this always means that the right equilibrium has not been attained or else destroyed. Now, man, however powerful, still remains a *child* of Nature; if he acts as her master only, repudiating his childhood if he behaves as her tyrant, she will take sooner or later a terrible revenge. We Europeans have realized that mere intellect, if developed at the expense of life, becomes its enemy bound to destroy it, as a quality first, and eventually as a fact. The creative powers atrophy. But American technicism presents a still greater danger. If only business counts—I use the term in its most general sense—then none of the purely human powers, as opposed to the animal forces, have any chance to grow. And since the life-source of man lies in the spiritual, this must lead to physical devitalization. To my mind, this provides the explanation of many things which every intelligent observer of America must notice when taking the measure of American man. Notwithstanding the tremendous energy shown in special fields, he is very much less vital than the European. If he is not infantile, he more often than not looks disproportionately old. We said that one possible goal of American civilization is a termitoid state. The termites are the most ancient of all creatures. But when they live their termite-life, they still live out their whole nature. Man as a termite would not. He would leave unexpressed, more and more, all human powers. And since his real essence *is* human, he would probably die out. A life which is untrue to its own meaning never lasts. These facts largely account also for the neurotic state of an appalling percentage of American business men. And many of them have become truly ant-like. They can see no other point of view than their own. They can do one thing very well and rapidly, but beyond that they can do nothing. Very quick on their accustomed lines of action, just as insects are, they are incredibly slow on all others. Will the Americans become ants after all?—We said that this could not happen because they would probably die out before. But there is a more hopeful outlook and with this I will conclude this chapter. Very likely the animal ideal of a high standard of living will lead itself automatically *ad absurdum*, making room for a higher ideal before it is too late. The higher the general standard of life becomes, the more difficult will it be to find human beings for the lower tasks of life, which will always have to be fulfilled. Then, one of two things is bound to happen. Either foreign slaves will be introduced in large numbers, or else the nation will make up its mind that it is not possible to continue for ever in the assumption that material progress must indefinitely go on. And in both cases the only possible solution will be to restore spirit to its true place. One can rule slaves only if man as such means more than the "thing," if initiative means more than adaptation. And man, as an essentially striving being, can inwardly put up with stationary conditions, and not very satisfactory ones at that, only when he seeks and finds satisfaction for his striving nature in dimensions where there is no question of comfort and success, because the mere idea would be contrary to sense.

## Socialism

IT IS a pity that the term Socialism has been associated with the least social of all social systems. Children, too, rarely are given a name which really suits them. The idea underlying the so-called Christian name is that everybody should have—apart from his family name, his titles, and so on, which symbolize his relationship to others—a designation expressive of his uniqueness; within the framework of our civilization the Christian name corresponds to that name which in Hindu civilization God alone is supposed to know and which is given in secret to each child by the family priest; and I consider it simply a disgrace that newborn citizens of the world should be baptized, as often as not, "after" somebody else. But there certainly never was a designation less "made to measure," as Bergson would put it, than the name of Socialism as applied to what it stands for. The psychological nature of man is built up out of primarily individual and as primarily social elements. Viewed within the connexion of natural evolution, not the individual, but the social stands foremost. In every domain of life the whole is pre-existent to its parts.[1] The expression of this truth on the plane of physiological nature is the fact that the individual, however unique it be, is not only the offspring of its parents but also an integral part of a group. But it finds its expression

[1] See for the full development of this trend of thought the chapter "Life and Death" in *The Recovery of Truth.*

likewise on the plane of psychological reality. There are primarily impulses within each which are the outcome not of individual but of a primary social consciousness —the term employed in the widest sense, so as to embrace the whole range of the social, from the sexual up to the ethical. That such primary social impulses should exist cannot really be understood; it is not possible, for the very simple and obvious reason that the first and last premise of all thinking is the individual, thinking being a purely personal process. But the existence of primary social impulses can be experimentally proved. Not only indirectly, through the fact that a purely selfish life always leads to trouble (external trouble need not mean anything from the point of view of inward experience) but precisely through the latter, that is directly. Whoever renounces or suppresses activities the vital root of which would be a primary social impulse, falls ill or degenerates or lives in a state of everlasting unhappiness, a kind of Hell from which there is no way out. All ages have been aware of this; here lie the foundations of the universal idea of sin. But former ages explained the facts in terms of religious or metaphysical premises, the validity of which may well be questioned. Modern psychology has proved that it can be explained without reference to any "Beyond" of Nature. It is, in particular, the merit of the Viennese psycho-analyst, Alfred Adler, and his school to have shown that in the structure of human nature the social impulses are elements as real as the individual aspirations. Man *as an individual* is endowed with non- or super-personal emotions, feelings, and impulses; they are intrinsically his, notwithstanding the unique individuality of each, in exactly the same sense as every man is in the first instance an expression among others of the genus "man" with all its typical characteristics. That there is a psychological correspondence to this physiological fact, is most convincingly proved by the approved methods of training employed by all religions. In order to promote strictly individual progress, they all employ symbolic images which we know today to be expressions of the collective unconscious. They belong as such to the sphere of the genus, not of the individual, but the individual must use them, if he desires to grow, because the process of growth can be started and accomplished only by means of generic forces.

This also explains why a man who does not live out his super-personal or social impulses falls ill. It is as though his heart did not beat or his bowels digest, while the brain alone worked. This explains also why a man who lacks these impulses to an exaggerated extent must be considered as pathological; in the extreme case, he is the born and unreformable criminal; and then he usually looks it. The latter fact, again, provides the proof of the reality of non-individual qualities within the individual: there could be no somatic signs of criminality if the latter did not denote something wrong from nature's point of view.

Man, thus, is always both a social and an individual being. *Accordingly, the ideal would seem to be a harmonious blending of the social and the individual side.* Such a harmony is obviously possible on the basis of various proportions between both elements; there can be a question of pathology only when either the individual or the social side is under- or over-developed to the degree of rendering impossible all harmonization. It has often been stated that every saint is potentially a criminal. He is indeed, and for two reasons: first, the essential quality of spiritual reality is its uniqueness; in his spiritual essence, no man is comparable to any other, nor is there anything he has in common with others; accordingly, as spiritualization increases, it must also enhance uniqueness-consciousness, and this again must enhance the individual as opposed to the social impulses. The second reason is, that owing to the law of polarity which rules in all life, the natural foundations of extreme selflessness and extreme selfishness are closely related, if they do not actually coincide. In any case, every man of exceptional individual endowment is physiologically an egotist by both spirit's and nature's will, because the purely individual side of his being is developed to such a degree that he is *of necessity* in the first instance conscious exclusively of himself, and not of his inner relation to his fellow men. The most potent hypertrophy of either the individual or the social element in man need not, however, disrupt his natural equilibrium; a man may be the greatest individualist and at the same time he may be inwardly impelled to use all his powers of individual initiative for the benefit of all. In his case *this* particular kind of equilibrium would mean the state of balance true to both nature and spirit. In the same sense, the man whose social impulses are so strong that he practically feels no interest in his own perfection, preferring to sacrifice his whole life for the benefit of others, cannot be called a pathological phenomenon as long as his will to sacrifice does not encourage and further the selfish aims of others. This accounts for the sternness of Jesus and most Saints. Their love of others never was good-nature in the sense of weakness. They never were like the Russian aristocrats who could not bear the feeling of being privileged and, therefore, gave away everything, becoming part of the dark mass, instead of using their privileged position to help the latter to rise. It follows, then, that *any* kind of equilibrium between the individual and the social side in man may be considered as normal as long as a state of balance actually exists; whereas every case in which no such equilibrium exists must be termed pathological. But it follows, moreover, that each given state of balance renders possible a high development of certain activities, while precluding an equally high development of others. To this limitation the relationship between man's and woman's psychology provides the prototype. From the point of view of the psychology of elementary instincts and impulses, man may be called the individualistic and, accordingly, the egoistic or selfish component of mankind, and woman the altruistic, unselfish, and social-minded. All initiative, all invention, and all variation presuppose a predominance of the self-assertive element; on the other hand, all preservation and all continuity in the two dimensions of simultaneity and succession presuppose a predominance of the altruistic impulse. Both impulses are equally necessary for the continuance and the progress of life. Without self-assertion mankind could not hold its own on earth; nor could there be progress of any kind. On the other hand, without self-forgetfulness as a ruling force, the only normal relationship between human beings would be war. Altruism is as little superior (in the absolute sense) to egoism as woman is to man. To have misunderstood this constitutes one of the most fatal fallacies of Christianity. The Christian era, in compensation, laid all stress on the values of feminine existence because they had been too little emphasized in pagan Antiquity. But since the Christian nations standing foremost in history were in reality of a very virile character, this conscious stressing of feminine ideals only led to all the more accentuated unconscious and involuntary selfishness, and to the worst kind of cant besides. It is perhaps true that the Christian nations have on the whole been less cruel than many Asiatic peoples; but, then, that was the case even before they were baptized. As far as selfishness, in the sense of exploitation of the fellow man, is concerned, no race can compete with those whose conscious faith over-stresses the value of unselfish love; and this could not be otherwise, considering the intrinsically masculine character of the Western nations. Thus, I am sorry to say one finds the greatest kind and amount of selfishness in charity-work and wherever organized women are the leaders; here, the will unto power really knows no limits, for then the banner of "unselfish Love" serves as an excuse for whatever people actually do. The solution of the dilemma is that altruism and egoism stand for *correlative* natural attitudes. Neither incarnates a spiritual value in itself; both are capable of doing so. What is really necessary in all cases is the right relationship between the forces of both which by their nature compensate each other. But man and woman doubtless have different tasks on earth.

This, then, brings us back to the subject of Socialism and to our argument that the social system called Socialism really least deserves that designation. The many possible states of normal balance between the individual and the social elements in man's soul are limited on the one side by a state of absolute predominance of the individual element and, on the other, by a state of just as absolute a predominance of the social element. This means, that in the first of these extreme states actual life (which is always individual life) is focussed wholly on the individual impulses, and in the other, as focussed wholly on the social impulses. This last point is important: in the latter case it is not a question of suppression of the individual, but of predominant social impulses *within* the individual, so that life is as much an expression of liberty in the latter case as in the former. Now the word Socialism should reasonably be applied only to a life-attitude which gives expression, both in theory and in practice, to a state of predominating social *impulses;* and this again means that a socialistic system should be as essentially based on liberty as is the most extreme of individualistic systems. A socialistic system founded on the social side of man which yet is compulsory in its essence represents a contradiction in terms. As a matter of fact, however, all socialistic theories and practices bearing that name are based on compulsion. The most obvious explanation would seem to be that they consider economic *i.e.* external forces as decisive; on the plane of these forces there is indeed no freedom; if man conforms to them, he must inevitably partake of their mode of existence; this is why workers in a too well organized factory inevitably become, psychologically also, something like cogs in a machine. But the fundamental reason is to be found in another direction. All so-called socialistic theories have been invented by members of individualistic nations, in order to make socialists of these. This explains why that which officially bears the name of "Socialism" could become a power only in those two races whose psychological structure renders a social life based on original and free social impulses most difficult: the Germans and the Russians. The German, as I have shown in *Europe,* is as a type without any direct contact with his fellow men; he represents an extreme case of the objective introvert type, as Beatrice Hinkle calls him;[1] if Leibniz called man a "monad without windows," this was not true of man in general, but it is true of the German. For this reason the latter cannot build up a social life based on free social impulses; even where these are predominant they cannot come into free play. Thus, if such a type of man comes to the conclusion that life of the community should be based on a greater degree of equality and equity than it possessed hitherto, he can think only of compulsory means to bring about such a change. We here find the reason why German Socialism and Prussian militarism seem to be animated by exactly the same spirit: there is but one way of organizing masses on a compulsory basis. . . . And the same explains why Bolshevism and Czarism seem to differ so little in their methods of government. The Russian as a type is not like the German, a "monad without windows"; but he incarnates a tremendous tension between polar opposites in his soul, ranging from the opposites of extreme passivity and ruthless energy to those of bestiality and superhuman spirituality. This tension inevitably expresses itself in the psychological structure of the nation too; the nation can never really be unified in accordance with the ideals of equality and democracy, because it is primarily composed of complementary types. The relationship of those among them who are capable of playing a part in political and social life—which is obviously not true of the religious type—to the majority is much the same

[1] One should read her truly excellent survey of the European nations from the point of view of the psychological type to which they belong, in her book *The Re-creating of the Individual* (New York, Harcourt, Brace & Co.).

as that between a small but sharp knife and a large piece of butter. Accordingly, some kind of minority will always rule in Russia; and every ruler-type among the Russians being of the knife-type, the rule must needs appear despotic, whether the ruler be a Czar or a workman. And here again, the only attitude towards butter being that of the knife, a dissimilarity in world-philosophy cannot lead to essentially different facts. The only method of establishing a kind of equilibrium in which the will of the people at large can have a voice is that corresponding to the idea of the soviet-system. In this the people choose an aristocracy, as it were, and are supposed to have the power to do away with it when it proves inefficient—the idea being not unlike that of the Chinese, that a dynasty has *juridically* forfeited its rights if it cannot live up to its task. But once it is elected, the aristocracy commands all the power. And good care is being taken that only the ruler-type should be elected. This being the case, I am convinced that the soviet-system will remain in Russia (unless she again becomes monarchical). Terrorism, of course, will cease, and Communism may be abolished as a state-religion, but the soviet-system is the right system for the Russians in exactly the same sense as parliamentarism is for the English.

Now, both Germany and Russia desire to be social in the very sense which in the case of the originally social-minded is the result of co-ordinated and co-operating free wills. This fact provides the final elucidation and justification of the paradox stated at the beginning of this chapter, *viz.*, that the term "Socialism" has been associated with the least social of all social systems. The socialistic system does not in any way take into account the reality of original social impulses; on the contrary, it seems to presuppose the non-existence of such impulses; it tries to impose its ideal by force, from the outside. If it believes, as even Bolshevism does, that the necessity of compulsion will cease some day, this is only due to the behaviourist belief that the new economic order will create a new type of man, essentially free from the curse of individuality. The actual result, however, is the following: the harmony between the individual and the social instincts, wherever this state has existed, is upset or else it is prevented from being born; the individual is thwarted at every turn. But not to the benefit of the reality of the group-soul which really lives in each, but to the benefit of a lifeless principle of organization. For this reason the German socialists appear as the least vital of all Germans; they are also the most resentful, the most jealous, the most envious; repressed impulses always find an ugly outlet. And as is only natural when the law and harmony of dead matter provide the standard, their one ideal is security as opposed to risk, the love of which is the first sign of inward freedom. The ideal of the German socialists would be a clockwork state in which everybody would hold his appointed office that required no independent thought and where there was no possibility of being discharged because of inability. But the ideal of socialistic Russia is avowedly "collective man," understood as a mechanical apparatus. Here the abstract concept of class takes the place of a living community; there is to be no individuality; the strivings and cravings of the unique soul are completely set aside. This is the essence of the Bolshevist hatred of sentiment of any kind—at school it is being systematically eradicated in the children. Even the leader of men is interpreted in terms of non-individuality. Pokrowsky, the official historian of Soviet Russia, when trying to describe to the proletarian masses the significance of Lenin for the revolutionary movement of mankind, wrote: "We Marxists do not see in the personality the creator of history, because for us the personality is only the apparatus through which history works. The time may yet come when we shall be able to produce this apparatus artificially, just as we build up our electrical accumulators today. As yet, however, we have not advanced so far, and for the time being these instruments through which history works, these accumulators of social processes, must be born and bred in a primitive way."

This, then, leads us to the understanding of the conditions which determine the mere possibility of a "socialistic" state in the true sense of the word: *the social instincts and impulses must actually, that is organically, predominate;* which implies that a socialistic life, if it is to deserve its name, must be as much an expression of liberty as opposed to compulsion as a life based purely on individual impulses. It must be admitted that in its beginnings Socialism was implicitly meant to represent just such a life. Originally, Socialism was the legitimate child of Liberalism. It sprang from the latter as a corollary or further qualification owing to the recognition that within the narrow channels of European life the motto *laissez-faire, laissez-passer* did not give everybody a fair chance. And at first it stressed quantity chiefly because it realized that in order that equity and justice should rule in countries of a definite cultural tradition embracing a hierarchy of values and its bearers, man as such, independently of all considerations of value, should be granted certain inalienable rights.[1] This had already been the idea of Rousseau; it was the idea underlying the activities of both the American and the French revolutions. Accordingly, in the socially gifted old countries of the West Socialism became only a qualified expression of Liberalism. In France it is not only Aristide Briand who can call himself *radical-socialiste*; even Poincaré might do so without giving up anything essential. The case is similar in England. The party as a body politic with its non-liberal program made in Germany or Russia cannot mean more than an opposing minority in those countries, doing wholesome work as such. The reason is that both France and England are fundamentally individualistic. It would be impossible to build up the whole of French or English life exclusively on the basis of the social impulses. But there is one white man's land where this could be, and has been, done. *That land is the territory of the United States.* The Americans are the only socialists I know of in the true sense of the term in the Western World.

AMERICAN Socialism is partly the effect of three causes one of which we have already examined and the others will be examined in later chapters: its youthfulness, the predominance of woman's spirit, and of a moralistic outlook. Woman, being the altruistic fraction of mankind, is primarily social by nature. Then, group-consciousness always precedes in time individual consciousness. Finally, the basic moralism of the American type of man must further the growth of the social

[1] The latter point has been explained very clearly in what I consider the best statement of the idea underlying Socialism, the pamphlet *Der Sinn des Sozialismus* by the Baroness Leonie Ungern-Sternberg (Otto Reichl Verlag).

tendencies, for morality is primarily concerned not with man as a unique entity, but as an "I-and-You"-relationship. There are even more of what one may call accidental reasons for American Socialism. The spirit of the revolutions of the eighteenth century, the essence of which was revolt against all hierarchy of values, still rules. It is the soul of the entire political constitution of the United States. Owing to the peculiar opportunities offered by a New World overwhelmingly rich in natural resources and the absence of counteracting traditions, it was able to expand and develop in intensity as it could have done nowhere else. Moreover, the American soul is still at bottom a pioneer-soul. And this means that the forces necessary for the primitive struggle for existence predominate—a circumstance which always makes for Socialism as understood in the context of this chapter; in fact, every army is and always was an intrinsically socialistic system. Last but not least, the majority of immigrants were poor peasants and workmen, and among the lower classes the social impulses naturally predominate; they have to, since the external frame of life which shaped this type granted little scope for individual development and differentiation. On the other hand, kindness and good-fellowship are essentials in primitive life; what hospitality means in the wilds finds among the modern masses its equivalent in a social outlook. There may even be more accidental causes for American Socialism. But its basic and essential root is the fact that in the American nation the social tendencies actually predominate over the individual tendencies. This is the reason why America is completely immune to Socialism in the European sense of the term: it has no *raison d'être* there. During my stay in the United States I had the opportunity of making a study of several "radicals" in the

European acceptation of the term: I found them (as far as they were honest and not merely playing the martyrs in order to make more money) completely unreal, for there is no national reality they stand for or represent; they oscillate between the types of Thersites and the court-jester, the irresponsible critic who may say anything because he lacks any influence whatsoever and who is even encouraged to offer the most offensive criticism in order to create within the soul of those in power an excessive and, therefore, irksome sense of security. The United States must obviously be immune to Socialism in the European sense *because of the fact, unheard of in Europe, that the very problem which the reformers undertake to solve appears solved from the outset.* From the outset there is no trespassing of the individual on the domain where the social impulse should rule. The most impressive and at the same time the most astounding experience a post-war European has when visiting America—I insist again and again on this point—is the (nationally speaking) total absence of jealousy, envy, ill-will, resentment, and revolt. There can be no question of explaining this by outward circumstances. "Unlimited possibilities" for individual advance may still exist in theory; they certainly do not in practice, if only because of the emphasis laid on quality in work, which precludes from the outset, the ascent of the incapable individual beyond a certain point, and the utter lack of sentimentality which characterizes American business-life. American life is based on competition. Accordingly, it is a perpetual sequence of victory and defeat; in principle, it offers a great deal more risk than security. Now European Socialism fights nothing more vehemently than a social structure based on competition; it does not admit that greater ability deserves better pay. If, therefore, external reasons counted at all, there ought to be an even greater percentage of socialists in America than in Europe. Moreover, the differences in position, wealth, in social standing and influence are very great; if envy and resentment were to awake, there would be food enough for them. Lastly, the social and governmental system is far from perfect: there are probably more "pirates" of society in America than in any European country; it cannot fairly be denied that the phenomenon of "graft" is universal. In spite of this, there is no general discontent in America, as there would be anywhere else under similar circumstances. And this, too, cannot be accounted for by the general high standard of living—man's consciousness is primarily one of differences, so that what everybody shares in does not normally evoke positive emotions; it is not felt as an asset. Under similar circumstances, the German or Russian, or even the French majorities, would undoubtedly seek out those who owned more and do their utmost to make their life miserable. Therefore, the lack of jealousy and envy in America must be altogether due to inward reasons.

Before I proceed further, I must ask my readers to recall what I have said in *Europe,* chiefly in the chapter on Hungary, concerning the lack of envy of the *grand seigneur:* only then will they realize clearly the unique attitude prevalent in the United States. In the above-mentioned book it was shown that the *grand seigneur* is constitutionally incapable of envy, jealousy, etc., because his consciousness is focussed on his uniqueness. The essentially unique cannot be compared with anything else in the world, hence there is no foundation for envy. Within the context of this chapter I can develop this idea in another direction. The *grand seigneur* is beyond envy because the individual side so completely predominates in his being that shortcomings on the part of the not-individual fail to mean much to him. To make the point thoroughly clear by over-stressing it: suppose there be a Heaven, as mediæval Christianity believed it to exist, and suppose it to be as overcrowded at the end of time as the Christians of those days anticipated: there could yet be no jealousy among the Blessed, whatever their respective places near God might be, because after death the unique side of each alone survives; any points of possible comparison would be lacking.—A similar world lacking all negative emotions can be produced by the opposite psychological causes: when the social side predominates as absolutely as the individual side does in the psychological structure of the *grand seigneur. This is precisely the case of the United States.*

What appears exemplary in the atmosphere of good-will in America is, indeed, almost independent of the perfection of its institutions. It is almost exclusively due to the psychological circumstance which I have condensed in the above sentence. Considering what human nature is, there can be a general rule of good-will, a general lack of envy, resentment, jealousy, and hatred under two circumstances only: one, that the consciousness of uniqueness, the highest expression of individual consciousness, should predominate; or else that the consciousness of social reality predominates as absolutely. In the latter case, what psycho-analysis calls "a process of identification of the individual with the group" takes place, and this creates, in its turn, the predominance of the feelings of solidarity with the fellow man as opposed to those engendered by the struggle for existence. However, if what has been stated until now were really the last word, the state of the American nation would be identical with that of an anthill or a beehive, as was more or less the case in the land of the Incas. But what we have said does not represent the final word. For on the other hand, the American mode of life does give scope to individual initiative, provided this asserts itself within the frame and to the acknowledged benefit of the community. This fact, then, proves that the case of America is essentially unique: it represents a *novum* in the history of mankind.

In order to realize this fully, we must turn to particulars. Current expressions or words are always deeply significant—I say "deeply" because they reveal better than anything else the depths of the soul. Some of the words one hears most frequently in America are "citizen," "the community," "the group." Speaking of a prominent man, the average American will involuntarily say, not that he is a great man, but that he is a great citizen. He will constantly talk of the part played by him in the community. And if he be a teacher, well acquainted with cultural tradition, he is almost certain to say at some stage of the conversation that progress has now led to the realization of the truth that man finds his fulfilment or accomplishment not in his perfection as an individual, but as a member of a group. In this connexion the most significant books of theory I know (no matter what their intrinsic value may be or what they consciously represent in American eyes) are those by Miss Follett, of Boston; I mean *Creative Experience* and *The New State*. She sees the goal of human perfection (to put what interests us in this connexion into a single condensed sentence) not in the full expression of individual uniqueness, but in the participation in the lives of as many groups as possible; to her, accordingly, individual uniqueness means only something like a mathematical point: the point of intersection of the many various social correlations. If we envisage these facts in the light of abstract theory, we are struck by the similarity of the American point of view with that of Roman and Greek antiquity. For the Greeks and Romans, too, man was primarily a citizen; in their eyes, too, there was no individual life apart from the functions within the group. We shall see in the next chapter that this parallel is not ultimately true because of the entire lack of political sense and interest in the American, a sense which was the primary factor within antique man. On the other hand, the essential likeness with the Bolshevik state is complete: to the Bolshevik, too, man is nothing but the member of a group; as such only can he attain perfection; there are no purely individual values; there is no uniqueness, nor should there be.

But I should think that at this point precisely we perceive with perfect clarity to what extent the American only, and not the Russian system, rightly deserves the name of a socialistic system. In Russia there is a conscious attempt to crush the individual in order to socialize him. There is nothing of the kind in the United States. The true importance of this fact will best be revealed when we envisage an analogous case: the moral quality of traditional Chinese life. Among the Mediterranean nations and their spiritual children, the Europeans, who never were moral at heart, the moral order was always supposed to belong to a plane not of this world, to be applied here as commandments (thou shalt). To Confucius morality never meant anything else but human nature educated, cultivated, and perfected in the spirit of its own laws. In the same sense, what is essentially compulsory in Russian Socialism is essentially free-willed in the American. This is the reason why in America it seems senseless to discourage private initiative and private profit-making: the American being at bottom a socialist —which means that in his psychological structure the social tendencies actually predominate—his private profit-making is, in principle, never turned against the interests of the community. This, then, explains that apparent disinterestedness of American rich men at which Europeans usually stare with incredulity and suspicion; the same explains why in the United States private initiative has already realized in many cases the most remote ideals of European Socialism: the workmen's banks, which have made of capital a truly social institution, were first established by the business-magnates, and they still further them. American millionaires pride themselves on making gifts to the community; at their death they usually leave a lion's share of their fortune to it. Private munificence has made a great many educational institutions rich enough to be independent of all income derived from the pupils. On the other hand, American Mæcenases always endow institutions or collective associations; they rarely confer such gifts on individual men. This is not at all due (in the generality of cases, whatever may be true of individual ones) to what most Europeans believe it to be attributable, *viz.*, that the American millionaires think it *safe* to sacrifice a part of their wealth in order to go on enjoying it. It is simply due to primary and predominating social, as opposed to individual, tendencies. The truth of this is perhaps best exemplified by the Constitution of the Rotary International. The latter's objects according to statement are, as every American knows, to encourage and foster (1) the ideal of service as the basis of all worthy enterprise; (2) high ethical standards in business and professions; (3) the application of the ideal of service by every Rotarian to his personal, business, and community life; (4) the development of acquaintance as an opportunity for service; (5) the recognition of the worthiness of all useful occupations and the dignifying by each Rotarian of his occupation as an opportunity to serve society; (6) the advancement of understanding, good-will, and international peace through a world-fellowship of business and professional men united in the ideal of service. To a European many of these objects sound as though they were dictated more by the spirit of sound business than by what is called the "common end" in the Old World. Yet there can be no doubt that the proclaimed belief in the ideal of service is genuine; so is the belief in Society as an entity superior to the individual. And both the ideals and the beliefs in question can be genuine only as the expressions of a socialistic as opposed to an individualistic spirit.

IT IS of the utmost importance that this point should be thoroughly grasped. For this reason I will enter even more deeply into the factual side of the case, although I am writing for Americans who obviously know much more about it than I do. First of all let us consider a little more closely to what an extraordinary extent the American system leads to the realization of the very goals of European Socialism and even produces the same general phenomena. The latter teaches that only he who works has a right to live; usefulness for the community provides the only basis of individual rights. This is the very belief of all typical Americans. However rich one may be, one *must* continue working. The usual phrasing of this commandment is this: one must continue to make money. But in America money is the symbol for all accomplished tasks; the American always thinks in terms of effects; as we shall see in the next chapter, he really cares less for money as such than any European. Again, the equitable remuneration of all work is one of the fundamental claims of Socialism. The idea underlying the whole scheme of American life in reality is that a life which is not useful to the community is an abomination. Here the specialized belief comes in, that, above all, producing goods means social service. In order to understand it aright, the stress should be laid on the ideal of service as such, not on the means by which service is performed today; these means may undergo a change at any moment, without anything essential being altered in the state of things. Here, we must enlarge upon what was said at the end of the last paragraph. The idea of social service is indeed the fundamental principle in America; it is only "accidental"—to use the terminology of mediæval philosophers—that it should express itself foremost in the production of material goods. It does not mean more than that any American may say to a fellow he approves of: "You are the goods," where a European would say: "You are a gentleman." Now, "social service" as the highest ideal is the very idea which implicitly underlies all forms of Socialism. And is not orthodox Socialism, too, materialistic in its creed?—But the similarity of the effects of the socialistic point of view on the one hand, and the American on the other, goes even further. One of the most vital aims of socialism is to do away completely with exploitation by capital. From the point of view of abstract and theoretical possibilities capital can nowhere indulge more freely in exploitation than in the United States; and indeed, American capital lustily acts that way abroad. But within the confines of the home-country the theoretical possibility is powerfully counteracted by the motive power of organic socialism—of a general state of soul fundamentally socialistic. Everybody naturally tries to make as much money as possible, and there also certainly are very many who try to "put over" on others as much as they can. But here the following considerations must be taken into account. Man being no machine, there can never be a question of everybody doing what the whole demands; nor is this indispensable for the specific quality of the latter. On the contrary, its intrinsic strength may be gauged by the amount of exceptions that can be said to prove the rule. In no aristocratic community was there ever a prevailing uniqueness-feeling in the sense of Rousseau's *volonté de tous*, but it has always existed in the sense of Rousseau's *volonté générale*, which is the one thing that matters if a group-soul exists in any way. For then that group-soul predetermines from within all individual actions by means of a code of honour, of morals, or ideals believed in. Accordingly, everything that Europeans believe of America, judging from Upton Sinclair's disclosures or personal opinions, is essentially wrong, *even though all the facts should be true,* because their meaning is not what Sinclair believes (or pretends to believe) it to be. There are, of course, many American capitalists of the pure robber-type; there also are socialists of the most radical Russian pattern. But they mean exactly as much, and no more, than criminals mean in essentially law-abiding countries like Germany and England. The point is not that they exist, but how small their number is in proportion to the whole and how little they signify within the latter. The "piratism" of individual Americans actually has no national significance whatsoever. One may even say that—owing to the frontier-tradition—it is joyously accepted as part of the game, of the adventure of life, and the game as such is always primarily considered as a collective game. Now, as development progresses, what is primarily true expresses itself to an ever-increasing degree in the facts. One may still "fire" every inefficient workman at a moment's notice. But today it is considered as immoral not to pay an efficient workman as well as possible, not to make him rise as fast as possible on the scales of salary and partnership, and not to think of the interests of the consumer or the public in general to any degree within reason. It is, of course, very intelligent to do so; it has proved to be much more profitable than any other method. Those "men of vision" who imperceptibly created an "orange-consciousness" or a "radio-consciousness," not to mention the "automobile-consciousness," were seldom individuals with whom the ideal of social service stood foremost. But if the American way of doing business were only, or primarily, a result of intelligence, the business-intelligence of Europe, surely not inferior to that of America, would long ago have used the same devices. Moreover, were it due to this only, the European capitalists would have prevented the very rise of the socialistic tide, as they are actually doing in America. As a matter of fact, man's life is always directed by primary impulses; man succeeds only in what he involuntarily does; he only is a successful business man who involuntarily experiences life in terms of business correlations, just as he only is a successful philosopher who involuntarily views life in terms of intellectual or metaphysical problems. Mere voluntary concentration never carries far. Socialism as a system of compulsion could become a power in Europe only because within the souls of the European capitalists the primary social impulses play a very inconspicuous part. As against this, the American business men are socialists at heart even when in practice they act like robbers. An amusing story which I was told by a prominent gentleman of the South, which may or may not be true (personally, I think it is), will perhaps bring us soonest to a full understanding of the case. "There is," he said, "no more satisfactory co-operation in the world than that between the police force and the bootleggers in our state. Whenever one of the latter gets pinched he can find a warm place in the Force; and whenever a member of the Force gets into trouble, he can pass over to the bootleggers, so that the wives and kiddies need never starve."—But to proceed: *why* did no European ever hit upon the idea that not the public should pay for the radio in the home, but those who advertise by means of it? *Why* has no European firm that I know of made a special point of winning its clients to become its shareholders? *Why* do all sorts of groups, which in Europe can hardly even agree to differ, co-operate in America as a matter of course, so that even frank enemies often co-operate along special lines? *Why* does the principle of co-operation work so very much better in America than it does in Europe? *Why* does it seem natural to even the greatest American business man—there are exceptions, but there are not many of them—to run the business not as an autocrat, but in agreement with co-directors? *Why* is there so much less untruth in American advertising than there is in European? *Why* is it really essentially built up on the principle of social service? It is not because it is primarily profitable—or else intelligent Europeans would have done the same long ago. It is because the social tendencies are *really* predominant in the American soul. There is no more instructive reading on that line than Claude C. Hopkins' book, *My Life in Advertising* (Harper & Brothers). This book rings true throughout. The writer really is essentially an altruist.

But let us proceed. *Why* does the idea that the workmen should profit not as little but as much as possible from the works, that they should be paid the highest possible wages, and on the first possible occasion be made shareholders, strike the American as essentially sound and the European as Utopian? Again, not for rational considerations, but by reason of the original psychological structure. Were it otherwise, Germany, and not America, would be the country of the greatest social contentment, because nowhere else do so many people think and express in writing what "should" be. But very unfortunately, mere ratiocination means nothing. In democratic Germany the citizen is ordered about to an even greater extent than he ever was in the days of the Empire, and in consequence there is still less of that general atmosphere of mutual good-will so characteristic of America, even where "graft" and "putting over" flourish most. Henry Ford, the best-known of high-wage-payers, is in reality the least social-minded of American business-kings of his type. It is true that he pays high wages; that he tries to raise the standard of living of those he employs, and that he has built up his whole business on the idea that the wants of the public should be taken care of at the lowest possible price. But I have the distinct impression that in his case it is much more a question of *intérêt bien entendu* than in the case of any other American who operates on the same principles—and there are thousands of them. The true character of a vital reality is always proved by its vital effects. There is no doubt that, in spite of all theory, to pretend that a man paid as the workmen in the Ford plants are paid and who works only comparatively short hours *should* be able to develop into a cultural being in his leisure hours, *is not true.* Whoever plays for eight hours a day the part of a cog in a machine to the extent which is there required, actually becomes a cog. Ford's ideal lies in the direction of man transforming himself into a termite—one of the great dangers of Americanism. And this, again, proves to him who knows anything of the human soul that Ford does not wish man to be free. He is an autocrat at heart, whose ideal it would be to rule—for their best, of course—millions of completely mechanized man-ants. What is good in Fordism is expressed in a very much better way in the principles followed by other, less conspicuous industrial magnates. However bent on personal profit—their last personal resort is never the individual, but the community. This is the reason why they give so lavishly to the latter, as soon as they can afford to do so. The same explains why, generally speaking, the poor in America do not feel envious of the rich. This is partly due, of course, to the irrational belief of the man in the street that he, too, can grow rich if he really wants to. The essential reason, however, is that he sees that the rich man feels at one with him at bottom, which is due to the predominating social tendencies. Human beings very rarely mind unpleasant individual facts, if only they feel satisfied as to the ruling principle.

But there are even more similarities, in the effect, between the original American attitude and the socialist ideal than those we have pointed out so far. Socialism demands a unified standard of living for each and all. This actually exists in the United States. However great the differences in income and fortune—all Americans live very much in the same way. It is so difficult to live in a style qualitatively differing from that of the majority, that those among the wealthy who still have individual idiosyncrasies spend some months a year in Europe, in order to be able to do so. The difference between the facts of Bolshevik Russia and America, in this connexion, only amounts to a difference in prosperity; the standard is different, but the standardization is identical. The same applies to the solution of the housing problem in America and Russia: if the richest in New York have to live in narrow apartments, while fifteen years ago they still inhabited palaces, this means even more of a revolution—considering the material means at the disposal of the respective nations—than the Russian law that no family should own more than one room.

It is one of the most instructive things I have ever come across, this extraordinary likeness between Bolshevik Russia and America. The difference actually amounts to a mere difference in language: the spirit is the same, whatever the causes which in each case brought it into empiric existence. Both countries are basically socialistic. But America expresses its socialism in the form of general prosperity, and Russia in the form of general poverty.

America is socialistic by means of the free co-operation of all, and Russia by means of class-rule. Can there still be a doubt that we have entered upon a socialistic era? There can be none indeed, since the socialistic tendencies are reinforced by the concomitants of rejuvenation and the rule of the animal ideal as well as by the rise of the masses all over the world.

AMERICA really is constitutionally a socialistic country. This is why it is able to consider itself a free and individualistic country in spite of all the standardization which makes it impossible to lead a free life as the European individualist understands it. I have dwelt upon this problem at considerable length because it seems to me that it is far from being generally understood and that here, if anywhere, right understanding may prevent serious trouble. There can be no doubt, for instance, that the two principal foci of historic life for the next centuries will be America on the one hand and Russia on the other—the latter standing, as I have shown in *The World in the Making*, for the whole awakening East. Now, if America continues to believe that it incarnates a principle entirely opposed and inimical to that of Russia, considering America's missionary temperament, portentous struggles will inevitably follow. But if America realizes that it is animated by the same essential spirit of a New Age as the European and Asiatic East, and that it only presents a different and perhaps a better incarnation of that spirit, then the inevitable struggle can take the form of a peaceful and completely productive contest or discussion—the word employed in the sense of the Introduction to this book.

But now the moment has come to tackle the problem of the prospects of American Socialism: its prospects of both good and evil.

Here we have to take up again and to follow to its logical end the line of thought which led us to the statement that *the American system represents something unique and entirely novel in history.* Socialistic though it be—*it yet gives full scope to individual initiative.* It does so to such an extent that the Americans believe themselves to be pure individualists and that even only a few foreigners seem to have noticed their intrinsic Socialism. This proves that in the case of America there really comes historically into existence an entirely novel state of balance between individual and social impulses. It proves, moreover, that there exists the possibility at least of an entirely new civilization blossoming forth on the territory of the United States, and that this civilization may become as exemplary in its kind, as was ever any previous great civilization.

This new kind of civilization would mean the polar opposite of a civilization based on the ideal of the *grand seigneur*—polar to the extent that the opposites actually meet. It would be a civilization in which all would feel equally free, in which, for the opposite reasons of those that make the soul of the *grand seigneur* impermeable to envy, the ruling spirit would be one of generosity; in which the state of all would be, in effect, equivalent to the state of the privileged in the Old World. This, then, constitutes its entire novelty. The social life of the ants and bees is a perfect life, and, for aught we know, a happy life at that; but it can be so only because there are no individualized ants and bees. In the same sense, the social life of the Incas and no doubt that of the

Egyptians as well, was a perfect and a happy life; when criticizing the rule of the Pharaohs, one should not forget that the Egyptian peasant toils even today under a very different rule, as heavily as he ever did beneath the menace of the supervisor's whip and that he was and is an essentially merry and contented man in spite of this. To put it in a few words: perfect socialistic systems have existed in past history, only they were based on the premise that the demands on life of the majority of men were those of poor peasants or tenants; accordingly, within these systems no generosity could develop, no broad and inwardly free type of man. It is exactly such a type of man which is growing up and taking shape to an ever-increasing degree on the North American continent. There is nothing like him to be found in Europe, nor can there be, because of the European's basic individualism. But the American type is undoubtedly akin to the Bolshevik with what they call in Russia the proletarian sense of honour; for the ruling Bolshevik type, too, is that of a free man. And on the other hand, the American too prides himself on not recognizing certain cultural and spiritual values; he, too, despises courtesy in the sense of formality; he, too, believes that, in principle, every American is as good as any other—which means exactly the same as the Russian idea that all comrades—but all comrades only—are equal; in America, the nation corresponds to what is still a class in Russia. And the typical American is just as intolerant, inwardly, of everything not-American as the Bolshevik is of the bourgeois. Yet there is a fundamental difference. Russia is class-conscious at heart; it has, moreover, deliberately declared the lower type of man to be the more valuable, if not the only valuable type. There is inherent in the

Russian nature a preference for what is low, the highest expression of which is a genuinely early-Christian type; but more frequently this tendency leads to the glorification of what is ugly and mean and even base and goes far to explain the unequalled horrors of the Russian revolution. For here it is not a question of mere cruelty—cruelty is, alas, a very normal thing among most men, and there was a very great deal of it at work in the American Civil War—but of fiendish baseness. The Satan which has been and still is at work in Russia is not Lucifer, but that same Devil portrayed by Dostoievsky: a shabby city intellectual with the soul of a lackey.[1] Though the American is not an aristocrat, he is not a plebeian. Thus, he actually represents a historically novel type. If we wish to find anything comparable to it in any way, we must revert once more to Antiquity. The ancient Greek, the ancient Roman belonged, body and soul, to his city; there was no question of liberty in the individualistic sense—the aristocracies in those countries and ages were really socialistic communities in which slaves not belonging to it did all the inferior work. Now does not machinery in America perform most of what slaves did in Antiquity? American Socialism really is a kind of aristocratic Socialism. And its tendency is to grow increasingly aristocratic from year to year. The general feeling is that there *should* be no low work to perform. The strength of this feeling is enhanced by the fact that even the negro shares it—even he is an essentially self-respecting man. Obviously, machines will never be able to do everything that slaves did in the past. Accordingly, since the servant-class is fast dying out, there will be more and more work of the lower kind

[1] Compare *Europe*, p. 387 (first American edition).

to be performed by all—a tendency in which America once more converges with Russia. But here the original American idea—which in general is showing a tendency to disappear, namely, that all work is equally honourable—sets in to overcome inner obstacles. And it derives new strength from another idea which is still thoroughly vital and is even gaining in vitality since everybody owns a motor car, namely, that manual work is not an inferior kind of work; on the contrary, every American takes pride in being independent of others in this respect.

We are, thus, face to face with a truly unique achievement. If it develops in the right direction and if it consolidates, it will some day stand out as an exemplar like any other great civilization. Whatever can be achieved on socialistic premises lies within the range of American possibilities. This range is very wide; it covers practically all that belongs to group-life, all that is not of the "unique" side in man. America's historical significance at the present turning-point in the destiny of man can hardly be overrated. We shall realize this clearly if we remember at this point what was said in the chapter "The Animal Ideal" on the dawning "Geological Epoch of Man." If this is so, then even the worst cultural disadvantages are no disadvantages in the absolute sense. The foremost historical problems to deal with at this juncture are precisely those which a nation of the American type is most fit to solve. Today any nation which resolutely bases its existence on technique without troubling much about past tradition is in a position of vantage as regards possible power and significance. And the same state of actual transition from one geological epoch to another gives a position of vantage to the young and primitive. But if now we envisage the period we are living in within the scheme of human evolution alone, then its primary significance lies in its representing the age of emancipation of the masses. Accordingly, its chief scope and tenet *must* be to achieve equality. There will be new differentiations, new mountains and valleys later on. But first the general level must be raised, and this cannot be done without a temporary equalization at the expense of the heights. Under these circumstances, even envisaged within the scheme of human cultural history, those frankly collectivist nations whose actual belief is in equality, occupy a position of advantage which no accident can annul. Here, then, lies America's great historical chance. If all goes well, the United States will, when what is the future to us will be looked back upon as a historic past, be remembered as *that* socialistic country among others in which individuals were most free and at the same time attained to the greatest amount of earthly comfort.

IN THE following chapter we shall have more to say about the problem dealt with in the last paragraph. Within the context of this one my task is only to finish the picture as it strikes the eye, when viewed from our present standpoint. And this means that, after having described the possibilities of further progress, I must now outline the limitations inherent in them.

There can, of course, be no question of any civilization being ideal in all respects; all perfection is one-sided. And in the case of the United States, this one-sidedness must assert itself all the more as it is built up on the social impulses. An individual may, in principle, lead any kind of life, he may even begin anew at any place; he is the bearer of the principle of initiative and variation. As against this, the group is essentially conservative, static, and exclusive. If there ever was an instance of wrong thinking, it was in the conception of a socialistic *Internationale* embracing the whole of mankind. The whole of humanity certainly might become corporate in spite of all antagonisms, as Christendom was in the Middle Ages, but this could come to pass only if each and all reached complete individualization; only the unique element in man is capable of all-sided and unexclusive relationships; this is why in all ages only the aristocrat could be a "man of the world" in the worth-while sense, a true cosmopolitan; he alone never lost himself by opening himself up to all the world. If the group as such is to predominate, which presupposes the predominance of the social impulses, then an inwardly closed system is the inevitable result, whatever the character of the group may be. One should remember here that every family is essentially exclusive, every army, every nation, every political party, every church, every co-operative in business or consumption. A family, though the most altruistic structure in the world within its own boundaries, is the most egoistic structure in its relationship to whatever lies outside of it; the most devoted mother is as divinely selfish where her children are concerned as any tigress. This explains the fact that even today there is no freer life than that of the American (or his invited guest) in the territory of the United States; but that American foreign policy, dictated by what the American people feel at home, must be singularly inclined to disregard the interests of others. This fact, very patent already, is still veiled by persisting eighteenth-century ideals. But if since Versailles the United States have withdrawn from all ideal positions they held during the War, they will withdraw all the more certainly in the future, wherever they find that the holding of them is contrary to their own interests. This cannot be otherwise; no closed system can be unselfish. There is but one alternative to an ever-increasing assertion of the Monroe Doctrine: world-conquest. A beehive can expand, in theory, into a world-embracing beehive; but it can never open itself up to the non-bee. Now for organic reasons it is impossible to make an exclusive whole world-embracing at the same time; the fate of all would-be world-empires and world-churches has amply proved this basic truth. They never remained world-embracing for long, especially because they were based to a high degree on the compulsion exercised by superior force, for only *inward* forces permanently hold a group together; and such forces are either organically existent, or they are not. This goes far to explain the general trend of the history of the human race. In the beginning, everywhere small tribes were the normal units, and these completely absorbed the individual; this was in accordance with the organic predominance of the social over the individual element within each and at the same time with the exclusiveness based on the lack of transferable elements of the life-form in question. In unison with the development of the individual and the intellectual elements, group-formation became at the same time more encompassing, less contrary to individual initiative—but also less organically coherent. Now any nation of an essentially socialistic structure to that extent resembles a primitive tribe; and this means that it cannot expand beyond comparatively narrow limits. Its life-form is essentially untransferable; for since it is based on actually unintelligible impulses—the only normal premise of all thinking being the individual—it is essentially non-rational. This is the reason why the rule of the International ideal in Russia has in reality made its consciousness more nationalistic than it ever was before. The same explains how the German Socialists, in spite of their avowed internationalism, came to be chiefly responsible for the preservation of German unity after the Great Defeat. Now the same obtains in the United States—and this, in its turn, proves how socialistic at heart the American type of man is. There is no less adaptable type in the modern world than his—just like the primitives, he considers what is not American simply "wrong." For the same reason he is incapable of colonizing; he would be able to do so only in the form of the Greek colonies which were new life-beginnings in the same sense as swarms of bees, leaving their original hive, found a new one.

From these simple considerations it follows that there can be no question of an "Americanization" of the world. Quite the contrary: the American, being the most insular type of the newborn world, the American Commonwealth cannot help developing in the direction of increasing insularity. Thus, what has been true of all cultures —*viz.*, their being exclusive, untransferable, and unique in both space and time—must come to be superlatively true of the American. It will very likely become an exemplar on its particular line—but no one will be able to imitate it, quite apart from the economic premises which obviously make for the same result. And here we have reached a point of the greatest historic and political significance: America being the *only* socialistic commonwealth based on prosperity and being exclusive as such almost equal to an ancient Greek city-state (herein we find the reasons for the entirely irrational, but all the more vital, idea of restricting immigration) it must inevitably stand in permanent opposition to all others. This growing state of things already expresses itself in a very marked way in the popular emotions on both sides of the Atlantic and Pacific and even southward across the Isthmus of Panama. The historic forces embodying the aforesaid truth are, further, reinforced by the fact that any social system essentially based on social (as opposed to individual) impulses is a closed system. Again, America's socialistic structure implies the increasing assertion of this closedness. But now let us follow up some other consequences of American Socialism. There is only individual initiative; the individual alone is the bearer of the principle of variation; the individual alone, too, incarnates the principle of speed. Hence it follows that socialistic America cannot possibly remain what it is today: a progressive country. Unless a new chain of causes interferes with the line of evolution she has started on, she will inevitably become as conservative, as static and traditional, as any family ever was and had to be if it wished to fulfil its mission of carrying on the life of a group as a whole. This development is bound to receive an additional momentum from the—equally inevitable—increase of the influence of woman; for woman is the conservative and routine-lover. Thus, in all probability, the present mobility and dynamism of American life must be looked upon in the same way as the mobility of the spores which represent the short initial stage of the growth of moss. But even today the American who has taken root in the soil strikes one as a basically conservative type; his mobility is all on the surface, or else it signifies a permanent characteristic such as the greater speed of the horse as opposed to the cow. The Americans would not cling so religiously to their Constitution were they not conservative at heart; every town would not be exalted to such a degree by its natives were they not born provincials and regionalists, in spite of all present-day nomadism. Nor would they be conventional to such an unequalled degree. Last but not least: they would not be so slow. For the mental slowness, not the quickness of the native American type first strikes the European who is capable of penetrating below the surface. All this, then, lends additional strength to the arguments presented in the first part of this book in support of the thesis that America's final centre will in all probability lie in the South: in accordance with the laws of the Symbolism of History (cf. the chapter thus entitled in *Creative Understanding*), that type always becomes representative and, therefore, dominant, the inward structure of which corresponds most perfectly to the external needs. If the United States are to settle down as a closed system, static in its essence, then the static type of the American will in the long run inevitably predominate within it.

SO MUCH about the limits set to America's future development by its socialistic structure, as regards the transferableness of its civilization and its further progress. The limitations inherent in its structure in other directions are more important still. It seems mighty improbable that America will develop anything of great cultural importance along such lines as presuppose a predominant individualism. The social is always at the same time the individually undifferentiated. If, in spite of all differences of extraction, all Americans are converging with amazing rapidity toward one single type, or a very small number of types, this is due to the fact that the growing social tendencies actually obliterate the individual impulses which alone make for differentiation. Wherever the social tendencies predominate, there must be very accentuated differences between the groups, but there can be hardly any between the individuals within each group. Thus, the American type must needs become ever less individualized as it draws nearer to its perfection. It may even become un-individual in the pathological sense. Owing to the ruling principle of competition, there are, of course, Adlerian cases in the United States; as every one knows, Alfred Adler has discovered that many nervous diseases are due to an hypertrophy of the will to power which always grows at the expense of the original social impulses. But there certainly are far more cases in the United States for which there is as yet no special medical term, but which well deserve the designation of "Anti-Adlerian" cases: they are characterized by an hypertrophy of the social impulses at the expense of the individual. Here, the will power—a very good thing in itself when put to the right use—seems repressed for the benefit of the will unto service; here, the personal atrophies in favour of the generic impulses. Moreover, the socialism of America belonging to an originally highly individualistic stock must naturally in many cases present pathological symptoms, for racial characteristics do not disappear as quickly as those who bear them (but would prefer not to have them) often believe. A great deal of the hustle and bustle and nervousness in American life seems to me to be due to this. In any case it provides the best explanation for that feeling of inferiority which is evident in most typical Americans when they get into touch with more individualized types. But let us set aside pathology: the fact is that the most genuine predominance of the social impulses, while making for absolute superiority in some respects, entails inferiority in others. If the "I-and-you"-relationship alone counts in the eyes of public opinion, and not the uniqueness-quality of the "I," then certain values simply cannot be realized. Here, the advertising business and its inherent ethics provide the most instructive illustration. Its supreme ideal is always to serve the public *as it is*. Since the community as such is supposed to incarnate the supreme value, and not, as within individualized nations, some independent supersocial or metaphysical sphere, then value must obviously increase with increasing numbers. But the larger the number, the lower must be the quality. It follows that in the normal course of events the lowest kind of type must some day provide the standard of value. Such a natural trend of developments makes cultural progress a very difficult thing to achieve. Cultural progress is possible only when there is no question of conforming to the average man, but only of trying to raise the latter's level. . . . Socialism indeed only too easily blinds the inner eye—man's organ for values. The writings of Judge Lindsey—to quote a very widely known example—provide a peculiarly instructive instance of this state of things. This man means well; moreover, he has great merit; and he really is one of the foremost champions of freedom in an America threatened with the loss of the freedom it originally possessed. Yet, even he cannot see that there are *intrinsic* values. He discards ideals he thinks obsolete such as those connected with the Puritan outlook. But he does not advocate new and equally high ideals instead—he does not understand that the real task is, as I have shown in *The Recovery of Truth,* to give the eternal truths a new setting in harmony with the new psychological state of the age. He says in principle: if I like this or that, why should I not do it provided it makes me happy and healthy? But then happiness and health are purely animal ideals. There is indeed a common denominator only for the wants of all men within the sphere of animal wants. Here we find the most deep-reaching explanation of the American habit of thinking of everything in terms of dollars and cents. Money really is the one common denominator for all wants man, conceived as an animal, can have in our modern age. The dollar-cult, thus understood, really is an expression not of individual greed, but of a predominant instinct for social service. And the same is true, *mutatis mutandis,* of the present-day American ideal of education. The colleges or universities are expected to "turn out" educated men, as factories turn out motor cars. What other ideal could education possibly have, when the group and not the individual is the ultimate terminus? Then, the necessities of group-life as such must decide. And this again to the common denominator of the animal ideal—the ideal of a higher standard of living.

The idea of the "I-and-you"-relationship meaning more than the individual, is, indeed, a dangerous ideal. It inevitably makes for the supremacy of things as opposed to living beings; it inevitably makes for a life ruled by routine. Let us here once more take up the trend of thought of the preceding chapter which dealt with the danger of America's becoming something like one great ant hill. There would be no such danger, however much technique might progress and even though the animal ideal were to rule supreme for a long time to come, were it not for the inherent Socialism of the American type. Socialism makes for a static state. It also makes for an ever-increasing division of labour. Its chief aim being to give satisfaction to all, it is bound to make for standardization, not only because there is no other way to provide everybody with goods at a low price, but because it must take the lowest type of man as a standard, and because this type is only happy in routine-work. Fortunately for the United States, many qualities of the pioneer days are still determinant: the love of adventure and of competition and last, but not least, a very healthy distrust of all mere learning. The typical native-born American is constitutionally afraid of the expert. In the Far West one still sometimes hears this slogan: "First comes the liar, then the damned liar, and then the expert." The best part of American enterprise is due to the belief, proved to be true in the pioneer days, that it is always best to trust in man's creative powers and in his individual initiative, seconded by the belief that everybody can in principle do anything, should the emergency arise. This is the reason why in America one notices those defects inherent in Socialism of the possibility that life may lose its quality of initiative, much less, as yet, than in Germany. But there is a danger that things will not remain as they are now; every development has its own inherent logic and momentum. And although the Americans are not men of routine in the German sense, the mere fact of their laying so much stress on what they call enterprise and promotion is bound to make for an increasing insect-quality in their social life. Here, Henry Ford's factories provide the model. If Behaviourism is ever right, it is in this connexion. Whoever concentrates so entirely on one single thing to the exclusion of all others must lose his inward openness. The great philosopher Max Scheler has recently pointed out that man is the one animal inwardly open to the whole world (*das einzige welt-offene Tier*); all the others are open to small sections of it only. But when he specializes in the Fordian way, man loses precisely this world-openness. If external activity and social service only count, and not inward expansion and growth, then man is bound to develop more and more into a specialist-type even as all insects are specialists in their essence. American life might thus become—not indeed one single repetition—but something like a moving picture: constantly changing, yet always for a mechanical reason only.

But I hasten to say that the fate outlined here is not inevitable. It is doubtless so that events are bound to take the described course if they are not opposed by conscious effort. Today, the general impression is that the American is individual exclusively in his business enterprise; in all other respects he appears thoroughly socialized. And even in business enterprise he seems less and less inclined to follow purely individual courses; he acts as a member of a group; the pioneer with his splendid individual spirit is dying out fast. The American grows more and more obedient to suggestions. A thinking in terms of social service also narrows the range of personal initiative: the millions have comparatively few and simple wants. . . . But enough of the dangers of the direction American evolution is taking. The first step toward wisdom consists in the understanding that all positive possibilities imply and are bound up with limitations. A perfect social and a perfect economic civilization is possible only where the individual side of man remains somewhat under-developed. The social and the individual cannot possibly be equally highly evolved at the same time. And whatever the drawbacks —the way in which the American type seems to be developing, provided only he escapes the dangers inherent in the field he has adopted, can lead to America's becoming one of the great historical exemplars of a social and economic civilization.

## *Privatism*

THOMAS PAINE said: "Almost everything appertaining to the circumstances of a nation has been absorbed and confounded under the general and mysterious word 'government.' Though it avoids taking to its account the errors it commits and the mischiefs it occasions, it fails not to arrogate to itself whatever has the appearance of prosperity. It robs industry of its honours by pedantically making itself the cause of its effects; and purloins from the general character of man the merits that appertain to him as a social being." This short sentence put the fundamental cause of one of the most original characteristics of America into a nutshell; I mean the primacy and supremacy of the point of view of private life. In America not the State stands foremost, nor the Law, nor anything else belonging to the range of the antique idea of a *Forum*, but the private individual with his inherent rights.

It is a state of affairs which developed by way of contrast to Europe. Since man usually lacks inventive power, he seldom hits upon a new idea except when the law of association by contrast compels him to do so automatically. Every people which is despised or persecuted or oppressed soon becomes convinced that it is the chosen people or that it has a messianic mission; the most recent illustration of this law of nature was provided by the Poles. Every new civilization stresses the points which were least regarded by the preceding, thereby upsetting the latter's scale of values. Thus, Christianity in its early days thought nothing of wisdom and worldly power, and believed exclusively in the value of love, a quality which had not been much thought of in Antiquity. Again, the hierarchical structure of the Middle Ages was the opposite of the equality which prevailed among the barbaric tribes during the Wandering of the Nations. Again, Democracy was the idea an unintelligent man was most likely to hit upon, if he had reason to dislike the aristocratic régime. I am not sure whether Rousseau was ever blessed by one single thought which was original in the sense that it originated in his own free nature, apart from surrounding circumstances; almost everything he taught was the result of his resentment and dislikes. But it is precisely for this reason that Rousseau has meant and still means so much. Only what is obvious to many men, can become a determining historic force. And this invariably is the idea automatically brought into the range of vision of the human mind by the natural law of association by contrast. In Europe, as in every old country, the new never could completely supplant the old; all evolution, though proceeding counterpointwise, always sooner or later settled down to a compromise between the old and the new; and the more such a compromise was aimed at from the outset, the more real and durable were the changes it effected, because under these circumstances the old had no chance of ever being restored in its original state. (This explains, incidentally, why the English have constitutionally—the word taken in both the psychological and the political sense—changed so much more than the French with their reason-born radicalism.) But in America, owing to unique historic circumstances, a clean severance between the old and the new could take place such as has never, to my knowledge, occurred anywhere else. There, after the critical point had been passed, development continued along the lines of the latter only. This fact is chiefly responsible for almost all that is original in the political and social structure of the United States. For in this respect nations are just like individuals: the differences already in existence between children must needs accentuate themselves more and more as they grow up.

We have already had occasion several times to point out that the ideals of the eighteenth century still rule America, whereas they have considerably faded in favour of new ones in the Old World. The reason is that the younger and, therefore, the more undifferentiated a living being is, the more it clings to what law and order it happens to possess. Hence the rigidity of all early religious and social systems; hence the extreme conventionalism of children. They are so keenly aware in their subconscious of their chaotic state, that they are terrified at the slightest possibility of a change; they are afraid lest Hell itself break out. It is in the first instance to this natural circumstance that mankind owes the exceedingly interesting phenomenon of the existence today of a nation the fundamental structure of which has its root in the opposition to those conditions its first settlers had fled from or resented in Europe. If we want to define these in the abstract, or find a general denominator for them, we had best call them *form* in general and *government* in particular. It is impossible to appraise justly American directness, the instinctive American distrust of all courtesy that is a matter of form and not simply of good-will, and the American incapacity to realize the truth underlying hierarchy, without remembering that the strongest motives alive in the American collective unconscious were born in the age when Nature was contrasted to Culture in the same sense that truth is opposed to untruth and when the "good Huron" was thought superior to any great gentleman. But we shall deal later with the problem of form. What interests us here is the entirely different view of the idea of government the American holds as opposed to the European and the consequences this has already led to and is likely to lead to in the future.

The Old World from which the first settlers fled was a thoroughly de-personalized world. It was not "objectified" as our modern world is; institutions and "things" did not rule supreme. But man did not dominate as a unique individuality, he dominated only in the sense of what he stood for in the spiritual scheme of things. He always was in the first place representative: of the Church, of the Government, of his class, of the guild he belonged to; even the purely natural relationships were supposed to have their vital roots in the spiritual world; for which reason the individual meant less than the family. Individual man as a private being really had direct business with God only. Accordingly, all hopes for a life in which private concerns counted most were centred in Heaven. This was true in general until America started her independent life. Then and there, irresistibly, the ideas and hopes connected with Heaven as conceived and held by simple and primitive souls materialized into forms and conditions of earthly existence; which circumstance largely accounts for the idea that America is God's own country. Man no longer desired to play the part of a representative; he wanted simply to be a man and to live out his own private interests. This tendency, then, inevitably resulted in a life religious on the one hand and essentially bent on success on the other. And as always happens, the original tendency got accentuated, as it evolved, and differentiated in the course of time. In eighteenth-century America and during the first part of the nineteenth century even, the Cavalier tradition of the seventeenth century, as opposed to the ideas the protagonist of which was Rousseau, played a large part. So did the Puritan tradition of patrician nature, which was as "cultural" in its own way as that of the Cavalier. For from the Puritan point of view wealth was not really a private concern—it was considered as an evidence of God's Grace. To that extent the American Puritan was as mediæval in his outlook as any Cavalier. But the more the two originally predominant types were outnumbered or lost prestige, the more emigrants of a different tradition sailed over from Europe, the more the point of view of the private individual asserted itself. For in the opinion of the emigrants America continued to stand for freedom *from* government, *from* caste, *from* hierarchy of any kind. Only in the course of time the governments and hierarchies and castes against which this feeling of opposition was directed grew to be different and more modern governments and castes and hierarchies; it was a more radical kind of freedom each successive generation of emigrants looked forward to, when crossing the water. The freedom which the fighters for independence had had in view was only a freedom from *arbitrary* government and from all restraint of class, guild, etc. In this respect, then, the "alien" has contributed more to the maintenance and continued predominance of America's original spirit than the native-born of ancient stock;

for eternal ideals can continue only by means of perpetual reincarnation in accordance with the changing spirit of the age. There is even no doubt in my mind that the new emigrants mean more in this respect than the pioneers of the frontier, for these aspired to no ideals; they lived in a world which was congenial to them from the outset and they were exclusively bent on practical concerns. But, on the other hand, the frontiersmen are all the more responsible for the increasing development of the purely private outlook, and in this respect it is indeed true that the native-born frontiersmen have made of America what it is today. They were the first in whom the purely private outlook predominated, and to that extent they really represent the consummation of the development started in the eighteenth century in opposition to European conditions.[1] This predominance of the private point of view increased in proportion to the growth of business in the modern sense and its importance. For business is always private in its essence, even if it be run by the state. The general result of all these components is an outlook—apparently unconscious with the most, but deeply rooted in all Americans—the like of which has never before prevailed on Earth. Since the system in which it expresses itself has as yet no name, I have invented one myself: I call it *Privatism*. Its vital spirit is the predominance of

[1] The true significance of the frontier has to my knowledge best been described by Frederick J. Turner. He shows in his brilliant pamphlet on the subject that American development "has exhibited a return to primitive conditions on a continually advancing frontier line, and a new development from that area. America's social development has been continually beginning over again on the frontier. This perennial rebirth, this fluidity of American life, this expansion westward with its new opportunities, its continuous touch with the simplicity of primitive society furnish the forces determining American character."

private interests over everything that cannot be classed as such, and the tendency to think of and treat everything in terms of private interest.

THE most obvious course for me to follow in my further exposition would be to state as many as possible of the "facts" of the American Constitution—the latter word taken both in its political and in its physiological sense. But I shall do nothing of the sort. And I even ask my American readers to think as little as possible of these facts while reading this chapter. They should remember Gustave Le Bon's fundamental thesis which I quoted in the first chapter to the effect that the peoples are not ruled by their institutions, but by their respective characters. Life always proves stronger than any imaginable external framework. It has not always the power—nor even the wish—to change it, but then the way the latter is interpreted and applied brings about changes; and very often conservatism with regard to the former even furthers inner transformation, as exemplified by England. Accordingly, it would be a gross mistake to attribute to American institutions as such anything vitally significant in American life. If some American institutions of the eighteenth-century style still appear vital, this is due not to their inherent virtue but to the survival of the eighteenth-century Spirit. But most institutions actually no longer mean what they originally did. To quote an American authority, Professor Carl Becker: "On the basis of popular sovereignty and national independence, in origin a protest against the divine right of kings, there has been created in our days the doctrine of the divine right of the state and the absolutism of the majority. Today this absolutism is at the disposal of the capitalist class; tomorrow it may be at the disposal of the proletariat." And another American, Professor Pollard, writes to the same effect: "The irresponsibility of monarchs to their peoples is a matter of detail compared with the irresponsibility of the state. If the state can do what it likes, form its own code of international conduct and dictate its own conception of truth and morals, it is immaterial to those who suffer whether that dictation comes from a despot or a democracy." . . . Indeed, vital significance gives power to all institutions. We shall, therefore, examine only such facts here as are vitally significant, and only as many of them as seem indispensable for the understanding of the underlying meaning. In order to get at the latter, I shall not even shrink from occasional simplifications and exaggerations.

In this connexion there are practically only a few facts which are of primary importance. I will begin with the most striking: the American attitude toward law. It sounds simply ridiculous when Americans speak (a thing, I must admit, they seldom do) of the "majesty of the law." No expression could be more true to the facts of the situation in England; it does not meet them in any way in the United States. The judge is primarily considered as the executive of the people's will, which only incidentally, as it were, coincides with the people's welfare. Never mind the Constitution: psychologically speaking, the American type of judge has evolved out of the sheriff of the frontier days; his task was to shield the community from all who threatened or were believed to threaten its life and property. Accordingly, the American idea of justice is, in principle, much more akin—

again a trait of convergence—to that of Bolshevik Russia than to that of Europe. Originally it was justice according to the point of view of the interests of a given group of settlers. Later it evolved more or less into party-justice. And it might become class-justice at a moment's notice, as it is in Russia, if corresponding classes existed in America; for the fundamental idea is the same. Let no one cite the "facts" of the Constitution against this, or the Courts of Appeal, or even the Supreme Court of Justice, which, from all I have heard, seems to be an exemplary kind of court. In American legal practice there certainly was a line of development which simply continued British legal tradition. And setting aside the Supreme Court, there certainly are institutions which function apart from the ideals the people may entertain; every institution as such, as an independent entity, may be established anywhere. Last but not least, the very fact that America considers law differently from the way Europe, the heir of ancient Rome, does, makes—in individual cases to be sure, but they are frequent—for a humanization of legal procedure and practice which is more akin to the true Spirit of Justice than can be said of any corresponding phenomenon in the Old World. But what counts foremost in this context is the *idea* of law the American instinctively possesses. The system of written constitutions counts here only to the extent that there is nothing in it to prevent the popular will, once it is clear what it desires, from having its own way. If, one day, this way should lead to an equalization in the distribution of wealth or to the establishment of a genuine social democracy, there is no power in institutions or even in men to prevent the achievement of these ends.[1] Exactly the same is true of all legal matters, even where it is a question of pure justice. Law is *not* a something that towers above private desires; it is inwardly accepted and countenanced just so far as it meets the latter. If—as it often happens—a law is countenanced in spite of its being fairly generally considered as bad, this is due to the traditionalism inherent in all young communities and to the primitive respect of an inwardly chaotic life for any kind of form—form meaning something almost magic to such a life. Law is conceived in the United States, first and foremost, as the expression of *the will* of the people. But, again, this will is not conceived as a something above private will, in the sense in which Rousseau opposed the *volonté générale* to the *volonté de tous,* but as the latter only. In theory this leads to the conception that the will of the majority is sacrosanct. But in practice no American really thinks that the will of the other fellow is more important than his own. And this inevitably leads to the idea that the concerns of the State and the Law are different from his own whenever they collide, in exactly the same sense as the interests of business-rivals differ. This explains a great deal of what belongs to the category of graft; the latter means something totally different from what dishonesty means in other countries. This explains in particular the attitude the Americans adopt toward Prohibition. The State is a private trust among others. Like every trust, it may, of course, try all it can to achieve its particular ends; it is its obvious right to do so. But there is no reason why the private individual in his turn should not do his utmost to satisfy his personal desires.

[1] Compare Professor Carl Becker, *Our Great Experiment in Democracy* (New York, Harper & Brothers).

That this point of view does not destroy all order is due not to legality or to political virtue of any other name, but to the morality and the inherent Puritanism of the American type. But here again one should remember that the original Puritan was decidedly unscrupulous in business and always thought it fair to use whatever "means" he found at hand.

All this taken together, as it seems to me, explains most of what strikes the European as extraordinary in American legal life. The judge is not independent; he is elected and can be deposed if the people do not like him; he has to conform to a very considerable extent to the wishes of his party. As often as not, he even knows little law. The juries play a distinctly unreasonable part. The most unreasonable laws can be established if the people so desire it. On the same grounds even lynching can appear as a legitimate course to take. Again, a sentence for life is very rarely really served: a strong current of popular opinion can commute it. On the other hand, this state of things gives the lawyer a positively inordinate power. Since there is no question of law and justice in the European sense, but only of an existing form always liable to be changed by the will of the people who cannot possibly understand much of its intricacies, everything depends on subtlety and astuteness in putting to use the legal forms on the one hand, and on the other, on the skill with which the instrument of the people's emotions is played upon. This state of things, gauged by the European ideal, is one of the most backward states in the whole civilized world. But everything becomes clear once one has understood that to the American law does *not* mean something beyond him, a form of spiritual reality. There is no "Beyond" of private interests from the American point of view. Why, under these circumstances, should the judge be impartial or independent? There certainly is a "Beyond" of individual desires. But this "Beyond" is the community. And in the opinion of the community authorities are not authorities in the European sense—quite the contrary, they are merely the executives of the community's will. This explains also the peculiar quality of the American police. It has more power than that of any other country I know; it is also more ruthless; that is, it has to defend the interests of the community. But since all interests stand in principle on the same level it means nothing irrational if time and again one hears of compromises or even of co-operation between the Force and gangs of criminals. Both are groups of human beings, and both have their legitimate interests.

This state of things may or may not lead to a reign of justice. The will of the people very often coincides with justice. If it does, then, as we have said before, this is due to morality and not to legality; it is due to that undifferentiated sense of equity and fairness which is inherent in all genuine group-consciousness; and since the social tendencies predominate in the structure of the American soul, the sense in question must be very highly developed. But, in principle, the will of the people and justice do not coincide because the natural sense of justice and fairness inherent in group-consciousness does not extend beyond the limits of the group. It really and ultimately simply stands for its cohesion; what it means by justice is the mutual adjustment within the group to the latter's benefit. No sooner does one group enter into conflict with another, than the same fundamental facts which make for justice and fairness with each of them, make for the ethics of strife. This is the reason why the decisive step toward the establishment of a legal state guaranteeing justice to each and all was to give the judge absolute independence even from the State and to make it a question of honour in his case that he should never yield to public opinion. This step may have been formally and officially taken in the United States as well—as a matter of psychological attitude it certainly has *not* been taken, although, the forms of American legal life have been derived from those of England, the most legal-minded of modern nations. This is highly significant. It can be explained only by the psychological fact that Americans do *not* admit a "Beyond" of the interests of private life.

Now what is true of the legal side of American public life is true of the whole governmental machinery. The State and the Government are *not* considered as institutions ranging above the private individual. On the contrary, they are supposed to be mere executives of its will. This is the foremost reason why so very few seem to think of calling truly remarkable men to governmental offices and still less to elect them to Congress. The State-life is obviously considered—whatever may be said to the contrary—as the least important part of American existence. There has, of course, to be something of the kind and to the extent that the will of the State is a manifestation of the will of the people, it is scrupulously respected. It is even very highly respected, inasmuch as the will of the community stands against the individual. But the State is primarily looked upon as a machinery of the same kind as, for instance, the Mail Service. No one dreams of calling a man of genius to become Postmaster

General (if such an office exists in America, which I do not know). And it is because of the essential *unimportance* of the State as the people view it that the President of a nation more jealous of governmental power than any other on earth, is allowed more real power than any king in modern days. If one considers the case from the other side, the result is the same. The best men do not enter government service because even the highest government post means less significance and real power than a leading position in private business. The picture is completed by the poor pay which government officials receive in a country that considers high wages not only the only fair, but also the only profitable, policy for the employers.

The truth of the situation is obscured by the fact that the United States today are a tremendous power precisely as a State and that they play a very active part in world-politics. It is, moreover, obscured by the circumstance that the Americans are very proud of their nation, very susceptible in their pride, and that they are as ready to fight for it, if the emergency arises, as are any other people. Nevertheless, things are what I have shown them to be. The objections to my argument which seems contained in the foregoing observations can be refuted by the one consideration that in the domain of life not the facts as such, but their significance ultimately counts. Even if the Federal Government of the United States were the greatest power on earth—as long as it does not mean more to Americans than it evidently does, then national appearance and national reality do not coincide. Moreover, we must always distinguish between what an institution means at home and what it means abroad. Considering their intrinsic power, the political institutions of America certainly are a formidable thing. And not only that: every American citizen delights in the fact and will do his utmost to insure their prestige in foreign countries. But for his own person he views them in a totally different light. Nor is this all that can be said in this connexion; the important point to be grasped, if we wish to understand the United States, seems to me to be that national consciousness and national pride need not have their focus or centre in the State. China always gloried in its culture, but never in its government. The Hindu Brahmins of the traditional type honestly look upon their British rulers in the light of domestic servants—they think them so inferior that they leave them to do the dirty work for them. The Americans' idea of State and Government is different from the Hindu and the Chinese; but it differs still more from the European notions. Theirs is that entirely novel outlook which I have named *Privatism*.

Privatism is the one offspring of the eighteenth century which bears only the traits of its direct parents. America was to be a free country with free men at its head, which meant psychologically—never mind the actual Constitution—that no government was to interfere with the private life of the individual as long as the latter respected the rights of the community. This was an ideal which could easily be lived up to as long as America was practically an empty continent. Prospectors and hunters need no state for their well-being. Nor is there any necessity of an authority superior to the will of the people as long as the communities are small and scattered. Later on, difficulties arose from various causes which stood in the way of the foundation of a nation in the ordinary sense of the word and kept the process going in the original direction, the most important of which were the movement of the frontier, which was not completed before the year 1880, and kept the participants primitive; the constant influx of immigrants, and finally the industrial revolution with its new and unlimited possibilities of national progress making for a free "frontier-life" of a new kind. But there were several other causes leading to the same effect. When the new life began to take root in the American soil, its local and provincial outlook with its narrow horizon precluded the possibility of really visualizing so immense a thing as a Great Federate Nation. And the finishing touch is given to the picture by the fact that American life could not be interfered with practically from without, so that the whole of the nation was actually safe from political troubles and its citizens able to live a purely private life. The result is that today, in spite of all their power and influence, the United States represent psychologically a gigantic Canton Appenfell—that is the most provincial province of Switzerland, and, therefore, are private minded.

This explains why there is so much to be said against it from the political point of view. The fact that the Americans themselves seldom recognize that is due to a cause which, again, is a result of the same state of things: the Americans look at their Constitution as historians; they only think of what has been or what should be in theory, completely overlooking the present-day phenomena. It is, moreover, due to the fact that the American primarily thinks of his State and not of the Union. At this point, I have to qualify in one particular respect the general picture I have drawn: the individual States very often are exceedingly well administered. But then they really are *municipalities;* they have no political concerns. The *Union* only is a political unit in the European sense, and here all that we have stated holds good. The English, in particular, with their keen political sense, simply stand aghast at the spectacle offered by America as a political unit. As an illustration I may quote a few passages from an article by Harold Laski, professor at London University (published in the June issue, 1928, of *Harper's Magazine*). No political system has ever been so

> vehemently assailed as that of the United States; nor is there any upon which criticism has produced so small an effect. There are no signs that a foreign observer can detect which indicate any widespread desire for alteration. So few politicians have anything like a national significance, so many are politicians because they have failed in other walks of life, that the inhabitant of Main Street is easily tempted to venerate where it seems an extravagant luxury to comprehend. Yet, if we assume that democratic government is desirable, there is hardly a canon of institutional adequacy against which the American system does not offend. It is desirable that the source of responsibility for government error or wrong should be clear and unmistakable; the American system so disposes responsibility that its detection is approximately impossible. It is urgent that the working of institutions should be conducted in the perspective of discussion which educates and clarifies the public mind; but the essential tasks of operation in America are almost wholly concealed from the public view. It is important that the occupants of high office should be chosen on the basis of ability and experience; yet both the President and his Cabinet are selected by a process which, if it resembles anything, is akin to a dubious lottery. A governmental system, moreover, should be sensitive to the opinions of its constituents and maximize the opportunity of translating a coherent body of doctrine into statute; yet it seems the purpose of American institutions delib-

erately to avoid that sensitiveness, on the one hand, and to prevent the making of coherent policy upon the other. . . . To any critical observer trained in the legislative experience of France and England, the House of Representatives must necessarily seem unworthy of a great people. Most congressmen are unsuccessful lawyers. . . . The legislative cannot get the executive which it wants, the executive is never sure of a legislative to its liking. Each has a certain interest in the failure of the other. . . . No verdict can be sought from the people at a time when a verdict should be taken; and when the fixed epoch of judgment arrives, events will have done much to obliterate the material upon which a verdict should be rendered.

And so forth. There is, indeed, no question of American political institutions being perfect; if, again and again, they are glorified, it is simply due to ignorance or hypocrisy. But the real point which explains everything is this, that in America the political system plays no important part. England put up, longer than any other European country, with a shocking system of general education because it did not care. America, for the same reason, puts up with its political status. And if it considers it as sacrilegious even to think of altering it, the essential reason is again the same.

America, then, is no political unit in the usual sense of the term. Yet it is not true that it is no nation at all, as a prominent Frenchman recently would have it. It really is a *novum* in history. But in order to make this point completely clear, I must for a while give another direction to our trend of thought and approach the problem from a different angle. By means of a general analysis of the course of history, I will try to show *why it is that the State must needs lose in importance all over the world.* What originally was and, at first sight, still appears as American backwardness or provincialism, really means the beginning first realization of a new and progressive state of mankind.

FOR the Greeks, the inhuman course of natural evolution meant Moira, or Fate; they had no power over it, hence it ruled them. Napoleon asserted that politics meant fate—and in his time they really did; for this formidable man so absolutely mastered every political situation, no matter whether he was the leading spirit or was himself driven by circumstances, that his political will took on the character of fate for the rest of humanity. But how is it in our day? Today economics undoubtedly mean fate in the very same sense. They mean fate for Europe in particular, because its most serious problem is whether or not it will be able to pull through the economic crisis which is the foremost result and aftermath of the World War. Therefore no international political treaty can be considered as finally ratified before this problem is solved; and economics mean fate in general, because the economic relations of the whole world have developed into such tremendous and completely independent forces that hitherto no will has been able to master them.

There was a time when the State meant little as compared with the religious community; during the Middle Ages Christianity in Europe represented something infinitely more important than any political formation, as the religious community does even today within the Islamic and Hindu worlds. Since then, the State as compared with the religious community irresistibly gained in importance; a thing most energetically carried through in France since the reign of Louis XI, but most striking in the case of Germany's Protestant states in which religion as a "national church" (*Landeskirche*) more and more lost its original independence. And up to a very recent date, the importance of the State steadily increased to such an extent that in Germany in particular the national community could no longer imagine any other expression for itself. Now in our days the importance of the State is in its turn steadily diminishing in favour of the significance of economic associations. Even before the World War the balance of importance was in reality shifted in this sense. One of the main facts which made for England's greatness was that it was backward in its political development in so far as, besides the State, a series of other free associations embodied the Imperial idea. And the true power of Imperial Germany—immeasurably greater than most Germans had the slightest idea of—was not dependent on its army, which was merely continental, but on the delicate meshes of the cobweb with which its economics had overspun the whole planet; it has been possible to destroy this power only because the Germans failed to carry on a policy corresponding to the true interests of economics, so that the real power was dependent on the spirit of what was relatively powerless. Now since the World War this historic momentum leading to a loss of importance of the State has become patent. In the first place, of course, in the case of the defeated nations. As long as the State was relatively unimportant, a defeat was likewise relatively unimportant; the loss of lives did not exceed the limits of what the people could stand; private property remained secure in principle;

also, the conqueror's power over the defeated was not inordinate. Today the conqueror wields greater power than in the times of the Assyrians *because in public opinion the emphasis lies on economics. For this results in the assumption, unheard of since the suppression of slavery, that all private property must stand security for the State.* Today a form of bondage of debt is considered as morally permissible in the case of nations, the mere idea of which as applied to an individual would be branded as criminal in the opinion of the world. Today even military subsidies are treated like business debts. Today the great capitalists are the wire-pullers, not often as yet as creative leaders—they are mostly too *naïve* for that or else they have not yet formed a correct estimate of the political necessities—but they are as representatives of world-embracing economic interests. The latter are of such paramount importance that purely political considerations in the old sense cannot compete with them. Since the industrial revolution the number of human beings has increased to such an extent that any disregard of economic necessities can result in a catastrophe similar to the Deluge.

Let it be clearly understood that here it is a question of a complete *novum* in history. Man's primary concern certainly has always been to live, and material life depends on material means of existence. But as long as the earth was sparsely inhabited, the question of starvation was not, properly speaking, an economic problem; for it could in principle always be solved by emigration or conquest. On the other hand, wherever this was not so it was a case of ineluctable Destiny; then, either superior natural or superior human forces prevented any change for the better. Furthermore, before science became the acknowledged director or inspirer of life, economic values could not be properly created. And they could not be created on a scale sufficiently large to affect the general condition of the human race until a very short time ago. A treasure could only be robbed or inherited or come upon by good luck; it bore no interest. Before riches became what one calls "capital," taking interest always meant usury. And on the other hand, interest had to be so high as to make it akin to robbery because there were no general foundations of life providing at the same time for the security and legitimacy of turnover. Only two hundred years ago the honesty of a merchant was looked upon as that of a conqueror. Thus, all great merchant nations of past history were, in the first instance, raiders and conquerors. Their daring, their love of adventure, their capacity for ruthless exploitation of the vanquished, were the qualities they really depended upon, not economic ability. The latter could not guarantee a free existence. The "economic man" of the past was either a conqueror and a ruler, deriving material advantage from his position of power, or else he was a slave, if not worse than a slave; think of the position the Jews had to endure for thousands of years. All this has begun to change since wealth has been thought of ever more generally in terms of capital and since scientific discoveries have made it more and more possible for economic life to exist in its own right. But since the masses have begun to awaken to scientific and economic consciousness—those very masses whose race-memory knows of no conquest, no rule, and no exploitation of others, but only of toil—the point of view of the man to whom war signifies *not* the last resort, nor, accordingly, politics either, begins to predominate. As far as numbers go, it predominates absolutely all over the world even today. The man in the street everywhere is intimately convinced that economics as such *can* guarantee a good life for all. He is equally convinced that war can only destroy material values—never create them—and that politics only help—or not help—to take advantage of economic possibilities. Accordingly, an irresistible, though mostly unconscious, inner alienation from the State is gaining ground; an alienation which, for the present, as long as the altered circumstances are not yet clearly understood, finds its expression for the most part in dishonesty—dishonesty in otherwise honest people always means a lack of adaptation and this generally lies in the circumstances and not in the people. But quite apart from the foregoing considerations, every organism has its destiny, the universal and organic destiny of youth, ascent, achievement, and ultimately of decay. Thus, after the organism of the State has passed beyond its culminating point, it can continue living, but it can never again signify something equally positive as it used to signify. Here, then, a new chain of causation sets in. No machinery is ruled and controlled by itself; it always serves some individual or group. Thus, the State was first the vassal of individuals and castes. Then it became the organ of larger associations; in its zenith it was the normal means of expression of the well-organized community. But since the masses have practically conquered the political power, the State is becoming increasingly the organ of the mass and its needs. It follows that it soon will serve almost exclusively the greatest happiness of the greatest number according to Bentham's idea. In so far as it does so, it certainly has a right to exist. The masses must be increasingly better off; a decent standard of life must finally fall to the share of each and all. And only law and a machinery strong enough to enforce it under all circumstances can guarantee fair dealings on such a gigantic and at the same time minutely differentiated field. But if the State thus becomes essentially a controlling-apparatus for the welfare of its citizens, how can it continue to pursue ends of its own? How can it remain the principle of initiative incarnate? It is bound to stand ever more and more for static as opposed to dynamic values. The consequence of this development is clear. The State will probably become more "useful" than it has ever been, but its exalted position will dwindle more and more into something like that of the Mail Service. Its destiny will be similar to that of its head, which from being thought of as anointed by "God," ended by being the office temporarily or permanently held by an ordinary man recognized as such.

We are thus doubtless living in an era of diminishing importance of the State. This certainly does not mean that any nation will give up its state and its government or that it ought to do so. Nor does it imply that the State will soon lose its power and authority: on the contrary, everything argues in favour of the idea that in many countries it will temporarily grow all too powerful and thus bring itself *ad absurdum;* unfortunately, what is reasonable does not often take place on earth because of anticipated significance, it usually becomes fact as the result of nonsense refuted by better experience. This applies precisely to Bolshevik and Fascist State-superiority. The final condition of which both the present Russian and the present Italian system represent embryonic phases obviously is of a syndicalist nature; the idea is that the producer alone should count politically and that the State should see to this. But both Russia and Italy are ruled today by revolutionary minorities; these cannot help—not only in order to carry out their new program, but simply in order to hold their own—overstressing the power and authority of what machinery for rule they have inherited from the past. The above statement—that we are living in an era of diminishing importance of the State—only means that the State is necessarily diminishing in *significance*, and since on the historic plane significance creates the facts, this cannot help manifesting itself more and more in the quality of the latter. Just as the religious community which in the past possessed sovereign independence, gradually became an integral part of the growing State, the latter will eventually become the organ of a higher connexion, which would then, in its turn, gain the prestige formerly appertaining to the State.[1] We are far as yet from any

[1] Europe is on the way to this condition. Even the present League of Nations, in spite of its most imperfect foundation, involves a diminution of the importance of the single States and the development of a higher super-national organization, the first task of which will probably be to protect the individual as such from the encroachments of his government. So paradoxical a necessity alone suffices to depreciate the traditional State: the spirit of most of the new States created by the Treaty of Versailles is such that the majority is absolutely determinant and legally deprives the minority of all its rights; an unbearable state of things which can be terminated only by the individual *as such being* internationally recognized as possessing inalienable rights. Cf. the detailed description of this particular aspect of the present crisis I have given in the chapter "The Baltic States" of *Europe*.

sort of final condition, and this is not the place for me to anticipate it. But this much is certain: at the present historical juncture all the real importance which exists in the idea of reconstruction lies in the economic and not in the political sphere. Today oil decides the grouping of powers in very much the same way as in bygone days religion decided it. However great the number of nations which still carry on a purely nationalistic policy, one need only glance at the lists of quotations, at the balances of trade, and the statistics on unemployment in order to understand that no state is really independent any longer and that all national weal and woe depends on super-national general conditions, the decisively competent of which are economic. And this will probably remain so for a long time. In all likelihood, events will again take the course which once led to the development of the Middle Ages. Fustel de Coulanges has shown that the feudal order in France developed out of the provincial civil law of Imperial Rome. When the machinery of the Roman state fell to pieces, the old economic system became the basis of the new political system. In the same way everything leads one to anticipate that the future political order in the West will begin by constituting itself as an economic order. One should not forget that even the germ-cell of the new German Empire was a customs-union (*Deutscher Zollverein*). When the present order will have been definitely done away with, then the recognition and correct interpretation of the economic order as the very foundation of community-life, and its further development of modern community-life, into a more encompassing order will gradually take place.

But if now we remember the introductory part of

"The Animal Ideal" and link it up with our latest observations, then we shall find that the historical development sketched here in general outlines really means only the detailed description of one aspect of the change brought about by the fact that now at last man has come to be the Lord of Creation, as the "leading fossil" of the Geological Epoch of Man. If only man who has grown scientifically and technically supreme really *is* man, as he was meant to be from the very first, *then, obviously, economics, understood in the sense of mastery over nature, must mean more than politics.* It must do so as long as mankind at large has not attained the status which really belongs to it within the cosmic scheme. And this leads us to a belief which seems paradoxical at first sight, although it confirms the most modern conviction of mankind at large: a human condition in which politics with their inevitable corollary, warfare, stand foremost, is *really a lower condition compared with a life centred in economics.* All animals really live by means of war and politics; wherever one species is stronger, it is utterly ruthless; symbiosis where it does not mean a pre-established harmony is always the result of an unwilling compromise. If now man succeeds in creating a general condition in which all men can lead a satisfactory life, this will, of course, happen at the expense of the other organisms; to that extent man will prove no better than any other leading fossil ever proved since the advent of life on this earth. But he will create a *human* basis for human life, as opposed to the animal basis prevailing up to now, and this would mean a state in which intelligence would overrule brute force, and a general feeling for solidarity dominate over the fighting instinct. The latter will certainly not cease to exist. Human nature never changes, and any loss of instinctive or elementary forces means vital loss in general. But it makes all the difference whether these forces rule or serve. Aristotle was right when he called man the political *animal;* politics really belong still to the animal sphere. So do economics, of course, if they are defined only as the activity which provides for food in general. But this is precisely what scientific economics no longer are, because here the emphasis rests on intelligence and spiritual initiative, and the furthering of human welfare at large as the end in view.

I CAN see no logical fault in the developments of the last paragraph; nor do I think that I have shown the facts in a wrong light. If politics *seem* to mean more today than ever before, this is due to the natural law that before going out the flame leaps up once again. I certainly do not mean to say that the new balance of power between politics and economics will be reached without long fighting and, possibly, new wars. In particular, many nations will probably have to fight for their economic independence; they will have first to use all the devices which traditional politics provide in order to make politics less important in the future. One should not forget that fighting in itself is not dependent on the existence or rule of politics or militarism, but that it represents the natural way for every man to get from the other fellow what the latter does not want to give away. Yet even at the time I write this, in the year of grace 1928, the real relationship between France and Germany cannot be gauged by the speeches made in parliaments, but only by the agreements between ore and coal on both sides of the Rhine—and here it is manifestly a case of agreements independent of all political treaties; this independence constitutes their essence. On the other hand, the agreement about the Outlawry of War could not have been signed exactly ten years after the World War, out of which the victorious nations seemed to emerge more militant than Prussia ever was, if national self-consciousness had not to a certain extent become disassociated from pride in state and power. But now let us return to American conditions. Does the present State of America mean an anticipation—however preliminary or even rudimentary—of the very goal of European development? It does indeed mean such an anticipation. And in this fact, in its essence not yet understood by public opinion, lies the chief prestige of the United States.

This prestige does not indeed depend on America's immense economical power as such, but on the fact that on the basis of it a new kind of commonwealth is in the making. From the point of view of tangible fact, the United States as a body are no doubt chiefly an economical unit; and as representative a man as Henry Ford has even gone so far as to pretend that a nation does not essentially represent anything else. But quite apart from the untruth of the statement as far as other nations are concerned—the United States would not be what they are from the human point of view if Ford's statement were true in their case. One single consideration will suffice to prove this. In the field of pure economics pure egoism is the very soul of life; a business or an enterprise which does not pay is as wrong and bad on its own particular plane as a crime on that of morals or an untruth on the plane of science or an ugly phenomenon in the sphere of beauty. An economic life in which the principle of profit does not rule supreme is a contradiction in terms. Accordingly, business cannot mean everything in the United States. This, then, is the moment to remember that in an essentially political community politics do not mean all in all, either. The soul of politics is will to power; political interest also represents a purely selfish side of life. But that does not mean that in every state the will to power should rule supreme; if that were the case, then Machiavelli's *Prince* could claim to be the Bible of all community-life. The fact is that in a well-organized political nation the political form provides only the *basis* or the *frame*, no more.—It is exactly the same in America with economics. If one analyses an American situation, the last irreducible element one finds is almost always an economic connexion. But the living synthesis contains a great number of other elements. Here, then, the essential socialism of the American character, both individual and national, stands out once more. If economics were the only decisive principle, American life would be the most individualistic and egocentric of all lives. As far as business goes, it undoubtedly is. Americans "play" harder here than any other nation; no sentiment ever interferes with business interests and if anyone chooses to be a *pendant* to Machiavelli's ideal prince, there is nothing in the code of American business-ethics to prevent him from becoming one. Such Machiavellians of business have, as a matter of fact, been more frequent in the United States than anywhere else on earth, for the same reason that the political Machiavellians have been most frequent in Italy: nowhere else has the one-sided principle underlying economic profit—as in Italy the principle underlying political power—found an equal chance to rule autocratically. But the outstanding fact is that this chance is growing less favourable with every successive year. With every successive year the innate Socialism of America is increasingly asserting itself, so that the conflicts between Capital and Labour, for instance, will hardly ever become acute—not because the problem will be solved, but because it is dismissed from the outset.[1] If, then, the basis of American life is doubtless economic, it is also true that in the soul of the modern American individual the social tendencies predominate: owing to this an adjustment of the conflicting interests can and does take place. Does it now not also become clear why the establishment of the supremacy of the economic and the socialist principles not only *could*, but *had* to coincide historically? A commonwealth in which economics form the basis of life can be a connected whole only if not the individual but the social tendencies predominate. On the other hand, any kind of socialist system can be built up only on economic foundations; for only if a high standard of living for all is the ideal, can a group as such hope to lead a civilized life.

And now let us turn our minds directly, without further détours, to the absolute advantage which the United States have over the rest of the world. Is it not an amazing fact that after "the war which was meant to end war" all those who still think in terms of politics as the final issue candidly contemplate future wars even more cruel than the World War? In reality, it does not seem amazing, once one realizes that the stress of importance has shifted from politics to other forces. For hence-

[1] Compare the chapter "Tension and Rhythm" in *The Recovery of Truth*, in which I have shown at length that vital conflicts can never really be solved, but only dismissed when life rises to a higher plane, on which the problems of lower planes no longer exist.

forth any hope of a permanent victory of the one nation can lie only in the complete destruction of the other. Unless this end is reached, a war never pays; for since the decisive power lies with economics and not with politics, a political defeat can in no time be transmuted into victory if the economic forces of the vanquished remain intact or capable of recuperating quickly, or if those belonging to other nations side with them—which in principle they can be prevented from doing only when the former are practically annihilated. The traditional outlook of the statesman really can hold its own only if gas war, the sinking of merchant vessels, the wholesale murder of women and children, and the subsequent enslavement of the defeated are contemplated as a matter of course. *Now within the scheme of the United States, war is really no intrinsic necessity.* War is inevitable only if the State leads its own independent life as an entity superior to its citizens; wherever and as long as this is the case, the abolishment of war is a logical impossibility, which fact, incidentally, explains all the recent failures of the attempts to establish peace everlasting on European foundations in general and from the premise of the League of Nations in particular. In the same sense, it is a logical impossibility to found politics on the idea of Justice, because politics belong to the plane of biology, and Justice does not. But if *private* life is considered the last resort, then there is nothing in principle to prevent the adjustment of conflicting interests in a manner becoming the New Geological Age; the less so, since then the human types chiefly bent on war, the statesman and the soldier, can no longer predominate. If these types appear today so sadly incapable of adaptation and understanding, this is partly a result of the adjustment to routine which must inevitably regulate the greater part of governmental machinery, but it is chiefly due to the adjustment to violence as the last resort. The possibility of violence and, more especially, the self-evident duty ultimately to use it, always blunt the intellect. Now it lies in the nature of things that violence can never decide in economic life. Rightly directed, economics adapt themselves to any kind of juncture, as any plastic organism adjusts itself to its surroundings. It is true that the United States have become militarized to a certain extent as a result of the War. But then there is a great difference between a healthy warrior-spirit, ready for self-defence, and imperialistic militarism. There is a difference *in kind* between the spirit in which France, for instance, understands security and peace and spirit of the Kellogg Pact. America really is in earnest about outlawing of war, because war in principle means an absurdity where the foundations of national life are of a privatist, as opposed to a political nature. For the United States war might then mean only an intrinsic necessity, in spite of the above, if the combative instincts of man, which are and always will be present, could find no outlet but in war. But American life provides such outlets. The Americans are perhaps more of a fighting nation than are many European nations; they are bound to be, since competition is the very soul of their life and the pioneer- and frontier-traditions are still very vital. Accordingly, they were eager enough to fight when the emergency arose in the World War; and should such an emergency again arise, they will again try to make a "good job" of it. But there can be no repressed combative instincts in America because those very instincts form the basis of American business life. Americans play and fight hard from principle; generally speaking, one can say that in America the adage "All is fair in love and war" applies foremost to business life. This accounts for many practices that seem dishonest to Europeans. But it accounts to an even greater degree for the fairness of business life, which is, after all, its salient point. In the United States, enemies on the field of business prove chivalrous as often and in the same way as enemies in war used to be in pre-war Europe. After having been at daggers drawn the whole day, they will meet as friends after six p. m. This is exactly what was expected of warriors belonging to hostile camps, or of duellists in the days of chivalry. And the reason is the same: the very impulses which worked themselves out in the fighting traditions of knightly Europe do so in present-day America in the way Americans play both hard and fair in business life. That such a transposition of the field of activity of the selfsame impulse was possible is something very remarkable; but there is no doubt of the fact. It is certainly true that the man who puts his life at stake is more noble than the business-fighter; life and property do not belong to the same plane. But then we must remember that modern warfare is no longer a noble, but a beastly thing; it amounts to wholesale extermination of the enemy as though they were mice or lice; it will never again be a noble sport. We must likewise remember that this age *is* an economic age, and that there is no evading the fact. It is, therefore, not a question of accepting this state of things or of trying to restore the supremacy of the outlook of the warrior, but simply of whether or not the economic field, too, offers an outlet for the combative instincts and whether there, too, a code of honour can be made to ennoble the expressions of these instincts.

And if in America the combative instincts can find an outlet in a life which practically excludes the possibility of war, the same is true of the spirit of adventure. One may even say that the latter finds more possibilities of outlet in America than it has in Europe for a long time past. The fundamental reason is that private life being accepted as life's essence, adventure was looked forward to there as well; and that since for more than a century there really was little possibility of adventure on the fields of state-life and military careers in Europe, the advantage is now all on the side of America. In the most civilized communities of America every boy can still start life with hopes of thrilling experiences, as youth did in Europe in the days of d'Artagnan. The love of adventure is increased in its turn by the standardization and uniformity which characterize everyday routine. All this taken together makes for a general love of risk, which is the chief reason why the American as a type strikes any unbiassed observer as a free type of man, in spite of all his prejudices. Although the foundations of his life are economic, he is hardly ever a "man of property" in the sense of Galsworthy's description, nor a bourgeois in the French or German sense. The most striking expression of this is that in the United States initiative plays a greater rôle in business life than anywhere else in the world. Experience, routine, and learning do not count, change of occupation and of fields of activity are not the exception, but the rule. This accounts also for the originality in all fields which really interest the American. There can be no question that the American economic structure is absolutely original. And there is no reason why ever more and more manifestations of American life should not become so, as the number of things and problems the American is interested in increases.

And now we have reached the point where we can deal with the most striking advantage of the inner state of the United States as compared with that of the rest of the world. In post-war Europe, too, the real foundations of life are economic. But the ruling ideals and prejudices *will* not have it so. Accordingly, in Europe one notices an overwhelming underlying greed for material goods, on the one hand, and on the other, a constant indictment of materialism, a condemnation in the name of idealism and spiritual values of all who strive after comfort, in which striving the Americans, of course, stand foremost. The results are hypocrisy and cant, and over and above, an appalling frequency of the phenomena of ill-will, resentment, envy, jealousy, and mutual condemnation. These phenomena are most frequent among those who call themselves idealists *ex officio*. In the United States, where the economic interest is consciously recognized as both primary and legitimate, the general atmosphere is practically devoid of these ugly phenomena due to repression and untruthfulness. I have already given several reasons for that generosity, good-will, and that lack of envy and jealousy one cannot help noticing in the United States as their most outstanding national characteristic. But the chief and fundamental reason is the reason stated above. Every normal man or woman desires to be comfortable, if possible wealthy; naturally so, because the highest possible standard of living is the normal ideal of the human *animal*. Only those very rare individuals in whom spirit predominates and who, moreover, belong to the ascetic type are genuine exceptions. Now in America everybody frankly admits this fact, both to himself and to others. There are, therefore, no repressions in this respect. And the result is — not an increase of greed, not dollar-madness of the kind the European subconscious projects on America as upon a screen, but a prevailing generosity, a general desire to spend and to give, an involuntary general application of the principle "live and let live." There are practically no misers in America; almost everyone spends freely, in Russian-fashion, what he earns. Those who grow rich do all they can for the community without pressure from without. The reason is that it is the *normal* thing to spend the money one has; it is the essence of unthwarted life to give; besides, money is essentially fluid, it *wants* to change hands, as it were, so that the law of man and that of money reinforce each other. Americans really care for money much less than Europeans do; they care less precisely for the reason that they admit to themselves whatever wish for it they have. This desire is never infinite, nor is it everlasting; as soon as it is satisfied in the proportion required by the basic equilibrium of the man in question, the tendencies which make for giving without wanting anything in return assert themselves all the more powerfully. The case is the same as in France with man's erotic needs. In pre-war Europe these were openly admitted in France only, with the result that the sensuous atmosphere of France alone was pure at bottom and that the phenomena it led to were beautiful and not ugly. It is repression only which makes the natural ugly. When leaving the United States I told my friends there, that I felt I had had a moral rest-cure. Very many things in the New

World certainly are not what they should be. Nevertheless, on the whole the moral atmosphere is purer than in Europe.

HERE, then, we can resume our considerations about the possibility of America's building up a truly peaceful civilization. Mass-conflicts really have no reason to exist where there are no repressed desires on the lines most likely to lead to such conflicts and where, moreover, the competitive instincts find sufficient outlets. Here we may once more call to mind ancient China. China, too, was peaceful and wonderfully contented for centuries without interruption; the general atmosphere of that country, too, was one of universal goodwill. The reasons for this state of things were partly different from those at work in America; the chief reason, no doubt--I have explained all this at length in my *Travel Diary*—was an innate feeling for harmony rooted in its turn in a development—unique in history—of the æsthetic sense into an organ for the perception of universal connexions. Nevertheless, the Chinese and the American type of man have striking likenesses. The Chinese, too, have an innate feeling for original equality; a marked preference for the ordinary as opposed to the extraordinary; a strong moral sense. They, too, show an extraordinary development of the social tendencies; a high respect for trade; a dislike of the soldier-type; a positive veneration for education; and above all, an inclination to consider government more in the light of a necessary evil than as a supreme good. The highest ideal of the functions of government ever conceived by the ancient Chinese was, that it should *not* govern. In my *Travel Diary* I suggested the possibility of an outlook akin to the Confucian triumphing all over the world. However this may be, in America one cannot help noticing an approach to this goal.

Even by now my readers will have perceived that on foundations differing entirely from those of Europe a very ideal community-life is possible. But only at this point can we grasp and define the core of Privatism. The term Privatism implies, not that business comes first, but means private as opposed to public life. And private life is essentially a life of the *whole* man. Any kind of life which is centred in a projection that becomes an independent entity existing in its own right, as, for instance, the State, the army, not to mention the person of an emperor or a pope, is somehow or other detached from its vital root and resigns some of the most human qualities as ultimately irrelevant. History has amply shown what it leads to when *la raison d'état* is considered as the last resort, or when a ruler is in a position to say *L'état c'est moi.* But it has also shown that it is quite as dangerous when a government-machine supposed to represent a government by the people and for the people actually leads an independent life; this is true today of most parliaments, not to speak of caucuses and the like. From the historical point of view the greatest epochs were the early ages. But they were so not because the old times were better than more recent eras, but simply because *whole men* were then the leaders and not partial projections and substantifications or objectifications of the inner life. *Now to this state Privatism leads back; or rather, it does not lead back to it—it clears the way to the same state of things on a higher level.* If partial projections and substantifications or objectifications are no longer believed to mean more than life conceived as a whole, whether in the case of an individual or a nation, then inhumanities inherent in the predominant king, or the predominant State, or the predominant army, or the predominant abstraction, whatever its name, in which lies the vital root of practically all inhumanities of previous history, will lose all moral support. Then the Christian outlook will really gain predominance. But again, this would not entail a loss of those qualities which in past history made of the man who lived *for* the State, or *for* the army, or *for* the law a higher and nobler sort of being than any individual leading a merely private life: it would mean that the same qualities would henceforth work themselves out within the framework of a new totality, expressing a higher state of integration. In a previous context we said that the aristocrat and the American are closer to each other than the former and the bourgeois. We have already given several reasons for this. But there is one more. The chief value of the aristocrat resides in his mere being; in so far he, too, is a Privatist; the wholeness of his existence means infinitely more to him than any office he may hold. This is precisely why every really superior man in history has belonged to his type, whether or not he was conscious of it and even though he pronounced "democratic" the very aristocratic virtues, as most Americans would have done up to a short time ago. To a great king, the people and the State always represented his private concern, he did not merely do his "duty" with some fraction of his being; he lived for them as the best of fathers live for their children. In the same way, the great lawgivers in history never belonged to the type of the modern judge or solicitor; their one concern was true justice; and no one who is personally neutral or impartial can ever be truly just; for being just means having the courage to side with what is more valuable; but then siding, again, can be the result only of a subjective and in so far a privatist attitude. The same applies even to the great military leaders, in case they were independent. Alexander the Great and Julius Cæsar were no specialists nor did they ever live and act on purely military premises: both felt the inner urge as whole men to fulfil a mission on earth. That no great work of thought or art has been created except out of an inner subjective impulsion, is obvious. And any relationship in harmony with God cannot possibly be other than a private one. Accordingly, there can be no doubt that, in principle, an inner state allowing for a purely personal and subjective life-centre is the higher as compared with a state characterized by the supremacy of partial projections and objectification. As a first stage in the course of differentiation, the rule of partial projections and objectification was both necessary and legitimate. The primordial wholeness, corresponding to the state of innocence, cannot persist as evolution proceeds. But here, as everywhere, after a certain degree of differentiation has been achieved, in integration alone can salvation be found. This new integration on a higher level is what Privatism in principle stands for.

This new integration and nothing else is the real inherent goal of American development. There are a great many defects inherent in American life; we have dealt with many of them and shall deal with many more in later chapters. But this much must be admitted—and I think that, as an aristocrat who in his childhood and youth lived that kind of feudal life which passed away in

Western Europe centuries ago, I have a right to judge—the same stress on the whole of life as such which in Europe one finds only among the aristocracy, is a typical American characteristic. One notices little of this in centres like Chicago and New York. But on the other hand—why do the men toil so much? In order to create a better foundation of life for their families. If one visits places resembling more the European country, then the predominance of private life becomes increasingly patent. Accordingly, politics cannot mean much; neither can law, nor can purely abstract considerations of any kind. At the present moment an ideal of Democracy wrongly understood (we will deal with this problem at length in the chapter "Democracy") makes for the predominance of private life in the trivial sense and a conception of the values of "Being" in terms not of value, but of mere material existence. But there is nothing inherent in the vital premises of Privatism to prevent a change for the better. Some day it will become clear to the national consciousness that man is not "whole" unless he is developed not only along the lines of ability and efficiency, but first of all as a cultural being. For that a true culture of Being can develop on privatist foundations can be conclusively proved by the sole consideration that all the deepest concerns of man *are* private by nature; whether it be his relationship to God, or love, or personal courage, or individual inventiveness. That is, all of them originate in the unique individual, who as such can never live himself out in a projection or partial objectification of any kind. This is why ultimately the value of all the different kinds of objectifications, army, or Church, or State, or law has always proved to be dependent upon the value of the individuals representing them.

The basis of all this possible progress is the shifting of the emphasis in national life from politics to economics. *Only* when there is less reason for strife, ill-will, and resentment; when there is more general comfort on earth; when the animal instincts of man have been turned into new channels ruled by the spirit—can a culture develop in which cultural values really are decisive as the last resort. But at this point we must qualify our bright picture of the future of mankind. It is, alas, out of the question that the whole human race should become americanized in the best meaning of a possible development of Privatism. Why not?—Let us remember what we have said before about the essential likeness between Americanism and Bolshevism. Their spirit is ultimately the same. But in the case of Americanism it expresses itself in the language of prosperity, whereas in that of Bolshevism it expresses itself in the language of poverty. Moreover, both Russia and America are socialistic; only the socialism of the former is a system of compulsion, and that of the latter a system of liberty. Our general conclusion was that Bolshevism and Americanism will counterpoise each other in the centuries to come, as did Catholicism and Protestantism during the age of the religious wars and the ensuing period. There will be as little question of a compromise between the former as there has been between the latter. The reason is the following: Russia would be only too glad to establish American conditions. I remember reading a poster on which was written: "Let us take the American organizations, animate them with the passionate spirit (*Doukh*) of Russia—and then there will be Heaven on Earth."

But a civilization based on the prosperity of all can develop and flourish only in a country which was practically empty when the industrial revolution began, so that it could grow in correlation with the increase of population. For this sole reason it is impossible to transfer the American solution of the economic and social problem into any over-populated part of the world, nor to any fully populated country with strong and vital pre-industrial traditions. There, only violence and compulsion could fundamentally alter the existing order of things and raise them to the height of the American system; again, violence and compulsion inevitably lead to a throttling of economic development which stands or falls with individual initiative. But there is one more reason why the American solution cannot be transferred. In order to "open up" or "claim" a continent as the Americans have done, a race must possess very strong original acquisitive instincts; it is not a question of material resources as such. Now in many peoples the acquisitive instincts are very weak indeed. The confiscation of property as practised by the Bolsheviks—it practically found no resistance—was possible only because no Russian, not even the most westernized among them, really believed in the right of property. The Russians never will toil for wealth, or even comfort, as the Americans do, simply because they do not care. And the same applies to all Asiatic children and nephews of Bolshevism with the one exception of the Chinese, who later on will probably gravitate toward the American solution of the problem of material life. Accordingly, everything leads us to believe that the case of America will remain unique. Her Privatism, such as it may appear after having reached perfection, will in all likelihood stand out as something essentially inimitable, as all previous great civilizations have done.

WE HAVE considered most of what is positive in the facts and possibilities of American Privatism. Now we must revert to its negative sides. These are obvious. They constitute the *raison d'être* of most justified criticism and complaint. But against the background of what has been said they will assume a new and more hopeful significance.

It has been rightly pointed out by an Italian philosopher, Luigi Valli, that the inner wealth and greatness of Europe are fundamentally due to the tension produced by the simultaneous co-operation of three entirely different and incompatible principles: Christian religion, the ethos of the warrior, and the bent for technical enterprise. Indeed, no common denominator is conceivable for these three principles, but each one of them expresses one of the fundamental positive tendencies in man. Europe's contribution to the human treasure-house of values is unique, because the interference of these tendencies, incompatible at bottom, made impossible both a one-sided development and a settling down in a final static state. Now there can be no doubt that present-day America is bent on economics alone with an insect-like exclusiveness. And this inevitably lowers the level of American life as compared with any life ruled by more than one ideal and, in particular, as compared with national lives ruled by spiritual ideals. The general reason to which this lowering of level is due has already been given in earlier chapters. All babyhood is materialistic; all youth is undifferentiated; and in this phase the prevalence of the animal ideal is necessary. However,

American one-sidedness is, nevertheless, a condition pregnant with evil, because of the *insect*-like differentiation it represents. Even here, to begin with, I will make a qualification in America's favour. Under no other conditions could general prosperity increase so rapidly; under no other conditions could the idea of social service so easily find an expression in general material comfort; under no other conditions could what has to be the ideal of the Geological Epoch of Man, namely, that all values should find their material remuneration, be so completely realized. It is only where matters are simplified as they are in America, owing to the fact that everything is viewed in terms of dollars and cents, that all money that is to be gained will really be earned and that money will achieve all that it is capable of achieving. But if there are good sides to the American one-sidedness I have described, the bad sides, unfortunately, predominate. If the rejuvenation of the white race which is taking place on American soil and the prevalence of the animal ideal make for uniformity and, therefore, spiritual poverty, this tendency is enhanced in a particularly dangerous sense by the fact that money is the one generally acknowledged denominator of all values. Wars are judged in terms of material losses and gains; churches in terms of the success they achieve, intellectual and spiritual values according to whether or not there is "money in them"—under these narrowing conditions, Privatism appears not as a state superior to that of the predominant Ethos of the warrior or statesman, but as a very inferior state. And if no other chain of causation, starting from different inner tendencies and ideals, interferes, matters must go from bad to worse, for every development has a logic and a momentum of its own. Nor are the drawbacks and dangers inherent in American Privatism exhausted when we mention those inherent in the habit of judging everything in terms of dollars and cents. If Privatism means that life's primary concern is the humdrum bread-and-butter question, it is just as pernicious. In this case, it is not wealth which provides the standard, but happiness, or comfort, or health, or likeableness, or popularity, or peace understood as the lack of all disagreeable tensions. Now all human progress depends on the capacity of bearing the lower kinds of tensions and of translating them into tensions of a higher order. If private life in the vulgar and trivial sense of the word with its inherent aims and goals provides the standard of value—how can inner progress, directed by spiritual as opposed to animal ideals, find encouragement? Other circumstances contribute toward this natural result of Privatism narrowly understood—circumstances to which we have already drawn attention or shall draw attention in later chapters: America's basic socialism, allowing the average with its needs to take the lead; the idea that any man is as good as any other, which practically amounts to the denial of all spiritual values—for men are equal only as far as their bodies and the latter's requirements go; further, the quality of youthfulness and the exaggerated estimation of the child; the prevailing animal ideal; predominating woman with her natural over-valuation of the well-being of the race as such; last but not least, American Moralism.

Even this is not all that can be said against Privatism as it stands out today. If business continues to mean practically everything to a great majority, then private life will forfeit all importance and all power in favor of "things." Then the law of *Enantiodromia*, of the reversion into the opposite, will set in. It has already set in in one very remarkable respect which may easily become symbolical and symptomatic for the whole of American life. The nation which today attributes the highest value to private life, carries on an existence of the most reckless and shameless publicity. There is nothing in America that may not be published. The significance of this phenomenon can best be realized by a comparison with English conditions. The English are an essentially political nation. Accordingly, the idea of the Forum and its materializations plays a predominant part. But since they do so in the right relationship to the whole of life, the very emphasis laid on public life guarantees more privacy to what is essentially private, than can be found in any other country. In the United States there is no public life acknowledged as such. But for that very reason, nothing is really private.

Yes, present-day American Privatism is not at all exemplary. And yet, with all its disadvantages, it is pregnant with a future more positive than any other State on earth I know of. All modern ideals of humanity, without a single exception, can be realized only on its basis; even the ideal incarnated in the League of Nations, even that reform of Law all progressive countries are working at—a reform the ideological premise of which is that the inner meaning of an action is more important than what it means in any abstract or formal scheme of things. Politics *have* to become unessential, war *must* be generally thought of as a disgrace, if the principle of solidarity as opposed to that of the struggle for existence is to predominate among men, if all are to be able to lead a decent and dignified life, if cultural values are to rule supreme and at the same time to become the privilege of every human being. Nor is this all: if spiritual life is to predominate, then individual life must mean more than collective life—and the first premise for this is that private life should mean more than official life; for all public life has a social basis.

It will no doubt take the United States a considerable time to disentangle themselves from the past difficulties which made for deterioration, among which their predominating economic position, due to post-war developments, is the most serious one. And it must even be admitted that all we stated in the last paragraph sounds more than serious: it sounds alarming. But I trust that Providence will bless the United States with the difficulties they stand in need of in order to achieve perfection in their own lines. No nation—no more than any individual—ever became great without undergoing periods of severe trial. And owing to the singular prosperity prevailing today in America, she stands in need of correspondingly great difficulties in order to outgrow or burst that shell of narrowness which is the inevitable fate of the satiated. For it is him and not the wealthy man as such that Christ cursed. Now the hard times that are necessary are sure to come. Up to the present Privatism was an exclusively American outlook; it was all very well as long as America kept to herself. But as a result of the World War she has become the greatest and richest power on earth. Now she applies her peculiar point of view to other nations. She looks on her loans to nations in exactly the same light that she looks on loans to business-concerns. She treats war-subsidies as though they were ordinary loans. But no other nation thinks that way. Most nations are as yet primarily political or warlike—the repudiation of a debt means nothing to them as compared with loss of independence or of self-respect. On the other hand, most other nations being poor and the United States being anxious to invest their money, it is inevitable that the former will more and more become the debtors of the latter. This state of things is bound to lead to conflicts, all the more so as no means of defence has been thought out as yet against financial oppression and invasion. Out of these conflicts, in this technical age, the United States might easily come off victorious without any inward gain, were it not for one circumstance which is, on the one hand, the vulnerable point of the present American Privatism, but, on the other, stands as the best guaranty of a better future. The idea of America today is not only that a high standard of living should be the privilege of all, but that there should be no low work to perform. Now this is contrary to the cosmic order. However much the general standard may be raised, however great the amount of labour of which machines may relieve man—there will always be *all* kinds of work to perform. Even today the current prejudice actually leads to the result that most educated Americans must themselves spend considerable time on household work which in all other parts of the world is done by certain classes only, very few representatives of which are really fit for other duties. Thus, in America today the real, though paradoxical result of the prevalent high standard of living is a lowering of the general standard—only the very richest can enjoy as much leisure as all those men and women, who are not "professionals" of manual work still do in the Old World. That the Americans do not see that leisure and the possibility of gratifying individual tastes mean much more than "big money" which cannot buy these privileges, is one of the most interesting cases of prejudice-born blindness I know of. This lowering of the general standard cannot help making for a certain convergence of the general outlook of the American type with that of the European small man who cannot see beyond the humdrum bread-and-butter issue; only think of President Coolidge's proclaimed personal ideal of owning a small shop at a street-corner in a good neighbourhood. . . . But it is not this aspect of the problem which concerns us here. We are dealing with the dangers inherent in America's position from our point of view. The fact is that America can maintain her own present standard within a closely inter-connected humanity only if the whole American nation attains a position more privileged than any single caste or class ever enjoyed on earth. But that is impossible. For in order to achieve this result many wars would have to be fought, which would in any case destroy all existing standards of security. Then, the conquering and enslaving of other peoples means a contradiction to all the ideals alive in the American heart. But even apart from this—as soon as a desire for culture awakes in wider circles, the present state will seem intolerable to the nation as such. A prosperity rendering impossible all individual variation would finally not only be a "disgruntled prosperity"—which it already is today in the eyes of most Americans capable of cultural aspirations—it would be resented as the worst of slaveries. And not only a desire for culture would soon have the effect of exploding present prosperity—*the same will soon be the effect of idealism of any kind.* A prominent American is reported to have said: "Economy is idealism in its most practical form." I do not contest the possibility of such "idealism" being the most successful along economic lines, but it certainly leaves all true ideal aspiration unsatisfied. Every development has its own logic and its own momentum, practically independent of individual men, unless they are very great. Thus, the present kind of narrow Privatism is bound to become ever more narrow if nothing interferes with the process. . . . But, as we have shown, fortunately it is almost certain that everything *will* soon interfere with it. In consequence, everything also leads one to hope that, after many struggles and many disillusions, to be sure, the American nation *will* find its way out of its present narrowness into that width and broadness in all respects which alone accords with the spirit of the American continent.

## *The Overrated Child*

WHEN asked why I do not dance, I sometimes answer: I am not yet sixty. It is, indeed, highly amusing for me to watch the same men, or types of men, whom a quarter of a century ago I used to consider with a feeling of awe as paragons of poise and gravity do their utmost today to be taken for boys. And at bottom they *are* boys. What a tremendous power lies in human imagination! Man actually becomes what he wishes to be. . . .

Now there can be no possible objection to the disappearance of the signs of senile decrepitude; in this respect I even hope for a radical change for the better as a result of the discoveries of the power of the endocrines put to intelligent use. But there is a great deal to say against any kind of shortening of human life, and the shortening in the psychological sense is not the least objectionable of the various methods of achieving this result. Man's life really is a melody. No period of life ever returns as it was. Each phrase of the melody has advantages and beauties of its own which are irrecoverable. Accordingly, if the type of the venerable octogenarian disappears, this means an absolute loss, for there are intrinsic values of human life which this stage alone can incarnate to perfection. The angelic beauty of childhood is due physiologically to the fact that certain endocrines do not play as yet any part in the child's organism. In the same way, the surcease of their activity only gives the spirit a complete chance of living according to its own laws. For the rhythm of spiritual life is different from that of the body; it continues growing as physical life declines.

What I have said of childhood and old age applies, *mutatis mutandis,* to all stages of life. And the development and perfection of each largely depend on what man or woman thinks about it, and on the inner attitude they assume toward it. In those early days when the grey-haired dancers of today appeared full of poise and gravity, childhood and youth were not valued highly enough; this led to the result that the young did not develop and make use of all the qualities of youth. That this appraisal of the situation is correct is being demonstrated by the counter-proof provided by our own days: within the memory of no living man has the physical standard of the young been anything like as high as it is today. This can be due only to the high appreciation of the qualities of youth; and very likely the same accounts for the exceeding beauty of the men of the Greek classic period. As opposed to this, the young ones of thirty years ago did not develop this virtual beauty because they always looked forward to being mature; and this, in its turn, led to a voluntary exaggeration of the symptoms of maturity. Even men of thirty were staid and grave then and took pride in their heaviness; the women almost gloried in the early loss of their figure and did all they could—by wearing bonnets and the like—to deprive their faces of all seductive charm. How long did life under these circumstances really last? No more, in the average, than thirty years, because a life fully assented to and, therefore, really lived, only began after the age of thirty. In post-war Europe youth alone counts; not the earliest youth, though; but a youth fully developed, both sexually and intellectually mature and conscious, with the emphasis placed on intellectual wide-awakeness or sophistication; a youth, therefore, in which nothing is left of the stage of the bud. But this stage corresponds to the natural stage of about thirty. Accordingly, even the youngest girls of this generation are, psychologically speaking, thirty. And since life beyond the age of forty is no longer associated with any values, human life really lasts, as far as its differentiated contents are concerned, only ten years; that is to say, about as long as the life of a dog.

In the United States the case is different. There also no life beyond the age of forty-five is inwardly assented to; the girls are as knowing as they can be. But the nation does not really idealize youth, the exclusive value of which is taken for granted; it idealizes the child. America is fundamentally the land of the overrated child. This, then, is the deepest reason of that infantilism one so often observes in grown-up Americans. We found that rejuvenation to thc degree of primitiveness is a fundamental trait of the nation as stands out today; to that extent infantilism can be considered as a necessary stage of development. But there is another side to the question. Whatever belongs to the domain of psychology is subject to the influence of man's thoughts. If the American is infantile as a result of a natural process, he will soon grow out of it because childhood never lasts long. If, however, over and above this, he idealizes this perpetual childhood, then he runs the risk of never growing up. The place or spot within his organism upon which man personally lays the emphasis is finally determined. For the soul is ultimately what I call a sense-connexion; significance creates the facts everywhere.

And it even can perpetuate normally short-lived stages, because the functions corresponding to the various periods of the melody of life never really die; in the depths of the octogenarian even the babe survives; for this very reason old age so often represents a second childhood.

The outcome of all these facts is the following: if man idealizes childhood to the exclusion of all other periods of life, he will remain a child to the end of his days. If he idealizes maturity as one-sidedly, then the qualities of the full-grown man or woman will predominate and reach their highest development—but at the expense of the other stages of life. If the wisdom of old age is most highly valued, then the whole civilization in question will appear essentially old; for all really acknowledged values will in this case be dependent for their realization on the physiological state of old age. This being so, I think it necessary, after having examined the natural side of America's rejuvenation, to consider it as subject to man's creative freedom. For if the American nation continues to overrate the child in the way it does today, there really is a danger that it will never grow up. Then, owing to the polar quality of life, it will develop senile characteristics before having become mature. For the essence of youth is that it soon passes away; and there are no cosmetics which can be applied to nations.

IN ORDER to get the right start, let us recall what was said about youthful idealism: it is essentially an idealism without an object, because the supposed-to-be object really only means a projection of the inner urge. For this reason the objectified ideals of youth can never be taken seriously if they are meant to represent more than ideals for the young. But in the same sense youth is, generally speaking, the most uninteresting phase in human life. The period of youthful *Sturm und Drang* which older people are so apt to relate to spiritual values is, for the most part, a result of typical organic processes; and youth's ambition, too, is a natural physiological phenomenon. It is likewise the result of physiological and, therefore, unalterable causes, that its interest in problems belongs more to the intellect alone, reflected in emotions and feelings, than to the *whole* personality; youth is never psychologically integrated; the various constituents of the soul play almost independent parts. Accordingly, its interest in problems is always a mental and not a vital interest. This is why the idealist is generally considered as unpractical and lacking in common sense: his ideals are not correlated to the other functions of his psychic organism. This also explains why the idealist usually is a hopeless radical: lacking the above-mentioned correlation, there is nothing to prevent his thoughts from following their own laws only, and the laws of abstract thought are purely logical; the pragmatic test does not apply to them.

Accordingly, a young person can be rightly judged only when considered as a being in the state of *development.* It follows that the real and basic value of youth lies in its plasticity as such and that only this plasticity can provide a true standard of value. It has nothing to do with any kind of contents. It follows, further, that youth loses not only its chief, but its one asset, if it loses its plasticity. In order to see what this means, let us have a look first at German conditions. As a consequence of the World War, German youth had to an extraordinary degree lost its plasticity. About the year 1923 a tremendous percentage of the university students in particular appeared to have definitely fixed their inner attitude—no matter whether on the conservative or on the radical side—in a way which is normal and right only for men of forty. Hence that fanatic clinging to traditions of every kind, and the older these traditions, the better, even up to the cult of Wotan; hence, on the other hand, the passionate adherence to futuristic dogmatisms like orthodox Marxism or Bolshevism. Thus these youths prematurely grew psychologically rigid. It is easy enough to explain this phenomenon. The shocks and disappointments of the War and its aftermath were more than the young organism could bear. In order to save itself, it pushed aside all possibility of original inner experience (*Erlebnis*) and tried to find a support in something which was secure, stable, and immutable; it wanted psychological security at any cost, and therefore in principle, any kind of security would do. But the same chain of causes also partly explains the well-known phenomena of demoralization. Even where it has crystallized into a state of rigidity, youth is young still. Accordingly, wherever some kind of inner attitude prevents the normal exercise of its effervescent sap and strength, these seek possibilities of expression elsewhere; for psychological reasons this "elsewhere" can in this case only be the antipole of rigidity and fixedness; that is, anarchy and whatever is hostile to laws. The demoralization of German youth, as far as it exists, is, therefore, only natural. But now let us revert to American conditions. American youth has not lost its plasticity on account of causes which temporarily robbed part of the German youth of this quality. But it has for another and a more serious cause: it has in a great measure lost its plasticity *owing to the prevalent static ideal of youth.* Youth is thought of as something permanent (therefore, to be made permanent by every possible means, however artificial). This must inevitably lead to the suppression of its dynamic, the aspiring and expanding quality. If youth really is to express itself according to its inherent laws and thus to fulfil its meaning, it must look forward and beyond itself; all its ideals must lie in the future only; it must, for that very reason, look forward to maturity and old age. For youth is nothing if not the stage of irresistible growth in all respects. And as soon as a movement comes to a stop it is therewith at its end.

This seems obvious. Yet there can be no doubt that the American ideal of youth is a static ideal. Now how is it possible that something essentially dynamic should become static? It is possible in this case because of the ruling ideal of childhood. For childhood actually is, in one sense at least, a static stage; a child is a child with specific childish qualities which remain essentially the same as long as childhood lasts. Both body and soul evidently grow, but they do so unconsciously and without voluntary effort. During this period the conscious dwells in a static state of paradisiac quality; the child plays, it does not work; it dreams and imagines, but it does not think. It has no set purposes. Now any kind of dynamic life must have in view an aim or goal. Accordingly, when the dynamic life first sets in, it does so in an exaggerated manner; hence the reckless radicalism of the first idealism of the young. But a child has no ideals. It does not live in the dimension of time at all. This must needs express itself in the empiric sphere as statism. This, then, explains the peculiar quality of American youthfulness. The whole of America confessing essentially the ideal of childhood, it thinks of youth as a permanent static state. And it is this idea which gives to its youthfulness its dangerous infantile quality.

Let us here call to mind some of the phenomena described in previous chapters. The ideal of social life in America is embodied in the kindergarten. The feeling for differences, for shades, does not exist; everything is either black or white. Nor is there any appreciation of mental and spiritual values. The ideals of likeableness, of a good time, of "popularity" in the kindergarten-sense, that is apart from all intrinsic value, predominate. So does the health-ideal. So does the ideal of conformity to social standards as opposed to the ideal of individual perfection. But there are many other phenomena of the same general significance, of which I shall mention only the most important here. There is no type of human being intellectually so passive as the American. He can "take in" as the desert sand absorbs water; in the worst of cases, he "takes in" like a sieve. This very fortunately applies to most of his newspaper reading; were it otherwise, its quantity would simply mean a sort of mental capital punishment. But the American usually absorbs as a child does. The latter absorbs with absolute passivity, because, on the one hand, the active aspect of spirit is yet undeveloped, and on the other, the state of the nervous system does not as yet allow of concentration. It is, therefore, a question of a lack of initiative, and at the same time of extreme suggestibility and physical weakness. Now there certainly are, expressed as percentage, as many people in the United States as there are elsewhere who *should* be capable of a permanent attitude of mental originality, initiative, and concentration as opposed to passivity—and this everywhere, not only on specialized lines; for of the latter not only the child, but the animal even is capable. But the general kindergarten atmosphere of the United States discourages their attempts to develop as they might. In order to remain in tune with their fellow men, even the best minds, with rare exceptions, keep to the general childish attitude, and this inevitably induces a corresponding process of retrogression in the brain. Very few Americans are capable of intensive concentration, except along specialized lines, and these lines are generally executive, in what Americans call enterprise and promotion; that is, lines which require the least amount of mental effort. If they cling to facts and things, to the point of having to touch them before they believe in their existence, this is chiefly due to the incapacity, typical of the child's mind, to remember and operate with abstractions. This also explains why Americans have such a cordial dislike for irony, wit, and satire. Here the French are their very antipodes. Langdon Mitchell writes (in his excellent book, *Understanding America*): "The Latin laughs and may be said to be gay, or appear gay, in the face of a clear and brief intellectual statement of some moral or other incongruity. He is moved to what we suppose is mirth by some discrepancy between the ideal and the fact, which the intellect perceives and makes plain; that is, wit makes him gay. Wit seldom makes *us* gay; rather, when the penetrative rational faculty throws its cold, dazzling intellectual light on some unacknowledged incongruity between the ideal and the actual, between what ought to be and what is, the American becomes restless and melancholy. It disappoints him. It is pessimistic. It ought not be that way; and he sulks." This is exactly the way every child's mind reacts all over the world. Salvador de Madariaga, that most brilliant of living

Spaniards, writes to the same effect (in *Harper's Magazine*, July, 1928): "Americans are direct, frank, and spontaneous like children. They want to know, because they are curious, not because they seek some advantage from the information they are asking. They just want to know. They are hungry and thirsty for information —facts, stories. But they dislike thought, as wholesome, healthy children do. Knowledge, yes. But principles and theories are quite another matter. Thoughts are dangerous things. God knows where they might lead. That is the way people turn radical, and once boys began to be radicals, the whole nursery would be agog, and the boys divided for good, instead of just for a game of politics, as they are divided now into Republicans and Democrats with not a pin to choose between them; but, oh! such fierce quarrels and such agitation and shouting and organizing and playing at politics and denouncing this and the other in dead earnest and choosing one particular lad and turning him into a hero, either because he speaks well or because he is silent, or because he is wet or maybe for being dry, or for descending from one of the masts of the *Mayflower*, or perhaps for being a self-made man—just some one to become a hero and a great man; and once chosen, they will work for him and shout for him and fight for him and die for him and forget all about him, while he is safely seated in his stately chair and the fun of the fight is over." To conclude, one more quotation from Langdon Mitchell on Americans: "What Americans need today is not what they already in such large measure possess, generous warm feelings, Christian kindness, the fraternal attitude to others. Of all the peoples of which I have any personal knowledge, we have the most of these expansive feelings, and it is a cause for just pride that we have them. In this respect our people are great and noble. But what we need, and need sorely, is to seek truer knowledge. And, too, we need the light of reason." The delightful human qualities of the Americans are partly due to their persistent childhood. But a nation can no more with safety remain a child among grown-ups than a child can safely handle its own fortune in Wall Street; if it happens to be more powerful than the grown-ups, then this must breed disaster for all concerned. The American situation is something very much like this. And it is chiefly due to the underlying idealization of the childish state as a static state which is meant to last.

Now let my readers face what follows squarely: however delightful childhood may be, it is not only unpractical to remain a child among grown-ups—*there are no spiritual values whatsoever attached to it.* This is the decisive point. Children are animals, as far as their developed conscious reaches. This is the reason why they have to be directed from without by such as are themselves inspired by spiritual values. Childhood is indeed the normal beginning of life. But it should not last a second longer than is absolutely necessary. For what Jesus meant when glorifying the children was not their immaturity: he meant their original creativeness as opposed to rigidity. This is indeed always needful. But when childhood as a phase of physical development has been completed, it is normal that original creativeness should manifest itself as originality of the mind. Then, bodily growth having ceased, mental and spiritual growth, which means pure dynamism and essential striving, should set in, as evidenced by the typical phase of youthful idealism. Then all statism should be radically abandoned, both as a fact and as an ideal. Whoever is still a child when the age of puberty is past is simply infantile, and infantilism is a real defect.

WHAT can be done to help America grow beyond its present state as quickly as possible? Here, as in all other cases, *understanding* alone can aid. First and foremost, it should be realized in what sense education in the United States is wrong; not only in regard to details and facts, but in principle.

The fundamental mistake is the American belief that the kindergarten is a better educator than the family. On the basis of what has preceded this can be conclusively proved in a single sentence: the American belief in question implies a fundamental mistake because the kindergarten is chiefly responsible for the persistence of the ideal of childhood as a static state, never to be outgrown. In the kindergarten the child's mind rules supreme. If every child adapts itself to it with such amazing ease, it is due to the fact that the kindergarten is the kind of social life which exactly corresponds to its primordial instincts. Though every baby seems at first a preposterous egoist, it yet has no ego. Its egoism simply means that the instinct of self-preservation rules supreme in the beginning. And it is quite right that it should do so, for in that first phase of its existence *others* have to take complete care of it, and its one business is to show them what it wants. The instinct of self-preservation obviously lasts through life. But the first kind of consciousness which can be called psychological, as opposed to physical or physiological, is not a self-consciousness, but a vague something out of which an articulated group-consciousness is more easily evolved than an individual consciousness which means more than a persistence of infantile egoism—because the latter presupposes a degree of differentiation not yet possible in a child. This explains why in the history of mankind we find articulated and well-governed groups at a much earlier date than we find individualities. It is, therefore, essentially easy to socialize children. If it seems difficult (the perfect kindergarten is indeed a very recent invention) it is because the case is too simple on the one hand, and on the other, too different from that of grown-up people. The taming of lions, too, is difficult, not because the task is complicated, but because it is too simple. Now the socialization of man is indeed very necessary. If he wishes to attain perfection man as opposed to animals has to learn, to be educated up to what he should be; in his case, it is not nature which completes the process of growth. Accordingly, left to itself, infantile egoism can very well persist, with the result that the individual suffers as much as the group, not only outwardly, but inwardly as well, because he remains out of harmony with himself. The socialization of the child is indeed most necessary. It even represents the chief value of education, of which I shall have more to say in the next chapter. But on the other hand, the chapter "Socialism" led us to the recognition that in regard to the social tendencies, those tendencies which make for a fully differentiated individual are independent entities. They are not identical with the instinct of self-preservation which accounts for the egoism of the baby; they are as much above the latter as are the social tendencies. Therefore, the development toward *individuality* cannot possibly be furthered by socialization. This explains why most truly great men have either been failures or, at least, not conspicuous successes at school. This also explains why the best minds of individualistic Europe begin to agree that, owing to over-education, man is over-socialized today, and that it is here that the real trouble lies, not in the opposite direction: modern man is inferior and not superior, as a "whole" individuality to most of his ancestors considered as types. Now America is a fundamentally socialistic country, and this is not likely to change; on the contrary, her basic socialism is almost certain to assert itself more strongly from year to year. Therefore, kindergarten and school will in all probability always mean more in the United States than they do, and ever will, in individualistic countries. But there is a limit to everything. If a system leads to predominant infantilism, then there must be something wrong with it.

The truth of the matter seems to me to be the following. The idealization of the child leads to the result that the adaptation to the kindergarten remains the ideal of all later life. And this is all the more so since the impersonality of what may be called "Life's Earnestness" in the United States makes every grown-up there subconsciously long more for the child's paradise than anywhere else in the world. The law of business rules supreme in the American world of grown-ups. It is more pure in its specific quality there than anywhere else. It specializes more than anywhere else on what can be mechanized and standardized. It gives less scope than anywhere else for the development of an all-round personality. This cannot help making, on the one hand, for a retrogression of the human side (for the same reason Americans are so often mawkishly sentimental—sentimentalism means the compensation of arid intellectualism by primitive emotionalism); and on the other hand, it makes for an all the more pronounced idealization of the purely and simply human, the most complete expression of which is the child. Thus all later life is really ruled from within by the kindergarten-ideal. Every girl wants first of all to be "popular"; the quality of the popularity desired was predetermined by the kindergarten. The same applies to the boys. What does it really mean, that "normalcy" is most highly valued at schools and universities, that the "highbrow" is disapproved of, and that each institution glories in the fact of its being more "democratic" than any other (whatever the facts may be)? It simply means that a boy should be *likeable* first of all. But a man can be a general favorite only in two cases: either if he is a saint or else if he is quite commonplace, without any signs of superiority of any kind. For the American fondness for likeableness and popularity does emphatically not care for values. It has a prejudice against anything of the sort; for any consideration of value makes for differentiation and this is the one thing a kindergarten cannot tolerate.

And now we have reached the practical issue in question. The inordinate influence of the kindergarten is due to the fact *that in America home life is generally little valued or neglected or misunderstood to the extent that it appears incapable of creating the values it should create.* To be sure, home life is to a great extent little thought of because it is a case of "sour grapes"—housing and other conditions making it almost impossible for the majority to lead a home life as it should be led. Thus, the best which parents not over-wealthy can do to comfort themselves is to believe that what necessity compels them to do is really the best from every point of view. But to a very considerable degree home life is so little valued because it does not develop the social side in man. Certainly it does not. *But precisely in this lies its intrinsic value.* If kindergarten and school represent the best of social influences, the home, or rather the right kind of home, alone develops the individual tendencies and thus lays the foundation for true personality. The influence of the kindergarten leads to nothing but socialization. The one individual impulse which it does not discourage is that of competition and, accordingly, this appears strongly developed in American life. But competition, too, belongs to social as opposed to individual life proper; the latter has no primal relationship to fellow man, it is unique in its essence. Accordingly, the typical so-called successful men in America are not personalities but social creatures, whose social life is based on competition as opposed to a static order as the German socialists would have it, who do not want the efficient worker to be better paid than the inefficient (a desire chiefly inspired by envy and jealousy and really due to an under-development of the primal social impulses). The general result is that in the typical product of American education the social qualities alone are fully valued. And since this state of balance between the social and the individual tendencies is normal only in early childhood, the picture which results from the various lines we have drawn and the shades of color with which we have touched it must needs be one of *a socialism of an essentially childish quality.*

American social life with its merriment and good-nature and brightness and playfulness is very delightful for that very reason. But for the same reason it cannot possibly be creative nor appreciative of values. A kindergarten is a paradise; and in paradise there was no question of good or evil—the question of value can arise only on the basis of a differentiation between these two. The same also accounts for the unique quality of modern American "immorality." Its directness and shamelessness and self-understood matter-of-factness, too, correspond to what one calls childish innocence. There is no question of responsibility, none of spiritual values, no understanding of the significance of inhibitions and of tensions borne for the sake of realizing spiritual values. The children want to get rid of the silly rules the grown-ups imposed upon them; they want at last to have a holiday. After my New York lecture on the subject whether freer morals would make for richer souls, a very intelligent American wrote to me:

Business men do not bother about morals. The matter is a fight between women on the one side and Puritans—mostly ministers—on the other. Were it not for the presence of policemen, the clergymen would soon be disposed of. But the policeman protects the clergyman, who in turn tries to protect morals. For some reason or other, however, the clergyman is not quick enough; by the time he protested against women exhibiting their ankles, the women had their skirts above their knees; and when the clergyman will protest against the knees, God knows where the women will have their skirts, if they will have any. . . . I can assure you that most of the women of your audience were there in the expectation of hearing from you of another good reason or two enabling them to dispose of whatever vestige, impression, or memory of morals might still be left in this country. If you had said to them: "Morals? Fiddlesticks! There is no such animal: It's all humbug of old Europe's stupidity. Do not bother about it and have all the good time you can get"—you would have made a hit and become the ladies' hero (this accounts, by the way, for the vogue of that most candid of writers on sexual matters, Mrs. Bertrand Russell). But you spoke of "freer morals" after rising to a higher plane of life by a long cultural training. That was too much for the ladies. They simply did not like that; a few left as soon as they realized that they were not getting what they wanted, and others commented adversely.

I think what the gentleman wrote is true of a considerable percentage of American women. Only he did not realize the real significance of the case. I mean that it is really a question not of depravity, but of childish innocence resenting the fetters imposed by grown-ups "who have no idea." That this is the only right way to look at the matter seems to me to be finally proved by the evidence of the man who knows and understands the modern youth of America so well that he involuntarily thinks and judges according to its standards; I am thinking, of course, of Judge Lindsey. His stories generally sound like nursery tales; for instance: Mildred's college-sisters found it immoral that she had sexual intercourse with boys while suffering from a venereal disease; and they sent a deputation to the Judge asking him to stop it. Or: Maud said that she would never go with Jack again because he was so silly that—think of it—*she* had to go to the drug store and get the contraceptives from the soda-clerk. And these stories, as often as not, end like fairy tales. For instance: And then Millicent had a baby which she could keep (after having disposed of one or two others for the benefit of childless couples), and she was happy with her husband ever after.—Exactly the same applies to all sides of American social life. Even the formidable tendency of American clubwomen to pass radical resolutions beyond appeal on all and sundry issues and the urge which impels them (and personally I am most grateful for it) to continue listening to lectures for many hours a day, from their college years up to the time they are great-grandmothers, has its chief roots in the foregoing.

I SAID that only understanding can help to overcome an unsatisfactory state consolidated by habit. I said also that only a strengthening and improvement of the home influence can counteract that of the kindergarten which perpetuates childish socialism. Let us then consider, before we proceed, what the influence of father and mother really means.

In his essay "Marriage and Self-development" in the *Book of Marriage* Alphonse Maeder has shown that the external relationship between husband and wife means the projection in the form of symbols of two complementary poles in man, inherent in every human being, and that marriage can frequently lead to the integration of self because the individual, whether husband or wife, draws the projection back into himself and by its means develops into a complete soul. Psycho-analysis has long ago discovered that father and mother represent the symbols of even more highly important poles within man's soul. But it has not as yet drawn one very important conclusion from its recognitions. It is the following. Man always achieves the integration of his self by means of projections; thus the artist achieves his by means of his works; thus, generally speaking, striving man does so by means of his ideal. Now the state of the child is essentially characterized by the fact that *here all determinant centres lie outside the sphere of its ego.* This is obviously the case as long as the child is in the mother's womb, and it is so later in the sense of its standing in need of guidance. But it is also true in the sense that father and mother really *are* for the child what purely individual functions effect in later years. The personality of the child cannot be detached from its connexion with the parents without a violent wrench. This is the reason why the earliest childish experiences are of such decisive importance. Herein lies the danger of any impressions received from the parents which distort or destroy the true vital connexion: for what seems to be external experience, in reality means a process in the child's own inner being. This being so, we have to ask: what attitude should father and mother adopt toward it, in order that its soul should become capable of the highest perfection? The answer can only be the following: *the mother should embody the principle of intimacy, and the father should represent that of distance;* for it is these two principles which they embody by nature. For the little child the mother "is" its own inner cohesion; and the father "is" its own superiority over the sphere of its animal nature.

I need hardly say anything about the task of the mother, for its meaning is obvious. She should be as close to the child as she possibly can; here the mother's womb remains the symbol for all stages of life. And then mothers so rarely fail, in the first years of a child's life, that there can be no question of a general problem here; in those periods in which woman exclusively fulfils the will of nature she is so close to the latter that irresistible instinct compels her to do the right thing. But the father's task requires a detailed explanation. It is generally said today that the authoritative attitude of the father has led itself *ad absurdum*. So it has. Not, however, because its significance was wrong; its meaning has stood the test of thousands of years. It has led itself *ad absurdum* because the traditional embodiment of this meaning no longer corresponds to modern psychological conditions. Distance must be maintained. But there is another and a better way of keeping people at a distance than that of the despot. To posit the problem in the right way from the outset: the greatest distance is not created by harshness—on the contrary, rough manners are always an expression of subconscious familiarity—it is created by courtesy. This is the reason why the peoples which are essentially bent on establishing universal equality so strongly resent polite forms. I will begin by giving two examples taken from Europe. That it is only the traditional relationship of distance, not corresponding to the modern psychological adjustment, and not distance kept as such which causes the trouble, is proved by the counter-evidence provided by those who understand their fatherhood as a function of intimacy. There are psycho-analysts who from the very beginning analyse their children and let themselves be analysed by them almost from the outset: the result is that these children lack steadiness to an unparalleled degree; they do not know how to keep their distance with regard to anybody or anything; they are incapable of self-guidance—and the only possible future open to them is eventually to become psycho-analysts themselves. Another instance is provided by the Austrian aristocracy, in which, as far as I know, the "happiest" of all family lives in the world is the rule, inasmuch as they suffer the least amount of tensions. This is due, in the first instance, to the fact that the fathers adopt something like the attitude of the mother toward their children. The products of this kind of education have all the feminine, but hardly any of the masculine virtues; they are incapable of shaping their own destiny. There is no class in the world which, considering its general endowments, has produced so small a number of important men, for the Austrian aristocrat as a type is by no means lacking in talents; on the contrary, he is generally mentally refined and, more often than not, highly gifted; but he lacks initiative and backbone.—And now let us turn to America. Is there more of the father or more of the mother about the American father? Nothing strikes the European observer more forcibly than the fact that it is so often the man who, on Sundays or holidays, looks after the children, while the spectacled mother is reading her books. Nor does he often find children who respect their father except as they would a more experienced playmate. American men very often are go-getters. But they very seldom are what they themselves call "he-men." They are a decidedly humble sort of folks. They are essentially infantile; that is, they lack precisely those qualities which make a man, as opposed to the child, which is intrinsically neither male nor female, but something particular of its own. Finally, their mother-complex is so strong that it really means a fusion with what should normally be the father-complex. The result is that American men very seldom bear comparison, as far as virility is concerned, with the Englishman—that most virile of the Whites.

Now is this really due to an irrational education? It is. The real meaning of the principles of intimacy and cohesion ruling all psychic life is this: that organic cohesion rests upon the principle of intimacy, whereas tension rests on that of distance; and it is thanks to tension only that kinetic energy is developed. Without tension there is not only no productivity, but no governing of the whole organism from one determinate centre. A human being is a man as opposed to a woman in her primeval state to the exact extent that in his psyche the democratic republic of cohesion is subjected to a hierarchy of ruling spiritual forces. Moreover, he is a man, as opposed to a child, to exactly the same extent; in this connexion, the relationship between the man and the child is this, that what originally appears as the masculine sex-character is sublimated into the spiritual principle as such in the course of development; therefore, it is quite natural that woman, as she develops, should grow masculine in the same sense. In so far as within the woman and the child the principle of cohesion is originally predominant, both are very close to each other (although we shall see later that woman as opposed to man never really is a child); and this explains why women and children, and not men and children, understand one another best. The father symbolizes the spiritual principle within the child; he *is* the spiritual principle in the form of a projection. Hence we can easily understand the practical rôle the father should play in the educational scheme. The centres of relationship of the child's own masculine and feminine principles are externalized in the persons of father and mother. Accordingly, the child can develop superiority over its own animal nature exactly to the extent that the father knows how to keep it at the right distance; and that means: to that extent precisely can the spiritual principle become determinant in man. For it is not a question of intellect or specialized initiative—of which woman is just as capable as man—but the embodiment of spirit in the sense of the word becoming flesh; of the centring in the spirit of the whole of life; of an original life built on the foundation of a consciousness of value as opposed to the qualities of the undifferentiated Eros. On the other hand, the distance kept by the father naturally demands a correlative intimacy on the part of the mother; for the mother is the symbolic embodiment of the child's *own* cohesion; this explains why disappointment with regard to the mother, without a single exception, entails serious inner deformations. But I will not here insist on the part the mother has to play, the significance of which is hardly ever misunderstood. Let us keep to the case of the father. The instances of the psycho-analyst and the Austrian aristocrat as well as that of the American have shown us the pernicious consequences resulting from the father's taking upon himself the rôle of the mother. On the other hand, it is typical that the strongest men in history emerged in ages in which the father was authoritative; thus America, too, in the great age of Puritanism was a country of essentially strong men. In the same sense, almost all the important men of all ages originated from families in which there was not Austrian harmony, but a strong state of tension of some kind; whether because the father was a harsh man (Frederic William I of Prussia in his relation to Frederic the Great) or that the mother embodied the masculine principle (Laetitia in relation to Napoleon), or else that a state of tension between the parents induced a corresponding state of tension in the child's soul. What we have just said may meet with the objection that an unhappy family life more often than not leads to pathological states. I certainly do not advocate these: though as a rule they have a creative influence on highly gifted personalities, they invariably have the contrary effect in the case of ordinary children. I mentioned the extreme case of the singularly gifted man only as an extreme instance. In the case of the latter, unhappy family circumstances *mean* the same as does the existence of a normal state of tension in normal cases. What is meant by the latter is perhaps most easily made clear by the instances provided by England and China. In modern England the patriarchal principle of authority hardly ever comes into play. But then the child's own will is recognized as a matter of course within the compass of custom and good manners. And since the latter demand courtesy, reserve, and consideration, the *actual* supremacy of the father, as viewed from the standpoint of the child, involuntarily leads to the result that the reserve of the father has the same effect as the assertion of authority, only with the advantage that, from the outset, the boy does not feel bound, but free. In old China the son felt free only after the death of his father; hence the lesser initiative of the Chinese people. But on the other hand, in China the patriarchal state of things led to none of the bad effects to which it has led in the West—for which reason a regular revolution of youth has of late broken out here—because the Chinese father used his absolute authority within the compass of a filial love demanded by custom, which nipped any possible countermovement in the bud. In the Far East, little children are treated with more love than anywhere else. They are never spoilt, but they live in an atmosphere of understanding love. This is why one hardly ever met naughty or crying children in the traditional China and Japan. Originally the child is most willing to obey. The only reason why it does not obey is, that as yet it has no control over itself and, therefore, stands in need of intelligent suggestive influence. Therefore, it holds in contempt every grown-up who cannot command obedience. To revert to the Chinese system. We said that the objectification of authority in custom prevented the personal relationship between father and son from being impaired. The difficulty which so often results from a compulsion to study was most wisely precluded by the fact that the father did not instruct his son, but committed him for this purpose to the care of a friend. At any rate, in old China the love of his child never prevented any father from creating that in the child which belongs to the proper rôle of the father: namely, self-command and the right distance with regard to its own nature, and therewith the supremacy of the spiritual principle.

Now it should be clear what is wrong with the United States, as far as the context of this chapter is concerned. I said that there is no need to insist on the mother's task, because this is obvious. And I did not get the impression, notwithstanding the many things to the contrary I have heard, that American mothers are less motherly than those of other nations. They must be just as motherly or else there would be no such general attachment to the mother as one meets with all over the country. All that can be said in this connexion is that children are too frequently sent from home. But this is due in most cases to external necessity and so there is no help for it. As far as free will is concerned, the fact that children are sent from home is due, again, to the peculiar type of American socialism. In all socialistic communities women concentrate more on social work than on their families, and this to the detriment of home life. This is a disadvantage, but an inevitable one. One cannot fairly ask of an essential socialist what one can rightly ask of an individualist. And whatever may be said in the abstract—the mere fact of the extraordinary attachment of Americans to their mothers seems to me to prove conclusively that *under the peculiar American circumstances* the women know their business as mothers well enough. The case is very different with the fathers. Owing to woman's predominance in American life, with which we shall deal at length in the next chapter, on the one hand, and to the idealization of childhood on the other, the father as a type commands no reverence whatsoever. At best he is the favorite older friend and comrade. But usually he is even less than that. Since he has to spend most of his time at the office, returning home from it dead-tired five times out of six, and is moreover compelled to do many things for his children, whenever he happens to be with them, which nature demands of woman, he is organically unable to induce in his children the growth of that superiority over nature on which both individualization and spiritualization depend and which makes the real difference between the child and the grown-up.

This, then, is my answer to the question as to what is wrong with America as we have considered it here: America is infantile; by reason of the wrong attitude of the American fathers combined with the other influences working toward the same direction, the young ones never grow up to be spirit-controlled individualities.

And it is really a question of the father. Woman always is essentially a woman; she never is a child as opposed to the woman she will grow to be; she never is a child in the true masculine sense at all—for she is mature as a woman from the outset, standing for custom, law, and order, whatever these may be. A girl of two years knows all about flirting and petting and mothering and educating—she only expresses her knowledge according to her age. If the kindergarten-socialism changes her, too, into something more childlike in appearance than she would develop into if educated in other surroundings, this merely means retrogression in the cultural development, it does not in any way affect woman's attitude and significance as a mother. But that which by the eternal laws of nature the father alone can inspire and induce in the soul of the child cannot grow under the American system. Man cannot really become a man in the highest sense of the word. The principle of distance cannot be inbuilt into his soul. Spirit cannot really rule. In the next chapter we shall find many more reasons for the fact that in the United States woman predominates psychologically. But one of them is this, that the father, failing to fulfil his task as a father, and the child remaining a child in consequence, its natural dependence on the mother is increased to the degree that the boy expects from woman everything he would normally expect from the man his senior in age; and this attitude lasts as long as he lives. For the two poles of human nature, the one standing for intimacy and the other for distance, *must* find their symbolization somewhere; and the only grown-up the American knows by experience is the eternally grown-up:

woman. I may quote here one more *boutade* of Madariaga:

> The boys have hoisted the woman on to a pedestal of admiration. Her power and privileges flow from the position she occupies as an idealized type of humanity. In her youth the inspirer, in her maturer years the leader of men. First, the sweetheart of the nation, then her aunt, woman governs America, because America is a land of boys who refuse to grow up. She it is who rises to the activities reserved for grown-up people: general ideas, æsthetic enjoyment, culture, understanding of the world. The boys around her live a life of fun and activity, caught in the "behaviourism" of club and school standards, which they scrupulously respect, faithful to traditions and to a collective earth their inexperienced minds are afraid to leave. She dares explore the Heaven and Hell of individualism, the wider responsibilities of thought and the wider liberties of experience. The boys look up to her—her beauty first, then her intelligence, her culture, her wisdom. As the sweetheart of the nation, she keeps the boys healthy and happy with her affection; as the nation's aunt, she made up her mind the boys were not to drink, and the boys were dry. Not that they like it overmuch, but, when asked, they sigh first, smile afterwards, cast a side glance at *Her* and concede: we are better off as it is.

Unfortunately, they are not. A substitute can never be the real thing. If woman really could mean everything the boys expect her to mean, the American would not remain infantile. From the point of view of the growing soul, man alone really stands for the principle of distance and, consequently, spirit-rule. Where man cannot act as the symbol and polarizer required, something remains lacking for life. When studying America, I realized for the first time that there was sense in the Greek idea of homosexual love as a means of education, however strange this may sound. It certainly was no exemplary idea. But when conscious Spirit was first born on earth in its intellectual aspect, it is not unnatural, after all, that it should have wished to guard itself by extreme means from any influence which might thwart its growth.

THERE are indeed reasons enough to account for the fact that the modern American is infantile as a type. But the chief reason undoubtedly lies in the idealization of the child. Even the last-mentioned facts derive their full significance from it. Do not women love children more than anything else in the world? Are not they chiefly responsible for the idealization of childhood? Man, remaining an eternal child, he longs at heart to grow up. But woman being essentially grown up from the very first day of her life, for that very reason—for we always admire what we are not or what we lack—must glorify the child. Thus, no help can be expected from her instincts in the task of accelerating the process of America's growing up. During my lecture tour I watched with keen interest the way the women reacted to what I said regarding the indispensable emancipation of the American man (a subject fully dealt with in the next chapter): wrath or anger or resentment was hardly ever vitally rooted in intellectual objections; most frequently it was the will to power which felt threatened. But there were numerous voices, too, which simply rang with the anguish of the mother fearing she might lose her child. Nevertheless, no mother is selfish to the extent of wishing to prevent her child from growing up, whatever she may feel, *in case she knows what she is doing*. For this reason I do not doubt that the American woman will be the first to give all her support to the dis-infantilization of man, once she has realized what is needful.

Let us, then, conclude this chapter by concentrating finally on the father's natural rôle, and on the change in the attitude of the father which seems necessary. The father should *for the child's sake, whatever his personal feelings may be, try to embody with the utmost distinctness the principle of distance, as opposed to the principle of intimacy.* He should completely discard the idea of being his son's comrade. He should certainly not try to re-become the patriarch of old; the latter's days are past. But we have already had occasion to observe that courtesy is a much surer way of keeping one's distance than bullying. My impression is that the best attitude a father as a type can assume toward his son in these modern days is something like the typical attitude of an eighteenth-century prince toward an *étranger de distinction.* I know that Americans do not like courtesy in the original sense of the word. Langdon Mitchell writes: "The French mean by politeness one thing, and we another. To us to be polite means to exhibit good-will. To the Frenchman politeness consists in forms; the formal use of the words 'Monsieur' or 'Madame,' with a host of other forms of phrases, are, they conceive, necessary. They are so, because they avoid friction. In America, save in the Southern States, we have no forms and dislike them." But in this, if in anything—I say this in all humility, but I am certain that I am right—Americans are absolutely wrong. Forms not only avoid friction—they create contents. At any rate, they create that inner distance, the feeling of which is indispensable for any human soul wishing to become conscious of and to develop its uniqueness. Accordingly, a father who really loves his son and wishes him to become a spirit-ruled being should rather communicate with him in the outward form of Spanish etiquette than thwart his development by depriving him of the condition required for his inner growth, namely, the stressing of the distance-principle within the child. The father should never be the tyrant; he should strictly respect every peculiarity; nor should he under any circumstances try to break the child's will. But he should all the more consistently keep the right distance between himself and the child and by fixing insurmountable limits, which through custom grow to be second nature, he should help self-control to become a matter of course for the child. In order to achieve this result he should, in particular, most strictly avoid weakening the *fated* character of distance by explaining and giving reasons for everything. On the contrary, he should help the child to learn to bear alone the tension between not-understanding and enduring. For man's freedom is only a minute pinion in the great mechanism of the universe; even the freest of personalities must accept ninety per cent of all events as destined to happen. Therefore, it is the task of the father to bring into unweakened evidence precisely the fated character of his superiority: thus only does he help the child to gain the right adjustment within the cosmos and therewith the right kind of freedom. *Amor fati* means indeed a great deal more than energy and enterprise in the American sense. It is a far greater achievement to face a hard truth than to be optimistic in spite of everything. Life is a synthesis of a great deal of thraldom and very little freedom; whoever perceives or faces the extent of the latter only remains superficial. In this sense, once more, the father has to incarnate for the benefit of the child—whatever it may cost him to do so—inexorable and even irrational Destiny. But this, in return, will help the father to inward growth. Since I have children of my own, I am more and more impressed with the fact that the education parents give their children is nothing as compared with the education they receive from them. Only think how parents have to behave before the keen scrutiny and the merciless memory of the little ones! Many fathers do not in the least like this preordained rôle of incarnating the principle of distance, and very affectionate fathers probably never did. But whenever, in the course of human history, custom forced them to acquiesce in this part, it has been for the good of all concerned. The American fathers, too, are of course being educated by their children. Only, since they do not understand, they are being educated the wrong way. They are being encouraged in their infantilism, by which process the vicious circle is closed.

I have tried to show in this chapter why and in what sense the present idealization of the child must cease if the American nation is to grow up. As long as this persists, no spirit-born culture can develop. In the paradise of the child's world there can be no question of culture—there, all that matters is to be nice and likeable and popular and "game"; the last idea relates American business-practice to the kindergarten. I think I have also shown the only way out of the vicious circle that exists. However general and efficient education may yet become—if personality does not develop, if the American nation remains fundamentally infantile, then even institutions of heavenly perfection would be of little avail. What is culturally wrong with America is that it has no sense of values. All values are of the mind and of the spirit. There are no values inherent even in the most delightful qualities of childhood. If primitive emotions, and even if they were of the angelic order, provide the standard, then no progress should even be necessary—for on this line no sage and no saint can compete with any child which is perfect as such. There is, however, one emotion which indeed does lead to cultural progress; it is lacking altogether, as a national characteristic, in the United States and it, too, can be induced to grow by the right kind of father only. That is the emotion of *reverence*. Reverence bears the same relationship to love as distance to intimacy. Love perpetuates an existing condition; reverence leads upward to higher ones. It is in harmony with the general condition of the United States, that the value of reverence is not recognized. Yet, there will be no culture there before conditions change in this respect, *because only the reverence for what is recognized as superior leads upward*. Goethe said that "reverence, which no one brings into the world with him, is yet that upon which everything depends, if man is to become a man in every sense." According to him, three kinds of reverence should be equally developed: reverence for that which is above us, for that which is below us, and for that which is like us. Goethe had to think thus because his one ideal was to grow; and there actually is no other way of growing than by polarizing oneself in relation to something recognized as higher. If a man meeting another begins by thinking "I am as good as he is" and accordingly treats him with familiarity, he will never learn from him, even though the other be a god. On the other hand, if reverence is the primal attitude, even the greatest can learn, and always does learn even from the humblest. This effect which reverence achieves is as much a natural quality as are the properties of electricity. It is not a question here of aristocracy versus democracy, but simply of understanding versus blindness. There is no doubt something sympathetic about the man who boasts that "he looks God straight in the face." But there is a danger of his seeing in Him a man in the street among others, and that would mean that his meeting the Supreme instead of some inferior being was simply wasted upon him. . . . I do not want to insist; the case seems to me to be clear. A certain class of American writers has of late set itself the task to "debunk" great men. Of course, they can be debunked. But with the debunking their creative value disappears. The private life of all men is equally uninteresting. But the spiritual life of one single great spirit, *when faced in the right way*, can uplift whole nations. This is how the world of the white man became Christian. . . .

To conclude, I may answer a question sentimentalists are sure to ask. If the principle of distance is to be maintained henceforth between father and son, will not love suffer? All experience of all ages goes to prove the contrary. The child *wants* to see in its father the "God Almighty," for only by polarizing itself in relation to him does it in the long run learn self-control. This is the reason why the child does not love the all-too-intimate father more than the severe father—instinctively *it holds him in contempt*. No child really likes the father to take upon himself the functions of the mother. The loss of authority of modern fathers is to a great extent due to the fact that the sons bear them a grudge for their lack of distance during the decisive years of their development. Sons who deeply loved their fathers were most frequent in those ages in which there was no question of the father's being a comrade to his son. Wherever the fathers try to adapt themselves to their revolutionary sons, filial love is singularly rare. For it is in the nature of things that love should for the most part exist in the form of reverence, and thus only can it exist.

## *Predominant Woman*

WE SAW in the first part of this book that the fundamental forces and processes of nature can be mastered and led into channels different from their original ones only by strong spiritual powers. Environment inevitably changes man; each continent, and even a mere landscape, creates a specific type. However, spirit-born rules can counteract and balance and sometimes even overcome the influences of nature. Hence the preservation of ancestral types on foreign soil, as exemplified most strikingly by the Hindus and the Jews. Now the most tremendous force of nature is incarnated in sex. Very few women who have borne children escape being ruled, at least for a time, by what one may call the "God-Almighty-complex." This is natural enough: the existence of God the Creator may be doubted; but if He does exist, and if He created the World according to the tradition of the Bible, He really did nothing that can be considered as miraculous: the creation out of nothingness by His will is only the heightened reflection of what every man performs at every moment; Man thinks of something—and there it stands at once, as a fact, in the world of mental images. On the other hand, the procreation of a child by the time-honoured means is an altogether miraculous process. And if the miraculous is at the same time the vehicle of the greatest earthly joy, every possible subjective support is added to the objectively existent power.

Hence the fact that no age of profound inner experience ever considered love a natural thing—it was looked upon as either sacred or sinful. Hence the other fact that the love-impulse was always the first impulse to be regulated by spiritual rules, and that, if these lost prestige, this always constituted a far greater danger for a community, than any other kind of revolution or anarchy. From the very first, man instinctively felt that if the tremendous force incarnated in sex were allowed to sway him, no order of life could be maintained. This is why he has always made it a part of his religious scheme. And he was right. Whenever religion—in the widest sense of things natural being related to things spiritual as their basic cause—lost power, a hypertrophy of sex-life was the result, a hypertrophy meaning a disruption not only of the spiritual, but of the natural order as well. Where that which we are accustomed to call vice becomes dominant, the race inevitably degenerates or dies out. The disruption in question does not take place in the life of animals, nor even in the case of primitive human beings who are still close to nature, because they have no self-consciousness; in their case the harmony of nature is preserved from within, free will playing practically no part in the process. But the power of sex in the hands of intellectually conscious man or woman, endowed with free will, really resembles a high explosive. Unless the person possessed of that power is a man or woman of high ideals and morality, this tremendous force cannot but do harm.

Sex is an essentially mysterious power. This is proved more clearly today than ever before by the fact that it preoccupies the mind and heart and soul of mankind at large more than it ever has done, *in spite* of all scientific explanations which attempt to strip it of its mystery. Boys and girls pretend that everything belonging to sex-life is perfectly simple and obvious and explicable, but in their heart of hearts they think very differently about it; the only exception I know of are those who are satiated: an overtired animal never thinks at all. The assertion of so-called progressive writers that the new generations are not sex-obsessed is sheer nonsense: if there is less of sex in their thoughts, there is all the more in their activities, I mean they over-stress and overdo things sexual in their actions as much as their parents did in thought. And the results prove that their behaviour confirms once more the ancient idea that sex is a sacred thing in the sense of the Latin word *sacer*, meaning holy on the one hand, and infamous on the other. The free-doers—as one may well call this type, coining a word in analogy with the word free-thinkers—always show signs of backward development, of which we shall have a good deal to say later on. The fact is that whoever does not view sex in the light of a profound mystery is infinitely more superficial and shallow and unenlightened than any savage who stands in awe of its power. Even if everything concerning the biological side of procreation is "explained"—which explanation cannot possibly lead further than to a bare statement of facts—in what way does this help toward *understanding?* It is altogether incomprehensible; it is as miraculous as any miracle any god ever performed, that by cohabitation and its consequences a mental and spiritual being can be brought into the world.

This is not the place to deal with the problem of sex in its entirety. But what has been said should suffice to make clear to all who are capable of thinking for themselves that any explanation of things or processes referring to the correlation of man and woman which does not start from the premise of a fundamental mystery is unscientific and irrational; and that, this being so, such an opinion must needs affect perniciously whoever holds it. For mental images invariably become realities, and ideas always influence the facts. Let us now consider the mystery of sex as far as the specifically American problem is concerned. I shall treat its purely moral aspect in the chapter entitled "Morality"; here I will deal exclusively with the natural relationship between man and woman irrespectively of all moral prejudices, both right and wrong. The fact that wherever in nature a division of the sexes has taken place the organic type in question is never fully expressed in one sex alone, but only in the synthesis of both, is as fundamentally mysterious as the fact of procreation itself; from the natural point of view, only man and woman taken together constitute the human being. That this is so as far as procreation is concerned is so obvious that no more need be said about it. But the same is true of individual life, quite apart from its continuance by means of children. Man needs woman not only sexually, but psychologically and spiritually as well; and in the same way woman needs man. Modern writers, on the basis of their experience with emancipated women, sometimes pretend that woman needs the companionship of man much less than he needs hers. But I think there is a fundamental error underlying this opinion. Sexually, the female *seems* to stand in need of the male less than the other way round, because it is her rôle to be expectant. But if she expects in vain, she is even more deeply disappointed than the man who fails in a particular pursuit, because his active rôle enables him to find new chances as soon as he sets out in search of them. Psychologically, however, woman undoubtedly stands in greater need of man for her full development than he does of her, because it is her nature to respond. Hundreds of thousands of modern emancipated women may think themselves perfectly satisfied without a man playing a principal part in their lives; but, in spite of an unusually vast experience, I have never met a single one among them—except in the case of exceptionally gifted individuals—who was not inferior, as a human being, to a woman of the same quality developed in correlation to the right kind of man. Even club-women will agree that the old bachelor is an inferior or defective type. But the same is signally true of the spinster. The fact is that both have lacked or are lacking the complement that would have made them complete by calling out forces which cannot manifest themselves spontaneously. The idea of that sexless "human being" pure and simple, which the up-to-date man and woman so freely indulge in evolving and glorifying, is all very well. There certainly is a sexless element in human nature which could and should attain as high a level as possible. (I am dealing only with human *nature* here, not with the spiritual part of man which is an entity whose plane of existence lies beyond the division of the sexes, but which has nothing to do with the former; as a matter of fact, no truly spiritual human being ever was sexless in this sense.) No reasonable objection can be made against the highest imaginable development of that sexless element, and I even entirely agree with the opinion that, the differences of the sexes having been over-stressed for thousands of years, it is a very good thing to focus for a while, with equal one-sidedness, on what is common to both and to develop what should be the apanage or privilege of every human being; it is not a question here of the emancipation of woman but, on the contrary, of the development within all human beings of that which is essentially sexless because it belongs to the type *homo sapiens Linné* as such. But it remains true, nevertheless, that the masculinity or femininity of a human being is a thing deeper than its quality as a human being in general; deeper, that is, in the direction of what Goethe called "the Mothers"—the earthly part of man—and it is that part only which provides the means of expression for the spiritual. All creative powers, on whatever plane, are inherent in these qualities of masculinity and femininity. And I never saw nor heard of a man or woman who did not know instinctively that creativeness is the greatest and deepest thing on earth. Thus, all gods were in the first instance thought of as creators.

It is true that man as such never is complete, nor is woman as such. But this is the very fundamental fact of life which has to be accepted as it is. And every superior man and superior woman has accepted it eagerly, instead of boasting of his or her self-sufficiency. No part of the universe is really self-sufficient; each and all parts depend on one another. Modern thought even over-stresses this quality of dependence and obligation of the individual as regards his fellow man or the group, where this stressing actually thwarts individual growth. Why then deny and repudiate it in the one and only case where incompleteness, inwardly assented to and rightly directed, makes entirely for happiness and growth and enhancement and inspiration, and where its non-acceptance can result only in sterility? Indeed, the one thing such attempts to make man progress by laying all the emphasis on the human being can lead to is the creation of a third type, corresponding to the sexless workers among ants and bees. Accordingly, the real solution of the problem of man's and woman's highest development can be reached only by establishing the best possible relationship between the two, and not by the isolated development of each. There is only one exception to this rule which does not represent downright inferiority: that is the genuine ascetic type. But in his case what really happens is that the essential polarity of life appears transposed onto another plane. Psychologically, the ascetic is always an inverted lover. And if he has no communion with the other sex (I need not deal here with homosexuality, because it implies no special problem; it is only a case of abnormal bi-polarity) he has all the more communion with what he calls his higher self or God, as the case may be, which psychologically amounts to the same. It is exceedingly significant that the language used by all mystics is of an erotic nature.

The fundamental fact, then, is that only man and woman *taken together* constitute Man from Nature's point of view. If procreation, which one may call the dynamic aspect of the life-process, takes place only by means of the co-operation of two poles, the same is true of life in its static aspect. Man and woman are essentially correlated. Whatever the particular position of a man or a woman may be, he or she virtually belongs, as one of two focuses, to an elliptical field of forces and never reaches perfection unless this virtual truth becomes actual fact. By this I do not mean to imply that everybody should marry or have a lover, but that the opposite pole should be occupied in each case in the appropriate way. Thanks to psycho-analysis, we know today that man is fundamentally a psychological and not a material being, and that, accordingly, the fundamental facts he lives on and from are not material things but symbolic images; this explains why almost anything may stand, in principle, for father or mother or mate, whether it be art or politics or science, or even the lap dog and the collecting of postage stamps. Yet the substitute does not represent a substitute in the derogatory sense in the case of exceptional and essentially spiritual personalities only. A Saint Theresa undoubtedly found her true mate in God and could not have found him in any living man. In the same way, the true antipole of most artists and philosophers lies in their world of images and ideas; this is the reason why they usually object to marriage and best live out their sexual and erotic impulses in *liaisons* which in their cases do not mean more than stimulants for their work. But at least in nine hundred and ninety-nine out of a thousand cases only a man-and-woman-relationship in the ordinary sense is a true expression of the polar situation. Here, then, the primary fact which stands out clearly is that both poles are (and, therefore, should be) essentially *equal*. It is as fundamentally ridiculous to speak of the superiority of man or woman as of the superiority of the positive or negative pole in electricity. No better symbolic image of the true situation has ever been created than that by Aristophanes, of which Plato's "Symposium" preserves the record, *viz.*, that originally man and woman formed one single individual and were later torn asunder with the result that ever since they long to reunite. Here we find the reason why every man and every woman has always felt that there was one and only one potential mate predestined for him or her from all eternity, no matter whether they ever met or not. This is not literally so, because man's soul is a very complex and manifold thing, the centre of which can lie in many spots, and each of them is the potential focus of a particular and exclusive field of forces. But it is so as viewed and judged both from each of the centres of consciousness in question and from the integrated individual whole. We find here the basic reason why monogamous marriage always was and always will be the ideal form of a man-and-woman-relationship. I have stated the case of monogamous marriage exhaustively in my introductory essay to *The Book of Marriage* and do not wish to repeat myself. But this much may be stated once more, because every opportunity should be made use of to bring home fundamental truths: Monogamous marriage is, for the overwhelming majority, the ideal expression of the man-and-woman-relationship, because here alone does the fact that man and woman are incomplete the one without the other, and that they belong to a bi-polar elliptical field of force find its most complete as well as its most adequate expression in a generally valid and applicable form. The expression is the most complete and the most adequate because it is permanent in its very essence and embraces all planes on which man normally lives; because it expresses itself not only as inter-sexual tension in its purely individualistic aspect, but also from the point of view of the race and its perpetuation; in correlative growth and decline; in the acceptance of destiny, of both joy and sorrow; in the interplay of necessity and freedom. Finally, monogamous marriage alone is an expression not only of the natural, but also of the moral and spiritual order. Monogamy has never really prevailed on earth because very few men and women are able to establish an ideal relationship; they either do not find their true mate, or they stand in need of several polar relationships, or they are incapable of integration to individual wholeness, or finally they lack the understanding and the moral stamina which are required to keep going so labile and fragile a thing as an intimate relationship between two human beings, in the right way. It is also true that the ideal of monogamy becomes more and more difficult to attain as differentiation increases and with it the importance of the uniqueness-element which is essentially solitary and incapable of seeing an ideal in any form of companionship based on what all men have in common. Accordingly, just as it was said of Russian Czardom that it was *une autocratie tempérée par l'assassinat*, it may be said of marriage that it always was a monogamy tempered by something else; this "something" meaning pre-marital freedom, or adultery, or easy divorce, or marriage representing less than a *liaison*, or official polygamy or polyandry, as the case may be. But that the ideal solution of the problem lies in a permanent union between one man and one woman, who complete each other absolutely, is proved by the one fact that precisely every differentiated soul treasures this and no other ideal in his heart of hearts. For ideals never mean illusions—they are the projected images of inmost subjective reality. Man and woman, then, are essentially correlated. This means that their unity is one of the fundamental facts of nature. But it means even more than this: it means that any change of one pole *necessarily* involves, by implication, a corresponding change of the other. The ideal is that man and woman should be absolutely equal. By which I do not merely mean to say that they should have equal rights as human beings (of course they should, but this question is only a surface-problem and does not concern us here) but that both should reach their fullest and richest possible development. This again, owing to their pre-existing correlation, presupposes the right relationship of a rightly developed masculinity to a corresponding femininity, and vice versa. But as a matter of fact they very rarely *are* equal. Here, then, the mysterious character of sex manifests itself most impressively. If the state of equality is disturbed for the benefit of one pole, the other inevitably deteriorates, and this for internal and *not* for external reasons. Let man predominate unduly—and woman will lose in quality and value however happy she may be; and the same applies to the opposite state of balance. Owing to the unfortunate topsy-turviness of modern American thinking, very few will understand from the outset what I mean to express here; and it is obviously difficult to make "clear" what is essentially mysterious. Therefore I can do no better than simply state the facts at the risk of remaining misunderstood. The facts are the following: The psychical correlation of the sexes is as primary a phenomenon as the physical. Public opinion is aware of this at least to the extent that it expresses itself in female adaptability and mimicry; woman always knows instinctively how best to appeal to the male. But public opinion misunderstands the real meaning of the situation. It is not a question here of outward adaptation: a woman will be up to date or rise to a particular occasion or emergency *as a matter of course.* The mere presence of a qualified masculine pole suffices to call forth these qualities within her. And it need not even be a question of actually meeting him: she will know from the outset, by the inspiration of the collective unconscious. What her so-called adaptability really means is an *anticipated* establishing of the eternal correlation between the sexes, or a re-establishing of it, if it happens to be disturbed by a change of one pole; and woman knows beforehand because, being close to nature, the centre of her psychical being lies in the correlation of man and woman; she never really feels single. Thus, woman took the lead, after the World War, in expressing in her mode of being and in fashion the new relationship between the sexes which had resulted from this war. Man *seems* more independent, because it is his part in life to represent free initiative; he incarnates the principle of variation and, accordingly, of instability and waywardness. Besides, in man spirit virtually predominates, for which reason what he calls "work" may mean a more fundamental expression of his being than his relationship to women and children. Nevertheless, man is only seemingly more independent. For wherever he is bound, he is more bound than any woman ever was or ever will be, in spite of his scantier and less developed emotional powers; precisely because of his greater independence, he is less well armed to resist the influence of the other sex if he exposes himself to it at all. The Christian and Buddhist ascetics who forbade their disciples any female intercourse were no fools.[1] It is diffi-

[1] I cannot resist the temptation to relate here a delightful story showing the deep humanity of the Hindus, a story which is contained in one of their Sacred Books. It is told there that the Brahmacharya may never have anything to do with women "unless," it is added, "woman proposes herself, for in that case a refusal would be discourteous. This, at any rate, is the opinion of the Rishi Vamadeva."

cult (in modern days, at any rate) to distinguish a married woman from a girl; indeed, the *jeune fille typique* was invariably a work of pure art. It is always possible to tell a married man. He is so helpless, psychically, if he is bound at all, that he really changes more in correlation to the woman who influences him than any woman is ever changed by a man. For it is well known that a widow or a wife who leaves her husband almost at once reverts to her original type. Those who doubt this greater susceptibility to influence of man should remember that woman is originally meant to be dependent, and man is not, for which reason the dependence of a man means much more, psychologically, than that of woman.

So much for individual cases. But there are generic phenomena of various states of balance between the sexes. The whole structure of a civilization may be such that either man or woman plays the predominant part. Both are equally natural. What matters from nature's point of view, is the correlation as such; and an identical state of correlation can express itself in an infinity of polar terms. We find examples of this throughout the animal kingdom. Among men, the extreme cases are represented by absolute patriarchalism, where man is a tyrant and woman a slave, and by absolute matriarchalism, where the reverse is true. Between these two extremes there are all possible shades and transitions. The purely patriarchal state is today not only on the decline, but even in the throes of death all over the civilized world, owing to the co-operation of the emancipation movement among women and to scientific enlightment. But there is one country in the world where that other state, a state of absolutely predominant woman, seems to triumph. This country is the United States.

WHILE travelling in America I made it a point always to say exactly what I thought, and in terms as provocative as I could make them, because this meant the shortest way for me to get at America's truth, by means of the reactions provoked. And all the reactions to what I had said in public about the man-and-woman-relationship that came to my notice confirmed my intuitions. Most of the thoughtful men and women agreed with me. No woman really minded my contentions, but very many minded what seemed to them the betrayal of a professional secret; like all ruling races or individuals, they did not want their subjects to know. The most significant reaction, however, was that an extraordinary amount of *men* were frankly angry with me. They could not have resented my opinion, had I been wrong. Their violent reaction was obviously due to their subconscious realization that I was right, together with the wish that things should remain as they are. Those who wrote in order to refute me always insisted, very significantly, on the most futile points. Of these I will mention only one because it best explains the case. In an interview published in many papers, John B. Watson, the behaviourist, said that man still holds the strings of the purse and that this circumstance alone suffices to prove that he still rules. In reality, this argument proves nothing. The superior or inferior position of a person depends, first and last, on the psychological influence he or she exerts. Mere material power in itself is of no avail, except when brute force decides—which is a rare exception in civilized communities. It becomes paramount only when people *believe* in it as the decisive element. It never was decisive in pre-war Europe, nor is it even today among those who count. Europe certainly never was like India, where a beggar belonging to the Brahmin caste is acknowledged by each and all as superior to a king of lower extraction. Nor has moral authority ever meant as much in Europe as in ancient China, where the whole governmental system rested on moral worth, and even less than in ancient Egypt, where the system really was one of oppression yet where the Pharaohs never needed an army to protect and support them because their authority was sufficient. In its own way, Europe always has believed in force. This is why in Europe force has always decided the destinies of nations, which never was the case in ancient India and China, in spite of all their conquests and foreign rule; here, the vanquished always assimilated the victors because their feeling of superiority remained unimpaired by defeat. But Europe never believed in *financial* power as the last resort. To hold this strange belief is one of the originalities of the United States. Its root lies, of course, in Privatism. In America, people really believe that the rich man is for that very reason a superior man; in America, the fact of giving money really creates moral rights. Even in post-war Europe, no Mæcenas who endowed an institution would even dream of thinking that this gave him a right to "control" its activities. Even in post-war Europe only the very lowest sort of rich woman who married an impecunious man would think for that reason that she had bought him and, therefore, had all the rights of a proprietress; the type of the "marrying sort of girl" who makes a fortune out of breach-of-promise or divorce suits, has not yet been born in the Old World. There was, in the May issue, 1928, of *Harper's Magazine*, an exceedingly clever article by Henry C. Beers "Woman and the Marriage Market," the chief argument of which is to the effect that woman originally looks upon herself as a merchandise and that most of her progressiveness can be explained on the basis of changes that have occurred on the Marriage Market. I feel certain that although Beers' thesis does not apply to the majority of American women, the instinctive outlook of whom is the same as that of all normal women over the world, very few Americans, both male and female, would object to the theory; and that a considerable percentage precisely of the leading women will agree with it even emotionally, whether they admit it or not. In Europe, on the other hand, Beers' point of view would meet with genuine and general horror. This difference in outlook, then, would seem to support, as far as America goes, Watson's argument which was originally meant to refute my contention. But it so happens that the position of woman in America is the one general exception to a general rule. It is quite true that she herself does not earn most of the money she spends and that in the case of wealth she is usually dependent on some man. It is also true that man *does* most things. But all the same, her position in the United States is that of the ruling race, very much like that of the British in India.

IN ORDER to make quite clear what I mean to an audience not accustomed to think of power in terms other than financial, I will begin by approaching the problem from a different angle. For that purpose

I will note down here, in a preliminary and sketchy way, some trends of thought that really belong to the chapter "Democracy," whereas others can only be fully developed in the chapter "Morality." Yet this is not a digression: the apparent détour will lead us to the goal in the shortest possible time.[1]

Two of the most important characteristics of the age of Democracy are its belief in differences of ability and its total disbelief in differences of states of being. The latter disbelief is natural enough; the old order which Democracy overthrew had been based entirely on the idea that there exist fundamental differences due to the original status of man, which no talent or merit could annul. These differences were thought to provide the only possible frame for a social system in accordance with facts; and they were supposed to be entirely a matter of natural heredity, except in those instances where the law of Divine Grace—superior to the law of nature—chose to assert itself, as it was supposed to do in matters of religious calling and—though very rarely—in regard to exceptional men of the world. This idea was obviously wrong in many respects. Heredity does not work as accurately as is supposed, nor is it safe to rely on Divine Grace always and inevitably manifesting itself at the right moment. Above all, a social structure exclusively based on differences of state of being disregards the rational side of life, that is the one part of it which can be directed by the intelligent will of man. Accordingly, a society like the mediæval cannot be progressive. It cannot breed efficiency as a

[1] The following considerations have been published by the *Forum* in a different setting.

ruling principle, since no individual can develop outside of and beyond his inherited position in life. It is not in accordance with the reality of life in the case of every individual whose inherited social position does not correspond to his true state of being. And it appears fundamentally unjust wherever the men belonging to the supposed-to-be superior castes are not actually superior. The democratic ideal could conquer the Western World chiefly because at the time when the struggle of the new with the old order became acute the mediæval hierarchy no longer expressed vital truth in this respect.

But though the expression of the idea underlying mediæval society was dying at the time when that society collapsed, and though the idea itself was wrong in several respects, it was not altogether wrong. As a matter of fact, there *is* such a thing as superiority in the sense of pure being, irrespective of any demonstrable ability. Roughly speaking, man's inward structure is the following. He is a vital creative spirit, a true spiritual "substance" in the sense the philosophers of India and our own Middle Ages would have it, which expresses itself by means of the psychological functions at hand, but is different from them in kind. This spirit, a purely subjective entity, unique in each individual case, stands for that in man which everybody feels to be his ultimate personal being. It radiates its own quality directly, from within outward, whatever ability a man may possess otherwise—we know of many whom everybody considered great in their time and who wielded tremendous influence but who were not endowed with any particular talent. Its activity is essentially involuntary; it corresponds to what the ancient Chinese called

*Wu Wei.*[1] It is incapable of objectification, incapable even of proof, yet it decides ultimately on whatever a man is to achieve even on the plane of ability; no great captain of industry in the most modern and mechanized sense has ever belonged to the average as far as personal weight and authority and magnetism are concerned. Now the quality of a state of being depends on the location of the inward centre from which a man rules the manifold manifestations of his life. This centre may lie in the depths of individual uniqueness, or in the collective unconscious, or even in what we term the Divine. It may lie on the surface so entirely that there is hardly any reality observable beyond purely instrumental functions; think of the superficial worldly type or of that other, so frequent in our days, who seems to express his soul completely in what a machine would perform equally well. Now it is obviously possible to base a social order on the differences described here, and not on such of instrumental ability; though they never are demonstrable as technical proficiency is, they can be perceived directly by anyone who has learnt to focus "being" as such; moreover, they can be proved to exist by the pragmatic test. It is a fact that being acts on being exactly as any force of nature acts on another belonging to the same plane.

On these differences of being all aristocratic social structures have been based. Their order must needs be a hierarchic order, for considering that the essence of being is its uniqueness, difference and not equality must be the ruling principle here. Now all *leadership* always depends on the state of being. Only he can rule others

[1] I have fully explained this term and what it stands for in the chapter "World-Ascendancy" of *Creative Understanding*.

personally—personally as opposed to rule by brute force or impersonal machinery—whom others involuntarily follow or obey; and this they do, in case their level of being is the lower one. Souls are not separated from one another as bodies are; accordingly, whoever controls his own nature inevitably emerges as the born ruler of such as lack the power of self-control. Aristocracy has, for this reason, a very sound foundation. Accordingly, in most countries the struggle between the democratic and aristocratic conceptions of life resulted in a compromise. Personal ability found complete opportunity to assert itself; on the other hand, differences in the state of being were accounted for in some form or other. In one country only the undisputable truth that there *are* differences in the state of being has been completely discarded: that country is America. There, and there alone, the whole social structure has been based on the assumption that men are born as equals under all circumstances and that all differences of quality can be accounted for in terms of ability. But American Democracy made one fatal mistake from its own point of view: it left *Woman* out of the social picture. Accordingly, the instinctive perception of the truth that there *are* different states of being, and not only differences in ability, found its outlet here. If all men in America are supposed to be equal, every American man instinctively admits, if not in his thoughts and words, then all the more in his attitude and in his actions, that woman represents a higher state of being than he does.

Women actually represent a higher caste in the United States. That they have gained this position has, of course, not been brought about solely by the fact that man necessitated an "abreaction" of his sense for differences of being, combined with the accidental circumstance of woman having been left out of the democratic picture. The foremost reason is that from man's point of view woman's distinctive characteristic is *in any case* the direct radiation of the quality of her being, so that in the case of American man it was not a question of the transfer (in the psycho-analytic sense) of a primary image from out of the unconscious to an indifferent object, but of a perception of reality. And American man, who in his own eyes stands exclusively for ability, must perceive all the more keenly the different adjustment of woman's original nature—which accounts for the otherwise paradoxical fact that the being of woman means most precisely in the country where woman is most active and thinks of herself foremost in terms of ability. But the decisive historical reason for woman's predominance in America is certainly to be found in what was explained above. Were it not for this, the American woman would not have been able to develop a self-consciousness so entirely different from that of man. It is the *respect* of man for woman which has developed it, exactly as in aristocratic communities it is the respect of the lower classes which makes for the perpetual rebirth of the superiority-feeling among the children of the higher ranks. The American woman originally *feels* superior; this *feeling* is the basic reason of her actual superiority and supremacy. For feeling is the immediate expression of being on the subjective plane, and it is actually impossible to feel what is not real. Thus she has developed those very qualities which have been characteristic of every ruling race. She wields immediate, direct authority; she need not prove her superior position, it is accepted as a matter of course. Accordingly, those who "hold the strings of the purse" give all the money they can afford to their wives and daughters, and the latter often spend it in exactly the same way as aristocratic libertines squandered the income derived from their tenants. Thus juries pronounce as a matter of course verdicts in favour of the woman in most divorce-suits. The same explains why the courtesy of the American man toward woman is so totally different from European chivalrousness: the soul of the latter was and still is the respect of the strong for the weak, whereas that of the former obviously bears all the marks of the respect of the lower for a superior class. And the same, finally, makes us understand why the "marrying sort of girl" is not considered an abomination pure and simple; as things are, the same allowances are made for her as for the occasional depravity of the *grand seigneur* in Europe.

Here, then, we find also the real *raison d'être* of the formidable power the women's clubs and other woman-organizations wield in the United States. Materially speaking, the men's organizations are much more powerful; but the women wielding the authority inherent in a recognized higher caste, their influence is out of all proportion to the facts. Let us revert here once more to Watson's argument that the men still "hold the strings of the purse." History shows that in most cases the ruling classes were not the rich classes; they often even made a point of not being rich in order to impress the masses all the more strongly with the fact that their supremacy was something unattainable; for everybody may grow rich through work, while no one can attain a state of being not originally his at least potentially. This, then, leads us to the final overthrow of the modern prejudice that working efficiency as such always leads to a position of superiority. It is precisely the American religion of work which has chiefly helped woman to attain psychological predominance. There are elementary truths which prove their validity in life in spite of all theory, and one of them is that the workman is inferior to the ruler—that is to the type which, owing to qualities the former lacks, can direct his work from above. In ancient Rome it sometimes happened that a comparatively poor man had a slave owning immense riches which the former had no right to take away from him—and yet the slave remained the slave, entirely depending on his master except in the one question of private property. Ruler-types are essentially not industrious in the sense of the working type, because what they alone can achieve depends not on toil, but on the involuntary radiation of their being. The English are essentially lazy, but others involuntarily work for them. Now the relationship of the American woman to the American man is very much the same as that of the English to their foreign subjects. Only that it is so extreme in her case that, again and again, while travelling in the United States, I was reminded of two similes which will sound monstrous to most American ears. The first of them is the relationship of the Egyptian slave or tenant to the Egyptian Queen. The Fellah never dreamt of anything better than of working for her day and night; and the Queen always made use of his earnings in whatever way she pleased, as a matter of course. The other simile is that of the Oriental harem. It is true that the women are not confined in America. But the men are. They are confined to the office, which psychologically amounts to exactly the same. The fact of man's inferiority, as compared to woman as such, is indeed the chief characteristic to the whole of American life. To the illustrations and demonstrations and explanations already given one more may be added here: the fact that the inferiority-complex of the American which is due to Puritanism, in particular his soul-fear, is much more developed in the man than in the woman, because Puritanism had a patriarchal outlook. Woman was not supposed to have any initiative, therefore she felt the burden of Original Sin much less than he did; she could not be primarily guilty. It is thus entirely logical that the restoration of the rights of the flesh has been initiated by woman in the United States. There are certainly millions of households where the position of woman does not differ much from that which is the rule in Europe; wherever husband and wife are partners within a narrow frame of life and dependent on co-operation for their living, the equality demanded by nature naturally asserts itself. This is true even in the Orient. But in spite of all prejudice in favour of equality, it is a fact borne out by all history that the type of a nation is never shaped by the obscure workers, but by those who have reached a prominent position; these, in the long run, influence the latter. At the time I am writing this, the daughters of the most old-fashioned parents develop into the flapper type if they come to live in the larger cities, and unless theirs is a very strong cultural tradition. And in any case the prominent circles of the big cities set the fashion. Influence always has the downward flow of water. Sometimes it takes a very long time to make itself felt. Thus I have been informed that the customs prevailing today in the lowest middle-class of Germany correspond to the court etiquette of the eleventh century. In the same way, what is true in the prominent American sets today of predominant woman, will inevitably be true, sooner or later in ever so mitigated a form of the average type, unless a great change interferes with the process. The general truth that influence always has the downward flow of water must inevitably assert itself in America as much as it has ever done anywhere else. Since democracy as Americans understand it means equality of chance, and wealth is generally accepted as a proof of superiority, it is out of the question that the wealthy classes in that country should not appear in the long run as its true representatives.

MY READERS should have grasped by now that in principle superiority and supremacy never depend on "facts," as such, but on significance; on authority, and not on actual material power; on psychological influence, and not on material data. Let all facts unite to prove that man still rules in the United States—the most complete set of proofs is devoid of validity if their meaning happens to be different from what those who collect them suppose. Nor is "history" of any moment. I know well how hard women had to fight in America up to a very recent date in order to get the vote, and how much oppression there was, as long as the patriarchal law really was in force. The all-important facts are that even in the days when public opinion was frankly patriarchal, woman in America held a superior position; that it was paramount long before she got the vote; and that today her psychological supremacy is complete. If this could come about so shortly after her legal enfranchisement, the vital forces in the United States must all make for Matriarchy.

Let us now consider more closely the significance on

the one hand, and on the other the details of the peculiar position of woman in American life. But to this end we must first recall to mind, with the utmost vividness the background of all these trends of thought, *viz.*, the fundamental truth that man and woman are essentially correlated; that their relationship is best compared to that of the two poles of a unified elliptic field of forces; and that for this reason any increase of importance of one pole *inevitably* entails the weakening of the other. The increase of importance of one pole is, of course, due in the first instance to external reasons; as a general phenomenon, life changes in response to stimuli. All patriarchal subjection of woman came into existence, as a general phenomenon, as a result of material force. In the same way, the former has been or is being disestablished by force—the emancipation-movement of women was a case of real warfare and it achieved final success exactly by the same means as those by which so many campaigns have been won, *viz.*, by taking advantage of dissensions in the inimical camp: all over the world the only real winners in the Great War were the women. Likewise, the American woman could not possibly have gained the predominant position she holds today, had there not originally been a scarcity of women in the United States, had the patriarchal and the Puritan tradition not made for comparative leisure in their case, promoting, in spite of all oppression in other respects, the development of being as opposed to ability; had the natural consequences of this state of things not coincided with a *Zeitgeist* favourable to the emancipation of women; finally, if most teachers in America were not female, which makes for the development in the American man of such an extraordinary mother-complex that it cannot help leading to a kind of perpetual infantilism. But all this is no argument against the *inner* reason for woman's superiority; every autocracy has arisen from original equality, and the inmost has always to be called out to manifestation by outward circumstances. One should remember in this connexion that, primarily, man experiences not material facts, but symbolic images; and that their power, which is a true magic power, ultimately decides. Looked at superficially, one might get the impression that patriachy or matriarchy came into existence in many cases owing to economic reasons; thus, in primitive societies, woman's prestige grew with the importance of her share in the maintenance of the household, her share consisting in agricultural labor and the tending of cattle as opposed to hunting. But then wealth meant *magic* power in those early days, as every other kind of power did; even if an African tribesman is successful in his hunt, he attributes this primarily not to his skill, but to the magic ritual carefully performed before he started out. Now the American soul having become primitive again, the significance of many opinions and activities which seem to be something altogether matter of fact, really belongs to the sphere of magic. Not only the belief of Christian Science—the belief in wealth, too, is essentially of this order; indeed, only if wealth be a magic power, can it transform by itself an inferior into a superior man. Precisely as primitive is the relationship of the American man to woman.

Let us now trace a background of meaning, against which the facts stand out with the utmost impressiveness.

American juries almost always pronounce judgments in favour of the woman. As opposed to this, not only no

European woman, but even no European man ever really believes that what happens to a woman was not actually meant by her to happen. In the Old World woman is instinctively appraised as the seducer, just as it was Eve who gave the apple to Adam, and not vice versa. In the same sense, European public opinion is instinctively in favour of man's waywardness, expressing itself in his reluctance to marry. The meaning of this is, that in Europe man's point of view predominates in the subconscious of both man and woman. In the United States the opposite is true. Absolutely everywhere woman's point of view predominates and her influence stands behind most of man's deeds. In the chapter "Socialism" we saw that altruism is woman's typical attitude—altruism is not morally superior to egoism; it is simply the expression of a different physiology; a race of extremely masculine pioneers would not have changed into a race of worshippers at the shrine of the ideal of Social Service were it not for the predominance, even in man's subconscious, of woman's outlook. The sense of property is primarily a female quality; it is she who owns, preserves, transmits; for this reason in many primitive communities woman alone had the right to inherit. Man's original bent is directed to conquest, but not to ownership. This is proved not only by the feudal and Bolshevik systems—both inventions of purely patriarchal races—but even by all great American money-makers; they all cared really only for the making, not for the owning of it. Yet today the American nation as a whole is the one which thinks most highly of property, to the extent that no bloodshed and no enslavement of others seem too high a price for protecting investments. This is exactly the way every mother feels where the interests of her family are at stake. The same applies to another side of American Privatism: woman's interests always were private in the personal sense, as opposed to the public interests of man; if a whole nation has a privatist outlook, if it thinks little of law and government, this is proof positive of woman's psychological predominance. The same is true in regard to what the Monroe Doctrine stands for: from the point of view of inner experience, woman always lives within a closed circle; her natural world is an isolated world; outside of it, her instincts make allowances for heartlessness and ruthlessness much more easily than do those of man. A further proof of woman's psychological predominance is the cult of the child. Proofs of the same also are, at least to a certain extent, the ideals, the chief roots of which lie, as was explained in earlier chapters, in American primitivity and the predominance of the Animal Ideal: woman is close to nature, she represents the earth as opposed to the spirit-principle. Accordingly, she prefers routine to change—her love of change in fashion is only a surface "abreaction," compensating her basic wish for stability; she prefers repetition to uniqueness, all of which goes far to account for the ideals of normalcy and like-mindedness. The tremendous number of laws and rules in America are also of female origin: woman wants to be protected; her instinct demands that there should be only fixed rules and customs and, above all, a minimum of risk. There certainly is a logical contradiction between this fact and the other that woman thinks little of law or government—but such is life. As an illustration of woman's natural longing for fixed rules I may give a singularly instructive instance. One more proof of the better state of balance in the South lies in the fact that woman does not predominate there to the same degree as in the North. Now Northern girls often complain of the Southern men that they are not safe; that they are apt to say nice things which they do not mean; in particular, they are horrified because in the South it is difficult to sue for breach-of-promise: this view of the South as held by Northern girls is a wonderful illustration of what woman's exclusive outlook can lead to in a mechanized age.

That the whole new morality is of feminine origin is obvious. Man certainly cares more than woman for freedom and variety in sexual life; in so far the new flapper-attitude means a reversion of the poles; with this most important problem we shall deal later on. But on the other hand, woman never thought anything of virginity. All the more has she always cared for respectability; and the American idea of divorcing and remarrying at the first sign of a new infatuation—not to mention the idea of legalizing what is essentially a *liaison*—is nothing else than a new expression of woman's desire to be respectable at any cost. A marriage may only last five minutes, but marriage there must be. And what about Prohibition? The Hindus and the Mohammedans in the days of their greatness did not drink, but this was due to obvious climatic reasons, to which religion only gave a spiritual interpretation. There is no reason of this kind for not drinking in America. All that has been said about the electric climate of that continent is sheer nonsense: it does not stimulate, it only enervates; accordingly, as a type, the American is less vital than the European, the Arab, and the Hindu. Therefore, if he objects to stimulants, this simply means that he prefers a lower to a higher kind of life. Man, as indeed every organism, needs stimulants in any case. Since he represents an essentially labile equilibrium, since he changes from one second to another and the life-force within him must be constantly restimulated to activity if it is to meet new emergencies, nothing whatever can be said, in principle, against drinks and even drugs as long as they work for good. There is nothing to be said against them even if they are noxious to the extent of harming the organism slowly, because life ends with death anyhow and an inspired life is always better than a dull life. Now the male is the bearer of the principles of variation and of initiative. Accordingly, he needs more stimulants the more inventive he is. This is why wine was praised as a gift of the gods from the very first; in the Bible the third curse recorded is attached to the first prohibitionist, to Ham who dared to disapprove of Noah. But woman never drank. Her rôle is not variation, but stability and repetition. The only stimulus she needs is man. Accordingly, she cannot see, from her point of view, why man should want others than herself. If woman comes to predominate, it is only natural that she should stand for Prohibition. It is all the more natural, as with power the urge for power grows; in a perfect matriarchy women will inevitably think that men have nothing better to do than to be good boys and to behave; and men obviously are obedient the less the principles of variation and initiative predominate in them; that is, the less masculine they are. (Even "predominant" women are in favour of physical masculinity, but the most manly man in this respect may be sexless as a spirit.) But from all that has been said it should be clear that the attitude of the prohibitionist is normal only in woman. The American fanatics of Prohibition among men are most of them psychologically feminine to a considerable degree; one need only compare their type with any Englishman, and the truth is patent; when I first landed in England, after visiting the United States, my impression was that all Englishmen belonged to the race of God Bacchus. My personal opinion is that the American stands in even greater need of that bottle of champagne in his blood which Bismarck thought necessary for the North German, in order to show himself at his best. If his conversation is so poor, if he is so extraordinarily passive mentally in everything excepting his business, this leads me to conclude that what he really needs in order to progress is legislation which would bring about a manner of living similar to that of the Frenchman and the Italian. I know well that there is little hope of such legislation ever becoming a fact. The North and the East of the United States are Puritan at heart. But then the South and the West are there. One may hope at least for a change of the Eighteenth Amendment to that extent that the individual States and not the Federation will ultimately decide upon the question of Prohibition or no Prohibition. The chief difficulty lies in the fact that so far Americans drink chiefly not in order to be stimulated but to be numbed. There is nothing, of course, to be said for numbing drinks. But even in this respect the chief argument of the prohibitionists that America produces more since it is dry, does not hold water. Man is no producing-machine. According to all standards accepted among cultured nations, the United States have more reason to be proud of Walt Whitman and Edgar Allan Poe, both men of questionable morals, than of all producers taken together, from the days of Pilgrim Fathers up to the year of grace in which I write.[1]

THERE certainly are other causes than the predominance of woman's point of view, which have eventually brought about Prohibition. The historian may even trace it back to Puritanism only, and with a certain show of right. However, the historian's point of view is the least adapted to help us see and understand life as it actually is. Life proceeds from one "now" to another. The quality of the now can never really be explained by what has happened in the past. But above all, owing to a new impulse from the spirit, the facts transmitted by heredity can gain an entirely new meaning. It seems that most native-born American men and women of sufficiently ancient lineage cannot see that woman predominates today. The reason is that in their subconscious man fights for his life—for he *was* predominant in the early Puritan days; this is the very reason why the "masculine protest" of woman has been so extreme in the United States. There never was so extreme a patriarchalist as the genuine Puritan. Up to a

[1] The most delightful involuntary persiflage of Prohibition I ever came across was a hymn sung at Geneva by little girls from five to twelve years of age, who belonged to the Junior League (Espoir) of the Blue Cross. They sang to the melody of "God Save the King" (which is also the national anthem of Switzerland)

*Je vois avec dégoût*
*L'alcool qui rend fou*
*Régner partout*
*Marchez sans crainte*
*Contre l'absinthe,*
*A sa voix sainte*
*Debout, debout!*

comparatively recent date the "home-and-mother-type" was more dominant in America than anywhere else. Very many modern developments in the direction of matriarchy can be explained only as a reaction against centuries of extreme patriarchalism. But we have to deal here exclusively with the *actual* soul of the United States. To the unbiassed observer, those women who even today fight against man's predominance present a spectacle akin to that of a fight against ghosts.

Let us now try to determine more closely in what sense the excessive predominance of woman must needs lead and actually does lead to the deterioration of man. I may remark incidentally that to anyone versed in the psychology of the subconscious, the glorification of types like the "he-man," the "go-getter" (not to mention these highly significant word-creations in themselves), alone provides proof of the fact that there really exists a certain amount of deterioration. But let us now simply examine to what results mere logical thinking leads when focussing the arguments put forth for the sake of proving woman's supremacy from the point of view of its effect on man: we shall then see that this a priori way leads straightway to the actual acts of life. If, owing to the ideal of Social Service, the fellow man means more, originally, than the self in question, the latter cannot develop. Man is originally not altruistic, but egoistic; this is his primary virtue, for all initiative and all creativeness depend on self-assertion. If, now, he renounces this primary impulse, then he must needs lose a considerable part of his virile force. Most probably American man is so extremely self-centred in the question of material pursuits, because this is the one outlet left to him for expressing this part of his virility. But this outlet does not suffice. The American man is specialized as a man, just as insects are on some particular line. A complete man in the sense of human world-openness cannot possibly develop.[1] And further: if property means everything and along with it stability; if repetition, along the lines of like-mindedness or standardization, becomes a national ideal, all this must of necessity lead to an under-development of the principles of variation and initiative which are the essence of man's being. Here again, the extreme development of the latter virtues along business lines only means that what should be the general characteristic has become a speciality. Further, if private concerns and the interests of narrow circles predominate, then the Promethean type of man, the type of the heaven-stormer cannot flourish. Yet all that is best in man finds its prototype in Don Quixote, Prometheus, or Faust. Here we find another reason for America's lack of artists. It is woman, not man, who is chiefly utilitarian. Man is the adventurer, the gambler, the eternal child. Since Mother Eve's days woman has always been terribly in earnest because she has always borne most of the responsibility; the mere fact that love is a game for man, and for woman, a matter of life and death, has made of her the essentially responsible creature. Now the whole civilization of the United States is utilitarian. All American standards seem to have been set up by the responsible mother. In such an atmosphere an artistic genius must deteriorate, all the more so, as he is the most wayward and sensitive of human types; he has always been the terror of the good housewife. And the creative artist, not the cave man, and still less the so-

[1] Compare the development of this trend of thought in the chapter "Man and the Earth" in *The Recovery of Truth.*

called he-man stands as the representative of psychological virility. Those whose prejudices are shocked by this should realize that man, and not woman, represents the romantic and idealistic portion of mankind. Woman has always been scientific-minded and matter-of-fact. If today her attitude toward sexual matters is completely crude, this does not mean depravity on her part, but simply that at last a *Zeitgeist* has become dominant which allows her to be sincere. I am sure that today among themselves, within a closed circle, millions of women gloat when they realize that at last they can do without that idealism which masculine stupidity, as they call it, imposed upon them for so many thousands of years: now this may be all very well from the woman's point of view. But it is disastrous from the masculine point of view. And I think it is equally disastrous from the cultural point of view. Spiritual values cannot be realized on earth if the earth-principle, of which woman as a type is the representative, predominates too much. It is true that American women go in for things spiritual even more perhaps than any other women on earth. But they do so only in reading; or else they do so by fostering education. But education as understood in the United States is a purely feminine business, too; it is the mechanized expression of what every female animal does when bringing up its young. All should be trained for life; all should become as fit as possible. Moreover, all should be as normal as possible, because normalcy alone corresponds to the routine of the earth. And first and foremost, all should have "degrees." This is only one more expression of the universal feminine desire for respectability.

Since the problem of education is of the utmost importance, I shall state here part of what I wrote about it immediately on my return to Germany, as a condensed result of my American experiences. One can educate only what has already been born; education is meant to develop and form what already exists. For this reason an instinct as elementary as that of bearing children has always urged women to educate. This explains why almost all born educators among men have had feminine traits. Hence also the predilection for repetition and routine inherent in every type of educator. Routine actually is the essential part of every kind of education. *Repetitio est mater studiorum.* Even as the heart works mechanically, in the same way all life, as a form both of nature and of culture, represents in the first instance a typical process. And since with man education has to effect, or at least to complete, what nature effects in the case of the animal, every education which does not lay the emphasis on the non-unique is simply an absurdity. These simple considerations should suffice to explain the invariable failure of every exaggerated individualism in education, and at the same time they should make clear why precisely an education which, in principle, takes into account only the typical but for all that does not prevent the development of the unique—like that of the Old English schools—should produce the greatest number of the best types of individual personality. At the same time, however, these considerations substantiate the fact that education is necessary. In one way or another, every young individual life must be made a part of the general rhythm of life and this is precisely the task of education.

But there is another side to the question. It is a well-known fact that there is hardly an original personality on record who in his young days was a model pupil. And it is an equally well-known fact that the routine of education is apt to destroy creative powers which exist. Hence, educational reformers draw the conclusion that the school in its present state is no good and that it must learn to foster precisely the creative powers. But every attempt along this line has hitherto proved disastrous in its effects. Where it was a question of little children in whom the quality of genius was to be preserved, the reasons are obvious. Every child up to the age of seven or eight is a kind of genius. Then a period of involution sets in; originality disappears; the generic side, *i.e.*, routine, comes to the fore. Whoever tries to stay or to cross this process is guilty of suppressing germinating life; for since it is a question of a natural rhythmic process, the child whose originality has been artificially kept alive becomes impotent in some sense when it grows up. On the other hand, this period of natural unoriginality is the very time in which to connect the child's personal life with the universal rhythm of life with the least amount of risk for its originality. For this reason the traditional school, as opposed to all innovating efforts, is absolutely right in this respect: since every kind of success in later life—with the exception of extraordinarily gifted individuals—depends on the harmonious relationship to the community, it is downright cruelty to withhold the education toward this harmony from the child; for here later self-education cannot, for elementary physiological reasons, make up for the loss. But on the other hand, it is true that education only too easily and too often prevents the development of the creative powers, or else that it gives them no kind of stimulus. At this point, then, we have reached the antipole of education: I call it *inspiration*. The fact that it is a question here of the antipole, and not of the ideal of education, is made clear when we consider that one can only educate, *i.e.*, develop and train and insert into the universal rhythm of life what is there, what has already been born, whereas to inspire means to stimulate the growth of *new* life. In other words: if to educate corresponds to the bearing of life already conceived, inspiration corresponds to fecundation. And fecundation is absolutely necessary, wherever it is a case of renewal. Once the sexes have separated, there is no such thing as parthenogenesis.

This gives us the psychological reason of the phenomenon why education has, time and again, been attacked in the name of creativeness. The feminine principle as the principle of constancy, of repetition, and of routine can work for the good only where fecundation has already taken place. If for some reason the creative impulse which called to life a formation has reached its natural end, education can work only as dead routine. This, moreover, explains why only *inspired* teachers lead their pupils beyond their original state; they are the teachers inspired by Plato's *Eros paidikos*, in whom the impulse to fecundate the soul lives as an urge and an inner calling. But this is the very reason why education as such can never be an expression of the principle of fecundation. First, a general necessity cannot be based upon the existence of the exceptional. Second, and this is most important, precisely that which does *not* require inspired teachers, namely the general, is the essential side of education. The creative individual forms and shapes himself under all circumstances, no matter whether he was educated or not. Since in him something new is striving to emerge, it is impossible that in his case education should be of any real importance. Hence the task set to inspiration is different in kind from that set to any possible form of education.

This leads us back to the particular problem of America. At present America is the most educationalist and at the same time the least creative of all countries of the globe. Both phenomena are interconnected: wherever the feminine principle absolutely predominates, the masculine and creative principle, if it exists, must dwindle or else it must remain undiscovered or otherwise ineffective. Now what can be the practical solution of this problem? Obviously, the solution is this: that within their respective spheres both the masculine and the feminine principle—that is the principles of inspiration and education—should assert themselves and co-operate in the right way.

In the United States the former principle practically asserts itself not at all, and in most cases its mere existence and the necessity of it are not even suspected. This explains why everything is expected from education. Now those who are ultimately responsible for all the progress of mankind belong to the inspirer-type. But the real inspirers, the bearers of the *Logos spermatikos*, were never educators in any way; they were exclusively fecundators. The Athenians were not far wrong when they considered Socrates more of a seducer than an educator. Plato, on the other hand, being a man of a more feminine nature, not only proved the high level of his Ethos, but also his profound insight by always teaching in the name of his spiritual father. Thus the founders of Christianity were right in referring everything to Christ. He, too, was anything rather than educator. He, too, was nothing else than a fecundator. The fish was chosen as the symbol of Christ because of its being the only animal which procreates without contact with the feminine sex. An even profounder meaning underlies this symbol: it is the one and only natural impulse of every genuine spiritual procreator to disseminate his seed; what subsequently becomes of it concerns those who received it.

I THOUGHT it necessary in this connexion to stress the true meaning of education even more than the context of this chapter really permits, because in my opinion it provides the best approach to the true understanding of feminine predominance in the United States. Let us now proceed further, or rather let us connect the contents of the last paragraph with the preceding ones. When man is not absolutely different from what woman normally is, then this means that he lacks the stamina of a man. Nor can this state of things be improved by an exaggeration of one-sided virility from sparrow-like sexual proficiency to over-smartness in the field of business and finally up to an excessive development of the gambling instinct. All these traits, so typical of America, mean over-compensations. The outstanding, the all-important fact is that man must of *natural necessity* deteriorate if woman's spirit rules supreme, because of the primary fact that from the natural point of view only man and woman together make "man," and that the over-stressing of one pole must needs entail a weakening or a recessive development of the other.

And man undoubtedly deteriorates even more when woman predominates too much than she does when the situation is reversed. This is a fact; and the reason is that he then represents the weaker sex. I do not know who it was who first invented the term of the weak sex as applied to woman, but I feel certain that it must have been a particularly cunning and unscrupulous female. Her greater vitality from the biological point of view is well known. She can stand a far greater physical strain in spite of being more easily fatigued; she is generally more long-lived, hardly ever degenerates, and practically never dies out. But apart from this, woman is stronger compared to man for the reason that it is her nature to wait and that it is she who decides whether or not she will give herself—violation is quite contrary to the order of nature and never happens among animals. Moreover, in the long run, passivity always proves a greater power than activity. Chinese philosophy is absolutely right here. There is no activity or movement of indefinite duration; sooner or later it must come to an end, whereas there is no reason why repose should not last for ever. Accordingly, the reposing or expectant one of two essentially equal partners sooner or later not only inevitably calls forth the strength of the other, but even drains it. Besides, man is sexually, and from the point of view of soul-companionship, much more dependent on woman than she is on him. Most women can much better do without masculine companionship than men without feminine. Finally, man is psychologically far more permeable to the influence of woman than she is to that of man. Since it is her nature to give herself, she very easily adopts the psychology of the man she loves or admires, but on the other hand she reverts to type at a moment's notice, when her emotional attitude changes. As to the material power she often lacks, she can very well do without it because she possesses the all-important authority inherent in psychological influence. It is probably true that man brought woman into subjection by physical force, subsequently objectified in the form of law, because this was the one way for him to gain and preserve a predominating position. But even thus he never really succeeded; only a short time ago a Turkish woman told American audiences that if a man had six wives in her country, this only meant, as a rule, that he was henpecked six times instead of once only. For this reason the emancipation-movement in our Western World necessarily led not to an equality of position between man and woman, but to a disproportionate gain on the part of the latter; for it is not the fact of "equal rights" that counts, but the results this formal equality leads to.

Now there is no doubt of the fact that woman is, on the other hand, essentially imitative, yielding, and submissive, and that, if she chances to love, her greatest happiness consists in the merging of her personality with that of her lover. But at this point precisely the second consideration sets in which proves that woman really does represent the stronger sex. She may be as submissive and imitative as she possibly can be: this being natural to her, she never is broken or thwarted in her development by playing the part of the object instead of the subject. On the contrary, as far as historic records go, she has always attained her highest development and perfection by giving herself to an ideal, whether it be a god or a man. This implies that man, however much he may predominate, never really robs woman of her intrinsic power, if only she is familiar with what the French term as *son métier de femme.* This is why highly feminine women, such as those belonging to the Latin races, show so little interest in emancipation, even when their legal status is undeniably bad. Most of them would agree with the answer of a sturdy Canadian pioneer-woman, the mother of about a dozen stolid sons, when she was asked whether she wanted to have the vote: "The vote? If there is anything in the world the men folks can do alone, for Heaven's sake let 'em do it." The most effective rulership has always been the one which was not overt and conspicuous. Of course, woman can be degraded or demoralized by oppression, and her intellectual development certainly suffered under excessively patriarchal conditions. But if one looks at the problem from a higher point of vantage, one cannot help admitting that degradation was generally the exception and that under-development of the intellect never did great harm because woman's really great possibilities do not lie on the intellectual plane. Even where woman's position was a hard one during her youth —as a mother she has wielded tremendous power in all times and under all conditions. Personally, I always see Eve not in the light of the naïvely innocent seducer, but in that of the mother and mother-in-law of hundreds of thousands of awed descendants. We know today, thanks to psycho-analysis, that no man ever emancipates himself from his mother-image. He is subjected to it as much in patriarchal as in matriarchal communities.

But now let us consider the opposite case—the case of predominant woman. If *man* is in a state of psychological subjection, corresponding to that of woman under the patriarchal system, then he gains nothing and loses the best part of his nature, because his whole value consists in his freedom and initiative. And the development of these qualities presupposes the recognized primacy of other than feminine virtues. An essentially altruistic, docile, routine-loving, and custom-bound man is dangerously akin to the ancestral type of the slave; he inevitably and to an ever-increasing degree develops the physiological characteristics of the subject-type, as opposed to the freeman. In my own experience, this development has proceeded in the United States with an uncanny rapidity. The words and the specialized activities of the average modern American still breathe the spirit of the pioneer. But how little do they correspond to the actual human type! American man's outlook, taken as a whole, is that of woman; it is symbolic in the highest degree, that ever-recurring spectacle of a husband minding the children while their spectacled highbrow mother reads some intellectual book. The American man's reverence for public opinion, his general bent to answer to, not to create, demands, is a feminine characteristic; it is one expression among others of the eternally feminine wish for respectability. So is his suggestibility and the fickleness of his emotions. The psychological emasculation of the American man is completed by the fact that he knows practically no solitude. Man is not only the inventive part of humanity; he is the solitary part in the sense that his best achievements are products of what he does alone and by himself. There is a deep significance in the fact that most creative men married late or did not marry at all. In America man knows practically no singleness once he has reached the age of puberty. He has, of course, an office outside of the home, but that is not what I mean. Woman, who does not stand in need of solitude, has imposed her law on him, whether in the form of "companionate" or merely too early marriage, so that a modern American youth hardly ever has an opportunity to develop as a single and unique being. For, being subject to the influence of woman in the highest degree, once he marries, man changes psychologically in a similar sense as a girl does physiologically in losing her virginity. All these conditions taken together must needs make for a deterioration of the American man *as* man. And this development must needs continue, entailing cumulative effects, if no new chain of causes sets in. Almost everything that still appears purely masculine in American man is only what woman wants him to be and to represent in a world ruled by her. One instance of this is precisely what American he-men and go-getters take such pride in: their excessive bent toward material gain. The philosopher-physician of Spain, Marañon, has shown that the acquisition of the means of existence really belongs to the *sexual* functions of man. Just as every male bird is urged by instinct to feed his mate and the young, even so it is natural for the human male that he should support his family; this is why woman instinctively feels that a husband "should" be well off, whereas a marriage by man for money is unnatural. Thus America's materialistic outlook is only one more proof of woman's psychological predominance. By encouraging him to centre all his interests on money-making, woman leaves to him only what is his own as a sex-being. The fact that American man very often is a wonderful male in the animal sense, strong, healthy, clean, athletic, is relevant also. This, of course, woman wants him to be. But physical virility means little as compared with psychological.

LET us now turn to the problem how the deterioration of man affects woman herself. Man and woman being inwardly and essentially correlated, it robs her, too, of her best qualities. One cannot really change the nature of sex; however great the number of transitions and shades may be, a human being is at bottom either a man or a woman; and if he or she loses the qualities characteristic of his or her sex, the new qualities which are gained thereby only represent substitutes or unnatural exaggerations. On the other hand, the law of correlation implies that the actually stronger pole spontaneously develops the qualities *normally* belonging to the stronger, and the weaker those normally belonging to the weaker. We need not say more about the progressive feminization of man if woman rules supreme. Only this much may be added: if the man who has lost his psychological virility converges as a type with the harsh spinster type, a type which is frankly effeminate is developing, too, less in America, perhaps, than in those circles of Europe where the young women are gaining supremacy in their turn; it is a flabby, fat, soft, cushion-like type of man, who could not even be imagined as ever wearing a beard. But now let us examine closely the masculine virtues of the American woman. When first I concentrated on the most masculinely efficient variety of that type, I was immediately struck by its likeness to that of the Amazon. I then made what studies I could in the ethnographic field, and what I found out was that this type of American woman does indeed belong to the same genus to which the Amazons of all ages have belonged. She is undoubtedly very superior in most fields of ability; but here it is less a case of masculinity than of a higher development of what woman, too, is capable of by nature. And then much of what is attributed to increased ability here, is really due to increased and better chances for expressing her original being. Thus, every woman is a born ruler; in fact, she is more of the ruler than man, because what she performs in her household is very much the same as what a king has to perform in the State; this explains the fact that most queens who really were rulers are remembered as having been great queens, whereas comparatively few kings have been great kings. Nor is there any biological reason why woman should not be physically strong enough to be a proficient athlete. And it even corresponds to one of her own most fundamental urges that she should work. As a matter of fact, *she* is primarily the working portion of humanity, man being the player, the gambler, the adventurer, the eternal child. She is also primarily the responsible and serious creature; in this connexion, nothing could be more contrary to the order of nature than the idea that woman should be a toy. That is what *man* would like her to be, because of his own inherent playfulness; no woman originally thinks that way; even prostitutes look upon their activities as stern professional work and if they "keep smiling" they do so because that is part of the business. In all these respects, then, the efficiency of the American woman simply means higher development which she has every reason to be proud of. But the case appears different if we take into consideration other aspects of this type. Here we find precisely those features which characterized the Amazon in the eyes of the Greek. The Amazons were known as hard and cruel and cynical; this criticism has been made of all the many women who enlisted as soldiers during the World War among all the nations. This is so because if woman, whose natural centre lies in the sphere of feelings and emotions, who is the born altruist, becomes that which is typical of the warrior- or statesman-type of man, her emotional nature atrophies by natural necessity. There is no egoistic man who can at all compete in ruthlessness and recklessness with a genuinely egoistical woman. We do not know much about the Amazons of earlier days, but we know a great deal about those of America, and what we know of them impresses me as the completion of the picture after the sketch provided by the tradition of Penthesilea. It is true that woman is matter-of-fact by nature, man being the idealist and romanticist; therefore, the scientific, and not the poetic, outlook is normal for her. Still, all woman's highest gifts lie in the sphere of the emotions. If now she renounces the ideal of ancestral womanhood, which above all demanded a high culture of the emotional qualities, she is bound to become more hard, more matter-of-fact, more cynical, and more selfish than any man ever was, with the exception of criminal or psychiatric cases. Almost every front page of American newspapers provides illustrations of this. The utter lack of sentimentality with which women leave and sue husbands, the openness with which they disclose intimacies, the ruthlessness with which they express, when organized, their social instincts at the expense of the individual, are all cases in point. So much for the typical side of the question. But the tendency which is normal in the Amazon must lead to simply appalling forms if the development of her type happens to take place in a scientific age. During the nineteenth century the men, bent on the conquest of the material world, for a while tried to explain everything in terms of material facts. This did not last long with them. But the women were so delighted with the feeling that their matter-of-factness had at last become respectable that scientific matter-of-factness became the very religion of advanced womanhood. Henceforth sex-life, and even love, were to mean nothing more than a biological function; henceforth all emotional ties were to be got rid of. The masculine "Why?"—the source of all progress in knowledge and understanding—was transmuted into the very different and very feminine question "Why not?" applied indiscriminately to all life-problems. The original instinct that man should provide for the family degenerated into the pathologic desire that man should simply be the slave of her sweet will. "Facts" mean everything for that type of woman, "significance" means nothing. Accordingly, she no longer discriminates between sex-appeal and love. Man, too, has always desired the woman who merely appealed to him sexually, but on the other hand he always knew that this meant only desire and not love; he always knew how to distinguish between soul-love and what he instinctively felt to belong in the category of vice. That is, it is natural for man to have pure animal instincts on the one hand, and a soul-life on the other; thus, both Dante and Petrach were perfectly sincere and true to themselves when they longed for Beatrice and Laura, and yet had numerous concubines. But woman's nature is different; it is more "whole." If she looks upon sex in the masculine way, her wholeness is disrupted and she then becomes sex-bent without any reserve. Thus we find the newest pattern of American girls, who believe in facts only, lead sex-lives such as the most immoral of males, provided he has a soul, would never lead. It means nothing to her to give herself to scores of men, even in the form of marriage. For marriage on the basis of mere sex-appeal is, of course, very much more immoral a thing than any *liaison*. The whole problem of morality and immorality is settled in her eyes by the "fact" of the existence of contraceptives. All this can only be explained by an atrophy of the emotional sphere. This type of the American woman is endowed to an exaggerated degree with that very crudity the normal woman objects to so much in the case of primitive man. She cannot love in the true feminine fashion—which is not an inferior way, but exactly that which men reverence most in woman because they are incapable of it themselves. But here again the natural fact that between man and woman there exists an essential inward correlation comes into play: among American girls, a most curious prejudice is developing in favor of what they call the cave man. During my stay in the United States an enquiry was made in the girls' colleges as to the type of man the girls would prefer; more than half of them chose the cave man; only a certain percentage, quaintly enough, added to the word cave man: "but refined." If woman idealizes the cave man, this can only mean that man is lacking in virile primitivity. It is he in America who shows most of what, outside of the United States, is considered as specifically feminine sentiment. He is docile, yielding, submissive; he marries or pays whenever he is asked to do so. And it is typical that he is left by the woman, and not vice versa. One need only remember the many cases mentioned in Judge Lindsey's book, where he had to comfort abandoned boys. This, then, finally demonstrates the Amazon-quality of the most advanced type of the American woman. Many of these women prefer to retain, after marriage, their maiden-name with the prefix "Miss," or they revert to the latter after having divorced. Such a course would be unthinkable in the Old World, where the status of the married woman is considered higher than that of the girl. It means that the unmarried woman actually represents the fundamental type. The marriages she may go through only mean so many episodes to her.

All this "progressiveness" of the American woman as opposed to the Old World type, thus really amounts to an unnatural over-stressing, on her part, of what should be the masculine pole. She has lost to a high degree the capacity to love as only women can. She now loves more or less as men do, which is a very good thing in its own way; but the disappearance of woman's specific manner of loving means an absolute loss, nevertheless. Whoever has known the highest type of a European wife with her wonderful development and culture of the responsive and yielding faculties inherent in human nature, which are as passive faculties as the active ones, will realize the truth of the opinion we pronounced without further explanation. But I may give one more illustration of the same truth: it is the public reply of a woman to things I had said on the same lines, during my stay in America. She replied that my contentions were disproved by the mere fact of the American women's social and charity work! As though love had anything to do with social work and charity! I readily admit that as a social worker, the American woman stands foremost. In that one direction, her feminine nature has not been atrophied; on the contrary, it has perhaps been more highly developed than anywhere else on earth. But what is under-developed in the type of the American woman I am speaking of, is the sphere of the specifically feminine emotions. This alone explains her absurd idea that all unsatisfactoriness of love is due to what she calls "Puritanism"; this could only be true if love meant nothing else and nothing more than sexual desire and its fulfilment. And the same overdoing of masculinity on the basis of emotional under-development is the psychological root of the modern American woman's view of home life. Man's instinct does not originally urge him to go in for marriage. But, the centre of his professional activities lying outside the house, he finds his best recreation in the home, once he has founded one. As opposed to this, woman, whose traditional work is performed within the home, has always looked for recreation outside of it; this is the reason why she always loved hotel life, which few men really like. In our days the emancipation of woman has coincided with housing difficulties; this, in its turn, has given an additional impetus to her masculinization. It is she today, and not man, who discards the ideal of the home; it is she who believes that the kindergarten provides a better atmosphere for children than the home; the "home- and mother-type" is fast disappearing. From man's point of view this means such a catastrophe that Lucien Romier has gone as far as to anticipate that the resentment of the American man may lead to a new enslavement of woman in America, which is, theoretically speaking, actually possible owing to his physical force. But the effect on the children of woman's discarding of the home means even more than a catastrophe, because all culture is the result of the influence of the home atmosphere on the subconscious. In this respect the point of view of the modern American educationalist is unmitigated nonsense. School-training is very necessary, but it belongs to the "animal ideal"; there has never been a great man who owed anything essential to public education. As to the average—it is precisely the type of the

American college-bred man which provides the proof of the truth that this kind of education signifies very little indeed from the point of view of real culture. Remember the *boutade* by one of the contributors to the Symposium *American Civilization:* "An American University is an athletic association in which certain opportunities for study are provided for the feeble-bodied." It is obvious that the effect on woman must be worse still should home life really cease to play a prominent part. Children are, after all, gregarious creatures, and the really important influences being those which work upon them within the first years of their life, they usually are influenced by some kind of home atmosphere; it is likewise natural for man that the most important part of his life should have its centre outside of the home. But this is not natural for woman. Being close to nature by the latter's command, from which she never can free herself in reality, she must needs lose many of her best qualities owing to want of nourishment, if she cannot develop in correlation with a home. A club-woman, who is essentially such, is as inferior, taken as a type, as a man-nurse. That is to say, in the case of the inner adjustment inevitably developed by a life which is chiefly public, woman's really creative powers atrophy.

HERE, then, we have reached the decisively important aspect of the problem. Up to now we have considered man's and woman's specific psychological qualities in themselves, referring to the mystery of their correlation only so far as it constitutes the vital root of all particular phenomena. So far as any kind of "executive" is concerned, the qualities in question can indeed be taken as independent entities; for here it is a matter of applying or exploiting differentiated functions of the psychic organism, which are as incapable of change and invention as a fully articulated physical body is incapable of acting as a germ-cell. As opposed to this, the creative part of man's mind and soul has precisely the qualities of the latter; and if one wants to assign to it any particular "place" within the psychic organism, one can only name the wholeness of the undifferentiated unconscious. This is why creative work and executive work actually exclude each other. Just as no genius has ever commanded his inspiration, but in many cases has destroyed the possibility of the state of grace it represents by trying to do so; just as no toil or labour on the mother's side can direct or accelerate the growth of the child in her womb, whilst it can easily endanger it by allowing too many forces to escape into the outside world, in the same way only the keeping back to a certain extent of the energies from the field of executive gives a chance to the creative powers which exist in every human being. For I repeat: all executive acts are carried out by the differentiated functions of mind and soul and, however wonderfully efficient these may be along their own lines, they are incapable of original invention of any kind. Accordingly, an artist cannot work regularly eight hours a day; the time he does nothing is usually the time in which he is best employed. This explains why in all truly creative epochs in history work as such was not rated highly; this also explains why our present civilization, while assigning to a far greater number of human beings the quality or the honorary title of producers, is essentially a civilization of enterprise, promotion, and executive nature *as opposed* to true creation: those who undergo any amount of routine work take the lead everywhere and they are unmistakably suspicious of the creative mind. Now if creative man's creative powers belong to the wholeness of the undifferentiated unconscious, then only a "whole" human being can be creative. And this not only implies that man dare not become a machine in any way if creativeness be the ideal, but also that his must be a real organic wholeness, which is impossible, man being ultimately always either a woman or a man, if he or she has lost the specific qualities of sex in question; that is, the qualities at hand then cannot become expressive of the depths. Nor is this all. If the merely instrumental functions can act as independent entities, the *whole* human being never is complete in the sense of self-sufficiency. Where the creative depths are concerned, the fact that only man and woman together make man, asserts itself with the same force on the planes of spirit and mind and soul as in that of the body. *It follows that the uncreativeness of one sex must needs entail the uncreativeness of the other.* Herein lies the real reason why American life seems so mechanical and so abstract. Herein also lies the deepest reason for the general dissatisfaction and unrest which characterize both American men and women. As far as the former are concerned they usually simply stand perplexed and helpless before the riddle of a basic unhappiness which impels them to work and labour and toil as long as their forces last; they are afraid of leisure as very few of our contemporaries are of Hell. As to woman, the most frequent psychological situation one comes across is this: She is indignant that marriage is not satisfactory; she is indignant that the new form of companionate marriage does not seem to yield all the interest with which her hopes had invested it; she is indignant, in individual cases, at the apparent unsatisfactoriness of free love. And since her fundamental instincts have not changed since the days of Eve, she holds that the whole fault lies with man. He is not as he should be. She then demands, as a remedy, still greater power for her sex. But what she really stands in need of is something entirely different. She wants a type of man able to complete her as her equal and to draw out and develop forces within her which she feels she possesses, but cannot express. She wants man to be creative on all planes in his masculine way, in order that she may become creative in her feminine way.

Now how can this creativeness be defined? Since it is a question here of the very well-springs of life, the essence of which is mystery, there can be no approach to them by means of exact science; here, symbolic images only can lead to understanding, by reflecting mirror-wise, in a form corresponding to the requirements of the mind, what lives on the other side of all possible human name and form in the depths of the soul. Thus, the Greeks used respectively the symbols of *Logos spermatikos,* spermatic, fecundating spirit, and *Eros kosmogonos,* or World-creating Love, for the determination of creative virility and femininity on the spiritual plane. The symbolic images of Chinese philosophy are more comprehensive still. For them, Yang and Yin both ruled and constituted the whole world's process, the former meaning "the Creative" in the masculine sense, and the latter "the Conceiving" in the feminine. Both are equal value; both are necessary for the continuance of life; and they must co-operate in harmony with the world-sense, if life is to progress on ascending lines. And indeed, on the physical plane, impotence or barrenness is obviously synonymous with death. But the same applies to the plane of spiritual values. Spirit, too, is a concrete, a live, a vital thing. Only creative spirit in its masculine variety can create values, and only creative spirit in its feminine receptive modality can understand and apply these values. Both Yang and Yin are omnipresent and all-pervading, to be found at the roots of all phenomena and situations. The only modern concept which applies to the creative spirit understood in the basic sense is that of *inspiration*—it very characteristically stands for a function and not for a substance. The underlying meaning is that the normal psychological functions can be animated or ensouled from a deeper region which may even not be of this world. This meaning is true to fact: "the Creative" in all cases lives beyond the range of manifested phenomena. Now we have already contrasted the principle of inspiration with that of education, the former being of masculine, the latter of feminine essence. But this is correct only on lower planes and within certain limits. As I have shown in the chapter "*Jesus der Magier*" of *Menschen als Sinnbilder* (French edition, *Figures Symboliques*, Paris, Librairie Stock), spirit is always masculine, whether it be understood in the sense of *Logos spermatikos* or *Eros kosmogonos;* thus, even the original Christian idea of love, which corresponded almost exactly to Plato's *Eros,* meant not man's loving response, but God the Father's power of creation. Spirit is always a power of inspiration as opposed to childbearing, which in each case is carried out by the earthly part of the soul. Let us recall here the profound Chinese idea of the omnipresence and all-pervasiveness of Yang and Yin, which anticipates for the universe at large the recognition of modern science that every human being consists of both masculine and feminine elements. Now what about woman's creativeness in the psychic field? *It also is a power of inspiration.* But whereas man's typical power of inspiration resides in the mind, woman's creativeness resides in the sphere of the emotions, which never have that quality in man. This is not the place in which to state an exhaustive philosophy of the emotions, but this much may be said: Just as the feelings, in the case of woman, are rational functions, that is, faculties leading to true understanding and judgment which for lack of differentiation they seldom are in man, similarly woman's emotional nature radiates creative suggestions.

This, then, explains why woman's intellect and intellectuality appeal so little to man. Woman can be as intelligent and intellectual as any man, but in that case her intellect appears particularly detached from the fountains of life. This is why an intellectual woman usually is an organizer or a manager—for organization and management no inspiration is necessary. Intellect in itself is only a surface-expression of life: everything depends on what stands behind it. True, there have been a few rare cases where something akin to genius has inspired woman's intellect. But the value of this kind of genius was never one that could be compared even in the remotest sense with the importance of woman's real creative power. This power has been known from time immemorial and, since all concepts have been invented by man, and this particular power cannot be clearly defined in their terms, it has often been reverenced as either divine or demoniacal. Modern Western idealism has misunderstood its essence to the point of believing it to be nothing better than man's—the male's—own illusions, reacting back on him. In reality, it is a power of the same kind as is the creative spirit in the sense of the Greek concept *Logos spermatikos,* the spermatic, fecundating spirit; that is, it is a thoroughly concrete and vital force which corresponds to that of procreation, to potency in the physical sphere. Mysteriousness is its very essence. It must appear more mysterious than man's because a creativeness having its source in the emotions, instead of in the mind, cannot be defined in intellectual terms. Now to this kind of creative power, not the Chinese, nor the Greeks, but the Hindus have found the nearest approach. Their symbolic image for woman's specific creative power is what they call *Shakti.* Those who want to know what the Hindus themselves have to say in explanation of it, should re-read Rabindranath Tagore's contribution to *The Book of Marriage.* Tagore himself translates *Shakti* by "charm." But it is not the kind of charm which corresponds to the current adjective "charming" that he means, and certainly not that very superficial attractiveness Americans call "it"; but charm in the original sense of spell, of sorcery. Masculine creativeness, too, is something mysterious; the prototype of creative man has always been God Who made the world out of nothing. Still, this kind of power does not seem so very mysterious, because every man possesses it at least in the sphere of imagination. As opposed to this, woman's creative power seems utterly mysterious because it cannot even be perceived by the eye of the intellect; because it has led to the most tremendous effects in all history, and yet these effects were never immediate effects. No inspiring woman ever gave out directly new ideas. Here, then, the fact that from the natural point of view man and woman form one single unit asserts itself again—only in a paradoxical form corresponding to the mysteriousness of the case. *If man is the inspirer, that is the fecundator on the physical and mental planes, woman is the same on the plane of the soul;* here man, and not woman, gives birth; for even intellectual creative work is ultimately emotion-born, all creation on earth having to be carried out by earthly means and the emotions belong to the earthly part of man. To resume and complete a sentence just written: an inspiring woman does not herself give out new ideas, but after fecundation by her feelings and emotions, man gives birth to them. Accordingly, all great works of art—taking the word in its widest sense—have been brought forth by man; but there has never been any creativeness if inspiring women were lacking, however little may have been known about them. Are we not now able to understand perfectly why America today is uncreative? Both man and woman instinctively see in creativeness the highest value. Both must accordingly feel inferior because they feel impotent. And both must instinctively attribute the fault to the other sex. Man depends on the inspiration by woman in order to create. On the other hand, woman desires man on the plane of mind and soul as actively as man desires woman on the physical plane. If now we look back on what we have learnt about the characteristics of American men and women, the whole case appears clear. The American woman has reached a very high development along masculine lines. But precisely because she has done so and has, moreover, lost that undifferentiated wholeness which is characteristic of the true feminine type, she has also lost her *Shakti*, her charm in the sense of inspiring power. This accounts for the mechanical and unartistic quality of all masculine work in the United States. But on the other hand, it is woman's nature to yield, to follow, to carry out. Therefore, if there is no man she can look up to, her best qualities cannot develop. She must needs lose her *Shakti*. The vicious circle is complete.

IS THERE no remedy for this state of things? There is. It consists, as everywhere, first and foremost in the true understanding of the case and its significance. A change of institutions and laws would lead to no improvement; this fact has been conclusively demonstrated precisely by the United States to all who have eyes to see; for the present state of affairs has come about in spite of all new and better laws. One may even say that the latter are in so far guilty of having brought about America's present unhappy state as they have drawn the attention of most Americans away from "significance," which is creative, to facts, which are without any vital power. The more Americans believe that bad marriage can be cured by better divorce, or soul-life improved by a more intelligent use of contraceptives, to mention only these two examples, the more freely the vital significance, which is the real cause of the sad state of things, can work itself out. On the other hand, understanding as such is the greatest force man commands. Wherever it reaches down to the depth of a problem, mechanical devices for carrying out the desired effects are usually unnecessary.

The first thing to understand is that all facts, rightly understood, seem to foretell that America will remain a matriarchal country. If it became matriarchal in a very short time, in spite of the fact that the whole tradition of the immigrants and practically all the institutions were patriarchal in spirit, there must be very deep reasons for this. These probably lie in the influence of the land itself, though I cannot offer any explanation of the fact; most of the Indian tribes who flourished in the territory of the United States were matriarchal too. But at this point one should also realize that matriarchalism in itself is no evil. As we explained in the beginning, it is as natural for the one pole to predominate as it is for the other; any particular state of balance between man and woman becomes pernicious only when it undermines the development of the best characteristics of the poles. Italy, Spain, and France, too, are matriarchal. European culture actually owes its birth to that period of the Middle Ages when woman was idealized beyond all reason and her judgment in all matters except political and military was the last resort; the cultures of the Renaissance and of the eighteenth century only meant more advanced stages in evolution of the same fundamental state of balance between the sexes. It is true that woman then wielded power not as an Amazon, not as the equal of man, but as his mysterious inspirer who wanted him to be supremely virile in a more refined sense than he could have become without her influence. But we shall soon see that nothing in principle prevents a similar evolution in the United States. What we have to retain at this point is that everything speaks in favour of the hypothesis that America will remain matriarchal, and that matriarchy in itself is not contrary to culture. Let us remember here what we said about the positive developments to which American socialism, privatism, and even the prevalence of the animal ideal can lead: if we link up these beliefs with those of the present chapter, we will perceive at once that these positive developments presuppose, as a matter of fact, a matriarchal adjustment of the nation. But there is even more to be said both in support of the theory that woman will predominate permanently in certain respects, and in favour of matriarchy: the modern social state with its motherly attitude toward all, its predominant interest in education, its prejudice in favour of the weak and the sick as opposed to the strong, and its inherent pacifism breathes the spirit of woman more than that of man. Therefore, it would be only a logical development if woman took an ever-increasing share in public life. Thus a country in which woman has evolved the characteristics of the ruling race has every chance of creating an exemplary social state sooner than any other country. The reason of the harshness of all patriarchal socialism, whether that of Prussian Militarism or Russian Bolshevism, rests on the fact that man is not an altruist by nature; he can make the group his principal concern only at the expense of the individual. With woman, feeling for the group and the individual do not exclude each other. It is accordingly in American matriarchalism that we find one of the chief reasons for that general kindliness, good-will, and happiness in free co-operation which is the most positive characteristic of American life. It is, therefore, not American matriarchalism as such in which the danger lies. *It lies only in the fact that in America the man-and-woman-relationship, adjusted in the sense of predominating woman*—an adjustment which is in itself as normal as any other kind of adjustment—*is distorted in its qualification.* Now how can this distortion be readjusted? The solution of the problem lies in the very opposite to what most progressive American women think: it lies not in a still greater emancipation of woman, *but in the emancipation of man.*

Man in the United States is, to put it roughly and exaggeratedly, in a position equivalent to what woman's used to be, *mutatis mutandis*, in the East. Whereas his material life is usually quite comfortable, he has to put up with a minimum of soul-comfort and inspiration such as the poorest European wretch would not stand. If the American man usually jests in his family, this means that he tries to laugh away the dimly felt sadness of his lot. For the moment American women behave and feel very much as all privileged aristocracies did. Failing to see that they are not isolated, but that they depend for their well-being on the corresponding welfare of other classes, they think that what is wrong can be mended by gaining yet more power; this, and not a legitimate demand for further emancipation, is the real *raison d'être* of most of the manœuvering of organized womanhood, under the pretence that woman still holds an inferior position. But the response to all I said in my American lectures with regard to the necessity of an emancipation of man, makes me anticipate the possibility that American womanhood at large will soon realize the truth of the situation. When I wrote in the *Forum* of woman as the higher caste, the *New York Times* commented on it as follows: "What Count Keyserling appears not to understand is that it was with the view of remedying this state of affairs that the Nineteenth Amendment was adopted. Now that the women have been granted the right to vote, it is confidently expected that they will soon demonstrate that they are no better than the men." This *boutade*, probably without the author's knowing it, actually hits one of the subconscious mainsprings of the emancipation-movement. American women really want to be less superior than they are. Most of those who have enough leisure to suffer from life are profoundly unhappy. Women would not leave one lover or one husband after the other; they would not take to drink, nor would they exhaust themselves in essentially uninteresting executive work, if all was well with them. The fact is that even the most masculine American woman is a woman still. And this means that she wants to be inspired by man as she has to be fecundated, in order to bear fruit; that she wants to reverence. Now woman can reverence only the man who is a true man in the creative sense. And she feels, ever so dimly, that the type which is ever more and more developing into the prototype of the American, is evolving more and more precisely those faculties in which she herself excels—at the expense of those she lacks. *She* is the working portion of humanity; *she* is by nature bent on economics; *she* thinks of security and maintaining and providing for the children; she, in a word, is created to incarnate the earnest side of life. Accordingly, it is only logical that she should want to win for herself all the posts and positions in life which are hers and not man's by the will of nature. And she desires as much power as possible in order to put man back in his right place, which is that of the creator, the artist, the adventurer, the eternal child. Under present conditions, this can really best be achieved by matriarchy of a kind.[1] This subconscious urge, springing from woman's eternal nature, cannot, of course, find its intended realization during the present period of the dawn of the geological Epoch of Man. This is an essentially economic age; thus, for a

[1] I have just discovered that a German philosopher, whose name I read for the first time, Ernst Runeman, has very cleverly exposed the same idea. See his article "*Auf dem Wege zum Matriarchat*" in *Philosophische Hefte*, Heft 2, 1928.

long time to come, man will have to give more of his attention to things economical than is good for what is best in him. Yet this much can be achieved: the more woman becomes man's equal in the economic field, the greater will be the loss of prestige of all that is not manly, but really female about the modern type of man; and the less, at the same time, will woman be ambitious to compete with man for proficiency along such lines of activity as have been his privilege for the last century. Thus, what is essentially valuable in man, on the one hand, and woman, on the other, would again be recognized as such. Woman would again find men she could reverence and man would meet women capable of inspiring him.

But how can this change be brought about or accelerated? In spite of all the initiative she may show along specialized lines and even in spite of her *Shakti*, which, after all, only few possess in a marked degree, just as there are few men of genius, woman is, in her essence, the responding part of mankind. Accordingly, she is fundamentally right and not wrong—though mostly in respects different from those she has in view—when she complains that all present ills are man's fault. If man is deficient, she cannot attain perfection by the law of nature. How, then, can a higher type of man be evolved? The answer is: precisely by means of the present predominance of American woman, provided she understands the real significance of the situation. The spirit of invention has not fallen to woman's share in the cosmic scheme. But, on the other hand, whatever woman has herself received she can transmit to man in a manner no man is capable of. Thus, all religions have really conquered through the women; thus, all reputations of spiritual creators have been made by them. Eventually, men always become what women want them to be. Thus, the woman-cult and in particular the mother-cult of the American men really is America's great opportunity. *If the American woman truly and profoundly understands —not only with her intellect, but with all her heart and soul—what is wrong with present American man, she will soon change him.* She may not be able to work a change in her husbands or lovers even then, but she will surely be able to make of her *sons* different and better beings than they would have otherwise become. She will in any case create a new cultural atmosphere—an atmosphere in which those values will rule supreme, the incarnation of which makes man grow and rise to his full height. This, then, leads us to a new positive aspect of American matriarchy, making it appear pregnant with similar possibilities and potentialities which led in the past to European culture. In America today the same cultural tradition belongs to women's colleges which in Europe belongs to the universities. One can never tell where a man has spent his years of study, for in most cases he becomes unfaithful to whatever tradition his university may incarnate in itself, as soon as he has left it and starts on an entirely different career; for instance he sells bonds, and soon forgets that he ever did anything else. But one *can* tell in what college a woman has been brought up. Accordingly, American women even today do incarnate a cultural tradition. What is required henceforth is that this tradition should be put to its proper use. At the present moment, most girls think that they have achieved all that can be expected of them, when they have become highly educated and continue to share intellectual and artistic interests throughout their later life, in particular in reading. But this means little from the national point of view. *Henceforth the girls should look upon their college days as a preparation for creating a cultural home atmosphere.* Culture *only* grows out of and within the home. It can emerge *only* if the sense of its values has been inbuilt into the subconscious of the little child. Men become cultured *only* when the mothers make them so. Thus, it really rests with the women to solve the problem of the raising of the level of American men, which is so badly needed. Here, then, I may say what I ultimately think of the American woman, an idea I have had to hide so far in view of the urgent problems at stake. I think that she represents a splendid human material. She need only abandon that wrong adjustment and outlook we have dealt with, and she may grow to be something truly magnificent. Even today when the flapper-type is enjoying a very undeserved prestige, by far the best thing I have seen in America is the American girl. The days I had the privilege to spend in women's colleges count among my happiest memories. Not because I dwelt among so many young people who were charming in the current sense of the term, but because I felt in the general atmosphere a true aspiration toward a better state. I never addressed more understanding and responsive audiences in any European town. My personal conclusion is very definite: the youngest generation has already passed beyond the flapper-state. It has likewise already passed beyond the harshness of ancestral Puritanism. It is eager to evolve that wholeness which alone can be woman's true ideal. And the moment such women exist. corresponding men will evolve of natural necessity.

## *Democracy*

THERE is, of course, no question as to whether or not democracy represents an absolute ideal. The only reasonable question to ask is, first, what the word democracy, which may mean anything, means to Americans; second, whether that which it stands for in the United States is really appropriate to their condition; and finally, whether the present state of things is pregnant with a propitious or an unhappy future. As a European, one must plunge back into the irrational bathos of mediæval belief if one wants to understand what democracy really means to Americans. Whether Walt Whitman sings religious hymns in praise of it, or John Dewey extols it as the only state worthy of mankind, or statesmen like Wilson and Coolidge and Hoover give out messages addressed to Europe which sound in European ears like the denouncements of prophets, unquestionably inspired by God himself—it always appears as a non-rational symbol of a still undifferentiated state; it is what the hieroglyphs and ideographs and the runic letters were in the dawn of history, and what in our own era the Cross meant to the early Christians. Hence the tremendous power of the symbol. Hence, on the other hand, the irrelevance of all arguments directed against democracy in the United States, and of all doubts as to its actual existence. Modern American intellectuals are even more inclined than Europeans to doubt both the fact of its existence and its value. One cannot, of course, speak of a government of the people, for the people, by the people, unless all decisions are taken unanimously. In the textual sense, apart from small circles, the only real democracy which ever existed was that of the early Christians, who held that the Holy Ghost manifests Itself by means of the unanimity of the faithful, which true democracy continued to exist up to recent times only in the Islamic world and determines even today the peculiar quality of the parliament of Angora. As soon as differentiation sets in, all real government amounts to class-rule, and it is only a matter of definition whether or not it is so called. For the only objection to this assertion which can be taken seriously, namely that in a democratic commonwealth the actual rulers are representative of the people, which is not true of all classes, can be refuted by the one argument that anybody and anything may be as representative of the people as a democratic government. Mussolini certainly is more representative of the true Italy of today than any elected political body in the United States has been of that nation within the memory of man. So were most of the monarchs fifty years ago. In this connexion, everything depends on the inner assent of the people to those who rule them.

Now, if democracy is taken to mean equality, then there is indeed more social equality in the United States than anywhere else in the West. The historic cause of this lies in the fact that America was settled almost exclusively by members of the lower classes of Europe who very naturally objected to any new "looking up" to "their betters." However, this social equality is not due to equal rights, but to an extraordinary like-mindedness. As a political and social system, none is less likely to make for permanent equality than the Constitution of the

United States, even though the unequalities peculiar to Europe may not develop there. With equality as with democracy, everything depends on the way the word is understood. The American idea of equality is not only originally, but essentially, that of the frontier: it does not imply nor ask for equality of rewards or possessions —what it claims is only equality of opportunity; the reward is to be proportionate to the merit. Hence the modern expression of this idea according to which not socialization of property is required, but socialization of will—equality of position need not exist, but giving and taking should counterbalance each other. That one should ever have imagined that this idea made for equality is the result of the unequalled opportunities provided, for so long, by America's "unlimited possibilities." Logically, this idea must needs lead to progressive *un*-equality and so it has as a matter of fact, with the one exception of social type. As soon as different merits, which are always due to different aptitudes, are accepted as deserving different rewards, unequality, and not equality, is accepted as a ruling principle, whether the people know or admit the fact or not. Sooner or later, the truth must take shape in the form of actual life. And this must be the case in the United States, even more than anywhere else because of the American belief in wealth as a distinction. If wealth counts in any way, then every dollar more or less must make for a difference of status and standing. Most Americans fail as yet to see this; the reason is that they are still labouring under the illusions of the liberal era. But it was a case of logical development that European socialism, which was the legitimate child of liberalism and turned out so different from the latter because it realized that liberalism inevitably results in plutocracy, should have dissociated, as a matter of principle, the idea of income from that of merit. There is indeed no other way to maintain equality in a world centred in economics. And it is equally logical that Bernard Shaw should consider the compulsory equality of income for all as the only possible issue: there is really no other alternative, *if* one believes in equality as an ideal. It will be seen in the course of this chapter why I cannot accept Shaw's premises. But however this may be, the natural development in America certainly tends toward ever greater unequality with regard to material standing. *Here* resides the real danger, because the privileged hereditary positions that are bound to develop, if nothing interferes with the process, will inevitably lack the basis of individual worth. If wealth means value; if property is considered sacred and if it can be inherited as a matter of course—how is a stratification according to more financial power to be avoided? American radicals sometimes hope for a revolution as a means to prevent the establishment of a plutocracy. But if there is a country where a revolution of the mildest kind is quite improbable, it is America. First of all, the American nation is growing more conservative in the Swiss sense of the term from year to year. And then there is no conceivable reason why prosperity—not of all, to be sure, but of a sufficient number precisely among the working classes—should not continue for a century. Even the complete ruin of the farmers would not, for years to come, mean the impoverishment of the United States taken as a unit, because an almost exclusively industrial civilization could be practically self-supporting for a long time in the present state of the world. And there never has been a social revolution the actual provokers of which were not empty bellies.

Nevertheless, there does exist a great deal of true equality in the United States, and this is not likely to change in spite of what has just been said. But the kind of equality in question here is not advantageous in all respects: among other things, it implies lack of differentiation and superficiality. It has been pointed out that the original root of standardization was the paradoxical situation that the citizens of the United States were from the outset so unequal that an external standardization had to be achieved by any means at hand, in order to preserve unity. There is a good deal of truth in this. Only it should be added that it explains more precisely the later development. The more immigrants from different parts of the world crossed over the Atlantic and the Pacific, the more did the unity of the nation become dependent on outward organization. This is the real reason why almost every type of man who settles in the United States becomes an extreme extravert: only by an almost complete extraversion of all interests, which imply a repression from the field of consciousness of all contents of the inner world not in tune with the new life, can satisfaction or happiness be gained. I have made a special study of this problem precisely with Germans and Russians, the most introverted of Europeans. German-Americans generally appear more materialistic and superficial, more devoid of intellectual and spiritual interests, than Americans of Anglo-Saxon extraction, simply because they had to repress what is profoundest in their nature in order to adapt themselves to the life-form of the United States. As to the Russian of the pre-Bolshevik type—if he becomes Americanized, he develops into the worst of hustlers and bustlers. The kind of extraversion peculiar to the American is so utterly opposed to the original adjustment of the Russian that he not only becomes superficial but neurotic as a type. For there is a kind of hurry and bustle that signifies only an attempt to escape from oneself.

The obvious kind of equality one meets with in America cannot, therefore, be attributed to democracy, in whatever sense the term be understood; it is due simply to externalization. And it naturally tends toward the opposite of true democracy. Here we find the opportunity to follow out a line of thought we developed only up to a certain point in "Privatism." We found there that an exclusive bent toward private interest makes for narrowness. But it implies an even worse danger—and this threatens precisely what is best in democracy. If all interests of private life are conceived in terms of money; if impersonal entities called corporations, aiming at the impersonal goal of production or social service, rule supreme; if thus all interests are de-personalized, as best exemplified by those agencies whose business it is to raise the "big wind," that is, to collect free gifts by professional technique; if even personal relationships are based first of all on community of interest and mutual service (no type of man or woman forgets former "friends" so quickly when they vanish from the radius of daily interest as does the American)—then two things are bound to follow: First, an ever-increasing standardization which will level down; for it is only to the lowest common denominators that all human beings can be equally related —the denominators we called the animal ideal and the mere externals of life. The second inevitable consequence is a chain of causes which works directly against equality of rights. Equality does not exist in nature's domain; here, superior force implies supremacy in the absolute sense. Nature is even essentially cruel; she knows of no compromise except as a chance result due to a struggle between forces which happen to be actually equal. Wherever one natural force succeeds in conquering the other, it puts an end to it. Now, a considerable degree of this natural cruelty is to be noticed in the United States wherever a man is unsuccessful; and this cannot help making for an increasingly clear-cut discrimination between the originally strong and the originally weak. Moreover, since the increasing rationalization of business makes for increasing concentration of capital on the one hand, and for an ever-increasing hierarchization of the leading intellects on the other, it is inevitable that present development, if left to itself, must lead to a general hierarchization of American society, the like of which even the Middle Ages never witnessed. And the resulting hierarchy would be really inhuman—not only because the standards of nature would predominate, but because practically no one would ever be in a position to act according to his own wish or judgment, since he would always have to think of the interests he represented. Mediæval society, too, was based on the idea of representation; to that extent it also was hard on the individual. Still, it was founded on a hierarchy of spiritual values. Modern industrial feudalism would be founded on material interests only, for which reason it would be inhuman in its very essence. Even during the World War and after we saw how millions of human beings were sacrificed with the best of consciences to the interests of coal and oil; this kind of de-humanization can only increase as time goes on. Now since most of the wealth of the world belongs today to the United States and there is no reason whatever why the capitalistic development should not continue there for a long time to come, there is obviously very little chance of America's remaining a democracy in the sense it is supposed to be today. As a matter of fact, the general belief no longer corresponds to the facts even at the time I write. If very few notice the truth, this is chiefly due to the fact that most Americans still think in terms of the eighteenth century. I said at the beginning of this chapter that in order to understand what democracy means to Americans, a European must plunge back, in his imagination, into the irrational bathos of the mediæval mind. However shrewd and matter-of-fact Americans may be in practical life—in their ideas and beliefs they are, as a nation, still in the mythical stage. But quite apart from this there is no possible equation between the ideas of the eighteenth century and those of the modern world. All Americans are certainly free and equal when judged by the standards of two hundred years ago. (I was even told once that whoever was not born free and equal must be a foreigner.) But the real foundations of the modern world are different. New formations have developed in the United States which no philosopher of the eighteenth century could anticipate and which are much more important and powerful today than any institution they conceived, the Constitution included. And every one of these formations tends to develop in the direction of increasing unequality.

ACCORDINGLY, the problem whether "democracy" will last in the form it is believed in by most Americans, as an ideal or a fact, does not concern us at all. Yet it is true that America *is* a democracy. It is a democracy in the one sense which really matters—namely as the normal life-form of the zoölogical genus *homo Americanus*, just as there are life-forms which are normal for beetles and stags. I had occasion to show in several chapters of *Europe*—and I do not wish to repeat myself—that it is at bottom a question of original structure whether the life-form of a nation is aristocratic or democratic. There are peoples within which the great majority of individuals belong to a unified type and in which, moreover, the social tendencies predominate; such nations are basically democratic, whatever their actual institutions may be like; in this sense, pre-revolutionary Turkey was as much of a democracy as republican America. There are other peoples in which a general feeling for equality prevails, but where an innate sense of quality and superiority allows for the recognition of exceptional positions in individual cases; such was the structure of ancient China. Other nations, again, are originally built up of various types which cannot be unified. In their case a democracy in the American sense can never be a success. The normal life-forms of such nations are either intricate caste systems, as they exist in India and Germany, with their rich variety of human types; or, in the case that they are composed of only two complementary types, such as make up the Russian nation, syndicalism like the Soviet-system; or finally, if the sense of value or quality predominates, aristocracies of some kind. England, too, is really an aristocracy; for only *gentlemen* are or consider themselves as equals there, and the larger proportion of the nation does not consciously belong to the gentleman-class; only the marvellous political tact of the latter made them re-insure, as it were, their very aristocracy in democratic institutions, long before it became imperative. Thus, with the political and social structures, it is primarily not a case of ideals or of morals, but of zoölogy. The deepest reason why the so-called ideals of the Allies, which materialized in the terms of the Versailles Treaty, made for increasing unrest and not for permanent peace was precisely that the fundamental truth stated above was not comprehended. Every definite structure, of course, facilitates the expression of certain values to the detriment or exclusion of others. But first it is not safe to say that the values apt to be manifested within a democratic system are of a higher order than those manifested within aristocracies, since all that is spiritual and metaphysical has its exponent in the unique, which democracy discountenances in favor of the social. And second, since the structure of a nation is primarily a question of zoölogy, it inevitably follows that until every nation has gained or regained its normal structure there can be no question of a permanent state of equilibrium.

Now the Americans undoubtedly belong to the democratic portion of the human family. But the roots of their democracy are different from those of British democracy, whence they inherited most of their ideals and institutions. They are not democrats from political insight and tact. Least of all are they democrats in the original Nordic sense that, all men being equally individual and self-assertive, universal liberty only combined with universal respect for the law, could guarantee the welfare of the whole. The Americans are democrats in so far as they are Socialists, Privatists and as the mother-spirit of woman predominates. One should remember here how little reverence law commands in the United States; this, too, can be traced partly to the predominating spirit of woman; if woman, on the one hand, out of her organic need of security and respectability is more in favor of law than man, she is always ready, on the other, to break it in individual cases. But here we can lead the trend of thought with which we ended the last chapter to its logical conclusion. We said that the United States were certain to remain a matriarchy and that, moreover, their best prospects for the future were bound up with this fact. The spirit of predominating woman is, indeed, the main root precisely of what is good in the American variety of democracy. For this spirit today is practically the only safeguard for the preservation of original liberty. If man's spirit still predominated, as it did in the beginnings of American history, and if, moreover, the American men of today were as ruthlessly masculine as were the early Puritans and Pioneers, the United States would represent even at the time I write an oligarchy of a harsher type than Carthage's; then the individual business-kings would be more ruthless than the financial magnates of ancient Rome. There is absolutely nothing in the American institutions to prevent this development; the effects which liberalism produced in Europe would have been a hundred times more violent in the United States. As a matter of fact, it has not done so and it is doing so ever less and less from year to year. The reason is that America is irresistibly changing from a patriarchal into a matriarchal nation. The organizations of women are sure to become ever more formidable powers as the years go on. Owing to

"Privatism"—the first foundation of national life congenial to woman's spirit—and owing to her natural proficiency on economic lines (for hundred thousands of years she has been earning and saving and calculating, while man only thought of hunting and playing and gambling) there is every probability that she will soon play not only indirectly but directly a leading, if not *the* leading part in public life. But even today the natural instincts of woman which are social and altruistic are irresistibly consolidating into the really vital roots of American national life. Thus, a chain of causes quite different from those which originally led to democracy—and almost opposite in spirit to that which still works in England—is now affording the guaranty for the preservation of liberty. Zoölogists would call this convergence of originally different types a case of pseudomorphosis.

THE essential features of American Democracy as distinguished from those of other democracies have already been dealt with at sufficient length in the chapters "Socialism" and "Privatism." It is, indeed, on the one hand, American Socialism unrecognized as such, as opposed to consciously advocated liberalism which guarantees democracy in the United States, and, on the other, the lack of political interest, *not* the existence of a singularly sound political system. Here I may say something more on the subject of the primacy and supremacy of private life and its specific outlook in the United States. The typical American dislike of State interference certainly has profounder roots than the prejudice against what Americans consider radical theories. One of its chief roots undoubtedly is that

Americans realize, however unconsciously, that this particular democracy can thrive only so long as the chief emphasis rests on private will as opposed to State compulsion. Now this is America's greatest originality and also the best guaranty for its future significance. *America is predestined to represent, in the new World in the Making, the polar opposite or counterpoint to socialism in the European sense of the word.*

Here I can do no better than oppose the American ideal to that of Bernard Shaw, as expressed most clearly in the book he has dedicated to the Intelligent Woman. It is really fortunate that Bernard Shaw has never crossed the Atlantic: had he done so, what I consider the most important book relating to progress on socialistic lines in the European sense would probably have remained unwritten, or, at any rate, it would have lacked that one-sidedness which alone makes for deep-reaching influence. Shaw rightly advocates general prosperity; he rightly sees in poverty a disease pure and simple, to be fought like leprosy. But he does not see that a great deal of what he advocates has already been realized in the United States along lines entirely different from those he believes the only possible ones. Shaw holds that a satisfactory state of social equilibrium can never be reached by means of free competition. (This is the reason why, like most socialists, he seems to anticipate revolutions on American soil.) According to his idea, all changes should be brought about by compulsion and law. There is, indeed, no other way to realize a socialistic state *if* a nation is at heart individualistic or else divided into ruler and subject types, like the Russian nation. But this is precisely why socialism cannot be a possible ideal for such countries. A far greater number of institutions and domains certainly can, or should, be socialized than have been up to the present; it is one of the most instructive sides of Shaw's book that it makes clear to all to what a considerable extent and degree not only socialism, but even communism, is the normal form of civilized life; what is true of the army, the police, the mail service, of public instruction etc., will very likely apply in the near future, all over the civilized world, to most matters of common necessity and concern. But in individualistic countries socialism can never be more than a substructure. The individualist is zoölogically defined by the fact that the individual tendencies within him predominate over the social; accordingly, he can reach perfection only if the emphasis continues to lie on what is individual. Moreover, the individualist's imperfections along social lines are nothing as compared with the deterioration which necessarily results from a thwarting of his native tendencies—an individualist cannot be changed into a socialist without such thwarting; hence the ideal of compulsion as opposed to liberty which even Shaw adheres to. Now if there is anything that has been proved once and for all, it is the fact that man can never develop his best qualities unless he is free. In any case, no man whose last resort is not his own deepest self ever attains personal superiority. For this, Shaw himself in his theories provides the most instructive example. His conscious idea is, of course, that, once the general framework of life has been socialized and the individual adapted to this general state, personality will develop all the more richly. But unconsciously he knows, exactly as Lenin knew, that personal superiority implying personal authority cannot thrive in a socialistic State. Accordingly, Shaw candidly explains that the real authority resides even today with the policeman who is entitled to arrest the King himself, should he drive his car too fast. . . . The policeman is the symbol of power and authority! When I read this I scrutinized my consciousness and found that, although I willingly submit to police regulations, this kind of authority means to me no authority at all. One has to submit to the power of government officials—that is how I feel about it—in no other sense than one has to submit to the law of gravitation. For me, the aristocratic individualist, authority can reside only in personal superiority and in no legal right. Now I think I am right here in the absolute sense; the whole of history proves it without a single exception that I know of; even Lenin has really influenced Russia as a personal being. Accordingly, should it ever come to this point that the ideas of power and authority should be permanently dissociated from personal value and become fused into the coercive force of routine and office, this would mean the end of all vital superiority in the individualistic European world; then the law of dead matter would rule supreme. It is natural that the emancipated masses should, for a while, extol the idea of state-power. One of the reasons for this has been very acutely pointed out by Bernard Shaw. He writes: "There is in British human nature, and I dare say in human nature in general, a very strong vein of pure inhibitiveness. Never forget the children in *Punch* who, discussing how to amuse themselves, decided to find out what the Baby was doing and tell it it mustn't. Forbiddance is an exercise of power; and we all have a will to personal power which conflicts with the will to social freedom." The lower classes have been ordered about as far back as human memory reaches. It is natural, therefore, that they should conceive liberty first as an opportunity to order about others in their turn. And since they originally think in terms of mass, State coercion is the idea of power most natural to them. But there is another reason for this deterioration of the underlying meaning of authority which has the same roots and makes directly for a lowering of level: as shown in "Privatism," the State as such is today the representative of the masses, that is of quantity and no longer of quality. How can anything else be reasonably inferred from this than that the State is progressively losing in value? Personally I feel certain that all that belongs to the State in Europe will become more and more an expression of socialism in the European sense. But this is precisely what proves that socialism (always taken in the European sense) cannot be creative of values. I quite agree with Shaw that we must get over our present commercialism and that some kind of socialism as a groundwork of national life is the only alternative in this mass age. I also agree with what Shaw says in the following: "The civil servant, the judge, the navy captain, the field marshal, the archbishop, however extraordinarily able, gets no more than any routineer of his rank and seniority. A real gentleman is not supposed to sell himself to the highest bidder: he asks his country for a sufficient provision and a dignified position in return for the best work he can do for it. A real lady can say no less. But in capitalist commerce they are both forced to be cads, that is, to hold up to ransom those to whom their services are indispensable and become rich at their expense." I remember well what I felt like myself when American lecture managers and literary agents first talked to me blandly about the possibilities of "selling me." . . . But I do not agree with Shaw in this: that State control as the last resort can ever lead to the kind of superiority which is typical of aristocratic communities; and by virtue of psychological law it is bound to become the last resort if it commands all distribution of income and if there is no hierarchy, independent of official position, which enjoys greater prestige than the functionary or the government machinery as such. It certainly never can in individualistic countries. But the case of socialism is different in America from what it is in Europe; American socialism is something different in kind from European. In the United States socialism would not and does not mean a compulsory system. Owing to the predominance of the social tendencies within the individual soul, American socialism is essentially a system of liberty, as most strikingly illustrated by the American lack of original reverence for the State and for the law. There exists in the United States, therefore, the very possibility which is denied to Europe: that a real culture may develop on the foundation of Social Democracy. One cannot expect this culture to create supreme values along lines presupposing an individual structure; its great achievements will necessarily be limited to the sphere and range of community life. But here we must remember, once again, that the chief task of this new age introducing the geological Epoch of Man is precisely the raising of the general level; to that extent, even European socialism is right in theory. Accordingly, America's advantages are of greater importance at the present stage than its shortcomings. And it is only a nation possessing the original psychological structure of the American which can achieve for itself, with more gain than loss, what every modern nation is aiming at.

NEVERTHELESS, all thoughtful Americans and all foreigners agree in this, that American Democracy today is far from incarnating an ideal state. I am not concerned here with minor and, in particular, with technical defects; such as these are always easy to remedy, and in any case they present no fundamental problem. My task is to make clear in what sense a general tendency is immutable and how it can be directed toward the good or toward the bad. For, as I have shown in the third chapter of *The World in the Making*, leaving things to take their natural course *always* means an active decision in favour of evil.

There are, as far as I can see, three fundamental defects inherent in present-day American Democracy which can and must be remedied. Here I shall have to repeat part of what has already been said at the beginning of this chapter, but clarity being my one object, I cannot well avoid this literary sin. The first of the defects in question is an exaggeration of the general defect of modern Western civilization: the rule of things over living men. (I have dealt with this problem in the abstract in the chapter "Culture of Ability and Culture of Being" in *Creative Understanding.*) This defect appears exaggerated in the United States owing to the following: The rule of the animal ideal has resulted in a general behaviourist outlook which, in its turn, is leading more and more to institutionalism—the latter word signifying that institutions are thought of as being more important than men. If all human development is supposed to depend ultimately on external influences; if the autonomous spirit is supposed to mean nothing—then, there being no "uniquenesses" in the material world, which is ruled by the law of routine and repetition, these external influences must needs lead to an ever-increasing standardization of man in the same sense as motor cars can be standardized. For even here it is really the *belief* of man which decides; if he believes in matter as the supreme power, it is bound to gain supremacy. Now the belief in externals as the ultimately decisive forces is so universal in America today that the whole of its life is becoming organized more and more as though it were one single factory, and whatever institutions still exist which are the creations of a different spirit are fast losing their original significance. This is true precisely of democracy: it is only because original significance has been lost that democracy could come to mean that everybody should be like everybody else. This has nothing to do either with the democratic ideal in the abstract, or precisely with the original American idea of democracy; on the contrary, according to the latter, man, liberated from the shackles of convention and tradition, should freely develop his full individuality. It is exclusively due to the belief, however unconscious, that the ideal of creative life is to be found in the Ford plant. This new development of democracy is evidently an unmitigated evil. Standardized motor cars are all right: standardized human beings are sub-human phenomena. It is from here also that we best realize the full and terrific danger of the present American ideal of production as an end in itself: if men are continually thought of as producing or consuming machines, then impersonal processes, directed by men who represent something impersonal and who, accordingly, are without a human conscience, *must needs* rule supreme in the long run. And this, again, must be the death of true democracy simultaneously in two senses. The first is that the machine and not man really rules; accordingly, there can be no question of freedom. Here we find one more evidence of the fact that Americanism and Bolshevism belong to the same plane as polar opposites: whether it be the State machinery or economic machinery which rules supreme—the result must be serfdom as opposed to individual liberty for all who are not employed in "controlling" the machinery. The second reason why the present development, if it goes on, must lead to the death of democracy in its original sense, is that only the representatives of the process of production count. This must needs make for class-rule. And the ruling class would be precisely the least valuable spiritually. The economic type is in itself inferior not only to the spiritual type, in the highest sense of the term, but also to the warrior, to the statesman, to the thinker, and to the artist. Of this obvious fact of natural science and spiritual hierarchy the American nation alone, in all history, seems unaware. But on the other hand, once man has gained the mastery of the forces of nature, the economic type is the most powerful in the material sense. Accordingly, the exclusive rule of the economic class would mean the most extreme expression of the supremacy of a single class, and this class, being inferior in itself according to all cultural values, its supremacy would necessarily lead to an inferior general state. It is true that their class-rule would amount to an aristocratic system of a kind, because mass-production can be directed only by exceptional intellects; thus, I think it highly probable that democracy will be made "fool-proof" to a considerable extent in the United States, as it already is as far as law goes in New York State—wherever the business spirit rules supreme it will be easier than where politics are of first importance to correct the most obvious defects inherent in universal suffrage. But this aristocracy would lack precisely those qualities which define the true aristocrat. There are many who are afraid that economic Cæsarism will become the final form of American Democracy. I do not share that fear. Firstly, Cæsarism would in all probability eventually lead to a true aristocracy, for when all greed for wealth and power is satisfied man naturally begins to look toward the other things and values he lacks. But my principal reason for not fearing the development of economic Cæsarism is that something very much worse is much more likely to occur: a two-class rule, the two classes together forming the higher unity of the economically productive class. Indeed, owing to America's organic socialism, there is as little likelihood of a development along the lines of Cæsarism as of a dictatorship of the proletariat, but it is all the more likely that capitalists and workmen will unite against all non-producers. Now this would mean the complete victory of the animal as opposed to the cultural ideal. And let it be distinctly understood: it is precisely the democratic Constitution as it is which would further its victory. This Constitution was established in another age, the spirit of which is almost as remote from the real spirit of ours as that of Greek Antiquity. Accordingly, there is nothing in the official Constitution to prevent what real forces there are from working themselves out; the less so since almost all Americans still think in eighteenth-century terms and as there is, therefore, no need to tell a lie when the existence of anti-democratic tendencies is denied.

Now let us turn our attention to the second fundamental defect of American Democracy: left to its own momentum, it will inevitably develop a true caste-system different from, and in addition to, the class rule described above, and different, too, from what I meant when I called the women in America the higher caste—a caste-system which is bound to become predominant in the long run. It has already been shown that it would have been a normal development if a caste-system like the Hindu had been established on American soil from the outset; in that case a stratification according to human type, however summary and rough, would have been openly acknowledged. As things are, the religion of democracy holding the spiritual sway, caste in America can only be a question of social exclusiveness. To give the principle its most extreme concrete expression: it can be only a question of the co-existence, intersection, and occasional conflicts of so many different ghettos. In our day it is easiest to wield and retain power when it is not officially recognized, nor otherwise manifest. I have developed this idea in the last chapter of *Europe*, but this much may be repeated here: it is much easier to wield real power today as a secretary-general than as a dictator; if modern kings are the humblest of creatures and have to put up with more humiliations and restrictions than any ordinary man, this is precisely due to their exalted position. On the other hand, the reason Lenin's corpse is worshipped as no dead ruler has ever been since the days of the Egyptian Pharaohs, is to be found foremost in the fact that he denied the very existence of any kind of individual power. In the same sense, the general belief in, and the affectation of equality is the best possible safeguard and breeding-soil for castes in the United States. For if they are based exclusively on social exclusiveness, they cannot be overthrown, once they exist. Now, such officially unrecognized castes are already to be found in all the bigger centres. They will inevitably continue to develop. And since everything clandestine breeds moral ugliness, there is little good to be expected from the final result if nothing interferes with the natural course of development. An American caste-system would inevitably be based *not* on ability, the latter finding a pre-formed channel for its activities in other social formations. Nevertheless, the castes could eventually acquire such power that they might dictate all American policy, on whatever plane. If fortunes continue to be inheritable as they are today; if at the same time the religion of prosperity and equality continues to prevail, the result must inevitably be, on the one hand, an inordinate power wielded by exclusive sets, and on the other, the complete dissociation of the idea of caste from that of ability, merit, and moral obligation. It is a truth, proved and confirmed by all history, that the descendants of self-made men, who by dint of hard work rose from very low to very high positions, are very rarely satisfactory in the biological sense; they usually degenerate in the course of three generations at best. Man must become immune to the effects of luxury almost in the same sense that he must be rendered immune to small-pox, if he is to survive. Here we find the chief reason for the indubitable fact that the older a civilization, the better the chances for the members of old cultured families. Any man can stand a life in the wilds, this being the normal kind of life for the human animal. But only traditional culture makes man fit to stand comfortable surroundings. This truth goes further than any other to explain the impression of devitalization produced by an extraordinary percentage of wealthy Americans as compared with Europeans. This also explains the fact that the native-born American of cultural tradition is not meaning less, but more, in American life as time goes on. But however this may be, the American caste-system is based not on ability and superiority, but simply on social exclusiveness. It is said that the aristocracies of Europe eventually fell because they no longer had any real social function to perform. Yet it was they who maintained, and even today continue maintaining, the cultural traditions of their respective countries. The American castes are not maintaining any cultural tradition whatsoever. The third and really the greatest danger inherent in the normal momentum of American Democracy lies in the opposite direction. There is every reason to expect, in spite of all caste-exclusiveness, that so great a uniformity of social type will develop as to preclude all cultural differentiation. And by this I mean something profounder than the mere effect of standardization. Equalization in the external sense need not destroy individuality, as is best exemplified by the army or by the religious orders. What I mean here is the vital type, the zoölogical genus, as it were. Now, precisely as types, the most exclusive sets and the most powerful financial magnets converge with the man in the street in the United States. Here I must ask my readers, should they have forgotten it, to reread the paragraph in "Predominant Woman" which deals with the fact that America is the only country which lays all the emphasis on ability only, completely disregarding the question of level of "being"; for this paragraph was really an anticipated integral part of the present chapter. Originally, democracy was established in the very hope that it would lead to a stratification according to true and not to imaginary differences of quality; equal rights were meant to constitute the basis for an all the greater diversity. Likewise, the legitimate heir of the ideals of liberalism and socialism, as best understood by Bernard Shaw, demands equality of income not in order that everybody should be like everybody else, but in order to give to differences of another order than financial ability and power a chance to assert themselves in the social picture—a chance which capitalism and plutocracy destroy. Even today idealists like John Dewey think that democracy furthers individual development. I shall try to show in what follows that within the limits set by an essentially socialist structure it could indeed do so. *Up to the present*, however, the exact opposite is true. It is an indubitable scientific fact that the belief that all men are originally and essentially equal has *not* led to richer individual differentiations and has *not* destroyed "type" for the benefit of "uniqueness," *but that it has led to the absolute predominance of one single type.* This certainly is one of the most amazing and instructive sights on earth: all the natives of an enormous continent, the official law of which is "free scope for individual energy," belong to or are tending toward the same type; or what is even more—if they do not actually belong to or tend toward the same type, they would like to. But this phenomenon, however extraordinary it may seem, is really the inevitable effect of a democratic system which lays all stress on differences of "ability" while completely disregarding differences in the state of "being." Man being essentially free, whatever parts and functions of his psychic organism he does not consciously stress, become again primitive or rudimentary, if they do not deteriorate and atrophy. And since man's being is something different in kind from his ability, no differentiation nor high development on the latter plane can raise the level of the former. On the contrary, if development along the lines of ability is over-stressed, it must lead directly to a lowering of the level of being. And this is a very dangerous development, because a man "is" exclusively what he represents as a being, for the latter alone expresses his uniqueness-principle, that is his only real self; everything else really belongs to the external world. Here we find the profoundest cause of American externalism. Unless a differentiated individual soul is both the root and the background of differentiated abilities, the latter can never rise beyond the plane of instrumentality. At best, they can become expressive of what the *virtuoso,* as opposed to the creator, stands for in music; generally, however, they are expressive of a non-existent soul—hence the supremacy of "things" over men in the United States. But what interests us foremost in the present context is that we find in the above described state of affairs the explanation for the predominance of the most incredible ideal mankind has ever believed in—the ideal of the man in the street. It is not a case, here, of an ideal representing an anticipation in the imagination of a higher reality to be attained by reason of its uplifting effect, but on the contrary, of an idealization of an actual state of fact which man feels unable to outgrow or to escape from—a device involuntarily adopted by the subconscious in order to compensate an otherwise intolerable feeling of inferiority. The average man always represents a distinctly inferior type. Nor is there such a thing as a nation of high quality. I will quote a distinguished Swiss, who certainly is a democrat according to all European standards, but who is at the same time the greatest living authority on Collective Psychology, Doctor Jung: "The level of a nation is always low, however high it may rise above its neighbours. A gathering of a hundred highly intelligent men, taken together, makes one single idiot, because every gift, whether intellectual or moral, is in the first and last instance a question of individual differentiation. But differentiation implies differences. Accumulated differences do not lead to a higher kind of difference, they annul each other. On the other hand, what gets accumulated is the generally human, the 'all-too-human' which is nothing but the primitive, the dark, the inert, and the devoid of free initiative." We find here the profoundest cause of the disastrous effects to which the ideals of "normalcy" and "like-mindedness" lead. Every individual is fundamentally unique. Accordingly, if he identifies himself with what is common to all, he voluntarily renounces his intrinsic value, and this inevitably leads to a lowering of his level. At the natural end of this development we find a type of man who actually seems to have lost his uniqueness-quality. This, then, leads us back to the phenomenon of the convergence of all types of men in the United States toward a single type, which is actually that of the man in the street. If the uniqueness-principle ceases to play a part, then of course that which all men have in common must determine the social picture. And since a state of soul in which uniqueness plays no part is possible only in the case of an un-individualized type of man, a process of progressive de-individualization must by force of natural law set in under the pressure of the social surroundings created by the American variety of democracy. Within my own memory the lowering of level of this process has progressed to an alarming degree, a fact most noticeable in the increasing idealization of what is low. When I first visited the United States colleges did not dream of praising themselves for being "democratic," implying that there was no room in them for superior types. Today this is almost the rule. Today we are face to face with the enormity (I am using the word in its French nuance) that American society really is a one-class society in spite of all differentiation, and that most Americans believe that there can be but one social truth—that any exception to the rule is a heresy in the same sense that a teaching differing from the official doctrine is heresy to the Catholic Church. This state of complete non-differentiation from the point of view of being is *the* outstanding characteristic of American Democracy. Since, where life is concerned, everything external has its real *raison d'être* in an inner state, the non-differentiation in question alone fully explains the fact (already dealt with in "Socialism") that in prosperous America there is almost as little difference between men's ways of living as there is in starving Russia. In both countries the ruling idea is that there *should* be no differences. But man being essentially free and creative in his freedom, this "should" inevitably lead to a corresponding organic state. And this state stands for something far profounder than for one human type among other human types: it stands for actual primitiveness from the point of view of being. To show what I mean I will give at the outset the most extreme illustration of the case: Americans glory in the "simplicity" of their great men. Every great man is simple as a matter of course in the sense of being natural and unembarrassed, wherever others do not prevent his being simple by failing to understand that he cannot help being different from them, as a matter of course. But if American great men really *are* "men in the street," it can only mean that they are not great. And, as a matter of fact, most of those whom public opinion extols as superior beings are very ordinary men, because the American man in the street usually thinks of superiority in terms of efficiency and wealth; and inward greatness leads to riches only in exceptional cases. On the other hand, the standardization of American life and the power of public opinion must in their turn lower the superior type, where it exists. The general effect of all this is an equalization unheard of in history, as far as the state of being is concerned. Here we find the profoundest reason for the lack of stimulation American social life provides; not only a social life creative of values, even a social life expressive of true happiness, is possible only where the unique being of each is focussed foremost, and the interplay of free energies radiating from the various "uniquenesses" makes for an expansion of each. But typical Americans of the latest pattern never even perceive differences of being. They can think only in terms of ability—whatever cannot be grasped within their framework is rendered ineffective as a creative influence by being looked upon as an "idiosyncrasy." Under these circumstances, it is only natural that American social life should present all the disadvantages of the social life one finds in Europe among the youngest races, such as the Czechs, the Esthonians, the Serbs. Personal superiority plays no part in it, no superpersonal scale of values is determinant. What is determinant is the infra-personal, the collective part in individual man, or worse still, brute material force.

This, then, leads us, from another side of the problem, to a definition of the American type. It is far easier to define "the" American than "the" representative of any other nation, simply because nowhere else are there more individuals true to type. Nevertheless, most definitions I know of miss the point. The American man in the street is not the brother of the European middle-class type. To attempt to identify them would be unfair to both. Unfair to the American because the latter is broader, more self-assured, self-respecting, generous; unfair to the European because, in spite of the narrow outlook of the middle class in Europe, it has been and still is the inexhaustible fostering-soil of individual talent; accordingly, the typification it represents cannot really imply a loss of individuality. Here, again, the only analogy to America is provided by Russia. The proletarian-consciousness and sense of honour of the Bolshevik really are closely akin to American self-consciousness; and there is an affinity between the two in this respect also that, by virtue of several qualities they have in common, both are more akin to the aristocrat than to the bourgeois. But their affinity lies chiefly in the fact that they are, both of them, unified types; and that, in both cases, the uniformity of the surface is not due to a ruling inner principle—as in the case of a religious order or an army—but to the crushing of the individual by the community. To that extent, then, both are superficial types. In both, the inner principle plays hardly any part. In both cases only that which in man can be summed up on general principles is taken into account; in both cases, whatever man is in and for himself is entirely disregarded. From this vantage-point we can finally understand why both in Russia and in America the rule is passing more and more into the hands of an aristocracy, and why, nevertheless, these aristocracies have little in common with real aristocracies. All differences in ability are readily taken into account. Mass-government can no more be effectively managed by fools than mass-production. And since it is not the individual as such, but only his social value that counts, there is no reason why individuals should not be entrusted with enormous power, wherever this seems expedient. But all the differentiation implied by this kind of aristocracy, however refined it may be or become, makes for a differentiation according to the standards not of human being, but only of human ability. All that cannot be directly put to use by the community remains undeveloped. Our final verdict on American Democracy, at this point of our investigations, must accordingly be: Americans are highly differentiated as far as specialized abilities and functions go; as beings, they are less developed than any race we know of. The standard is provided by the lowest average type. And the latter's suggestive power is so immense that it either crushes the individuality of those who might be truly original, or else forces them into some kind of eccentric position or attitude which inevitably, in its turn, thwarts their inner growth. This is partly the natural expression of organic socialism. It is partly due also to the rejuvenation which in itself is an excellent thing, provided it signifies the prelude to a maturity of a higher kind. But, in the first instance, it is an effect of democracy, wrongly understood.

WHAT can be done to make of American Democracy something better than it is today? The best way to find an answer to this question is to start from the fact that life is, always and everywhere, a phenomenon and a process of polarization. That is to say, its equilibrium being always unstable, its vital quality depends on the quality of the tension it manifests. Just as there is positive and negative electricity in inanimate nature; just as the continuation of physical life depends on the co-operation of those polar opposites, man and woman—in the same way does the vital quality of life, as opposed to what life has in common with dead matter, depend on unequalized tensions. And this means that its vital quality is directly proportional to the variety of its molecular structure. This is the reason why most great epochs in history have been what one calls aristocratic ages; the stress lay on manifoldness and not on similarity. For man is a creature of differences in this also, that consciousness demands the influence of something which is unfamiliar to it, in order to become fully conscious of itself. In this respect the idea of equality is contrary to the very spirit of life, for it really corresponds to the law of dead matter. Hence we realize once again that, since those who first advocated the idea of equality as a progressive one were no fools, equality as such can never have been their ultimate ideal. They wanted to destroy unequalities which were irrational, inasmuch as the appearance did not correspond to truth. Democracy in its beginnings was intended to create or further an even richer diversity than was manifested in the social body of the Middle Ages. Accordingly, what is required if democracy in America is to become again a progressive element in the human, as opposed to the merely technical, sense (and it undoubtedly was progressive in the former sense in the eighteenth century and even later) is *that diversity and manifoldness should henceforth be stressed more than anywhere else in the world.* The creed of the new generation should be—in contradistinction to the traditional creed which can be summed up in the sentences: "I am as good as you are"—"I being what I am, you should and must be different." "Normalcy" and "like-mindedness" should be officially stigmatized as degrading epithets; the wonderful advertising machinery of the United States should for once be put to use for something better than the creation of an orange-consciousness or an automobile-consciousness; it should promote uniqueness-consciousness. Indeed, in regard to this, as well as to all other problems dealt with in this chapter, a change of attitude is required at this turning-point in history of the American nation, as radical as that which Jesus Christ demanded of the Jews. But on the other hand, Christianity could spring from the roots of Judaism. Similarly, America certainly need not deny her history. While I was lecturing in the United States, the concrete situation of the country led me to emphasize wherever I went the intrinsic value of the unique: the response I met with was so great that personally I am convinced that the American Democracy is inwardly mature and ready even today, as far as its best representatives are concerned, to go through the required inner change. And what the best do will be repeated in due course by the majority all the more easily as the external framework of this democracy requires no alteration. Democracy is the zoölogical life-form of the genus *homo Americanus.* He is a socialist at heart; that is, the social means more to him than the individual. Therefore, whatever spiritual values can be embodied in American life will have to be incarnated in the bodies of the existing primary tendencies, which are all of them social. Hence it is easy to find that formula which can again make American Democracy progressive: *in the future, the individual as such, in his uniqueness, should be considered as the real social unit.*

This phrase has led us back, all at once and perhaps somewhat unexpectedly, to the bright picture visualized in the first part of this book. We said there that America was not likely to develop an intellectual, or an artistic, or a philosophic super-culture; but that it was all the more likely to evolve an exemplary social culture, practical in its expression, moral in its outlook, and religious in its roots. This is indeed the only kind of super-culture imaginable on democratic foundations as they exist in the United States. But on the other hand, there is absolutely nothing to prevent the development of such a high-culture if only the present ideal of equality dies its historical death, for the means of incarnation presented by the psychological structure of the American nation to the spiritual values certainly are of no inferior quality to those provided in their days by Egypt, ancient China, and Rome. And I am glad to say that all my observations tend to confirm my impression that the present ideal of equality *will* die. As is always the case wherever a great change is impending, many causes one might call accidental are co-operating to bring it about. Foremost among these rank the increasing influence of the Catholic Church with its deep understanding of all that is human and its strong sense of hierarchy and values; the disintegrating effect caused by the Jews, and the developing spirit of criticism among the American intellectuals who, however small a minority they may represent, are steadily gaining in importance. But it is the inward law directing the growth of the American nation which is the primary cause of the change. On American soil, too, the ideas of the eighteenth century have done their work and had their day. The process of radical rejuvenation is now imperiously calling for new aims and goals. In America these can have nothing to do with individualism of any kind. But socialism, too, can become profound; on socialistic lines, too, a one-sided differentiation may gain a new dimension and along with it a new vital background by means of a process of integration. And this integration actually is already the aim of all the best minds of the United States. I will again mention M. P. Follett as an example and quote at random several passages from her books *Creative Experience* and *The New State;* I have every right to do so, no matter whether these books are known to many or not, because they are truly representative: "Within every process is its own momentum; therefore the guiding power is always within—and this is the vindication of Democracy. Every living process is subject to its own authority, that is, the authority evolved by, or involved in the process itself." This is quite true—but up to now American Democracy has been the expression of the very opposite principle, the supremacy of externals. However, let us proceed: "Whoever advocates compromise abandons the individual: the individual is to give up part of himself in order that some action may take place. The integrity of the individual is preserved only through integration. Integration might be considered a qualitative adjustment, compromise as a quantitative one." When has American Democracy thought before of quality and the integrity of the individual? And now let us see what kind of integration M. P. Follett really has in view. It is not an integration of the kind that would spontaneously present itself to the mind of an individualist like myself. This is another quotation: "In society every individual may be a complete expression of the whole. . . . I do not believe that man should serve his fellow man. . . . We cannot transcend Self by means of others, but only through the synthesis of Self and others. . . . The exposition of the self-and-others fallacy has transformed the idea of self-interest. Our interests are inextricably interwoven. The question is not what is best for me or for you, but for all of us." This Chapter XI of *The New State* entitled "The Self-and-others-Illusion" destroys the mistaken ideal of service. Yet Miss Follett is a convinced American democrat. According to her idea, the free man is he who actualizes the will of the whole; man has no liberty, except as a member of a group. Only, it is not the majority that should rule, as it does today: "Majority-rule is democratic when it is approaching not a unanimous but an integrated will." And now—with Chapter XVIII of the book—we touch the core of the new problem: *Democracy should no longer mean the rule of the crowd;* the crowd should be entirely supplanted by the vital group. "Democracy is everyone building the single life, not my life and others, not the individual and the State, but my life bound up with others, the individual which *is* the State, the State which *is* the individual. Democracy is an infinitely including spirit." But at this point (p. 157 of *The New State*) we see also in what respect Miss Follett's solution is an essentially and exclusively American solution. Whatever she thinks good or ideal, she instinctively associates with the term Democracy, as I would associate it with the term Aristocracy. And this does not only mean that we use different words, but that we have different ideals. She says: "We (Americans) have an instinct for Democracy, because we have an instinct for wholeness; we get wholeness only through reciprocal relations. . . . We believe in the influence of the good and the wise, but they must exert their influence within the social process; it is the *process* which purifies, not the 'influence' of the perfect on the imperfect." If spiritual or cultural or artistic or intellectual values are thought supreme, if higher quality is supposed to mean absolute superiority, then every word of the last-quoted sentence is untrue. Culture and quality depend for their existence on uniqueness-consciousness—this is a fact of natural history not to be removed by any argument. The influence of higher quality has always worked from above; and no human being ever progressed along the line of individual integration by becoming part of an ever-increasing number of different groups. Modern psychology has shown that, on the contrary, the process of socialization has already advanced too far even in Europe and that *individualization*, a purely solitary process, is what really matters if there is ever to be a new Western Culture. But, on the other hand, what M. P. Follett stands for actually means a higher state than the one prevailing today, *along the lines and within the range of American possibilities.* If social consciousness predominates over individual consciousness, if the structure of a nation is organically democratic, then there is indeed no better ideal than to make each individual the representative of the whole. Then the expressing of the macrocosm will lead to such development of the microcosm as is possible along socialistic lines. I think that it is true that *if* man's essence is supposed to be constituted by his membership in a group, or his citizenship, and not by his individual uniqueness, then no better general plan can be thought out for him than the one outlined by Miss Follett. To carry it out would actually mean to establish a commonwealth ideal along specialized lines. America, then, would not be what Rome was, but it might be as good as Rome. It would not be what the British commonwealth is, but as good as the latter, only on new lines. Yes, American Democracy may yet become one of the great expressions of human perfection.

I cannot say more on this subject before having dealt with the problems of morality and the new bodies required for the incarnation of the eternal spiritual values. Yet this much can be stated even now. The resulting picture would be, on the one hand, very Christian. If the present differentiations along the lines of social service and co-operation were related to an integrated whole, which would result in the deepening of even the most socialized individual, then the true Spirit of Love might more easily become predominant in America than in any other country. This development would be all the more likely to take place because Privatism involuntarily makes for a stressing of the uniqueness-principle in everyday life, thus preparing a vessel fit for the reception of a profounder Spirit. I said in another context that the Americans are probably among Westerners the only really Christian nation because their subconscious does not reach back beyond Christianity. What, therefore, means a lack of tradition or wealth, may also mean the necessary premise for a new start. There can be little doubt that the Christianization of Europe has, according to ideal standards, been a failure. The religion imported from the East, with its totally different traditions, never really fused with the native tendencies within the souls of those European races which already had evolved traditions of their own. The vitality of Roman Catholicism is really due to the persistent vitality of antique Pagan tradition, and the deepest psychological significance of the Protestant Reformation lies in its being a rebirth of the original Nordic outlook. In any case, Christian Europe never got over and beyond that state of inward brokenness and insecurity which is characteristic of every hybrid or bastard. But there is no reason why the American soul should not reach a state of genuine wholeness and individual integration on purely Christian lines.—Again, our trend of thought has led us to expect that the American nation, after having reached maturity, will bear a strong likeness to ancient China. Does not that which we hinted at then almost take the shape of a completed picture now? Ancient China, too, was a democracy. In China, too, the social instincts predominated. The Chinese are so democratic by tradition that the ideas of Bentham today appeal most strongly to them. Yet the ancient Chinese culture was one of the greatest the world ever saw, because the socialist and democratic structure was yet made the means of expression of all the values which have their opponent in uniqueness. China, too, in its own way believed in normalcy. China, too, idealized like-mindedness in so far as all Chinese believed in the same fundamental truth incarnated in the same general forms. But then the ideal of Chinese democracy was not the man in the street, but the normally gifted man *who had reached such a state of perfection that the utmost depth found its expression in perfect harmony and even grace of the surface.* And Chinese like-mindedness did not mean that everybody believed in the same slogans and quoted the same headlines, *but that everybody was supposed to reach personally Eternal Truth, which is indeed eternally the same.* China laid all the emphasis on significance as opposed to the means of expression, which are always mechanical in this world. Accordingly, Confucius taught: "The noble one is no tool." Accordingly, China thought little of external organization. Its central idea was that, if Spirit becomes supreme, a perfect external organization follows as a matter of course. Up to now, America has lived according to the opposite idea. That is America's present conception of democracy. But there is no reason why things should remain as they are. Understanding works wonders. When prosperity will really have become the obvious thing—it is not so as yet, or else Americans would not boast of it so much—when America will have found for herself that kind of external organization which suits her type in all respects—and this has not yet been achieved—then that strange law of nature I have termed the law of historic counterpoint is almost sure to make for a reversal of many values. America may yet emerge as the nation least bent on externals and most strongly ruled, as a social organism, from within.

## *Morality*

I HAVE yet to come across the problem which Americans do not regard primarily as a moral issue. And one has no right to say that this particular way of looking at things is logically wrong, however odd the effects and results may often be. Life being fundamentally a sense-connexion, in which each particular sense corresponds to, and mirrors every other, it is in principle possible to use every single "sense" as a general denominator. And that there is vital truth in the American way of positing the problem of life is proved precisely by the undeniable sentiment which attaches to Prohibition as a moral issue: of however doubtful a value its aim may be, the feelings and emotions involved are genuine and even deep.

The *raison d'être* of this American particularity is, of course, that American civilization is fundamentally Puritan. But if one wants to understand the United States, not merely to explain how things have come to be what they are (which kind of explanation never really explains anything), one must leave history alone as much as possible. The real problem is not how Puritanism originated and how it shaped American life in the days of its greatness, but what it means vitally today. And this, again, has little or nothing to do with beliefs consciously held—it refers to the psychological reality Puritanism stands for in the unconscious. Here, then, one may say that the reality of Puritanism was never identical with its strict theological definition. In my *Travel Diary* I have devoted some space to a comparison between the original Puritan and Islamic types. Both the Puritan and Mohammedan religions developed in their prime a similar kind of simple and strong and heroic character. This has continued to be the case with the undegenerated Islamic races, because with them the emphasis continued to rest on the pathos of man's littleness before God and because in their conception of heroism there was never any thought of reward or earthly success on earth. In the United States precisely the latter idea soon became predominant; accordingly, the great and heroic qualities of Puritanism soon dwindled. And since there was success along all lines, the material outlook of the later Americans could not preserve that tension between the Commandment of God and man's perpetual shortcomings, which is the *raison d'être* of the spirituality of the Jew, who is a child of the same primal spirit: the pathos of the hero changed into the tenacious optimism of the business man. Yet the general quality of the Puritan outlook remained prevalent. And this is true precisely of its essential moralism.

Now what are the psychological roots of this moralism? We shall come to them most quickly by remembering a saying of Trader Horn, that old African tramp who overnight became, as a writer, an American best-seller. He says that the cannibals are the most moral race on earth. "The cannibal lives as nature taught him —kill only to eat, keep your women moral, hold no man as slave; and be content with your side of the river; cast no eye across the water." What Trader Horn means is, of course, that the cannibals are more moral than other African tribes, although they are less humane. Hence it becomes clear why I thought of the cannibals in connexion with the Puritans: the Puritan spirit, too, is in the first instance a cruel spirit. It is a child of hatred, not of love. The conscious idea is, no doubt, that one should hate oneself only and love his fellows; but Christ Himself knew well that such an attitude is impossible; this is why He taught "love thy neighbor as thyself" and not "more than thyself." In any case, in the domain of the subconscious, hatred signifies the same whatever its object may be. And this psychological truth has found its irrefutable historical proof in the Puritan condemnation of joy. Joy is the normal expression of love in the sphere of the emotions. And there is no real joy even today in American life; that is, no joy like that known to antique Pagans and European Christians and Confucians and Hindu Bhaktas. There are contentment and what one calls the "good-life" and the kind of brightness which is the natural result of good-will and kindliness. But real joy is lacking. There is no primary sense of the value of beauty as an end in itself, no psychological connexion between what the Greeks called ecstasy and the Divine. What real joy exists is of a childish quality. Naturally enough: Puritanism granted irresponsibility only to the child. For this reason the sons of its spirit instinctively feel inclined to behave and, if possible, to feel like children, whenever there is no serious work to be done. This explains the curious glamour of nursery-happiness one finds radiating sometimes from successful American business men, and more often still, from business women; now that they have achieved success and are manifestly blessed by God, they can afford to have a good time and to make others have it too. Here also lies one of the psychological roots of the universal commandment "Keep smiling." However, infantilism is never a positive issue or solution for grown-ups. The paramount fact is that American happiness stands out against a psychological background of bad conscience, self-hatred, and fear, which one notices most perhaps in that modern youth which thinks itself freed from all Puritan shackles: there is erotic emotion in their faces, instead of the bland blankness of previous generations; but its expression is cramped, stern, and even bitter. This lack of real happiness is noticeable throughout American life. We found in the first chapter that American humour even is at bottom an "abreaction" of hatred and fear. And the same emotions lie at the root of most traditional American views and ideas. If one must work without being allowed to enjoy the fruits of one's work; if no value is attached to leisure; if morality is considered a greater value than life itself; if nothing apart from that which the beliefs originating in Puritanism demand should or need exist; if sex-life is a sinful thing on the one hand, but, on the other must be worked out as an expression of God's will—that is, sternly, simply, directly; if there is to be no variety in life, whereas variety is the one thing man needs in order to enjoy it—all these phenomena can be explained only by a basic, though unconscious cruelty. And we certainly find here also the deepest root of the excessive American optimism. Whoever is in harmony with himself and the world sees things in their right proportion. This means among other things that he does not think of the future more than of the present and the past, and that he accepts and acquiesces in the fact that there is, on the whole, more sorrow and failure than pleasure and success in earthly life; life conceived as success is refuted by the fact of the inevitability of death, for both the individual and the race. Now if the Americans stand out as pure optimists, this can only mean an over-compensation of unconscious gloom and despair. Yet let no one imagine that the Americans desire to be different. Sadism and masochism always go together. If America is at bottom a Puritan country and might build up a great civilization on that basis, if it could even gild that brazen vessel with what looks like happiness, this signifies that the instinct of cruelty actually forms a very important part in their psychological structure. The same is true of the cannibal. But the same is true also of all Nordics. There have never been world-conquering races which were not cruel at heart.

So far, so good. But what does it mean when a man can enjoy being cruel to himself? Here it may be recalled what I developed at length in the chapters "The Ethical Problem" and "The Religious Problem" in *The Recovery of Truth.* Good and Evil are related to each other in the same way as Yea and Nay. That is to say, every Yea demands a corresponding Nay for its limitation; there can be no positive form on earth without a correlative negative. For this reason construction and destruction always go together, because they actually represent different aspects of an identical process. For the same reason the principle of Evil not only stands for destruction, but also for renewal and initiative. Nevertheless, there can be no question of Good and Evil belonging to the same plane of values. Destruction, limitation, and definition there must be. But the emphasis must lie on the positive; that is, on creation, pouring forth, building up. It follows that wherever limitations or definitions as such are thought to incarnate what is good, the principle of Evil predominates as a matter of fact, whatever the intentions of the individual or the group in question may be. Now this is true precisely of the just and moral man; if the emphasis in his soul lies on justice and morality and not on love, then he is, at bottom, an evil man. This explains why Jesus hated the just and the doctors of the Law. This, then, gives the final touch to our picture of the Puritan as a kinsman of the cannibal. Morality, understood as a system of things one "should" or "should not" do, can be nothing but limitation; and the emphasizing of limitations is of necessity an emphasizing of the principle of Nay. I know that all this will sound very paradoxical to most Americans, because nowhere does life on the surface show more kindliness than that in the United States. But we have already found that this smiling surface stands out against a dark background of gloom. The foregoing provides the metaphysical explanation of this fact. Indeed, no true understanding of life can be gained before one has realized that the stressing of limitations—even if they are supposed to express an absolutely true doctrine—means the stressing of the destructive principle. Yet in spite of the aforesaid, there is no question of our having to condemn even the most orthodox Puritan as a type. Without destruction there is no rejuvenation and no progress. I will say even this: however narrow a Puritan outlook a man may hold, if it corresponds absolutely to his nature, then the man in question can stand forth as a very great man. He may be the greatest of all heroes. But there are not many born heroes in the world; that is, not many men in whom the principle of cruelty makes almost exclusively for the Good. Generally speaking, its predominance causes only impoverishment. Now this impoverishment expresses itself chiefly in two respects. It makes an all-round development impossible. And it gives so much power to the accepted limitations that they emerge, as it were, as independent essences. Hence those social structures in which the military spirit as such, or the State as such, or the moral law as such, or a Church as such, rules supreme. These supremacies always represent the reign of the Law of the very sort Jesus Christ wished to abolish.

This is the one essential side of the problem of Puritanism. The other is contained in its very wording. Words, spontaneously formed out of the meaning, understood by creative unconscious, are always profounder than all theories and interpretations. The word Puritanism in the first instance denotes purity. Now purity is, as such, a distinctive psychological quality; it can attach itself to practically everything and, for the selfsame reason, make practically anything stand for purity. In this sense, the Puritan is essentially the pure man. The Mohammedan was the first physically clean man in the Near East, the cannibal is the most moral African. But the men of the French Terror, too, called themselves *des purs;* that is what they really were. At this point, then, we perceive that modern American immorality does not by any means prove that the days of Puritanism are at an end. Quite the contrary, it evidently means that the psychological quality of purity has now attached itself to sex-life pure and simple. Today the young people live out their sex as "purely" as the older generations lived out their stern morality. This explains also the candour, the extravagance, and the unequalled shamelessness of those who in America believe in sexual liberty.

Indeed, the pure is essentially candid; there is no limit imaginable and still less desirable for purity; nor is there any reason to conceal it. This is, incidentally, the place to refute a current prejudice. The Puritans' outlook on sex was always more matter of fact and more common sense than that of most other Christians. This is due, on the one hand, to the fact that purity implies also simplicity, and that the stressing of purity in any sense of necessity gives a similar quality to all other psychological functions; on the other, it is due to the innate sense of what is possible with which all Anglo Saxons and Scotch are endowed. It is in Scotland, I believe, that "bundling" was invented. Free intercourse between boys and girls was from the outset much less discouraged in Puritan communities than anywhere else in Christendom. And although as a matter of course it was always pretended—setting aside the question whether the pretence ever corresponded to genuine belief or not—that the limit never was transgressed (it is highly characteristic that exactly the same idea obtains even in the most advanced flapper-sets, only sometimes with the qualification that intercourse without the use of contraceptives constitutes the limit), the essential point was that one should *marry*, which, after all, is the predominant practice even today: one mother, one sweetheart, one wife; legality —not sexual innocence was what mattered. Under these circumstances the reckless sex-life of these days is only seemingly a revolt against Puritanism. Purity meaning the essential quality both with the Pilgrim Father and the flapper, their spirits are more closely akin than that of any American to any European of non-Puritan antecedents. In our day the pendulum has simply swung to the other pole for a while. At bottom, the most "advanced" of the girls Judge Lindsey describes are Puritans at heart.

Viewed from this angle, it at once appears clear that what is unsatisfactory in American love-life, etc., is not a result of Puritanism in the sense most of those who write against it think it to be. And that charming lady, Dora Russell, who exhorts the young, sometimes from the church-pulpit to get all the sexual experience they can both before and after marriage does not give a remedy for the ailment she wishes to cure. A "pure" sex-life or a "pure" religious life or a "pure" moral life comes to very much the same, psychologically. In all these cases it is a question of narrowing the range of life, of attributing a value to one side of it only, and of laying the stress on the principle of Nay instead of the principle of Yea. God only knows what the conventions the latest pattern of the flapper believes in really are; but as far as my information goes, these conventions are adhered to as rigidly as any Puritan ever conformed to the law of his Church. The type has not really changed. The modern girl with possibly the freest sexual outlook the world has ever seen is no freer inwardly than her pious grandmother. Nor is she any happier. It is probably true that the new generation is less sex-obsessed than the older. But it is not freer otherwise. This new generation, too, is essentially narrow. And it is certainly poorer as regards its soul-life. For the whole world of feelings, emotions, and imaginations is dependent on inhibitions.

THEN what is fundamentally the matter with Puritanism? It is simply the predominance of the Nay-principle. This again, looked at from the other side, means that Puritanism does not allow man to express the whole of his nature. But it means something even more dangerous: since it lays the emphasis on the negative (whoever does not understand the word purity as synonymous with ingenuousness cannot help laying the emphasis there) the Puritan outlook actually cuts off a small part of man from the rest, as it were, and thus forces him to express all his energies within this fraction of his being. Such a cutting off is a cruelty; hence the cruel outlook of every Puritan, however little he may be conscious of it and however much he may overemphasize love and kindliness by way of compensation. But this cutting off is also a very dangerous surgical operation which must needs lead to pathological deformations except in a few fortunate cases. This explains why such a tremendous percentage of Americans seem in need of psycho-analytical treatment. The original Puritan was certainly not pathological, no more than the true Islamite. But then the Puritan religion really corresponded to these hard and great and simple characters. They were Puritans by the will of nature, just as others are cannibals. But it is only now that we perceive the chief danger of Puritanism: *it inevitably drains the soul.* If only rigid law is to rule, if the forbidden is emphasized, if absolute truth expressed in abstract formulæ is to mean more than life itself, then the emotional, or feeling, part of man cannot develop. And according to the law of compensatory retrogression, it must become more rudimentary or primitive as differentiation proceeds on other lines. The highest intellectuality can grow from Puritan roots. All Western science is really of Protestant origin, and the peculiar sharpness of the American intellect is most probably due, in part at least, to the excessiveness of American Protestantism. The utmost efficiency can grow from the same roots. If there is but one channel through which the whole of life may pour forth and express itself, all its energy must needs rush through it; this is why the Jews, the first Puritans, were the inventors of the religion of work. Puritanism can, in particular, produce giants of will. But it is precisely this possibility that makes us understand why the Puritan's soul-life must needs be so poor. Gigantic will power and differentiated emotions actually exclude each other. No Genghis Khan was ever a Shelley, and no Shelley could ever be a Genghis Khan.

What may make only for greatness in individual cases does indeed make for poverty pure and simple with the majority. Generally speaking, a man is a representative of humanity (in all the shades of meaning this word may have) by virtue of his world of inner experience. This is the soil in which grow the roots of religion, philosophy, art, culture, and, last but not least, of love. Love as we understand it is by no means a natural emotion: its existence depends on inhibitions allowing the quality of "longing" to become creative on its own plane. Now there is no doubt whatsoever that the Puritan type of man is deficient precisely in the field of inner experience. Hence the quality of non-vitality in all his manifestations on this plane. His religion is purely dogmatic, there is no room for creative freedom within it, far less than in Catholicism; accordingly, there has never been a Puritan mystic. His idealism is purely abstract, or detached from this world. Whatever belongs to the lyric domain is endowed with some weird transcendent quality; there is nothing more ethereal in the world and, therefore, nothing more unreal, than the romanticism or the lyricism of a typical New Englander.

The same is true of all American ideas of love up to a very short time ago. American women would talk of the "divinity" of sex; they would think of themselves as priestesses and attribute a priceless value to woman's natural surrender—which alone suffices to account for the fact that marrying or not marrying could lately become such a lucrative business for her. Now all the sentimentalism of American love and all its idealism can be completely explained by what we said above: that Puritanism means the cutting off of one part of man. If man expresses his tendencies in a field of unreality, this always means—the case of the genuine poet excepted—that he has lost touch with his vital roots. This is why American women so often seem almost incapable of love in the European sense: what should be an expression of woman's whole being, is in their case nourished only by a small fraction of it. Compared with the differentiated soul of a cultured European or Oriental woman, that of the American woman I mean here is almost a perfect blank, a thing so incredibly simple—though for that very reason often most pure—that the richer soul sometimes feels urged, unconsciously, to fill it, and accordingly to make a goddess of an empty vessel. But this again shows us how the idealism of the American woman could change so brusquely into materialism pure and simple in matters of love: if soul-life leads a separate existence, actually cut off from the whole of life, then the same must happen to physical sex-life. The way from pure spiritualism to pure materialism is much shorter for an American idealist than for any other type of woman in the world. Everywhere the key to the problem lies in an under-development and a state of one-sided differentiation of what we call the soul. How could love and marriage be satisfactory under these circumstances? Human nature being what it is, how can there be anything but a rush from one experience to another in the hope of gaining from without what is really lacking within? It is only natural that an enormous percentage of American women belonging to the leisured class should look neurotic, and the corresponding men exhausted or worn-out; it is indeed man's natural instinctive urge, wherever he does not predominate too strongly, to make happy the woman he cares for; and whoever is empty in soul always tries to compensate this want by intellectual or physical effort. The aforesaid even partly accounts for the excessive estimation in which sport and athletics are held in these days. Nor have I enumerated all the defects and drawbacks of the present state of things. If the emotions are not differentiated, then the emotional nature of woman and man, which belongs, as Jung has taught us, to the rational side of their being, must lack *understanding*. Let me cite a few significant instances to illustrate this fact. It is extraordinary how rarely Americans know how to distinguish between infatuation and true love, to say nothing of more delicate shades. If a man or a woman falls in love at all, then there must be marriage. On the other hand, a woman thinks nothing of leaving a husband as soon as she feels only physically attracted by another man. This is, of course, an expression of the Puritan outlook: the moral law must be observed at all cost. But how is it possible not to see that there are dozens of different kinds of love, and that it is nonsensical to force them all into the same channel? How is it possible not to see that man cannot prove equal to all the many vital issues in question from the exclusive point of view of some accepted moral code? There is only one explanation: an under-development and lack of differentiation of the soul. For a man or woman of differentiated emotions it is a physiological impossibility *not* to distinguish between the many different facts and issues in question; these differences seem as patent as those between the colours red and blue. But if the development of differentiated emotions is lacking, then indeed it is natural that a woman should not think twice before marrying a man simply because he is blessed with sex-appeal; that she should destroy a married life based on all sorts of ties simply because of a momentary infatuation of hers; that it should mean nothing to her to inflict a mortal wound on the souls of men and children—she simply does not realize that soul wounds may mean anything; that she can go through the ordeals of divorce suits, with the publicity attached to them in the United States, without harming her own soul. One particularly interesting aspect of soul-under-development is provided by the American cult of frankness. The newest pattern of the American woman thinks she may do anything if only she tells her husband. She cannot see—what is obvious to any differentiated soul—that a frankness which hurts is always a crime except in the case when nothing but a cruel operation can solve an impossible situation; that when she does not realize that jealousy is a fact of nature to be respected she is guilty of sheer coarseness; finally, that the mere fact of wanting to be in the right at any cost is moral cowardice. This kind of frankness is almost worse than prostitution from the point of view of a refined soul. I know of no more instructive example of the fact that any Good, falsely understood or applied, may turn into Evil. Veracity and sincerity are indeed the very pillars of Western civilization, and a frank man is, generally speaking, the better man because he is courageous. But here frankness is nothing but moral cowardice. If a man or woman feels that he or she must do something that would hurt the other partner and cannot bear the guilt alone, rather dying or even going to Hell than ever letting the other know—then he or she is contemptible precisely on the grounds of the Western ethics of courage, rightly understood. I certainly do not mean to encourage polygamy or polyandry. But I do believe, with Christ, that the *soul* is supreme in importance, and that all other considerations, physical, intellectual, and moral, must stand back. I first understood what was really the matter with American love-life when the following story was reported to me. One of the prominent court of appeal judges of the United States is alleged to have said of my introductory essay to the *Book of Marriage:* "I think what Keyserling says is true. But I am used, as a judge, to sum up things. So I would sum up his whole doctrine in the following sentence: *More and better adultery.*" Of course, he did not mean exactly what he said. But his *boutade* was not only witty, but profound. Only an American could have said it. What the judge in question means was that the chief trouble of American love-life is a lack of emotional differentiation. Now at this point we can complete what was said in "Predominant Woman" on the same subject. If the American woman as a type is, comparatively speaking, hard and soulless and unable to inspire, this is undoubtedly due to her Puritan heredity or to the influence of the Puritan atmosphere. The same partly explains why neither the American woman nor the American man is really vital and why they appear to lose vitality with every succeeding generation. The tying off of a limb prevents the blood from flowing into it. The psychic life of the Americans is bloodless in the sense that it is not nourished by the whole of the emotions. Yet it is in the emotions that all vital power resides. It is on them that all creativeness depends.

But I cannot conclude this argument before having drawn attention to the Puritan roots of two more typically American phenomena. One of these is the missionary spirit. I have never yet met an American of Puritan antecedents who was not a missionary at heart. In the modern world this spirit usually expresses itself in salesmanship and advertising. Now what is the chief psychological characteristic of the missionary-type? No other than lack of poise and self-assurance. The man who feels in harmony with himself and the world never thinks of meddling in other people's business; "Live and let live" is his motto; and even where he is sure that he knows better, he never tries to *enforce* his own opinion. He does so all the less, the more intelligent he is, because then he knows that no one can be converted against his will. He will certainly stand up for the truth, he will proclaim it, but his will never be the foremost desire of the missionary: the will to *persuade*. Now if a person is out of harmony with himself and the world, then he must conquer it in order to feel safe. And if, moreover, the major part of his being is cut off from his conscious, if he is ruled by some narrow principle, and if he is cruel by nature, then his only salvation lies in the conversion of the whole world to his ideas. This also accounts, to a considerable extent, for American standardization. These successful business men and salesmen are, all of them, unhappy missionaries in their hearts of hearts.

And for this very reason they never really persuade anybody who does not belong to their own type, unless indeed a man be so exclusively bent on material gain that the mere likelihood of "big money" makes him a sincere convert.—The second phenomenon, the Puritan roots of which I want to reveal here, is the American fear of public opinion and the ensuing inordinate power of the latter. This fear or dread simply means the projection on the community—a projection inevitable in an essentially socialist nation—of the fear of man of the cut-off entity within him, which actually rules and keeps the rest of the psyche in a constant state of abjection. In the early days of Puritanism there was something heroic even in this: there is true pathos in Hawthorne's *Scarlet Letter*. The reason is that in those days the written Law was absolutely believed in by strong and stern souls, and public opinion was its obvious executive. But today? What used to be akin to the splendid proud humility of the Bedouin before the face of Allah, has become mere cowardice in the face of possible material damage. Here, that topsy-turviness I dealt with in an earlier chapter has led to real moral degradation. If one has always to meet demands instead of creating them, if the public or the majority is always supposed to be right, where does the dignity of individual man come in—of man, who stands and falls with the fact that he is the *non*-conforming animal, whose ideal exemplar is Prometheus, who disregarded the will of the gods themselves; or Jesus Christ, Who thought nothing of the laws of His own people; or Don Quixote, who kept to his own ways and ideals in the face of all reality? What about the loyalty to that much-praised Nordic race, the chief characteristics of which were its tragic heroism, its radical Protestantism, its intrinsically aristocratic outlook—the outlook according to which a man would rather spit in the face of a whole nation than be untrue to himself? I will not dwell any longer on this dark spot—the only really dark and distinctly ugly blot on American life. Here, only a complete reversal of recognized values can prevent an otherwise inevitable downfall. This term is by no means too hard: the rule of public opinion as an ultimate court is more detrimental to the moral stamina of a nation than any drug. Only remember what the American press *can* do in the way of libelling. Fortunately it very often does not make use of its power; but when it does, it merely gives a more extreme expression to the right to which every American community lays claim as a matter of course. This fact proves beyond doubt that if anything is utterly wrong and bad and inexcusable on any ground in the constitution of the American people, it is this tyranny of public opinion.—But fortunately the Pioneer spirit is still alive. On the other hand, Puritanism in the negative sense of the word is dying fast; finally, the later immigrants are ever more ready to discard what they begin to realize as wrong in the tradition. So I trust that this cancer within the moral body of the American nation will be cured, however deep-rooted it seems to be. But on the other hand, it should never be forgotten that this very cancer is the direct outcome of what was originally sound in its way and certainly pathetic. . . .

I HAVE not been afraid to state freely what I think wrong with Puritanism in a book the aim of which is to help, and not to judge, because at this very moment America is struggling hard to liberate herself from its one-sided and excessive sway. In many respects one cannot speak as yet of a true liberative movement in the revolt against Puritanism, but only of a swinging of the pendulum to the opposite pole. Thus the "Revolt of Modern Youth," as Judge Lindsey describes it, will not lead to liberation; and it is more likely that the freest among the modern flappers will end as all-too-strict Puritans (any one-sidedness being liable at any moment to turn into another) than that a really liberal outlook should be the final outcome of this revolt. But, generally speaking, it is certainly true that what is objectively wrong with the Puritan outlook is in the process of being conquered; less in thought than in more rationally directed activities. From roots different from those of Puritanism—in particular, from the spirit of the continent, which is making for breadth, and those of Socialism and Privatism—an essentially humane attitude is developing. More and more are kindness and psychological understanding becoming prominent traits of the American type; and these are certainly not the characteristics of the Puritan. But perhaps it is precisely the Puritanic part in the American psychic body which makes, according to the law of historical counterpoint (explained in *The Recovery of Truth*), for ever-increasing humaneness; even so, Christ's religion of love seems unthinkable without its Jewish antecedents and background. On more than one occasion I have called attention to the fact that America is the one exclusively Christian country in the Western World, because it is the only one in which the psychological roots do not reach down to Paganism. Thus it is quite possible that in this sense a progressive Christianization of America, understood as its conquest by the spirit of what Christ really meant, would be a natural development, because the Puritan spirit is an almost pure expression of the spirit of the Old Testament. This accounts also, incidentally, for the evil side of American materialism and success-cult: here the Jewish and the American spirit meet. The de-Puritanization of America is, moreover, greatly accelerated by the dying out of the New England type, the rebirth of the prestige of the Cavalier, and the influence of non-Puritan immigrants, in particular the Roman Catholics. Extreme outbursts of seventeenth-century narrowness as illustrated by Fundamentalism would be quite unthinkable if Puritan narrowness were not as a national phenomenon on its deathbed.

Yet for all that, the United States still are essentially Puritan. Their entire civilization bears the stamp of the Puritan spirit. All the organic life-forms that have developed there bear its caste-mark. And these forms are so strong and so vital that they are quite unlikely to die out, however much they may compromise and amalgamate with others. That they should die out is all the more likely as, somehow or other, most of the other spirits of any moment in the United States are akin to the Puritan. The Irish are born Covenanters. The efficient type of the German—and he alone prospers on American soil—is even more of a worker than the Scotchman. Last but not least, the American Indians, too, were Puritans of a kind; theirs was an ascetic type, they knew little joy, thought little of emotion in general. This seems to show that there exists a kind of pre-established harmony between the spirit of the North American continent and that of Puritanism. Those who are opposed to Puritanism today should not forget that not only the prevalence of aristocracy and the prevalence of democracy are fundamentally zoölogical questions, but also the prevalence of a Protestant or a Catholic outlook; as I have shown in my *Travel Diary* and also in the chapter "The Spiritual Unity of Mankind" in *The Recovery of Truth*, it is primarily a question of psychological adjustment and not of a definite religious belief. Now, the Puritan is undoubtedly one of the best adapted types among physiological Protestants. In his higher expression he is a distinctly superior type; and though he has never ruled for any length of time, he has always been foremost among the conquerors. This is why he has predominated, again and again, among the Jews as well as among the Mohammedans, the Confucians, and the Hindus of the Protestant type, whether they are Jainas or Buddhists. King Acoka must have had distinctly Puritan traits, or else he would never have thought of forcing Buddhism upon his subjects. Now there is no doubt whatsoever that the Puritan has achieved great things on American soil. His is all the prestige of success. Americanization means always, to a certain extent, Puritanization. All the efficiency America stands for in the eyes of the world presupposes psychologically a kind of one-sidedness allied to strength, to which only Puritanism of some kind can give a moral support implying its permanent vitalization. Therefore, that which is being struggled against, and will no doubt soon be outgrown, is only *the element which is decidedly wrong* in Puritanism and can accordingly be psycho-analyzed away. Its orthodox doctrine certainly is no longer tenable, nor is its narrow morality. But the type of the Puritan as such will no doubt survive. It will survive because there is not one bright prospect which we might outline for America's future development that cannot be related, somehow or other, to the spirit of Puritanism. The general quality of the American civilization is sure to remain socialist, moralist, Protestant, and "pure" in the sense of an essential simplicity and sincerity. Of all the many "genes" (hereditary factors) that will make up the final American type, the Puritan will in all probability remain what Mendelians call the "dominant," and will thus be responsible for the general quality and the specific outlines of the whole.

Accordingly, all I have to do in this chapter is to help toward an understanding of what American morality as an expression of Puritanism means, to show the right connexion between this particular meaning and the integral meaning of life, and thus to help to induce an inner readjustment where this seems necessary. In what respects orthodox and traditional Puritanism is irrational has, I think, been made sufficiently clear. We said in the beginning that life, being a sense-connexion in which each particular "sense" mirrors all the others and can, therefore, rightly be chosen as a common denominator, there is nothing to be said in principle against a life-configuration in which morality plays the essential part. But in order to render impossible a development which is contrary to sense but which might easily come to pass as the result of what is in principle a possible adjustment, it is necessary, first and foremost, to understand what morality really means and what are the limits which the application of its idea cannot overstep without leading *ad absurdum*. As a matter of fact, morality is a very different thing from what the orthodox Puritans believe it to be. In its essence, it is not an expression of the divine or spiritual, but of natural law; and this natural law, moreover, is not the supreme law, but only one among others. There is a German saying: *Das Moralische versteht sich immer von Selbst* (Moral behaviour is always self-understood). The greatest representative of the most moralist nation of the world, Confucius, once said in the same sense (I do not recall the precise words): "I don't know what is the matter with morals. Superior men think too highly of them, and the opinion of the inferior is too low. Really, morality does not mean more, as it seems to me, than cultured nature." Both the German proverb and Confucius' saying are expressions of the truth. *The fact is that morality in the case of man endowed with free will means nothing else than what form, law, and order mean in the case of the animal which is not free.* There has never been an immoral animal. The animal's conduct is always true to the specific meaning of its life; its organism is always perfect in its shape and workings. As opposed to this, what makes man, from nature's point of view, is his capacity to err. In his case free will, inspired by understanding, must complete what compelling nature does in the case of the animal. From this there follow two things: first, that there are, in principle, many systems of good morals; secondly, that immorality is contrary to nature. There can be no doubt that there have been many great civilizations with moral outlook widely differing from one another, and no pragmatic test has ever proved one of them to be truer than another. On the other hand, only a limited number of moral outlooks have ever stood that test. The significance of this is the same as the significance of that other fact, that there is only a limited number of types of organic life. Moreover, all systems of morals which have stood the pragmatic test have agreed as to fundamentals. This again runs parallel with morphology: all organic forms are expressions of a general law of life which is ever identical. Now as to the second point that immorality is contrary to nature: it is indeed, because it corresponds to the dissolution of form in the organic sphere; and life without form cannot endure. Accordingly, there have never been prolonged periods which were really immoral ("really" as opposed to what the prejudice of a particular sect would call immoral). There could not be, because nature punishes immorality with the penalty of death. Immoral classes always die out within a very short time. Throughout all history, whenever one part of a nation became immoral, this part soon ceased to have any descendants, and life was continued by means of more moral, that is, of sounder stocks. But on the other hand, immorality is for the very reasons outlined above a *normal* phenomenon in times of transition. Morality simply meaning form and order, it must deteriorate or disintegrate when an ancient order is exploded and a new one has not yet become consolidated. Here, the prototype is war. War means a state of transition from one balance of powers to another. To render this transition possible, all the laws obtaining in times of stable order must needs be temporarily annulled. This is why murder is then, of a sudden, thought moral, destruction meritorious, and rapine and robbery venial sins. (War as the exemplar of immorality shows also incidentally most clearly why the latter can never last beyond a certain limit of time: it inevitably leads to mutual destruction.) In exactly the same sense, every transition in history has been attended by phenomena of immorality at which the champions of the old order stood aghast. The early Christians were, from the Roman point of view, frankly immoral because they denied the supremacy of the state, the foundation of all Roman morals. The Reformation was attended, at least in Germany, with outbursts of sexual laxity no modern flapper could beat. We can now also understand the real significance of present immorality: it is only a *normal* symptom of the dawning of a new age. That it should express itself chiefly along sexual lines in the United States, is due to the fact that the sex impulses have been the most repressed and checked by the Puritan order. Besides, the sex impulse being the strongest in life—along with hunger—it is naturally the first to run wild whenever form and order disintegrate; in this connexion one should remember what I wrote at the beginning of "Predominant Woman." Now the most important result of the foregoing within our present context is this, *that immorality*, being on the one hand essentially short-lived, and on the other, a normal symptom of a state of transition, *does not present a problem at all.* Whatever is really immoral today will soon cease to exist, as has always been the case with all immoral states, and always will be. But on the other hand, the new morality will inevitably be different from the old. The law and order of the future will correspond to the new state of life.

This new state is one of disbelief in all tradition founded on blindly accepted authority, and of greater intellectual understanding. From this it does not follow that America will cease to be moralistic at heart. There is no reason why a nation should not consider the law and order of life as the essential issues. Many great nations have done so in the past. In this respect a moralistic America would only continue the tradition of ancient China and Rome and even of our own eighteenth century. However, since understanding reaches down deeper than it ever did before, it is out of the question that morality should continue to mean what it meant to orthodox Puritanism, *viz.*, the supreme spiritual law and issue in life. It is equally out of the question that America should put up for ever with a narrowing of life which, as experience shows, inevitably leads to devitalization and pathological deformations. The American will undoubtedly remain Protestant at bottom, bent on the conquest and the organization of the material world on the one hand, and on social service on the other. This inevitably makes for a one-sidedness which demands a common denominator of life residing in the moral, as opposed to the intellectual or artistic spheres. But once the Americans understand the truth, they will no longer emphasize this common denominator so far as to cause the disruption of the normal optimum-order. Nor will they any longer be satisfied with a form and order of life which prevents many of its profoundest tendencies from expressing themselves. In this sense, it is undoubtedly true that Puritanism is on its deathbed. In particular, it is highly probable that sex morality in America will remain more free in the future than in most other countries. Too many chains of causes co-operate toward this end: the tradition of the original common-sense view of the Puritan of sex matters, the amazonization of woman, the general scientific and matter-of-fact outlook (only owing to this can the existence of contraceptives mean so much to American morals), and last but not least, Puritanism once more, which has made the demand of "purity" an essential psychological motive. It is very doubtful whether virginity will ever become again an actual as opposed to an imaginary ideal. A circumstance not yet mentioned in this connexion works against the old morality: the loss of prestige which the married state as such will inevitably suffer to an ever greater degree as the difficulties of keeping up a real home increase. And these difficulties must increase from year to year if no way is found to get cheaper servants. If the greater number of people cannot afford such, even the most perfect mechanization of household work will not prevent the state of the girl remaining more enviable in many important respects than that of the married woman. But this apparent revolution in sexual morality is not really so very important. I have my strong doubts whether the "innocent" girl which the older generation still glorifies as the normal type ever predominated except perhaps during the reign of Queen Victoria. Woman always knows all about sex in her unconscious; given her psychological structure, it really makes very little difference whether or not she knows consciously as well. Sex is something so fundamental, so all-permeating, and so obvious to her that she can be or appear equally innocent whatever she may know or do. In the European Middle Ages, it was the custom that when a knight visited a castle the girls had to undress and bathe him; and it was commonly told in those days how bashful the knight had been and how little abashed the girls. Likewise, up to the seventeenth century—and in the lower classes even up to a very short time ago—there was only one bed in North European homes, in which the whole family slept completely undressed, and guests, staying for the night, were invited into it as a matter of course. All these phenomena, which eventually resulted in the formation of the innocent girl of the nineteenth century, certainly were more alarming than can be fairly said of any kind of modern co-education. No, there really is no danger that permanent immorality is inherent in modern emancipation. The moral law will simply change, as it has so often done. This change is the result of a profounder understanding of life as a whole. Better understanding and nothing else is undermining today what is untenable in Puritanism. Only because it is not sufficiently deep and thorough as yet, does it lead to destructive processes. Therefore, what is wanted is a *thorough* understanding of the place morality should hold within the general scheme of life. Our next object must be to prepare the way for this. But this can be achieved only from a vantage-point which will allow the Puritan problem to be viewed from the outset as a partial expression of a more general problem.

ONE of the expressions of the profoundest understanding I know of is contained in the Hebrew prayer: "I want to serve God with my good impulses, and I want to serve God with my evil impulses." It is indeed of no use to deny any part of oneself that exists. Psycho-analysis has taught us that there is a real hell within each man's soul. This, of course, all saints and sages have known. But what they could not know, and what today is a certainty, is that this hell forms the *normal* nether-world of every human being; it is as indispensable for the organism as a whole and, in particular, for its highest part, as the unpleasant processes of the bowels are indispensable for the brain. There can be no question, therefore, of abolishing what is ugly and what many religions have thought sinful. Nor is there any use denying it, because denial only leads to repression, and repression to the ugliest of all formations.

What is wrong in this respect with the modern freer outlook—which wrong idea is chiefly due to a lack of understanding on the part of the psycho-analysts—is that it wants to turn the down-side upward (if I may use such a transposition of terms), that it is topsy-turvy: the hell in man is right only when it remains the nether-world. Just as the sex organs are meant by nature to be hidden, in the same way every exhibition of what belongs to the nether-world is a perversity; this is why love exhibited becomes obscene. Now man's best self certainly is not identical with the hell within him. But this best self can express itself only by means of the phenomena in existence, and it can express itself completely only by means of the whole of the latter. It is of no use to deny or cut off some part of them. What happens in the latter case is this: the whole expresses itself all the same, only in a perverted way. Accordingly, the one reasonable thing to do is to co-ordinate harmoniously all the various parts and formations of the soul, just as the various parts and functions of a healthy body are harmoniously correlated. At this point, then, the moral task sets in. Man, having to complete by his own free will what nature does in the case of the animal, there can indeed be no harmony unless man makes a moral effort. This is the basis of the truth of the idea of Original Sin. Man's nature certainly is not originally good. It might be good only if nature took care of man as she does of the animal.

It is obvious that if man was able to invent independent systems of religion and politics and law, it was much more natural to him to invent independent systems of morals. This was, in fact, the first thing he always did. In this case it is a question of such fundamentals that even today it is irrational to found a moral system on epistemology: obviously, the moral law is recognized as a reality before all rational thinking.[1] But why is it that all systems of morals are one-sided and most of them so narrow, that if they really ruled life, little would be left of it? How could it happen that from the very outset the moral law was accepted as unconditionally valid, and yet everybody expected its transgression as a matter of course? The reason is very simple. Some of the natural impulses are so overwhelmingly strong, as opposed to those belonging to the spiritual sphere, that primitive man simply could not co-ordinate them. Nor could he realize that his feeling of identity need not be destroyed by the acceptance of the fact that many different and conflicting entities lived within him. Accordingly, he made a choice. He tried to organize his life in such a way that only those impulses which he accepted as positive had a chance of expressing themselves. In the wisest of cases he invented a caste-system in which each caste had a different morality. Had it not been for the over-stressing of the principle of heredity, there would be little to say against the idea of caste; very much less, indeed, than against any uniform moral law. Human beings *are* one-sidedly developed; accordingly, their form and order must be different in each separate case. And the old castes really were true to the fundamental types of possible morality. This then, leads us to a new conception of Puritanism. We said that Puritanism is essentially cruel. Now we can add: *because* the type of man in question was cruel and violent and fundamentally that of a man of predominant will with only

[1] This fundamental truth has, as far as I know, first been explicitly stated by Albert Schweitzer.

slightly developed emotions, he had to evolve a peculiarly strict and rigid and hard morality; instinctively he felt that for him there was no other way to achieve form and order. From here we also understand why savages have the strictest rules of conduct and why in civilized communities people are conventional in exact proportion to their primitivity or lack of differentiation.

From this vantage-point we can see at a glance in what direction the ideal lies. Since there is no use denying or repressing nature, since man's spirit is bound to express itself by means of the whole instrument of his body and soul, the only spiritual goal he should strive after is to reach an inner standpoint and adjustment which make it possible to co-ordinate harmoniously the *whole* of a given nature, to rule it from within, and to express by means of the *whole* given instrument his spirit-directed life, as a master-musician expresses what he wills by means of even the most complicated instrument or orchestra. Accordingly, the alternative of narrow morality is not immorality, but a morality of a higher order. Morality as such is nothing more than form and order. Nature always remains what it is. Consequently, the one sensible ideal should be to give the *adequate* form and order to the whole of one's nature.

This is just what the Jewish prayer I quoted refers to: "I want to serve God with my good impulses, and I want to serve God with my evil impulses." And it corresponds also to the last part of the quotation from Confucius, namely that morality means cultivated nature. Culture never means anything else than nature become a direct expression of spirit. Accordingly, since man is essentially spirit, morality, as the expression of the *right* form and order of a given life, cannot possibly mean anything else than cultured nature. All conceptions of a moral order which is contrary to nature, or in which man must fight against his nature, are untrue taken in the absolute sense. They are true enough in such primitive cases in which man can express his spirit only by repressing nature. But this being a question of a primitive state, no mature culture can maintain a morality expressive of such a law, however sanctified it may be by religious tradition. Here may be found the chief reason why Puritanism in its original form is bound to pass away: its morality no longer corresponds to truth.

But the conception of morality as a value in itself must pass away, too. Form and order certainly is indispensable. But the form and order of life does not exhaust itself in the moral order. It has several dimensions, each of which is independent of the others. Truth and Goodness and Beauty and Love and Courage are necessary, all of them, but it is impossible to find a common denominator for them in the moral sphere; the less so, as the moral order is essentially expressive of the principle of Nay and not of Yea. A railway train cannot be defined by the rails on which it runs, but only in terms of its intrinsic power and motion. At this point we understand once more why Jesus Christ could not but hate the just and why He taught nothing about morality as such. During the few years of His public activity He shocked as many Puritans as He could and apparently He did so with gusto; the few events of His life recorded show that He, too, like all true reformers, was intentionally provocative. He was also one-sided; the structure of Life, if it is meant to last, must be erected upon moral foundations; it is not possible with safety to found the whole of it upon love and grace. But morality can be only one chord *among others* in the life's harmony. And the fuller and the more differentiated a life, the more difficult does it become to judge it in terms of morals. Every superior man has really been beyond Good and Evil. This phrase is not Nietzsche's invention: it was coined by the Hindus for the definition of the Sage; and Christ, too, denied that He was good. Every single record of His life shows unmistakably how very skeptical He was about the current notions of Good and Evil. The sinner was more in His eyes than the Pharisee; He forgave Mary Magdalene because she had loved much; He changed water into wine, etc. Christ really recognized individual and unique situations only; and there can be no rule for the unique.

And indeed, the higher the development a man has reached, the more important the part his uniqueness-principle plays within him, the more decisive must be the question not of what is good in general but of what is good in his particular case at the particular time. Hence the a-morality of every superior man. He accepts the whole of his nature as it is; he accepts also the world as it is. And then he tries to make the best of it by incarnating the profoundest and best significance he can grasp into the phenomena at hand. He very often is a moral man in the ordinary sense of the word, because the moral order every human being instinctively recognizes as valid is the minimum of law and order on the one hand and, on the other, it applies practically to all human beings. But just as a great poet is allowed poetical license even to the extent that he may violate the laws of grammar and syntax, just so there are times when a superior man does not conform to the general norm. First of all, he usually has extraordinarily strong instincts and impulses, these being the steam, as it were, of the engine he represents; and every engine is in need of a safety valve. But above all, very often he cannot conform to the norm of the majority because by doing so he might forfeit the meaning of his life. If he be a soldier, how can he avoid killing? If he be a statesman, how can he avoid acts which would be criminal in the case of any private person? I was once asked in America to lecture on the subject why most great men have been immoral. The question was well worth discussing. Very many great men have really been immoral according to the standards of their nation or class. In addition to what has just been said, the reasons are as follows: The first is a general reason: a great man, being different in kind from the ordinary person, the moral law expressive of his true connexion with the world must also be different. What is generally called "morality" is really only middle-class morality. The middle-class type of man must have rigid rules of conduct; first, because he is not sufficiently differentiated to centralize and direct his nature from within; second, because he cannot rise to a superior kind of form and order. The second reason why great men so often seem immoral is that all creative geniuses are of necessity artist natures. This implies not only advantages, but idiosyncrasies as well. The spirit-principle, being opposed to the law of matter, will not endure executive life and routine; and most systems of morals presuppose a life of routine and executive actions as a matter of course. Then, they must be extreme individualists, and there is no common denominator for individual ethics and social morality. Above all, however, they are in *need* of stimulation. Stimulation is the very food of creative life—but on the other hand it is opposed to all routine. This, then, leads us to the profoundest cause of the artist's so-called immorality. The artist really lives for his work in the same sense that the pregnant woman lives for her child. Accordingly, that only is the right thing for him to do or to submit to which helps the child to grow. Now the birth of a poem is far from being valuable to the man in the street. It is said that Laura thought Petrarca no gentleman because he did not wish to meet her; for since he addressed passionate poems to her, she very naturally inferred that he was in love with her. In reality, he simply wanted the inspiration of her idealized image to enable him to write poems. In exactly the same way, the so-called immorality of Goethe which so many American writers have objected to corresponded to the only possible law of growth of his great soul. He needed stimulation by women, but he could marry none. If this man, who was conventional enough in other respects and obliged to be careful as a high official of the state, made up his mind to live with Christiane only and not to marry her (he did so very late and never really meant it) this was an expression of a feeling of ethical obligation as imperative in its peculiar kind as that of any Puritan ever was.—But the profoundest reason why great men have almost always been "immoral" resides in their very spirituality. Spirit is essentially not of this earth. It needs earthly tensions in order to manifest itself, just as the strings of the violin must be tightened if they are to send forth music. The more spiritual a man, the greater these tensions. As opposed to this, the normal moral man is precisely he whose nature is in the best possible state of harmony with the earth. Accordingly, mankind in its earliest days realized that the law of the spiritual man must be different from that of earth-bound man. This is the *raison d'être* of all rules made for monks and priests; they define a life frankly immoral from the worldly point of view, and, therefore, Protestantism was quite right when it fought the institutions in question as immoral. But Protestantism was essentially wrong nevertheless, because the law of the spirit is not identical with the law of the earth. Now what applies to spiritual man, in so far as his law demands a life of renunciation of all earthly laws, is true of anyone in whom spirit plays a paramount part: there must be an unusual lack of balance between his spiritual and earthly natures. His equilibrium must be abnormally labile. Only when endowed with an extremely strong physique has any great spirit ever been physically healthy. And in every single case we know of, there have been the same objections to his morality that the Pharisees raised with regard to Jesus.

It certainly does not follow that morality is a prejudice. On the contrary, even a very narrow middle-class morality is better for the man in the street than moral laxity. But as morality as such never means more than law and order, there must obviously be different kinds of law. Here, a true understanding of life is best possible in terms of the Hindu idea of Dharma, to which I have given the new setting required for the modern world in the chapter "Hindu and Chinese Wisdom" of *Creative Understanding*. A great man has a right to live in a way differing from the average man. If, owing to a life the average would call immoral, he creates eternal values, then he obviously has a right to this kind of life even from the social standpoint; for he achieves more good than millions of moral citizens taken together.

Even the superior man can certainly never claim the right to harm others. But on the other hand—I have explained this at length in the chapter "History a Tragedy" in *The Recovery of Truth*—no life is without guilt. No man can do more than the utmost good in his power by means of his specific nature and destiny. Every good life—even if the word good be taken in the ordinary moral sense—leads to evil in some respects. None can do more than take all the guilt his life involves upon himself, as Jesus took upon Himself all the guilt of mankind. Everybody can thus find salvation—with the one exception of the man who, relying on a good conscience, believes himself absolutely in the right. The so-called good conscience which justifies the condemnation of others, is indeed, as Albert Schweitzer puts it, the one thing certainly invented by Satan himself.

WE CAN now proceed to the final synthesis. In this we shall best succeed if we put the question in the way it was put to me in many American towns, namely, whether freer morals would create richer souls. After all that has been explained so far it must appear clear that a rich soul and a superior man cannot possibly have a narrow moral outlook. What makes a superior man is, in the first instance, the fact that within him the emphasis lies on his creative spirit and, accordingly, on the principle of Yea and not of Nay; but morality as such is always an expression of the latter. Again, a rich soul must needs feel that every form and order that does not permit complete self-expression is contrary to the truth it holds. Now there is no more a majority of superior men and rich souls in humanity today than in any previous age. But a general rise of level has taken place on the plane of understanding. What was known to every superior man as a matter of course—this knowledge merely reflecting the unwritten law of his being, *viz.*, that there is a "beyond" of morality in the sense of a higher order which can be realized as such and of which the moral order forms only a part—has today become a matter of objective knowledge, which every person of normal intelligence can comprehend. Owing to this, there can be no question of a return to traditional morality.

But it is as impossible that the present state of frank immorality, which is normal only as a state of transition, should last. We have shown in the beginning that modern sexual liberty does not represent a higher state as compared with Puritan strictness, but that it really represents a different expression of the same narrow spirit. Now we can even add: If that which makes superiority is the ability to see things in their right proportion and to rule them from within so as to produce a harmonious general state, then the flapper is decidedly inferior to any woman who genuinely believed in the truth of the old order. Why? Because she believed the requirements of the soul and its high development more important than the contentment of the flesh. To my knowledge, there never was a generation poorer in soul-life than the youngest American generation. There being no inhibitions to the impulses, soul-life simply cannot develop. Since the behaviourist outlook makes for a general conception of life according to which man appears as an animal among others, the physical is supposed to decide. Thus, for the first time in history, do refined women judge the value of love by its effects on the health. All these disadvantages are enhanced by the general rejuvenation the race is experiencing just now and by the idealization of youth. The life of the young always is poorer than that of mature persons. The whole instrument of their nature has not yet developed, a few primitive impulses play a predominant part and, the spirit still being embryonic, it has no power over them. Accordingly, the young are physiologically incapable in any case of living out the fulness of their lives. This was the reason why in all states of mature culture they were subjected to wholesome conventions which furthered their development. Now the all-important part of man is his soul, understood as an expression of the whole of the emotional sphere. If this sphere is not richly developed, then free morals are absolutely wrong, because a primitive soul needs some kind of rigid discipline. Here, then, we have got to the root of the matter. It is not primarily a question which of the opinions concerning morals is the best, *but of whether the concrete state of a given human being renders it capable of living according to the highest truth*. Children must be told all sorts of reasons for good behaviour which do not correspond to scientific truth. In the same way, the question with adults is not which form and order of life is the best in theory, but whether a given person is able to incarnate it or to live up to it as a matter of fact. Accordingly, the real issue is not whether freer morals are required, but whether human beings can stand more freedom. Now all facts go to prove that the overwhelming majority of modern American youth is not in the least ready for a freer outlook. Most of them are Puritans the other way round. And since man is first and foremost a physical being, an under-development of the soul is something very much more damaging than a repression of bodily desires. For the latter always leads, somehow or other, to a compensatory soul-development, whereas a purely physical life is perfectly satisfactory in itself and must needs lead, when thought of as the only thing of value, to the progressive animalization of man. This is the truth about these healthy boys and girls Judge Lindsey delights in. They may be healthy as bodies; I dare say they are. I will even go so far as to admit that the new generation seems to be blessed with a better physique than that of any generation for centuries outside of savage tribes. But their souls are often almost subhuman. Here we find the least pleasant phenomenon of the convergence between America and Russia. There is very little difference between Bolshevik and neo-American soul-life.

Still I am entirely in sympathy with modern American youth. It is normal that a generation called to overcome the narrowness of Puritanism should begin by going to the other extreme on the same plane. And anyhow in these days of dying belief and ever more awakening intellect, free experimentation is the only thing that can lead to ideas really corresponding to the facts. In this connexion, I sympathize most particularly with those who suffer harm from their experiments: theirs is a true case of casualties in wartime. With morality, as with every other problem of these days (I have given the general outlines of the new psychological state of mankind in *The World in the Making*) the fundamental trouble is that intellectual recognition has developed far ahead of all the other functions of the soul. Here, too, the fundamental problem is that of the new union between mind and soul, as I have entitled the central chapter of *Creative Understanding*. Perfection will be reached only through organic growth. But on the other hand, true understanding alone can give this process the right direction and accelerate it. Here then we come up, once again, exactly as we did at the end of our survey of the problem of Democracy, against the recognition that America's entire cultural future depends on a deepening of individual self-consciousness. This is so precisely because of the extraordinary development of its social consciousness. For on the plane to which the problems of Good and Evil belong, there is absolutely nothing to be expected from social progress. There is no common denominator for the personal law and the law of the community.[1] I must explain this fundamental truth, already hinted at in an earlier paragraph, a little more in detail here, because owing to her inherent socialist outlook, America's future depends to a considerable degree upon its realization. The form and order of the community applies exclusively to a multitude of men taken as an ultimate terminus, exactly as the form and order of the single soul applies solely to its wholeness, whatever the particular impulses and functions within it may desire for their complete expression. But whereas these impulses and functions really belong to a lower plane, as compared with the wholeness of the soul, for which reason their particular desires can be discarded from the point of view of the whole man, this is not true of the individual as compared with the community. In his essence man is unique; and his unique soul really is the ultimate terminus. The community actually bears the same relationship to this unique soul as do the im-

[1] I may mention here, incidentally, that I stated and demonstrated this truth, at the age of twenty-six, in my book *Unsterblichkeit* (*Immortality*, not yet translated into English).

pulses—only upon another plane. *That is, the community as such has no soul, nor is it a soul.* It is held together by what is really subhuman. Hence the low level of any collectivity as compared with any single intelligent man. Now the community being all the same composed of unique souls, it has naturally to a certain extent taken the individual side of its members into account. But it always draws the line at the point where the interests of the individual and the community clash. This is why it never could accept any genuine innovator and reformer; this is why it always objected to the particular ways of the superior man. It cannot recognize the individual soul as the ultimate end. Now, since every individual soul is essentially unique, and since the greatness of a soul is proportionate to its lack of "normalcy," since, on the other hand, there must be a community-life considering itself as a last resort, the result must be a tragic conflict which is insolvable in its very essence. There is no common denominator for the personal law and the law of the community, nor will there ever be; this is a fact which man must accept as the basis of his life. And the only solution—explained at length in *The Recovery of Truth*—lies in the fact that the acceptance of tragedy creates a new level of existence, on which the problems of previous levels cease to be vital and significant. And only on this higher level can there be any hope of really harmonizing the conflicting interests of the individual and the group. It is indeed possible, on that level, to express one's uniqueness in harmony with the social order. But it is altogether impossible on the level of under-individualization. Of this the present condition of the United States provides the conclusive proof. Social consciousness is more highly differentiated there than anywhere on earth. But the individual is under-developed to a degree unheard of among civilized nations in any age. And since all spiritual values are created by the individual, and can be created only by him, there is no possibility that even the most perfect social system, incarnated in men of the highest social morality, can ever compensate for the non-existence of fully developed individualities.

IN CONCLUDING this chapter, I want to explain a little more fully what I have said concerning the possibility of building up a great civilization on foundations essentially moralistic. I mean "moralistic" in contradistinction to moral, for the foundations of all good community-life are obviously moral, morality meaning nothing but form and order in general. To this end I will show what is already exemplary on its own particular line in present American life. In order to achieve this, I can do no better than comment on a passage written by a very acute French observer, Lucien Rémier, editor of the *Figaro*, in his book *Qui sera le maître, l'Europe ou l'Amérique?* He says (p. 158): "The American democracy educates the masses by moralism, whereas the European democracies feed them with intellectualism. The cult of the (good) conscience and the rules of practical life have proved more efficacious, socially, than abstract knowledge and intellectual prejudice. The definition of the social condition of the United States can be given in a few words: liberty of thought, but uniformity and dogmatism as to conduct. Morals, too, are standardized." And on p. 160 he continues: "To Puritanism are due both the individualism of thought and belief, and moral collectivism." It is indeed impossible to make intelligent people like-minded in ideas, except by robbing them of individual intelligence. But it is quite possible to create a like-minded community in conduct and habits. In this sense all unified cultures have had an unintellectual foundation. Now if the moral element contained in conduct and habits is stressed, and if the morality in question is, on the whole, true to man's best nature; if, on the other hand, ideas and beliefs and opinions as such are considered as practically irrelevant—the most diverse, nay, the most antagonistic individuals may feel *as* one. In earlier ages religion often provided the cement in question; thus, Constantine the Great, that most unscrupulous of all Machiavellians, made Christianity the State religion because he saw no other way to reunite the centrifugal forces of the Roman Empire then in a state of ever-increasing differentiation. In the United States religion, too, plays a great part. But it is peculiar that in this country the churches stand principally not for dogma, but for morality; this is why the Roman Catholic Church can co-operate there with the Protestant Churches. This, then, shows us that "moralism" really means the predominance of "habit" over thinking, which fact alone serves to account for the fundamental concepts of American philosophy; and habit is the most conservative and uniting thing within the whole domain of Life. Now here the decision as to value depends on the quality of the habit involved, and in this respect there is indeed a good deal to say against American morals; from the point of view of spiritual value of any kind, habits which work against an increase of differentiation and an enhancing of the uniqueness-quality are assuredly not good. But then we must remember that the American civilization is essentially a mass civilization; that it stands and falls with its success in amalgamating the most diverse elements. If we take this as a starting-point and remember at the same time that a mass age is emerging all over the globe, and then compare the American lack of inner conflicts with the strife and bitterness in most other countries—then we must admit that America presents the first satisfactory solution of the community problem on modern premises in the modern age. It has laid the safest of all social foundations so far in existence. There is no reason why upon these foundations great and beautiful buildings should not arise later on. One of the most promising signs of this possibility, I should think, is the fact that in America alone until now women enjoy the company of their own sex, and that the feeling of solidarity or the feeling for the common end in view seems to outweigh that of rivalry. Human nature as such never changes, least of all that of the woman, the conservative part of mankind; woman never was gregarious by nature and never will be. Therefore, if the American women collaborate so much better than those in all other countries, there must be a particular reason. The reason is no other than the basic American moralism. If only habit and conduct count, if everything else is left to individual discretion, if, moreover, every woman feels moral obligation to be the mainspring of her life—then there really is no reason why she should not play a part in public life she has never played anywhere else. The under-stressing of intellectual and artistic values, which is psychologically concomitant with predominant moralism, certainly has very serious disadvantages. But they are not the only values in life. And all I wished to show here is that there are great prospects in store even for the present very one-sided American civilization, if it develops in the right spirit.

And there is one element in moralism the mention of which I have withheld on purpose until the end—an element which makes the right kind of development highly probable. This is American optimism. So far, we have dealt with it only as in the light of a compensatory phenomenon. But it can be considered in another aspect. Optimism is one of the natural effects of moralism. The European eighteenth century was optimistic; so was the outlook of ancient China. The reason is that a pessimistic moral outlook as such is a contradiction in terms; this is why such an outlook never lasted long as a factor in history, however great the number of individual spirits which may have stood for it; even the outlook of the Southern Buddhist is optimistic, in spite of the letter of Buddha's doctrine. The idea underlying every kind of moralism is that life should be made better than it is; and this obviously presupposes that it *can* be made better and that it is not an evil in itself. If life's centre lies in Knowledge, or Faith, or Love, then a basic pessimism is possible; not so, if the centre lies in morals. This helps us to understand how the heredity of the grim Pilgrim Fathers could evolve the kindly, good-natured, exuberant American of today. If now the influence of deeper understanding is brought to bear upon this same moralistic heredity, then the native optimism is almost sure to lead to a betterment of life which will stand the test of the very criticism which present moralism is not yet able to stand.

## *Culture*

ONE of the results of the preceding chapter was the recognition that the moral order does not express the whole order of life. There is no reason why, in the case of a specifically one-sided race, the former should not be made the common denominator of the latter. In itself, however, the moral order is an integral part of a more general order. It was the latter which the Chinese and the Greeks really meant when they spoke of morality. When Plato, the most perfect representative of Athenian civilization—the most radically æsthetic civilization which has ever existed—taught that the idea of "the Good" was the ultimate idea underlying the world; when the ancient Chinese, one of the most broadminded and artistic peoples that ever lived, defined morality as "cultured nature," both obviously meant something vastly more comprehensive than what the Puritans call morality. What they really meant was what we today call *culture* as opposed to raw nature on the one hand, and mere technical training on the other. Now, does culture actually stand for the ultimate end which human striving after perfection can attain? It does indeed. The spiritual ideals have their home beyond the range of possible earthly fulfilment. Unresolved earthly tensions are their means of realization; the ethical problem is unsolvable in its very essence; life is fundamentally a tragedy, which means that that which is better, or superior, never conquers on the material plane yet at the same time can never avoid the burden of earthly guilt.[1] What is true of individual life is equally true of ideals: there is no positive earthly solution of the problem simply because it ends with death. Nevertheless, it is not impossible to build permanently spiritual values into historic life; this can be achieved if these values become generally recognized as ultimately determinant; if exemplary incarnations of them act as universally accepted models; and if, accordingly, on the one hand, all material manifestations of life are made part of, or related back to a spiritual scheme, while on the other, all individual striving after these values finds predetermined channels corresponding to the actual state of the souls. We have herewith defined culture as a plane superior to nature, and our definition states by implication that all orders of life, not only the moral but also the religious, to say nothing of the æsthetic and intellectual, are integral parts of the more general order of culture. But what has been said is not enough; we must get a complete and clear view of the situation. This is all the more necessary in the context of this book, as there is high idealism in America, on the one hand, and at the same time, as yet no national striving after culture.

The task we have set ourselves in this chapter is not difficult to achieve, because by explaining what the term morality really stands for and what can be its highest expression and aim we have already given a concrete image, as opposed to a mere abstract formula, of the true meaning of culture. The cultured man is he who organizes from within the whole multiplicity and mani-

[1] Compare for a detailed exposition of these problems the chapters "History a Tragedy," "Death and Life Eternal," "The Ethical Problem," and "Man's Place in the World" in *The Recovery of Truth.*

foldness of his nature into a harmonious whole, and rules it as a master-musician conducts his orchestra. The moral man, not only in the highest but in the only true sense of the word, is he who uses all his powers for the good, whether they are good or evil in themselves. The æsthetically accomplished man is he who expresses all his impulses in so true a harmony that even what is ugly in itself becomes beautiful as an integral part of a whole beautiful in itself. The man whose vital centre lies in understanding has reached perfection when he has grasped the meaning of everything in its right relationship to the integral meaning of the world. Likewise, the emotionally perfected man, the great lover, uses his natural instincts and impulses in a way analogous to that in which Chopin used the waves of sound. And so on. Now obviously the values and the empirical means of their realization we have mentioned here are, *all of them*, the apanage of man; there can be no real perfection where any one of them is lacking. This is true independently of all particular metaphysical or religious doctrine; man *is* "whole," foremost and essentially; therefore, "wholeness" must be his primary aim if he wants to realize himself. Whatever there is within him which does not belong to him inasmuch as he failed to relate it to his inmost centre, sooner or later develops into something like a foreign spirit by which he is obsessed; he is then ruled by what is not essentially himself, he is not truly autonomous. This single line of thought seems to dispose finally of the myth of the intrinsic value of any one-sided civilization. If a civilization, which is based on moral law, however high it may be, does not stand for Beauty, Love, and Truth as well, it is a crippled or a diseased state. Of this, precisely Puritan America provides the most striking example. In its stern early days it looked upon beauty at best as a superficial thing; at worst, as a downright evil. Today the value of beauty seems as often as not over-emphasized as far as conscious intention goes. But since the unconscious is still organized and ruled from within by the principles underlying Puritanism, one hardly ever meets with a genuine sense of beauty. Nothing in American life bears originally the mark of a primary and involuntarily acting sense of beauty. The mere idea of a possible standardization in things æsthetic proves this: that beauty always means true proportions in relation to a ruling centre. No drawing-room can ever be beautiful, however valuable the objects it may contain, unless it is attuned to the unique personality of the woman inhabiting it. In the same way, the women Americans themselves call beautiful are hardly ever more than pretty—and prettiness bears exactly the same relationship to beauty that popularity in the kindergarten sense bears to spiritual value. It is interesting in this connexion to follow up the historical antecedents of Puritanism. Its idea was founded chiefly on those of Jewry and Early Christianity. Now the Old Testament stands exclusively for the tension between God's Will and man's inadequacy; accordingly, the Jews never developed a culture of their own and they never reached a harmonious adjustment to the world at large; hence their intrinsic ugliness. On the other hand, the spiritual principle they recognized to the exclusion of all others—the principle of Ethos—made for perpetual motion and uprootedness from the earthly point of view. Here we find the spiritual roots of the one-sided dynamism of the American. As to Early Christianity—its specific discountenancing of beauty provides the spiritual background for the American idealization of "the man in the street"; the fact that the ordinary man is, in principle, supposed to be better than the extraordinary and the superior man is a reincarnation of the idea that the humble stand first in the sight of God. But precisely Early Christianity provides the best illustration of the truth that a one-sided civilization cannot stand the test of understanding. Among richly gifted peoples Christianity could remain what it originally was only as long as it occupied a position of contrast to an actually ruling culture based on beauty. No sooner had it conquered, than the profoundest representatives it ever had—the early Greek Fathers of the Church—understood that Christian Love was not opposed to beauty and wisdom, but was rather a partial expression of the same basic spirit, Beauty, Wisdom, and Love thus really forming a trinity. If we translate the intrinsic meaning of their teaching into modern terms, disregarding for the moment all religious dogmatism, it amounts to this: what had been wrong with antiquity was that the emotional side of man's nature had remained under-developed. The ancient Chinese gave to this basic truth which the early Greek Fathers of the Church had just touched on a more complete and, at the same time, a more scientific expression: they held that profundity is not profound unless it expresses itself in beauty and grace of the surface. This accounts chiefly for the difference between Chinese and Puritan moralism; it was always taken for granted in China that moral perfection must needs express itself æsthetically as well. Thus ancient Chinese life had one spiritual co-ordinate more, as it were, which determined life's external manifestations. Hence the all-roundness, the "substantiality" in the sense of mediæval philosophy, and the broadness of the ancient Chinese type of man—whose spiritual antipode is represented in this connexion by the Puritan. Now in our days the philosophy of significance makes it possible to arrive at a perfect understanding of the truth expressed more or less vaguely in earlier ages. Within the whole of life the law of correlation between meaning and expression obtains; that is, no meaning is truly realized unless it is perfectly expressed. But, then, perfect expression always means beautiful expression. And the highest expression of perfection obviously is beauty sublimated into grace. Why? Because lightness of touch is the one true symptom of the final victory over clumsiness; clumsiness always means that matter has not been conquered by spirit. Thus, the triumph over the force of gravity is not symbolized by some towering massive building, but by the flight of the bird. This explains why the most sublimated forms of moral perfection have always involuntarily been described as expressions of "moral beauty," even by Christians of the severe type averse to everything that was not stern.

There is indeed nothing beyond beauty on the plane of expression. This cannot be otherwise, since beauty alone implies perfect proportion and harmony, and since, inversely, the latter inevitably manifest themselves as beauty. Now since even the moral ideal is incarnated in the man who conducts perfectly the whole orchestra of his vital forces, all of which are perfectly attuned to one another, there can be no doubt whatever even at this point of our investigation that it is culture and nothing else which represents the supreme ideal of a good life on earth. However, this is not the last word to be said on the subject. The chief and the deepest reason why culture stands for the supreme ideal can be revealed only now: it is not only a question of harmonizing and integrating the diverse and conflicting natural tendencies of man within himself and with respect to his fellow men according to principles pertaining to the æsthetic order, but of *establishing the best possible harmony between spirit and matter in all their varying aspects in the dimension of simultaneity, on the one hand, and between present, past, and future in the dimension of succession, on the other.* We shall deal first with the dimension of simultaneity. The mystery of incarnation cannot be explained. But there is no doubting the fact that man is, on the one hand, a spiritual being and can never be complete or happy unless he is true to spirit; and that, on the other, he is as deeply interwoven with matter as a thought is with the words expressing it. Accordingly, the harmonization advocated here really is *the* first vital necessity. We shall define the ultimate significance of what the word spirit stands for in the concluding chapter. But at this point no final definition is needed, because everyone actually experiences himself first of all as a spiritual being. It is a unity of spirit in the widest sense, and not of matter which the consciousness of self-identity mirrors. Whatever parts of the lower soul—the emotions, passions, affections, instincts, impulses—have not become thoroughly permeated and animated by the underlying spiritual unity and by this represent symbolic means of its expression, have in all truth remained parts of the external world. The non-permeation in question cannot be avoided beyond a certain point in the case of the body and its functions; here beauty and grace, at any rate, cannot be commanded. But it *can* be avoided in the case of the soul; hence the commandment "thou shalt" of all religious and cultural systems with regard to everything that immediately touches the life of the soul. As a psychological being man *can* become "whole," that is completely integrated; the underlying spirit *can* become all-permeating and omnipresent. And again, that is what it "should" be, because man being "human" only as spirit incarnate, he is disloyal to his self if he fails to conquer the lower orders. Hence it should be clear why a state of culture only, and not a state of nature however perfect, is truly "natural" in the case of man. He cannot live in the right relationship with the universe, as an animal can, unless he has made all matter an expression of spirit. Only the cultured man, who rules all his vital forces in their right reciprocal proportion, as a master-musician conducts his orchestra, equals the animal in perfection. The truth of this statement is finally proved by the irremediable unhappiness of all those who do not succeed as spirits in conquering and harmonizing their natures. Life is always a tragedy; no one has ever escaped outward misfortunes and disappointments. But the then spiritualized man is joyful amidst his sorrow; he never finds reason to complain. Whereas permanent unhappiness is the inevitable lot of those who seek to find external remedies for a lack of inner balance; there is no help for them because, man being endowed with free will and understanding which can transmute reality, their state of unhappiness actually amounts to a sinful state.—So much for the dimension of simultaneity. As to that of succession, a true sense of proportion makes us realize at first sight that it is contrary to the meaning of life to detach any of its facts from the whole. Life really is a melody.[1] The whole melody is pre-existent to the single bar. Accordingly, any form of life the present existence of which is not consciously attuned in the right way both to the future and to the past is necessarily a failure, which sooner or later vital experience is bound to reveal as such. This is why every true state of culture is consciously based on tradition, on the one hand, and on the other feels responsible for the future as an integral part of itself.

LET us now recapitulate the chief points which seemed to us to be defects in the present condition of the United States. Up to now, America has been too exclusively moralistic. This is all very well for a simple race of conquerors, such as were the early Mohammedans; but as soon as life grows richer, exclusive moralism means a thwarting of many of the best tendencies of life; this is why later Puritanism is insincere in a very high degree, although the chief virtues of the original Puritan were precisely his veracity and uprightness. No one is really sincere—nor can he be—if he has to repress or conceal what actually lives within him. Then, America is ruled by the animal ideal; for this is the true significance of the ideal of a high standard of living. But the standard of living has as such nothing whatever to do with man's real goal, that is a life expressing the right proportion between spirit, mind, soul, body, and external world, which is the one real goal even of the animal and the plant; for what they desire is also in all cases a perfect state of balance between the inward and the outward. As opposed to this, the ideal of a high

[1] I have fully developed this trend of thought in the chapter "Life and Death" of *The Recovery of Truth.*

standard of living appraises life exclusively in terms of the one co-ordinate of surroundings, supposed to be beneficial in the abstract. But there is even more to be said against this ideal: is a high standard of living as conceived by the inhabitants of the United States really the best standard? History gives us every reason to doubt it. All races whose existence became too frictionless and comfortable have soon degenerated. On the other hand, there have been high cultures based on practically any kind of standard. A high standard is certainly better than a low one—but what is of first importance always is the quality of *man* and not of the surrounding world. Now there is so little question of the predominance of man's inner life in American civilization that in the eyes of the overwhelming majority the ideal of a high standard of living practically includes all ideal aspirations of this time. This implies that the spirit of matter, and not the autonomous spirit of life, rules supreme. Hence the belief that surroundings and outward conditions are of the first importance. Hence American institutionalism and educationalism. American civilization practically ignores the existence of autonomous spirit in man. This fact alone means a complete distortion of the true connexion. Accordingly, there not only is no genuine American art, there *can* be none—negro art excepted, for the negro alone so far has established the right kind of relationship between his inner being and the external world. There is no American philosophy which is more than one expression among others of the animal tendency of man to adapt himself to surroundings and form the most adequate habits. There is no original sense of beauty. Utility is everything. Never has there been a race on earth which took so little advantage of the natural beauties of the country it peopled and which thought so little of æsthetic values as aims in themselves in the building of its towns or the organization of its life. This, then, is the final proof that the modern American is out of harmony with both himself and the surrounding world. He considers himself the master of nature only, her child—never; he merely exploits her. He completely ignores the fact that Mother Earth was there æons before man and that she will outlive him; and that a true sense of proportion, synonymous with a true understanding of life, obviously demands that man should primarily feel himself a part of nature. Accordingly, it is inevitable that American life today should lack all beauty. The same which, along different lines, causes the intrinsic ugliness of the Jew, makes for the ugliness of a whole continent which was really meant to be beautiful; for the American scenery is grand. I have quoted the opinion of a Russian philosopher that the Demon of Comfort is far more dangerous than the Demon of Terror. Thus, I was never more shocked in all my æsthetic sensibilities than by the sight of standardized American homes. Sometimes, in order to keep my inner balance, I had to concentrate with longing on the contrasting picture of the very worst kind of Russian sordidness, which at any rate, on its own low plane, denotes a true sense of proportion. Beauty is the normal expression of meaning perfectly realized; and it will be easier for the Russian chaos than for American nicety and neatness to evolve cultural beauty. How totally distorted the prevailing American view of all these problems is, is most strikingly illustrated by the generation of American girls of which the flapper represents the type. It seems to do absolutely all it can in order to lose its charm. The

American girl is naturally pretty, if not beautiful; she is healthy and essentially young. But why, then, does she paint herself at the age of eighteen which would be æsthetically justifiable only in the case of an octogenarian? Why, in particular, does she paint her lips with so unnatural a colour as to deprive the mouth, the most expressive part of the face, of all expressiveness? The explanation is that this generation believes in "abstract" beauty, as earlier ages believed in abstract morality. These misguided children treat their own complexions very much in the same way that American engineers treat grandiose scenery.

But let us proceed in our comparison between the prevailing American ideals and a true sense of proportion. How can anyone believe that production is an end in itself, or even the consumption of material goods, or simply the possession of ample means of existence? What is the use of wealth and possession if there is no self-centred and outpouring original life to give it a meaning true to its own significance? In particular, what is the good of money, if man has no aims apart from it for which to use it? The ideal of property as an end in itself is no longer valid when we consider that man never thinks long of what he has got; unless he is a miser, he never dwells inwardly on what he already owns—he only uses it as a starting-point or basis for new conquests or achievements. Dostoievsky was right when he taught that man is the one animal that can get used to positively everything; he can feel contented even in prison. But, then, contentment with him never brings happiness; for man knows happiness only when his inner creative urge is given full scope. This leads us to another inherent defect of American life. Since not only objective value, but also subjective happiness depend entirely on improved *inner* conditions, where they were unsatisfactory —what is the use of all ability and efficiency unless they lead to such improvement? In the same sense, information without understanding is of no value whatever, because only information comprehended is raw material assimilated and spiritualized by man—and comprehension proceeds from within to the outside, not vice versa. This seems to dispose finally of the present American ideal of education. The kind of education the United States glory in simply means training, as animals can be trained; it makes men more or less fit for the struggle of life: it does not produce culture. The real reason why Americans are constantly talking of education as a supreme goal and why they spend unheard-of sums on it is that they are glad to have something obvious to focus as an aim. This goes a long way toward explaining the persistence of the pioneer-ideal of the completely uneducated man who yet has attained to high financial and social position. How little education is envisaged as a road to culture is proved by the fact that most Americans talk of the institutions they have gone through as though they were the stages of an official career, and that their foremost educational ideal seems to be to pocket degrees. No doubt the case is not so bad with the girls; but what has been said is certainly true of the overwhelming majority of the men. Their real inner attitude toward culture is finally demonstrated by the rhythm of their life, which demands a holiday in the wilds as the ideal change after business life in town. Technical and animal life really belong to the same plane. Accordingly, the American predilection for hiking and camping does not mean what the love of occasional weeks of half-wild existence means to highly cultured Europeans: it means that the plane of true culture still lies beyond their horizon. The American at one time surrounds himself with every imaginable comfort, and at another he camps out like a red Indian, just as the nomad peregrinates from the summer to the winter pastures. There would be nothing to object to in all this *if* man were an animal, as Behaviourism and Pragmatism will have it. But he is not. With the exception of races incapable of higher development and of such primitive conditions as make it impossible for man to shape them according to his own image, he can reach precisely the same perfection within himself and with regard to the surrounding world as the animal incarnates as a matter of course, only by establishing the needed harmony by spiritual initiative and sense-bestowal on the plane of culture. The zoölogical reason is that man is characterized as a type by free will, inventiveness, and the capacity to err. Therefore, he will never reach perfection as long as he tries to live up to an animal ideal. It is precisely when he considers health, naturalness, etc., as everything, when he discards as "bunk" the spiritual and moral order, that he is out of harmony with nature. And this is the more true, the more advanced he appears along specialized lines. The final result of this mistaken attitude is a caricature—a deformation which involves devitalization. Life in the United States is unnatural not because it is too technicized, but because *inward* man has not yet succeeded in building his newly acquired proficiency into an organic whole, ruled from within—which the Babylonians and Egyptians succeeded in doing on their own plane. For, comparatively speaking, those early races were even more advanced in the technical field than we are.

But let us proceed. The full significance of what we said in the preceding chapters about American lack of joy becomes quite clear only when viewed from the angle of the ideal of culture. Joy is the *natural* expression of a harmonious relationship between the inside and the outside; this is why all normal children are joyous. But then children are animals—for the adult civilized man to attain to a permanent state of joy the general outlook must be such as to allow for free interplay of all his energies. Wherever this interplay is made impossible by psychical fetters of whatever kind there is no more joy of life. I do not mean to say that there should be no discipline and no inhibitions; a child even enjoys the right kind of discipline because its law is the very thing which renders possible a harmonious life. Likewise, every adult who has not reached such a level of inward superiority as enables him to create *ad hoc*, at any moment the form and order requisite for a given situation, stands in need of some inhibitive system. Moreover, inhibitions are as necessary for the development of soul-life as the tightening of strings is for the production of musical sounds. Soul-life has developed on earth only where obstacles were put between longing and realization. What modern psycho-analysis teaches on sublimation as the result of repression amounts to the same. So, inhibitions there must be. However, when a system thwarts the energies, instead of liberating them or creating new ones, it is wrong, whatever ideals it may be believed to incarnate. And the most evident symptom of a wrong system is precisely the lack and the discouragement of joy. It may be that today there are not very many conscious Puritans of the narrow type left in the United States among the people to be taken into account, but the spirit of that type is all the more potent in the subconscious of the whole nation. Hence the conscious utilitarianism, which feels obliged to prove the legitimacy of any kind of joy by its usefulness. Accordingly, in the generality of cases mere contentment holds the place of joy, and real joy is thought possible only in the primitive sense of childhood. Here lies the root of the mistake of American aversion to stimulants. Life must be stimulated every moment in order to go on. Accordingly, aversion to stimulants as such constitutes a misunderstanding of life's fundamentals, and aversion to stimulation into a state which rises above the norm actually amounts to aversion to culture. Here we find the basic reason for the fact that social life in America is so dreary. Originality of thought or ideas or behaviour is objected to, where it should be the ideal. A man who wants to be brilliant tells stories—he tells them indefatigably, interminably. There is no art of conversation. When Americans meet a guest who is expected to be interesting, they often treat him like a criminal in court: he is exposed to a merciless fire of questions; he is "called upon" until he feels squeezed dry as a lemon. As opposed to this, every cultured society has always realized that a festivity arranged in a manner which elevates its participants beyond their normal state and makes them forget the banality of daily life is of infinitely greater value than any serious business transaction, because it stimulates men and women who are capable of being inspired to rise above themselves and it rouses them to higher achievements. Thus, the wonders of Greek philosophy were to a very great extent the result of inspirations received at banquets graced with the arts of supreme culture. All the great women in history have known that to fail to provide for beauty in the arrangements of an entertainment, to ask people together who do not harmonize, or to give the wrong things to eat and to drink, is a sin against *spirit*—because spirit inspires only when the lower orders of life have received the right kind of stimulation, and now think of American official dinners, dry in the physical, intellectual, and spiritual sense, when one has to listen for hours to after-dinner speeches which sometimes might make our Creator curse His omnipresence and omniscience. But then the stimulants which are in common use are equally anti-cultural. Here again the impossibility of expressing oneself in true proportion leads to caricatures. The American loves sensations and eccentricities because he is not allowed to be original. Over-suspicious of true inspiration, he is given to superlatives in his passing moods and is the most enthusiastic creature in the world as far as words go, because his real life is matter-of-factness itself. The same applies to the beverage most in use. I wish some one who really knows would write both the history and the psychology of the cocktail. It certainly is one of the most extraordinary inventions ever made. Not only that it numbs instead of stimulating—its essence is the mixture of the incongruous and the incompatible. I think there is a very profound intention underlying this: the cocktail *is intended* to do harm and not really please the taste. It is, in a word, a somewhat eccentric expression of Puritanism. America knows indeed no joy, but only contentment; she thinks comfort synonymous with culture. This denotes a truly depressing lack of sense of proportion. And the same applies on all planes. A socialistic national structure is certainly as legitimate as an individualistic structure. But if it is socialistic to the point of thwarting the individual tendencies, then it is inwardly diseased. In the same way, a democratic structure can be as rational as an aristocratic one. But if the ideal of equality leaves no room for the recognition of the value of uniqueness, the result is more contrary to the spirit of life than the effect of any system which disregards the rights of man as man, but stresses value. Life then gets disorganized inwardly, however happy its outward condition may appear; man ceases to be in tune both with himself and with the world. This explains the overwhelming number of phenomena in American life which can be explained (and fortunately also cured) by psycho-analysis. A cultured state or a superior state or even a truly moral state is impossible on the assumption that equality is an ideal and that existing differences are irrelevant. Men are *not* equal. They can be made so by force, and this is precisely what America succeeds in doing. The fact that the force employed is not brutal force, but the weight of public opinion or the material necessity for every man to adapt himself to existing circumstances, coupled with the reward of speedy success offered to every really conforming individual, does not alter the situation. But the outcome is what it inevitably must be. Since men are fundamentally unequal and yet desire to be equal, they become so in the form of what is at first an artificial state. This state can be realized only by means of an externalization of all interests. But this, again, renders culture impossible.

NOW we have reached the point where we can realize what American progressiveness really means. There is no doubt that the universe is the most conservative thing imaginable; it seems to delight in repeating itself for trillions and trillions of years. This applies to life to the extent that, if it is to endure, it has to adapt itself to the routine of dead matter. This explains why the lowest order of creatures seems, on the whole, the best adapted; and it explains also why a routine life always seems more successful in the sense of permanence than creative life. Nevertheless, life is essentially *not* routine. As opposed to dead matter, it stands for the principles of creation, freedom, initiative, variation, and innovation. The higher the quality of life, the more does it represent an expression of freedom as opposed to routine. Now this and nothing else is the *raison d'être* of the fact that man has been able to become the master of nature. Since the latter contains no principle making for change, the slightest change brought about by man could lead to effects of an immensity out of all proportion to the effort applied. Still, progress as understood in the United States does not correspond to life's whole truth. First, there can be progress in the generally accepted sense of the word only along intellectual lines; its concept applied to art, philosophy, religion—nay to life itself—is irrational. We need not dwell on this here, because we did so at length in the chapter "Youthfulness"; there we also saw why the age of progress must be and is as a matter of fact a short-lived one. But there are more points to consider. Man is not an intellectual being only; therefore there can be no real progress, unless the *whole* man progresses and not only his intellect and its creations. Now we already perceive that here again the real issue is higher culture as opposed to mere progressiveness. But there is a third reason why the idea of progress as understood in the United States does not bespeak the whole truth of life, and this third reason is of decisive importance precisely in the context of this chapter. *The idea in question is untrue to life because it discards both the fact and the value of tradition.* Here, then, we have to turn our attention to the second part of our thesis on culture, *viz.*, that it means right proportion not only in the dimension of simultaneity, but also of succession. Life is essentially a melody. The whole is pre-existent to every single bar. Accordingly, every present state is inwardly one with the whole past and the whole future, and this means that if the present does not feel itself responsible as much for the past as for the future, then its outlook is distorted and the error in understanding which it implies will not fail to bring about unhappy consequences in facts. The nobility in Europe has always shown greater longevity than the *bourgeoisie* because each new generation always felt at one with the whole history of the family, both past and future, and accordingly responsible to both. If it has often stood for reaction and has opposed progress, the reason was that the tradition in Europe laid the stress on the past as such, failing to see that what matters is not the number of centuries a family can look back upon, but the unbroken *unity* of past, present, and future. This is a fact which has perhaps best been realized by the ancient Chinese; their idea was that the dead ancestor rises and falls with the social rise or fall of his descendants. Americans today do not realize the fact in question. They often pride themselves on having no past (or rather pretend to do so: as a matter of fact, no race in the world is prouder of whatever family history it can boast of). They are all the more sure that the future is theirs. Now there was nothing to be said against such an attitude in the beginning of American history; I am sure every young race invading a territory inhabited by an older race, proud of its past, has felt that way. But the time has now come for the American people to realize, what every nation has realized when it became mature, namely, that life is a melody. And the need for better understanding is urgent because an outlook bent exclusively on the future is more dangerous than a moderate kind of ancestor-cult. The past is a long space of time in any case, whereas the future is as yet inexistent; therefore, a conception of life centred in the future practically amounts to little better than the *carpe diem* outlook of the libertine. Here we find the basic reason of those American phenomena which make a thoughtful observer feel most anxious about America's prospects of development. Foremost, its irresponsibility. Very few Americans think of the future in any sense, however much they may talk about it. The men do not save, the women do not want to have children. What is that much-vaunted love for children worth when all comprehension of the sacred mystery of the continuance of life is lacking? Most young people marry on the basis of a mere infatuation; they leave a husband at the first sign of a new fascination and think that all is well for the children when they are "taken care of," when they receive a "good education," and are made the objects of that sentimental kind of love which American public opinion demands so much as a matter of course that I have sometimes wondered whether the parents' conscience with regard to their children is not analogous to certain responses to advertising copy. American disregard of true family-life, in all its aspects, cannot indeed claim to be an opinion among others and least of all a progressive opinion—it is a sinful thing in the sternest sense of the word. Family-life belongs to the plane of culture because it presupposes a sense of tradition as distinguished from natural instinct; it is a matter of a spiritual connexion. Here, then, a few more words may be added concerning American marriage. What I really meant to convey in my *Book of Marriage* and what the American nation at large totally fails to see at the present time is, of course, that marriage belongs entirely and exclusively to the plane of culture. The whole meaning of that particular relationship between the sexes which bears the name of marriage stands and falls with the recognition that it is something *superior* to all the various relationships it includes. It is not a question of sex-appeal, nor of children only, but of common destiny, of joy and sorrow borne together and above all of a cultural tradition continued. My readers should at this point recall the concluding pages of "Predominant Woman." We tried to show there that America's whole future depends on a better understanding on the part of the women of the meaning of life, because only the right kind of home atmosphere can build spiritual values into the permanent framework of a child's soul. Unless the wives and mothers *know* (as they instinctively have known in all great ages) and must now come to know understandingly what their real mission is, *viz.*, that it lies wholly on the cultural plane, that is the plane where the facts of biology become means of expression of a spiritual connexion comprising all the partial orders of spiritual life, such as the intellectual, the moral, the æsthetic, and the religious—the prospects for the future of the American race are decidedly bad. Heredity in the case of man never means blood-heredity alone, but a synthesis of the latter and tradition. At this point, then, America herself, in spite of the shortness of her history, provides the proof that man's biological plane is that of culture and not of nature. It is the lack of a sense for the spiritual meaning of the family that explains why American families are so astonishingly short-lived, not only as social but as biological units—contraceptives or no contraceptives. If there is no sense of continuity on spiritual planes, there is no real will unto continuance. And the will to life being both the wellspring and the mainspring of life, disregard of the future is also one of the chief reasons of the progressive devitalization of the American type. The fact is that a form and order of life as sketched here is irrational on all planes. This applies to the purely spiritual part of man as well. As man is constituted as a child of the earth, he inevitably thinks of the eternal in terms of great spaces of time; this is why all early religions found their expression in some kind of ancestor-cult. On the other hand, man seems unable to realize the reality of spirit unless he thinks in centuries and millennia. American materialism, as far as it goes, is certainly to a very great extent due to the superficiality implied in the thinking in terms of the present only; for America's consideration for the future is purely fictitious.

But now let us once more focus the problem of culture as such. In order to find the right kind of transition, let us first look from another angle at the problems dealt with in the last paragraph. Then the situation is this: If thinking in terms of the present and future only denotes a lack of a true sense of proportion, it is obvious that the corresponding defect in the form and order of life must needs tend to render the achievement of a cultural state impossible. Here, then, we find the most striking illustration of the truth that life is a melody: *there never was a culture which was not traditional.* Why? Because the true form and order of life demands that present, past, and future should be related to one another in the right proportion. This implies a definite relationship between the principles of tradition and progress. Individual life is always unique, and the very essence of spirit-directed life is uniqueness, initiative, and variability. But just as even the most original man belongs, both psychologically and physically, to some organic type, even so must every individual variation have for its backbone, so to speak, a traditional state which it continues, even where its form is mutation. In the chapter "Socialism" we saw that in every man there live equally real individual and social tendencies. Likewise, every man is not only unique but is at the same time representative of something very general; and he is rightly adjusted within the cosmic Whole only when the principles of type and variation are in due proportion to each other. Now, if one surveys life in its large outlines, one must admit that the typical is of greater importance than the individual. The element of variation and novelty which even the greatest genius adds to life is a very small thing as compared with what seems to posterity only a continuation of tradition. Judged from a sufficiently high point of vantage, even whole periods of variation and progress mean only short intervals within the regular course of tradition. Indeed, no innovation ever led to a lasting state unless it was linked up with the past. Revolutionary periods are never of long duration; extreme radicals never have a historic future. As to what seems a complete solution of continuity the results of which endure, it amounts to the same as mutation on the plane of biology in all cases where a whole people did not lose its historical significance; that is, tradition actually continues, only in a new form. Christianity broke with Judaism, but had not St. Paul fused it with Greek tradition, Christianity would hardly have lasted more than a century and certainly would never have become a vital force. Besides, it never even really broke with Judaism: the Old Testament still continues to be considered as sacred as the New, in spite of increasing Anti-Semitism. In the same sense, democracy which became an explicit force in history as a result of the American and French Revolutions, could become a lasting power only because what it stood for had been slowly preparing ever since the thirteenth century. It is precisely Americans who should re-read De Tocqueville; for it is he who has shown in the most illuminating manner how long and how thorough has been the process of preparation of the modern State. Moreover, when reading that book, which was written about a hundred years ago, they will profit by being shown how *slowly* evolution has proceeded since; most of what De Tocqueville stated about democracy still holds true, and much of what he predicted has not come true yet. That progress itself depends on a sense of tradition is finally proved by the type of the great innovator. Consciously, he does not stand for tradition; consciously, he is a revolutionary in however mitigated a form. But as a matter of fact, in his subconscious depths he *embodies* the tradition more than any conscious traditionalist. Obviously so: a man could not be representative of the new needs of a whole nation or age if the historic foundation of the required change was not alive within his own soul. For historic changes are vital phenomena like the change from childhood to maturity.

Even these brief observations should have made clear why a cultural state is bound to be traditional. The following trend of thought will complete the mental picture. Life is not only a rational process, to be comprehended exhaustively in terms of the intellect: for progress of any kind to be lasting, "the word must be made flesh"; that is, the variation in question must be built into the pre-existing scheme of life so as to become part of it. This most emphatically is not favourable to the present American ideals of normalcy, like-mindedness, and standardization as true vital forces, because they take into account only what the intellect can grasp and because their way of influencing life as a whole is the mechanical device of suggestion. On the contrary, the aforesaid contains the very reasons why standardization can never lead to culture, although unity of tradition, too, implies like-mindedness. If standardization leads to more than an equalization on the plane of life's externals —against which there is nothing to be said in principle; for, as a matter of fact, most human beings belonging to the same class in the same country have always lived much in the same way—this can only mean an externalization and, accordingly, what one may call "superficialization" of life. And once a life loses touch with its vital depths, it loses most of its vital strength. This explains why traditional culture has always proved stronger than any progress based on one-sided development, as long as the cultured race in question was not declining in vitality. This also applies to the United States. Their real strength is based not on their progressiveness, but on their traditionalism. Were it only for their prosperity, education, and machines—to say nothing of the advertising technique and the flapper—they would not in the long run be a match even for Mexico. And who knows whether they will be? . . . The American beliefs that life *is bound* to progress, that prosperity *must* increase, that every new year *should* be better than the preceding, that there *should* be no evil on earth, are contrary to the World-Sense; and they give to the body of the United States a quality of extreme vulnerability. Should years of hardship and bad luck come, in whatever sense, as they are bound to come sooner or later, then the rich and progressive American may easily fail to show himself the equal of the poor and backward Mexican, who for centuries and centuries has continued the life congenial to him against all odds. But however this may be—it should be clear by now that the real and most vital and most urgent problem of the United States is the development of a cultural tradition.

WE ARE now prepared to turn our attention to the most fundamental aspect of the cultural problem. At this point, I must ask my readers to remember what was said in "Predominant Woman" and "Democracy" on different states of being as opposed to ability and about the decisive and ultimate importance of the former. I cannot here treat the question of principle at the required length; I have done so in the chapters "Culture of Ability and Culture of Being," "Hindu and Chinese Wisdom," and "World Ascendancy" of

*Creative Understanding;* to these I refer those of my readers who feel the need of an exhaustive comprehension of the subject. On the other hand, the very concreteness of this book may have prepared them to understand vitally, without further explanation, what is at stake. If being cultured means that a man is able to harmonize the diverse and conflicting tendencies of his nature and to guide them from a superior inward centre, this signifies nothing else than that a higher state of being as opposed to any kind of progressive ability is the one thing needful. When I say "being," I do not mean anything mysterious or transcendental and certainly nothing the existence of which is doubtful in any way: I mean *concrete* man as opposed to imaginary abstract man, the last premise of the philosophy of progress; I mean what the Middle Ages realized so vividly as the soul of man. This last expression, which is perhaps the most suggestive of the whole truth, implies that concrete man is both spiritual and material, that he is a timeless spirit as well as a passing phenomenon, in a word, that he is the *whole* man as distinguished from the mere fragment which corresponds to the idea of abstract man invariably the same, the premise of all prejudices of equality. Being ultimately means "the word made flesh," to whatever plane of being an individual may belong; for since man's essence is spiritual, he can never be ultimately identified with what he has in common with the animal. Being is that unity between spirit and flesh which has been the ideal of all ages and creeds—the ideal, because that unity is never attained by nature's command, but only by man's conscious effort. I may refer here, once more, to sexual matters, because the mystery of the continuance of life provides the most intelligible symbol for all corresponding processes. Why did the ancient Hindus, of all men the most spiritual, look upon physical love as on something fundamentally sacred? Why does it mean so much precisely to spiritual man to possess a woman he profoundly loves, and to spiritual woman in the same case to give herself—whereas on lower planes of inner experience both may look upon the manifestations of love in an entirely different light, indulging in occasional adventures for instance without giving them a serious thought? Because the physical act, profoundly realized, means the very incarnation of spirit on earth; as shown by the fact that it can lead to the birth of an immortal soul into the world. Precisely in this sense, being is always a synthesis of spirit and matter, it is always "the word made flesh." It is the ultimate end thinking man can attain to when trying to fathom the mystery of life. From here we arrive at a final and clear comprehension of what distinguishes culture from mere civilization. Culture is a higher state of being generalized. This generalization can be achieved, in spite of the essential uniqueness of each spirit, in the same way as thoughts and emotions can be permanently materialized in poems and philosophies or religious rituals. That is, it is possible to create expressions of a particular meaning of such perfection that, owing to the law of correlation between meaning and expression, the latter almost inevitably evokes the realization or experience of the former. In the case of culture this amounts to the following: what we may call the lower soul is organized from the outset in a way to make it transparent for specific spiritual values. This is why specific forms of noble-mindedness or honour or ethos can be hereditarily transmitted; it is never a case of physical but of psychical heredity. Hence it is easy to realize the difference in kind between culture and any sort of intellectually born civilization. One of the rare truly "spiritual" spirits of our age, Victoria Ocampo, once put it thus: "With Spirituality I have the impression of sweet, melting fruit, whereas things intellectual are made of dry wood, only good to be cut." In the same way, culture participates in all the vitality and, therefore, in all the softness, transmutability, and flexibility of life. But from here it becomes apparent also why American civilization today so strongly conveys the impression of being made of "dry wood." The modern American identifies himself completely with the differentiated and ready-made functions of mind and soul, entirely disregarding vital spirit. And since the significance attributed to them reacts upon the facts, this inevitably leads to loss of soul, relapse into primitivity of some kind, and a general feeling of emptiness which truthfully mirrors if not actual lack of spiritual substance, then, at any rate, a disconnexion between consciousness and being. This gives the final explanation of the instrumentalism of American life, and gives the final touch to the picture showing the progressive convergence of America toward Bolshevik Russia. In Bolshevik eyes the individual is nothing but a social instrument. I have quoted a passage by the official historian of the Soviet State expressing the hope that some day great men like Lenin, who really are nothing but social apparatuses, may be turned out at any moment in the required quantities by factories. The outlook of an enormous number of Americans is actually the same; and certainly at the time I write those who know better are *not* representative of the nation. If this outlook has not led to the discarding of Christianity, to say nothing of the possibility of Satanism it implies, this is due to the happy circumstances of America's material life, which make even the worst materialists among Americans feel no antagonism against ancestral beliefs. But that the state of peace has little spiritual significance is proved only too clearly by the progressive institutionalism of the Churches—not to mention such aberrations as the belief that Jesus Christ Himself was the model of the good salesman. The fact is that the American, exactly like the Bolshevik, appears soulless because he does not believe in being and does not lay the emphasis upon this. Here, then, we reach final solution of one of the chief problems we dealt with in the chapter "Democracy." American Democracy is the one social structure in history which was based on ability exclusively, completely ignoring the fact that there are such things as differences of state of being and that these differences are of supreme importance. *Why* are they of supreme importance? *Why* has there never been a great age in which the emphasis did not rest on being? *Because being alone stands for individual life.* Any kind of mere ability belongs to the plane of those general forces of nature which provide the means of expression and manifestation for life, just as the alphabet does in the case of thought, but which for themselves have no individuality; even where they cannot be said to belong to the domain of dead matter, they never represent more than the elements of life. Now, as a being, every man is unique. In this uniqueness lies all the vital value of every individual. But this does not preclude the possibility of communion with others. Being acts upon and reacts to being, as any force of nature acts on any other force belonging to the same plane. As beings, men are unique but no more isolated than any other integral parts of the cosmos. Owing to this, a general state called culture is possible. On the other hand, culture only, as opposed to external civilization, means a truly *human* unity. For only the cultural state has its vital centre in the human essence of man. At this point, then, it becomes obvious, that the ideal of equality is both fundamentally and ultimately a false one. Every individual being essentially unique, a state true to what Schiller called the "humanity in man" can never be founded on the basis of equality postulated, but only of differences perceived and recognized.

Now how do beings which are all of them unique in their essence communicate? They do so according to the scheme called *polarization.* The prototype of polarization is the man-and-woman-relationship. Man and woman can never really understand each other, but by virtue of the mysterious bond uniting them they influence and inspire each other for that very reason—and the result is a new form of life, on whatever plane they meet. Likewise, all differences recognized create polar relationships, acting and reacting creatively on all concerned. For this reason a state of culture always appears original, just as every new-born child is something entirely new however much it may resemble its parents, because here the vital quality decides and not the quality of the elements by means of which life manifests itself. For the same reason, to quote once more the saying of Victoria Ocampo's, culture is always "sweet soft fruit" as opposed to "dry wood," inasmuch as it always is as flexible and mutable as life is opposed to dead matter. The scheme of polarization of differences, accepted and emphasized as such, makes for perpetual originality and novelty and surprise. Accordingly, the first postulate of the cultured man is not that of the modern American: "I am as good as you are," but "I being what I am, you should and must be different." Indeed, culture stands and falls with differences perceived and recognized. Only where the law of polarization as opposed to equalization obtains can there be culture.

And now let us say the last word on the subject of culture that can be said before we have dealt explicitly with the eternal spiritual values. In the first chapters of this book I tried to make clear that the present ideal of the United States is an animal ideal and that the current theories concerning progress would be valid only if man really were no more than an animal. Now it might be thought possible in theory that a state of culture, on however low a plane, might be achieved even on these assumptions. Why is this idea refuted by the facts? Because the American outlook is wrong even from the point of view of zoölogy. If one insists on defining man as a peculiar kind of animal, then one must say *that the nature of this animal, as distinguished from all others, is ever aspiring, ever progressing beyond the limits it has reached, never satisfied, and thus in a perpetual state of unstable equilibrium.* A perfectly contented man is really a contradiction in terms. I cannot recapitulate here all I have said on this subject in the chapters "Life and Death" and "Man and the Earth" in *The Recovery of Truth.* But I may say this much: Any system of morality or civilization or values or education is untrue to human nature if it fails to take into account first and foremost the perpetually striving nature of man. Even the best system which does not foster his inward growth and expansion is essentially wrong. This truth recognized disposes once and for all of all ready-made codes and dogmas. Now if this is so, then education should be something different in kind from the training of animals; then a civilization which does not encourage and further inner growth in all respects cannot pretend to stand and make for culture. A culture is deserving of the name only if its ruling principle is perpetual growth. This has been the case involuntarily, without conscious understanding of the facts, with all previous cultures. The emphasis with all of them resting on being, the latter's perpetually active and dynamic quality necessarily impressed itself on the whole order of life, however rigid it may have appeared sometimes to the superficial glance. And since it was the differences between beings, and not what they had in common, which were visualized and stressed first and foremost, the law of polarization could set in and create new vital forms instead of standardized manufactures at any moment. Let us revert here to the simile of music. Life is a melody. It passes from one state of unstable equilibrium to the other. This is true on all planes. Christianity made its first great step beyond paganism when it realized that ill-health and sin are not disgraces and checks, but phenomena concomitant with growth and which can be turned into means of growth. Is it now finally clear in what sense the present trend of American civilization is diametrically opposed to culture? There can be no question of attaining to a state of everlasting happiness; nor would an ideal state be reached in any way if everybody were made contented and prosperous. The only ideal true to the meaning of life is to found a law and order of earthly existence giving expression to man's inmost being, *which is perpetual striving*, by means of the right co-ordination and correlation of all his thoughts, feelings, emotions, desires, and involuntary impulses. Everything else is ultimately irrelevant.

I think I have said enough on the subject. So let me conclude by stating that it is my belief that an American culture *is* possible along the general lines American life has developed on hitherto, in spite of all the dangers inherent in its present state. Every nation, like every man, is one-sided. There has never been all-sided perfection on earth nor will there ever be, and one kind of perfection generally excludes all others. As far as human foresight can tell, America will always remain a practical, social-minded, matter-of-fact, and moralistic nation. Likewise, democracy is certain to remain its specific life-form. But then democracy in itself does not, in principle, prevent the development of unique individuals, nor does socialism. It is possible to imagine a state in which the unique soul is recognized as the ultimate social unit, "uniqueness" and "quality" thus meaning in the social system what efficiency and office and service mean today. In the same sense, the very craze for information and education may represent an excellent preliminary stage, *if* the stress be laid henceforth on understanding. A high standard of living is decidedly desirable—only it should cease to be considered as an ideal. Certainly all should have a share in whatever good and noble things life can offer, but the emphasis should lie on what is highest and not on what is lowest. At this point let us think once more of China's cultural ideal. Ancient China, too, was democratic; there, too, the social emphasis lay on the ordinary man. But the Chinese ideal was not the man in the street, but the noble one; that is the ordinarily gifted man who had reached such a state of inner harmonization that what was ordinary in itself could serve as a mouthpiece for the Divine, and that all possible depth expressed itself in the form of beauty and grace of the surface. And the general law of life in those great days did not command a man to conform to the ways of others or to "what the people want," not to mention things purely external, but to conform to Tao only, that is to significance. This great culture has stood the pragmatic test as no other has. Under its rule, life was both full and profound. The tone was given by the truly great. The principles of spirit and of matter were correlated and co-operated harmoniously. And the results were an unequalled longevity, an unequalled peacefulness, an unequalled beauty, and an unequalled general happiness.

## *Spirituality*

THROUGHOUT this book we have either asserted or at least surmised the reality of spirit; without, however, ever focussing the problem of spirit as such. In the last chapter we came to the conclusion that most of what is unsatisfactory today in the United States is the result of an ignoring or understressing of spiritual reality. And if we now survey at a single glance all the particular problems we have been dealing with, we find that the last chapter is only an integration of the differentiations previously analyzed. Our next and final task must accordingly be to make explicit what has been only implied so far and to disengage the positive, as it were, from the many negatives described. We have seen in what respects America has failed or is failing. Let us now see what she has to do in order to fulfil the great promise Destiny has laid in her cradle. For this is how the question ought to be put. One of Goethe's most beautiful sayings runs thus: *Was das Leben mir versprach, werde ich ihm halten* (The promise Life has given me, I shall keep).

I think the quickest way to make clear to an American circle of readers what fundamental change must take place in the inner adjustment of the American nation if it is to start on a line of truly progressive development is to begin with a short statement of how life in general—not only spirit-directed life—is related to the material world. And to this end I can hardly do better than repeat, with the necessary modifications, what I wrote on this subject for the *Forum* several years ago; for the essay in question proved to be intelligible to very wide circles in spite of its abstract and metaphysical subject. If we look at life with a serene, unbiassed eye, we find that its fundamental difference from what we call the lifeless consists in this, *that no fact of life can be understood apart from its significance.* Stars and stones may be exhaustively described, for the requirements of the human mind, as the purely external phenomena without any subjective inner being, which they appear to be. But in order to understand the smallest cell within a living body, not to mention complicated organs, we must find out what part it plays within that body. Here, the phenomenon is not the ultimate end, nor can its *raison d'être* be found within the range of the laws of cause and effect, or function, in any external sense. Here, the vital root of the phenomenon lies in what is not phenomenal, in an immaterial, creative entity, a pre-existing whole to which one may give whatever name one likes—the most popular designation at the moment is "entelechy"—but which one can only *understand* as a sense-connexion. On the other hand, the immaterial source of material life-phenomena *can* thus be understood. There are two very simple reasons for this. In the first instance, man is alive himself and consciousness mirrors vital reality. But above all, understanding as such reaches down to and is an expression of vital significance; here, the fundamental principle of life appears incarnated and focussed in a specific human faculty. Thus, a true comprehension of the workings of the understanding (as distinguished from the merely thinking or constructing) mind inevitably leads to a comprehension of the fundamentals of all life-processes.—Everybody knows that the meaning of a sentence, as meaning, is not inherent in the letters which serve to express it; further, meaning is always pre-existent to its expression and creates the latter out of itself. The case is exactly the same with the articulation and functioning of an organic body. Here, too, the whole is pre-existent to the parts; it directs its processes from within, and the whole is something not material in itself—it is an entity of the same kind as the unity underlying an inspired work of art. If we now look, from the angle of this insight, at any kind of life-phenomenon, we shall find that the relationship, the prototype of which is the relation of the meaning of a sentence to the words and letters expressing it, obtains on absolutely all planes. The life of each individual human being must appear to have a meaning in his eyes, not only in order to seem worth living but simply even in order to continue; individuals who have lost their aim in life, or nations who have lost their gods or their ideals, always sooner or later develop suicidal inclinations. Again, it is the significance of a particular person within his social surroundings, not the person as a fact, which gives him his social position. Again, significance, not fact, is the essence of historical greatness; a man of a particular type rises to power only, then, when his personal tendencies are representative of the whole.

Let us now consider another aspect of the same problem. How is it that meaning incarnates itself in letters? It is by a centrifugal process. We have to *give* meaning to the letters ourselves, from within, if they are to express any; and this applies as much to the reader or the listener as to the original creator: if the former is to grasp an intended meaning, he has to put it himself into the letters; for what he gets from without is nothing but a combination of paper and printers' ink. Thus, meaning exists only in the dimension of creative activity; if the latter ceases, all meaning will seem to have vanished from our world. It is at this point perhaps that one best realizes how complete an analogy there exists between the relation of thought and alphabet on the one side and that of life and matter on the other. Physical life, too, goes on only as long as the processes of inorganic nature are being vitalized from within; no sooner does this cease, than the living body becomes what we call a corpse; that is, the processes of nature, left to themselves, now use the same forces which built up the organism to destroy it. In the same way, if a thought has become a dead letter, whether in religious belief, or in a particular law as an expression of acknowledged justice, or simply in an idea which cannot be understood by him who hears, it *is* dead; it can no longer work, or if it does, it works along the line of self-destruction. At this point we must consider a further aspect of the problem. The fundamental law of life is that which I have called the law of correlation between meaning and expression.[1] This law implies, on the one hand, that every meaning, in order to manifest itself fully, must have found its adequate expression, and on the other, that every *new* meaning must create *new* facts. Just as every new idea manifests itself in a new arrangement of letters, words, and phrases, a new historical spirit finds its expression in novel institutions. And from here let us pass at once to an idea which seems to lie very far removed from this: the idea of the Resurrection of the

[1] See for full particulars the second chapter of *Creative Understanding*.

Flesh. What does it mean? According to St. Paul himself, it means that spirit eventually forms another corresponding body which cannot help being the same as the old one in so far as the soul has not changed. This, in principle, means only what is done by all of us whenever we utter again an idea which for a time was non-existent in the world of words. If the latter fact is a reality, little can be said, in principle, against the possibility of the former. I have, of course, no intention of insisting here on this particular subject. What I wanted to do by drawing attention suddenly to the strangest conceivable expression of creative life, was only to make my readers realize in the most effective manner—that is by surprise—the following: if the relationship between life and matter is everywhere essentially the same as that between an idea and the letters of the alphabet which serve to express it; moreover, if meaning, not fact, is the primary principle, and if the former comes into existence in the world of phenomena by a centrifugal meaning-giving process, then facts in principle never are the ultimate termini. Then spiritual man ought, in principle, to be capable of creating such facts as he pleases, in proportion to the spiritual power he embodies. Then the whole of nature's processes cannot signify anything else or more from the point of view of creative spirit than what the alphabet means to the thinking man who makes use of it to express his thoughts.

Let us dwell upon this metaphor, which is really more than a metaphor. For the last hundred years people have believed in facts to which they had to adapt themselves in very much the same way and sense as religious ages believed in the necessity of fulfilling the will of God. In reality, no previous century had created so many new facts, which alone should have proved to man that the latter cannot be his last resort. And these facts from the point of view of his own philosophy, he actually had created "out of nothing"; for realized "meaning"—that is something immaterial, the existence of which he denied—was the source of all his huge material output; all great inventions were pure ideas first, which only later materialized into "facts." Therefore, the ancient magician who, on the whole, achieved less than do modern inventors—even if one bases one's judgment on the information contained in the fairy-tales accepted as true relations—was in his outlook much nearer the truth. Our present dominion over nature *is* the work of magic; it is nothing else than imagination become fact. Now when we have really realized this a truth dawns upon us which I consider all-important: namely, that the last sentence of the last paragraph ultimately does not express a metaphor, *but the truth in the sense of scientific exactness.* By learning to make use of nature's laws, man had learnt, as it were, nature's grammar. But his inventions mean something different in kind from any sort of grammar: they mean what man has to say himself in the language he has acquired. In what sense, then, are philosophers right in calling our modern age a mechanistic and materialistic, as opposed to a spiritual age? In no other than that modern man *believes* in the ultimate reality of facts and matter; this *belief* has given them a power which in themselves they lack. Thanks to this belief, spirit really *had* become powerless and matter omnipotent. For meaning belongs to another plane than the alphabet, and it is necessarily impossible that the ultimate terminus should *not* be the meaning freely given by man. Now let us look at this state of affairs from the angle of the inter-relation between alphabet and meaning. Then we shall realize that the true significance of modern materialism is this, that the so-called scientific age really was an age of belief in *grammar;* much more so even, than the age of scholasticism. Instead of simply using the Alphabet of the World for saying what he meant to say, man regarded this alphabet as his ultimate resort. He imagined that right spelling already meant speech. So much for this aspect of the question. But there is another. If the state of things is what we have described it to be, then there can be no difficulty, in principle, in getting beyond mechanism and materialism. Since all material inventions really are "meaning" expressed in "matter," nothing can prevent man from incarnating a *deeper* meaning in the world of facts. This depends entirely on him.

FROM here let us return without any transition to the facts of American life. In "The Animal Ideal" we succeeded in connecting almost all that is wrong with the United States with the general denominator of "topsy-turviness." It is indeed the very essence of American civilization that it should understand life in a way diametrically opposed to that which, in the last paragraph, we showed to be the only true one. Most present-day Americans believe that facts and not their significance count first; that institutions mean everything, and not living men. And we have already seen that the whole aridness and dryness and unoriginality and insect-like quality and, finally, the progressive devitalization are results of this wrong way of understanding life. On the basis of the insight contained in the last paragraph (the full development of which, I repeat, may be found in *Creative Understanding* and *The Recovery of Truth*), we can understand why it cannot be otherwise. Life's very essence, its concrete vital essence, is that illusive entity I call significance or meaning or sense. Now if the way of life were analogous to the working of a machine, it might proceed in the right direction all the same—understanding or no understanding. But life is essentially creative, it is a "machine" which mends and changes and adapts itself spontaneously from within. And this mysterious creative essence being precisely its underlying meaning, where consciousness has become connected with, and focussed in it—thus sharing its creative power—*mis*understanding must needs lead to distorted facts—distorted, because they are contrary to sense. For if on the plane of invention, which means a superstructure on life, imagination may more or less do what it chooses without working much harm, a false view of fundamentals endangers the very foundations of life. This explains the correspondence between life's objective and subjective aspect. A life which is a true sense-relation is not only vital and creative, but also full of joy. On the other hand, it is impossible to be happy in a wrong adjustment within the general scheme of things. But the same explains, in particular, why American life seems to be progressively deteriorating. Every misunderstanding breeds new fixed automatisms embodying misunderstanding, and the resulting distortions become increasingly accentuated as time goes on, precisely as heredity progressively enhances the defects and not the virtues inherent in a physical type, once it has passed its vital zenith.

From here we can proceed to a preliminary definition of what the word spirit stands for; it is not, of course—

since spirit stands for ultimate reality—a question of definition in the usual sense of the word, but only of a description of reality which may or may not spontaneously call out understanding. Man's primary experiences are not material, but psychological. Therefore, they all of them belong to the side of life which cannot be described as "fact" in the usual sense. Only a mature mind perceives "matter" in what seems to us a natural way, because for that purpose a process of abstraction must have taken place. Children and primitive peoples know of no natural events in our sense; their real life corresponds more or less to our dream-life. It is only in later periods—in the history both of the individual and of peoples and cultures—that external facts are primarily experienced as such; early races, in the first instance, experience sequences of inner images of a mythical quality which their unconscious projects on the external world, which they refer exactly to the extent that is indispensable for the continuance of existence. Nor is it necessary that the relationship in question should be of a rational or matter-of-fact quality. Levy-Brühl has shown that with primitive tribes what he calls *participation mystique* almost completely takes the place of that which causation stands for with us. But it is not even necessary to study primitive tribes or children in order to realize how little demonstrable facts may mean: owing to the rejuvenation which the Western World at large is experiencing just now, we can observe the same phenomenon of a primary myth-life in our very midst. The mythology of the World War, with its ideas of absolute right and guilt and progress and retrogression, transferred by each nation upon some other according to the position it happened to hold in the struggle, had nothing whatever to do with facts; were it otherwise, at least some of the ideal aims would have been attained and at least some of the results would have come up to the expectations of the participators in the struggle. In reality, the warring nations lived as much in an imaginary world of their own as did the Greeks when they believed that the gods took an active part in the war of Troy. The fact that what then were gods are today called ideals makes no psychological difference. In exactly the same sense, the immense power which wealth wields in America is due not to the facts as such but to the belief in its magic power. A man who has achieved success or owns millions can "control" so much in the United States because he exercises the same mystic authority which was, or is still, exercised by priests or kings or great men in other civilizations. That it really is a case of primitive superstition, to be understood only according to Levy-Brühl's category of the *participation mystique*, is conclusively proved by the simple consideration that in America wealth is supposed to create a "great man." If this is so, then it is no less mysterious a process than trans-substantiation.

This much for primitive conditions. But the same is true in principle of every man. We have said that man's primary experience always relates to psychological and not to material phenomena. But it is not what one may call "subjective fact" which forms the ultimate terminus of this experience; it is something more subjective still. A Something, the very essence of which is that it can never be objectified. *This is the very thing I call meaning or significance.* Its reality is still more subjective than any subjective experience for the following reason: the contents of the latter can after all be conceived as objects; inner experience may have the same contents for many people, and these contents can be externalized in permanent forms. But the *significance* given or attributed is unique in each individual case. It is as impossible to imagine an understanding which is not strictly personal as that there should be impersonal love, or that one man could take upon himself to breathe for another. Moreover, any bestowal of meaning is an act of initiative; it amounts to the same process of vitalization from within which is the essence of the processes of physical life, where matter and forces, dead in themselves, are forced every second into channels not originally theirs, just as an original artist creates something strictly and exclusively personal by means of forms and colours everyone may use. Of this, precisely American life provides the most striking illustration. Mentally, the average American is the most passive type of man I know; he is the most obedient creature in the world, he simply craves for guidance. Hence his unequalled gullibility and suggestibility—a fact on which rests the existence both of the American advertising-technique and of standardization. What people mistake for a national quality of initiative is, in reality, mere speed on predetermined lines, such as belongs to insects; no nation as a whole is less inventive and less adaptable—these two qualities standing for the lowest degrees of spiritual initiative. Whence, then, the opposite impression so many observers seem to get? It is due to the very fact of the general passivity. Owing to this, the comparatively small number of men of real initiative wield inordinate power and are equally inordinately conspicuous. Now this state of things is entirely due to creative *mis*understanding. America gives a wrong significance to things—and lo and behold! significance creates the corresponding facts. Behaviourist America *believes* that man can do nothing but respond: so he re-creates himself according to the image of his belief. The sons and grandsons of the most active races of Europe belong as a matter of course to that very type which rushes through Europe as a unit of so-called caravans, obediently following the suggestions of the guide and never doing anything they are not told to do.

FROM the vantage-point we have here reached, it should be possible to state as clearly as may be reasonably expected which kind of reality the word "spirit" stands for. It stands, in the first instance, for life as such, as opposed to inert matter. It stands, in the second instance, for human as opposed to animal life. However, man is, with most of his earthly forces and instincts, an animal among others; this applies even to intellect as such with which the so-called higher animals undoubtedly are endowed. Hence a third qualification. The word spirit stands for that creative meaning or significance which is the vital root of all that is called the "higher life." *It has, therefore, a positive quality of its own.* Of this, the ideals and values are the exponents on the plane of phenomena. Intellectuals may doubt their reality as much as they like—as a matter of fact there never was a man or woman of generally accepted higher quality, who did not want to be good and beautiful and loving and truthful, and did not accordingly attribute to beauty, goodness, truth, and love an intrinsic or absolute value; this fact admits of as little doubt as any other fact of natural history. Only the fact-side of the problem was obscured so far by the association with religious and other commandments, according to which human beings "should" strive for goodness, truth, etc., for the latters' own sake, without thinking of a reward. *Why* should they? It is only natural that after the intellect awoke and grew more and more impatient of irrational authority it should have doubted the *rationale* of the Commandments, the more so as they were associated—in spite of all that the great seers and sages have done to prevent this association—with promises of reward which have seldom if ever been fulfilled on earth. But in reality it is quite easy to explain why man feels that he "should" strive. Let us remember that the very essence of life is creative significance, a thing as unmaterial from the point of view of the body as of the soul. This significance tries to express and manifest itself on all planes by assimilating all matter so as to make of it living flesh; this is as true of the poet who makes the words reproduce his personal rhythm and render his personal meaning, as of the material body, or of true culture which connects all manifoldness of life to a specific soul and animates it therewith. Now there obviously is a spiritual significance belonging to another order than the motives directing the development of body and intellect and lower soul; only think of the great peace a soul may radiate in spite of all torments, as opposed to mere good health, or of the love of Beatrice as opposed to that of Paolo and Francesca in Dante's *Divine Comedy*, or of the personal significance of a life as opposed to all logical theory. This spiritual significance gives to man's life its *ultimate* meaning. Whatever a man may do or achieve—if he does not feel that his activities and achievements give expression to spiritual ideals, he feels dissatisfied, unhappy; he feels as a matter of intimate understanding that his life lacks an ultimate meaning; and since meaninglessness is nothing other than Hell itself, there is no way out of his unhappy state. This fact must again be considered as much a fact of natural history as any fact of physical discontent. Accordingly, the spiritual ideals must be the expressions of man's *ultimate* nature. And the latter must be man's ultimately *real* nature, or else that which religion stands for in the case of most could not be man's ultimate concern. But on the other hand: it undoubtedly is a question of "human nature" in the widest sense and *not* of anything opposed to the latter, as philosophical idealism will have it. This is conclusively proved by the fact that it can be surveyed and understood in the abstract within the framework of the same scheme as all vital phenomena. Dissatisfaction is dissatisfaction whatever be its objects, so is significance. If we now consider the quality of obligation inherent in all spiritual ideals, which, nevertheless, is not felt as something external but, on the contrary, as a paradoxical expression of an inmost personal urge, then we shall find the required formula. *Man's inmost subjective essence, for which the term spirit stands, has qualities of its own. But these may or may not develop.* As far as the earthly qualities are concerned, both the material and the psychological, nature has taken care of their development. Not so in the case of the spiritual. Here the same applies which we explained in the case of morality, *viz.*, that the form and order of life must be realized by man's free will. *This* part of man is not only incidentally, as it were, and to a very slight degree, but essentially and absolutely free; think of the second thief on the cross, to whom the Saviour Himself could not open the gates of Paradise because the thief would not open his heart to Him.

Here, free choice or initiative or free consent only can achieve what necessity achieves on the natural plane. Here, therefore, the form or category of "freedom" circumscribes the "natural" way of development. It is this freedom and nothing else that is really meant by the "should" of all religious commandments. Only the expression is clumsy—and it cannot help being so, as long as a higher stage of understanding has not been reached, because it is very difficult to find a formula acceptable to the intellect which would express that certain actions are both good in general and yet only to be accomplished in a way true to sense by strictly personal initiative. Buddha was the only man I know of who avoided the fallacy of every commandment relating to freedom, by simply stating: if you do this, that will happen; if you do that other thing, the other consequence is inevitable. But then Buddha's was the greatest mind among all the founders of religion.

There actually is no question of commandments, nor can there be. If God Almighty actually commanded that a certain general course should be taken, it would be generally taken; if, on the other hand, free choice constitutes both the essence and the value of an action, the word Commandment is devoid of meaning. In the above truth lies indeed the *only* solution of the dilemma contained in the idea of God's omnipotence confronted with man's constant failings. Now what, under these circumstances, do the eternal, spiritual values really stand for? Let us turn back to a sentence already stated. We said that man's inmost spiritual essence has qualities of its own which may or may not grow and develop. *Under these circumstances, the eternal spiritual values cannot be anything other than the exponents of the laws of this growth.* Man wants to be good, truthful, loving, etc., because then only does he express his own spiritual nature. This *growth* is the ultimate end, the end in itself. This is so quite independently of whether individual man personally survives death or not: if he only feels his life to be rational when he is living up to eternal ideals, then our explanation holds true in any case; for Eternity is contained in every single moment; its dimension lies at right angles to the horizontal plane of Time.

From here, then, many things become clear—in fact, all the most vital among those which have ever puzzled mankind. To state the most important argument first. There can be no question of material success or failure proving or disproving the validity of the eternal spiritual values or ideals: they belong to an altogether different dimension. And still less are the illusions: they are the most vital of all realities. *Man does what is good, in order to grow better; he strives for Beauty, in order to reach perfect self-expression; for Truth, in order to set free his own inmost reality from all that is unreal, and thus to help it to develop unhampered.* From here, then we arrive at what one may call an actual description of spiritual reality, imperfect though it must be. It can best be achieved by contrasting its specific reality with that of the material plane. Whereas on the latter, the laws of action and reaction, of correspondence between cause and effect, of give and take rule supreme, the case is totally different where spiritual realities are concerned. Spirit is essentially radiating, outpouring; here it is a question only of giving, of taking—never. And such giving enriches, it does not impoverish. Everybody may know this to be true at least through his own experience of love, when the more a person gives—without thinking of what he or she receives, the more he or she expands and grows. But the same is the case with absolutely all spiritual energies, without a single exception. There is a slight physical analogy to this truly stupendous phenomenon: muscles grow the more they are exercised. But in reality the laws of the spirit defy all comparisons taken from other dimensions. It really seems to be a case of a reversion of all tested standards. Here the more a man spends, the richer he grows. It is the same phenomenon that Christ specified with respect to certain aims of His own by saying: "He that loseth his life for my sake shall find it."

It is not always, as in the case of love, that the giving away is unalloyed by pain. But the gain always is infinitely greater than any loss. Whoever renounces his ego, thereby gains his self.[1] This, then, is why a life of the spirit always appears disinterested. It is necessarily so from the point of view of external success, because here there can be no question of the latter nor does it constitute an issue in any sense. But properly speaking, the term disinterestedness is not correct; one should rather speak of spiritual self-interest. Here Hindu wisdom comes nearest the truth. When teaching that the wife or husband is not dear for the wife's or husband's sake, but for the self's sake, it correctly states the law of this deepest essence in man we call spirit. This explains also why spiritual natures more often than not have the reputation of being selfish. As a matter of fact, they are neither selfish nor unselfish in the usual sense of the word; they simply radiate their own quality as does the sun. To a certain extent, one may

[1] Cf. the elaboration of this thesis in the chapter "Death and Life Eternal" in *The Recovery of Truth.*

call them selfless, because they actually never think of themselves. This is how God's love has always been understood; this is also how every profound human being understands love. Goethe has said: *Wenn ich dich liebe, was geht's dich an?* (If I love thee, is it any concern of thine?). But again, since it is the nature of spirit to radiate as the sun does, it is impossible to understand it within the framework of earthly interests. This, then, explains the intrinsically paradoxical character of all truly spiritual religions. They all thought exclusively of inner growth, but tried to express it somehow in terms of earthly welfare, which could not help sounding contrary to worldly sense; think again of Christ's teaching that one should lose one's life in order to find it, or of the commandment of renunciation in general. But this explains also why humanity has always felt that religion teaches the truth, however irrational its teachings may appear. The fact is that religion does not in any way deal primarily with the Beyond, but with as real a part of man as the body is. This finally explains why man has always instinctively felt that a religious life *does*, after all, stand the pragmatic test. It certainly does not stand it in the usual sense. If a religion has ever made a success in the world, this was due to its non-religious qualities; these are political in the case of the Roman Catholic Church, and economical in the case of Calvinism. Early Christianity, as it still lives on in its Russian expression, was not right in condemning worldly power as such, but it undoubtedly was when condemning any blending of spiritual and temporal power in such a way as to make some kind of power now appear as an integral part of spirituality; it most emphatically does *not* form a part of it. The essence of spirit being freedom, the concept of force does not apply in its domain. This truth is the real root of the Christian as well as of the Buddhist and Taoist ideas, that to be weak or humble or poor is better than to be one of the great of this world. Thus, religion cannot possibly lead to success in any external sense. But religion does indeed stand the pragmatic test in its own dimension, that is in the dimension of inward growth. It is a biological fact, that man grows inwardly only when living up to the eternal values which are the exponents of the laws of the spirit, and which at the same time show the way for fostering that growth. Now it should appear clear why religion has always had the last word in all understanding ages. It is not a question of what may happen after death; nor is it a question of the truth of any particular religious doctrine. The crucial point is contained in the very word *religio*, understood in its original Latin sense. *Religio* stands for the binding or the joining of man to his spiritual root, for his ultimate self-realization. As long as his spiritual substance has not pierced through and pervaded, assimilated and transfigured all his other parts, he is not really himself.

WE NOW see that spirit is not only as concrete and real a part of man as the body is—it is actually more real. The true correlation was much better understood by mediæval Christianity than it is by modern science. For mediæval man, the immortal soul was the supreme reality; nature was thought of as a province of the supernatural order which was accepted as existent as a matter of course. But for that very reason nature, too, was considered as intrinsically real, as the adequate means of expression of spiritual reality;

there was no question of the flesh being unreal as earlier —and again later—ages held it to be. But still less, of course, was there a question of spirit standing for something abstract or of being a mere product of man's illusion: mediæval man believed in an all-round reality which was supernatural or—as we would rather put it today—metaphysical in its essence, and of which spirit formed the core. His idea was fundamentally true. However, modern minds will better realize the very same truth when the whole order of life is defined not as a supernatural but as a natural order. In that case one might say that spirit belongs to biology as much as the body does. There can be no doubt of the fact that the profounder a man grows—which term does not stand in need of definition since every unwarped mind directly understands what it means—the more does spiritual as opposed to material welfare mean to him; in a spiritual man, physical health or ill health not only depends—as it does with many—on psychological, but on spiritual conditions. Such a man may actually die if his life loses its spiritual significance, or if his spiritual part gets injured (it is to this that Christ's saying applies: "For what is a man profited, if he shall gain the whole world, and lose his own soul?"). It is obvious that men in whose psychological structure the spiritual principle plays no paramount part—to say nothing of those who are actually spiritually blind, a defect as natural and frequent as physical blindness—must fail to realize this. But this is no refutation of our thesis. Man's component parts may be related to one another in various proportions. Moreover, the field of consciousness being limited and restricted in any case, that which is consciously stressed —whether for inward or outward reasons—inevitably plays the predominant part. This explains why it is so much a matter of man's self-culture whether physical or spiritual food is of first importance to him and likewise material or intellectual or spiritual problems. The history of asceticism proves that the spiritual part can gain predominance through actual starvation of the body; in the same way, spirit can be starved out through lack of nourishment. Nevertheless, there can be no question here of equal rights: the various ways of laying the emphasis do not lead to the same resulting value. It is never necessary to do the right thing, because man's essence is the freedom of his spirit. But if he voluntarily renounces or disowns spirit, he deteriorates exactly as, under given circumstances, a body dies or putrefies. But then, again, since man is essentially free, the natural law sets in, in this case, owing to his own fault. We find here the root of the idea of sin. Thus, no logical argument can do away with the *real* differences of quality—as real, indeed, as the differences between chemical elements—which every person who is not spiritually blind perceives between a great and a small, a profound and a shallow, a materially- and a spiritually-minded soul. And in the long run right adjustment only stands the pragmatic test; right adjustment meaning, as already explained in the chapter "Culture," the rule of the spiritual principle. Spirituality certainly never breeds success, because it has no exponent in the material world. But then the reverse likewise is true: no success on the plane of phenomena necessarily finds an echo in the realm of significance. This is why no man is permanently happy who does not primarily live up to the eternal spiritual values. He can be happy as long as individual forces or functions of his being sway him—whether sexual passion or will to power or even the lust to kill; but here satiety is the inevitable final result, because of the finiteness of all the forces of the lower soul; and satiety always breeds disgust.

But, on the other hand, there is no truth either in flesh-denying spirituality. Man can attain perfection only by pervading and transfiguring all matter with the spirit, without denying any. This is the Mystery of Incarnation. Just as the greatest spiritual love between man and woman which does not illumine the senses as well is an imperfect and crippled love and must needs lead to unhappiness and a thwarting of life, even so does it hold true on all lines of life. Here again, the prototype of all the situations in question is to be found in the relationship between meaning and expression: only meaning perfectly expressed, so that each letter bears the stamp of its uniqueness, only such a meaning is perfectly realized. That is, spirit which does not permeate matter is not realized *as spirit.* It is for the sake of the spirit that the word must be made flesh.

LET us now revert once again to the particular problem of the United States. The American nation at large tries, at present, to live up to the animal ideal. The Privatist outlook has had the general effect of laying the emphasis, in a degree unheard of in history, on the means of life as opposed to life itself. The natural trend of American Democracy follows in the same direction. The predominance of woman's matter-of-fact spirit gives additional force to the material side of life; so does the general rejuvenation the race is undergoing, along with the idealization of the child. Since the hereditary narrow moralism cannot stand the test of a deeper and clearer insight into the general connexion of things, it is unable to prevent an increasing materialization.—In former contexts we have drawn various conclusions from this state of things. But on the basis of an understanding of the true nature of spirit, implying that it actually belongs to the domain of biology, we can qualify the last conclusions arrived at, *viz.*, that what America lacks and needs above all things is *culture*, the word denoting the right kind of proportion between the various component parts of man. If America lacks culture, this denotes organic disharmony. With the majority this disharmony is due to an over-stressing of the material principle. But is there then no spiritual life in the United States? There is indeed. But, as far as it is a question of an original phenomenon representative of the nation at large, this spiritual life is equally one-sided and out of proportion to the whole. If, roughly speaking, the majority believes in matter only, a minority denies its very existence. If the members of the former are passive as spirits, those of the latter believe in the omnipotence of spiritual initiative. Now, both types of one-sidedness are so closely related and presuppose each other to such a degree, that it becomes immediately clear that it is a case of polar opposites; they obviously belong to a unified psychological whole where the law of correlation which rules all organic life obtains. On the physical plane, all organs and functions actually counterpoise one another. On the psychical plane, these organs are, moreover, essentially transformable, as dream-figures are, with the result that the psychic processes conform to two laws (among others, but these others do not concern us here): the one is *the law of general determination*, meaning that all processes can be related to a common denominator; the other is *the law of compensation*, implying that a balance disturbed in one direction is always re-established from some other. When dealing with American morality, we met with a classic example of the first law. Morality is the common denominator of American life, so that all issues appear as moral issues; again, the quality of "purity" inherent in Puritanism gives a particular colouring to all manifestations of American life, down to the shamelessness in matters of sex. Now the law of compensation is best exemplified by Christian Science, the prototype of American religiousness; and the example of this religion, again, provides the best proof imaginable—for such as want proofs—of the reality underlying its idea. *If* matter is over-emphasized in the United States, and *if* there is such a thing as spiritual reality, then it follows *a priori*, from the general knowledge we have of the human soul, that spirituality in America should differentiate with equal one-sidedness. So it actually does; the quality of "purity" determined by Puritanism, in its turn, adds to the clearness of the contours. Further: *if* the fundamental attitude in the United States is one of spiritual passivity, then some attitude which is all the more pronounced in its activity must needs compensate it in the general system. This is precisely the meaning of the uncompromising affirmations and denials of Christian Science. Within a nation individuals play the same part as do particular functions within the individual soul. We thus find that every spiritual American who can be considered as representative, actually belongs, whether he knows it or not, to the wider circle of Christian Science. It would perhaps be more correct, from the point of view of fact, to say that somehow or other he belongs to New Thought. Emerson, for instance, undoubtedly did, whereas one could not have called him a Christian Scientist. But on the plane of significance, Christian Science and no other expression of American religiousness stands out as the prototype—no matter whether New Thought may have preceded it in time—because it best conforms to the law of correlation between meaning and expression. At this point, some may object that the primitivity of the notions of Christian Science makes them unfit to express truth in any way. But this objection is not valid. Primitive people can be true only to themselves, and, accordingly, express absolute truth, when believing in the primitive or giving a primitive utterance to their experiences; this must be so, if the word spirit stands for reality and not a mere construction of the intellect. There is nothing more irrational than to apply to matters of the spirit the standards of intellectual valuations. Since it is a question of the inmost reality beyond all name and form, as the Hindus would say, only symbolic images calling out the corresponding vital response as a matter of natural necessity represent adequate means of expression. Accordingly, in principle, every man should have a strictly personal and untransferable way of realizing the spiritual, and this is actually the case as far as concrete understanding goes. But since every unique individual also belongs to a type, there are typical expressions corresponding to typical states; these latter account for the permanent attraction the established churches have for large majorities. It follows that in the case of primitive races these expressions must be primitive precisely if they are to convey absolute truth; with them, the grossest superstition and the most patent error may yet represent a truthful image of truth. But there is even more to say for what is primitive in itself.

Primitive expressions are the most transparent and convincing in the absolute sense. They are because they give the general outlines, without any disguise, in the original form of those primary images which continue to live in the unconscious even of the most differentiated soul. This is why all religions which continue to sway the world are expressive of a primitive state: even the cultured man directly realizes, by their means, the underlying truth, if he has any organ for experiencing it. When at two of the sessions of the School of Wisdom I wanted to show what the Christian doctrine really meant, I had to apply to Russians who are still early Christians or else have reverted to their type under the weight of what they experience as Satanism. Early Christianity found its form by way of contrast to pagan antiquity; accordingly, it over-emphasized what the Greeks call *Pathos*, that is submissiveness, long-suffering, meekness; and it did so with radical and archaic one-sidedness. But precisely for that reason these forms are generally convincing as symbols of absolute truth; they express it integrally by means of the passive modality of life.

Such a kind of spirituality could not possibly develop in the United States, albeit the psychological state of their inhabitants is about as primitive as that of the Russians. Here, the general adjustment of the spiritual part of man being one of passivity, qualified as a belief in things as opposed to living man, it could be compensated only by an over-stressing of spiritual Ethos or initiative. This accounts for the one-sidedly active quality of American Christianity. Every quality of life expresses itself in two opposite ways, actively and passively, as Ethos and as Pathos. In the form of Ethos,

American Christianity corresponds exactly to the Russian as the representative of Pathos. Here, then, we find one more example of the laws of correlation and compensation. On many previous occasions we have come to the conclusion that materialist America and Bolshevik Russia are closely akin in spirit. But for that very reason spiritual America and early Christian Russia are as closely related. Europe often regards Russian religiosity with awe, even expecting it to be the salvation of the world. But then it ought to assume the same attitude toward American spirituality. Of this one hears little. Yet the great successes Christian Science can boast of even on European soil are due to a psychological situation which is primarily identical with that of Russia. Christian Science is as far removed from a normal European religion as Russian Christianity is. But it is as representative of pure spirituality. If, accordingly, an intellectual and over-sophisticated European feels that his salvation lies in the direction of primitivity, he will find it in America as well as in Russia, his choice depending on whether his soul is more of an active or a passive quality. From the European point of view, Russian spirituality stands out with unique impressiveness because it is concomitant with savage nature; for the Russian there are no intermediary stages between nature and spirit; that is, he acknowledges no cultural values. But American spirituality really stands out as impressively because it is concomitant with massive materialism, which is no less savage since it is a question here of mechanized as distinguished from raw nature. In the United States, too, there is no intermediary stage between materialism and spirituality; cultural interests there are within small groups, just as there are in Russia, but there is no national realization of the value of culture. At this point I may qualify a statement I made several times concerning the United States—and this will complete at the same time the picture of the analogy and kinship between them and Russia. I said that America was the only basically Christian country because it has no pagan heredity. But it really is the only Christian country among *Western* nations only. Russia, too, is basically Christian; that is, there are practically no pre-Christian elements alive in her subconscious. Whatever is not Christian in the Russian soul, belongs to the Spirit of the Russian Earth—and the same again is true, *mutatis mutandis*, of the American. Now the essential Christianity of both nations is representative of true spirituality in one more sense with which we have not dealt as yet, and which is all-important in the context of this chapter. Spirit as such can never be institutionalized because its essence is significance on the one hand, and free activity on the other, for which reason it can never be objectified in any sense. This, world-bent Western Europe has failed to realize from the outset. But Russia always knew it. Accordingly, Russian Christianity always regarded the idea of authority in spiritual matters as anti-Christian; it always held that a dogma is true in so far as it is believed, and that belief is always a matter of pure freedom; in the same sense, it considered the idea of an *imitatio Christi* as anti-Christian—the image of Christ can never be more than a model and mould for personal realization. Therefore, the Russian Church was never an institution in the Western sense: its idea was analogous to that of a symbol of meditation—the *raison d'être* of all its objects and objectives was to call to life subjective spirituality. Now the official churches of the

United States are institutionalized enough. But the first original and true American religion, namely Christian Science, does not belong to the plane of possible institutions. It stands and falls with purely personal and subjective spirituality. That its organization has at present the outward appearance of a church is a phenomenon akin to what one calls a freak of nature.

HEREWITH we have reached the point from which it seems possible to spiritualize America: it is possible precisely because of the exaggerated and one-sided quality characteristic of whatever spirituality exists. For here there can be no mistaking the merely intellectual for the spiritual, nor of denying the independent reality of the latter. This explains the otherwise paradoxical experience I had when lecturing in the United States, that spiritual (as opposed to intellectual) truth was much more easily and completely apprehended by a greater number of people there, than anywhere in Europe. The whole of modern Europe is today "cursed with the literal mind," as Rabindranath Tagore has put it. It lives on the intermediary plane between pure matter and pure spirit, and the "names and forms" of that plane are so completely differentiated and congealed and hardened that for Frenchmen, for instance—the most intellectualized of Europeans—it seems almost impossible to understand what spiritual, as opposed to intellectual, truth means. But, on the other hand, American spirituality is as impossibly primitive, as a type, as is American materialism. There is no remaining behind the objective Spirit of an Age, if a nation wants to play a progressive part in human evolution. Today, even in the countries of the oldest and profoundest cultures, the traditional setting of spiritual truth no longer carries conviction for those who belong to the vanguard of mankind. The fact is that all historical religions were founded in Ages of Faith, whereas we are now living in an Age of Intellectualism. Hence the necessity to restate the problems of spiritual progress. This, then, would seem to be our next task. But in order to achieve it intelligibly, I must first describe shortly the general trend of spiritual history at this turning-point, which is no doubt the most important turning-point in history since the advent of Christ.

In the era preceding our own, when Western humanity knew that the things of the spirit are as real as the processes of nature—I mean the beginning of the Christian era—the Christians themselves held that the Age of the Son was not to be the last age on earth. There was still to follow the Age of the Holy Ghost. It is true, that this was not the official doctrine of the Christian Church, and only the best philosophers among the Oriental Fathers with their exalted intellectual tradition, ever avowed it frankly. But such was the early tradition. And quite naturally so, for the early Christians held that the return of Christ was imminent, and this would properly put an end to the strictly Christian era. Now what did they mean by their belief in the Age of the Holy Ghost? The answer is to be found in the outpouring of the Holy Spirit at Whitsuntide. The day would come when not the Man-God alone, but every man would serve as the mouthpiece of the Divine. Christ Himself had foretold that others, in the days to come, would do as much as He and more. After the age when only belief in the Saviour could bring salvation, there would come another age, more mature, when every man who had attained a certain level would be able to work out his own salvation.

Let us, from this point of view, examine the period of disintegration through which we are passing at the time I write. All over the world belief in tradition—religious tradition no less than any other—is dying out. And all the traditions—Christian, Hindu, Confucian, and Mohammedan—were founded, so far as the majority was concerned, on faith. Nor does it seem possible to regalvanize the corpses into life. If regalvanization does succeed, it is only in the case of individuals and classes—these, however, because they are crystallized and form exclusive closed systems of their own, do not count in the general progress beyond the present state. But, on the other hand, wherever the *meaning* of religion is being realized by the individual—the meaning of that which in former ages was blindly and naïvely accepted—a rebirth of the old is taking place on a higher plane. The individual, master of himself and freed from the bonds of tradition, then begins to realize for himself those truths, in so far as they are truths, that earlier man simply accepted on authority. Thus, at the very time when the old forms are disintegrating, their essential meaning, that is their vital and immortal substance, is beginning to be understood by the happy few more deeply than at any time since the Golden Age of Christianity, when Greek philosophers worked out its philosophy.

This means nothing less than that the Age of the Holy Ghost is now at hand. Truth can be found in the seemingly most irrational mythical images, if one knows how to interpret them psychologically, that is as projections of inner states. Thus seen, prophecies that come true are the most natural things in the world. The vanguard of early Christianity actually anticipated in its soul that which would not be realized, as a general state, for another two thousand years. Of course, the term "Holy Ghost," like the term "The Age of the Holy Ghost," belongs to an age that used mythical imagery rather than scientific formulas. But the term does not matter. I have used it because it is consecrated by the tradition of centuries; and in any case the underlying meaning of the ancient term was true to fact. But in this case mythical imagery and psychological truth correspond to an even further degree. That same Christian doctrine taught that before the new spirituality which would characterize the Age of the Holy Ghost could assert itself, there would have to be a period of tremendous struggle. Far from believing in uninterrupted progress, these true seers held that before the return of Christ an anti-Christian spirit would temporarily sway the earth. And they believed, moreover, that the Anti-Christ would by no means bear the aspect of a diabolic being: on the contrary, he would be the symbol of all that man longs for—not only in the material sphere, but in the intellectual and moral spheres as well. Now has not this actually come to pass? Is not prosperity—not only in the sense of wealth but also of information—the very hindrance in the way to spiritual progress? There can be no doubt that in the case of the overwhelming majority the original immediate sense for eternal truth and eternal values seems temporarily lost. All over the world the awakening masses are either irreligious or anti-religious to an extent previously unknown in history. In their majority neither Christians nor Hindus, neither Buddhists nor Confucians, really believe what they profess for the sake of expediency. The true religion of the masses of this age is the religion of the machine. Bolshevist Russia has actually turned the machine into a sort of god. There are pictures created by Bolshevist painters —works of art of evident sincerity and, therefore, of convincing power—in which the machine is represented with all the attributes of divinity; there, it takes the place of the ikon in the otherwise unchanged Byzantine Church. Nor can there be any doubt that for millions of workers and peasants such pictures *are* adequate expressions of inmost faith. The one ideal of this unhappy starving race is to be fed and to be better fed. Before the Revolution they looked to God for the fulfilment of this ideal; now they look to the machine.—The official and expressed faith of most Americans is different. But the psychological significance of the American machine- and efficiency-cult is the same. The psychologist who compares the distribution and the quality of belief in the machine with the distribution and quality of belief in the traditional religions must come to the conclusion that today true religious feeling, as a world-phenomenon, belongs to the machine.

We are thus undoubtedly entering on a decidedly anti-religious period. True Christianity, like every true religion, has again become the belief of a minority, as was the case in the days before Constantine. It is even being persecuted again, and this not only in Russia but in Europe, not to mention Mexico; indeed, such persecution may occur wherever radicals or socialists come to power. The masses are growing less religious from year to year. They must continue to do so for a psychological reason in the face of which all argument is futile. As I have shown in *The World in the Making*, in the psychic organism of all men, the centre of gravity has shifted from the emotional to the intellectual. Where the emotional element does not play a prominent part there can be no dominant religious feeling; on the other hand, a realization of the truth of the traditional religious doctrines by means of mental powers calls for a very high level of understanding—and it is characteristic of the chauffeur type (man become primitive again, but commanding all the mechanism of our civilization) that he knows everything and understands next to nothing. Thus, the more education they receive, the more the masses all over the world are bound to become irreligious. This process can be arrested only if the masses reach a new state of inner culture.

Yet, on the other hand, the spiritually-minded minorities are more spiritual today all over the world, and that in a deeper sense than ever before. A remarkable inversion of what obtained in the eighteenth century now prevails. In the eighteenth century the masses believed in everything, the *élite* in nothing; today even those of the *élite* who twenty years ago were at best indifferent to spiritual questions are either grasping the reality of the spirit or groping for it. And from the point of view of the future, these spiritually-minded minorities count more than any minorities have ever counted in the past. Now what is it that characterizes these spiritually-minded minorities, as compared with spiritually-minded groups in former ages? What is their aim? Are they the bearers of a new religion? They are not. The spiritually-minded minorities are necessarily akin to the anti-religious masses, for the vital spirit of an age is always one. In the psychological structure of the masses thought has replaced belief. In correlation with this, in the psychological structure of the minority, understanding plays the ruling part. Religion in the Christian sense stands or falls with the attitude of submission, of Pathos (in the true Greek sense of the word) in the presence of higher powers outside the soul of man. But as soon as the ruling centre is not in this Pathos, but in the Ethos of the individual—the spirit within man as the bearer of all responsibility—there should be no more talk of a religious attitude; this is why the early Christians refused to recognize any religious spirit in the pagans, for in the pagans, too, the Ethos dominated over the Pathos. Nevertheless, the new spirit which is at this moment in the process of birth does not mean a relapse toward paganism: it means just what the early Christians knew to be inevitable—it means the dawn of the Age of the Holy Ghost. It means not an attitude that is religious in the traditional sense, but an attitude that is not less deeply rooted in the spirit and not less permeated by it. This is not a pre-Christian, but a post-Christian state. It does not repudiate Christian truth; it is not even opposed to Christian belief as such: it means a psychological state of a higher level than that which found its world-symbol in Christianity. Compared with the Christian point of view, it is an attitude as new as the Christian attitude was to the pagans. It is a new original attitude toward the Eternal—the same Eternal toward which Christianity points. A new attitude necessitated by the new state of evolution into which the vanguard of humanity has entered.[1]

I trust that my readers now finally understand what I tried to explain in the first chapters, namely in what sense the present age represents something entirely novel.

[1] The trend of thought here sketched has been fully developed in the chapter "The Religious Problem" of *The Recovery of Truth.*

We are entering, first, upon a phase of darkness; this is the period of conception, incubation, and gestation. The soul of mankind must reconstitute itself, and this cannot happen without a period of sickness, disorder, and disease. But the outcome may be such an Age of Light as the world has never seen before. Still, no door leads out of the old house into the new light. Man as a psychological being has changed, and his first task is to realize the direction and significance of the change. Then he must create a new relationship between his surface and his inner depths, between the conscious and the unconscious. Today we are probably at the very climax of the crisis. Two alternatives and no more lie before us—the one leads to life, the other leads to death. There is no third alternative—and herein again we perceive the psychological accuracy of early Christianity. Either there will be an irretrievable decline toward the materialistic and even the Satanic, or else the Spirit will find incarnation in each and all of us, so that personal understanding and personal initiative will lead to the same results in us as belief in Christ led to in the highest representatives of the Christian era.

THIS is the general trend of spiritual history at this turning-point, the most important since the advent of Christ. What can America's particular task be in the new phase of human adventure?—This depends obviously on her present state. For all tasks are given to man in correlation with the life-basis actually defining his existence, and his endowments. We have by now surveyed and scrutinized the Soul of the United States in all its main directions. It should not be difficult, therefore, to give to our picture the finishing touch.

The great task of the next centuries obviously is *to develop a new spiritual life as the basis of the new technical age.* We have seen that what the latter stands for is not a period among others in human history, but a new geological epoch: the epoch of predominating man, as the leading fossil. Accordingly technicization is not a thing to be fought, whatever its temporary disadvantages—it means that man has reached a new biological stage and position; it means, moreover, that this stage represents something intrinsically positive, for only *technicized* man has reached that state of true equilibrium between himself and the world around him which is embodied by every animal as a matter of course. But on the other hand, all, even the highest technical achievements, belong to the animal plane. Hence it was possible to prove that the outstanding ideals of our age are animal ideals. Now man is no animal; ultimately, all we found to say against American conditions came to a single proof of this. In the preceding chapter we found a formula condensing both the situation and its significance in a few words: man as man attains self-realization only in the state of culture, in the state of nature—never; and culture presupposes the sovereign rule of the spiritual as opposed to the animal principle. The last doubts as to the truth should have vanished owing to the observations of this chapter which provided the proof of the reality of spirit as a biological element. Hence it is clear that the technical civilization which is in our day beginning to sway the globe, as the ways of the saurians swayed an earlier epoch—a civilization which has hitherto reached its zenith in the United States, *means not a last word, but a first word.* The real work has yet to be done. If man is rightly adjusted within the cosmic scheme as an animal only, he is ultimately *not* rightly adjusted. He does not live out of, nor up to the intrinsic meaning of his life; and since what I call "meaning" stands for its very well-spring, not unlimited progress, but devitalization and, eventually, the end of the civilized human race would be the inevitable outcome if the process were to continue much longer. This is the all-important point which should be realized. It is not a question of theory or idealism or religious dogma; it is a question of *human nature* in the all-embracing sense of the word. A civilization without spiritual roots consciously realized as real is not only incomplete—it is actually without vital roots. It resembles, at best, the blossom in a vase.

The great task, then, of the centuries to come is to develop a new spiritual life on the foundations of the Technical Age. That it is a question of a new spiritual life is self-evident as a necessary corollary to the knowledge that spirit belongs to the biology of man: if the basis changes, or the psychological structure changes, then obviously spirituality, too, must find an expression different from previous ones, if it is to be directly expressive of the truth. This is why the traditional forms of spirituality are decaying all over the world. In their own time the religions and philosophies in question were true enough expressions of man's position within the universe. But their time was prior to the beginning of the geological epoch of man. Then, man was—apart from his spiritual potentialities—just one animal among others. Of this, Hindu and Chinese wisdom represent a single testimony; they never have considered man as superior to nature. But even Christianity, little though it thought of the latter, never looked upon man as the Lord of the Earth; on the contrary, man in its eyes was essentially weak and powerless. Today man is beyond all doubt essentially powerful. Consequently, the expressions of man's position within the universe which make no allowance for this state of things are no longer true to fact.

Here, then, we must remember what we said about the Age of the Holy Ghost. Spirit being an integral part of the human organism, it must express itself, as an earthly power, in correlation with the whole. If man has grown powerful on all lines and planes, then spirituality too has to manifest itself, as a matter of historical type, in the modality of power and not of submission, of Ethos and not of Pathos. There will, of course, always be scores of individual human beings who will find their right relationship to the spirit in the form of humility; this was so even in the golden days of pagan antiquity; this is what that Father of the Church meant who spoke of the *anima naturaliter christiana*. There may even be entire nations whose spirituality will, in this technical age, thrive all the better under the sign of Pathos, owing to a need for compensation. But on the whole, and in any case historically speaking, the law of compensation does not apply here. Antique spirituality bore the caste-mark of the general spirit of Antiquity; Hindu and Chinese spirituality that of the general life-modes of the respective nations. In the same way, Christian spirituality was in harmony and correlation with the general structure of the Christian soul. The latter assertion may seem subject to doubt because of the bent for world-conquest and world-mastery which, in the eyes of the whole non-Christian world, is the outstanding characteristic of the Christian peoples—much more so, indeed, than of the Mohammedans. But then this bent for worldly power is due foremost to race instincts. And then, what characterizes the Christian is precisely his lack of wholeness, his "torn-ness" between spirit and flesh. Owing to this, the law of compensation could set in, in his case. The state of torn-ness of the Christian made his worldliness all the more aggressive, whereas his spiritual part had, in corresponding proportion, to express itself in the form of long-suffering, submission, and humility. But there can be little doubt that the Christian era was only a stage in the development of the Western nations. Among Europeans, the Russians only can be called truly Christian in the original sense; and the original sense undoubtedly is the only authoritative sense—Jesus and His immediate successors obviously must have known better what they meant than modern interpreters of their teaching do. Within the Roman Catholic system a great deal of pagan antiquity survived. But with the Reformation de-Christianization practically set in, because with it the principle of Ethos as opposed to Pathos began to predominate.

What the Western World is really made for is, indeed, not the Christian Age, but the Age of the Holy Ghost. The Western races being all too worldly-minded by instinct, they badly needed an education inspired by a fundamentally unworldly spirit; and it is very fortunate that it fell to their share. Since the emancipation of the intellect, however, the West has finally started on its own particular road. As yet it is groping, by many ways and byways, for a light visualized somewhere far off, in the heavens, in the past, in the future, but which really shines within the soul of each. But since all images belonging to the collective unconscious are Christian, it is obvious that even a "mutation" should see itself, as a first impression, in the light of a reversion to type. This, then, explains both the fact and the success of Christian Science on American soil. Although it is consciously entangled with all sorts of gross misunderstandings and prejudices and, in particular, honestly believes itself to be representative of the true teaching of Christ, Christian Science actually expresses, in a rudimentary and one-sided and distorted form, the Spirit of the Age of the Holy Ghost. Hence its affirmative attitude. Significance actually creating the facts, it is inevitable that mere affirmation should work wonders with such as are able to believe sincerely in Christian Science doctrine. But the principle underlying Christian Science means something much more important still than what I have shown it to mean in the above: given the psychological condition of the American race, it represents the very point of insertion and at the same time the very instrument for transmuting a state of equilibrium in which all power belongs to externals, into another in which the spiritual principle predominates. For modern Americans being as passive in spirit as they are active along external lines, an extreme affirmation of the active side of the spirit is the only way to make *them* spiritual. Still, Christian Science cannot be more than just a door-opener. For intellectually mature man there can no longer be salvation by blind belief: there can be salvation only through understanding. Understanding is just as affirmative a process as that of Christian Science. One can only understand from within by giving the experience one first has to submit to a positive meaning of one's own. On the other hand, every kind of Ethos is bound up with a corresponding Pathos; just as one has to open one's mind, woman-wise, in order to understand the affirmation of

Christian Science presupposes the Pathos of faith. However, understanding towers at an almost immeasurable height above belief of any kind. The reason is, that according to its very idea, *it can only be an understanding of the truth.* Here, it is not a question of suggestion, that is of a superstructure of imagined reality which can become a reality of a more fundamental kind only accidentally; it is a question of identification and ensuing essential union between the subject and the object.

This, then, leads us to a definition of the new kind of spirituality which alone, in the Age of the Holy Ghost, would be true to both fact and sense. It was the tragedy of all spirituality in the ages preceding the geological Epoch of Man, that it could assert itself only in the form of a flight from this world, for the latter was overpowering on its own plane. But even the Sages of the earliest days knew that the ideal does not lie in a dissociation from nature. Confucius said: "The Tao is not a thing apart or sundered from the world." Buddha, who began his career as an ascetic, did not end as one. Christ never was an ascetic. The fact is that, owing to the law of correlation between meaning and expression which rules every life-phenomenon, the richer the means of the latter are, the more meaning, the more spirit can be built into our world. If, up to now, this has not seemed to be the case, it was not owing to the spirit but because of man's failing to realize its full meaning. Thus, paradoxical though it may seem, only the conquest of matter, as it has been achieved in our days, could, in principle, lead to a sovereign reign of the spirit on our earth. Thus, present-day materialism represents in principle the very threshold to a deeper spirituality. It represents the threshold to a *complete* spirituality, not spirituality as a speciality among others, as it has prevailed so far and as it finds its caricatured expression in Christian Science. Here, then, we are face to face once more with America's chief defect today: its "dry wood" quality, as we put it in the preceding chapter. There can be no complete spirituality which does not resemble in sweetness and softness a ripe fruit. Language is always deeper than all theory. Thus, it is deeply significant that in most languages the word "sense" stands for two things which seem opposed to each other on the surface—signifiance and sensuality. It is equally significant that the Bible calls the possession of a woman "knowing her" —knowing in the sense of understanding—and that the metaphor "odor of sanctity" has been in use in all spiritual epochs. Indeed, spiritualization always means —to use the consecrated words of Jesus Christ—not to destroy, but to fulfil. Now the responsive aspect of fulfilment is understanding, and nothing else. Understanding has nothing whatever to do with explanation. It is not subject to the law of cause and effect. It is a direct union between spirit and spirit, or soul and soul, or flesh and flesh. It is again when starting from the flesh, that we best realize the real significance of that which is no longer of this world. On the plane of the flesh and the lower soul, mere incompatibility already means misunderstanding. Hence its disastrous effects: nothing wounds more deeply than misunderstanding, because misunderstanding means the denial of one's identity. The fact is that there is no other than *vital* understanding; understanding in the abstract, as it is thought to exist by modern science, really amounts to a contradiction in terms. Spirit is no abstraction; it is as concrete an entity as the flesh. This, then, is the reason why *love* has at all times been chosen for the ultimate symbol of spirituality. Not because of its unselfishness—true love never is unselfish, it is selfless, because it radiates like the sun, and for that very reason it can burn and consume; but because there is no more vital understanding than that incarnated in love. Leonardo da Vinci, in a famous sentence, has misstated the case. He said: "The love of anything is the daughter of its recognition. Love is all the more fervent, as knowledge is more certain." It is equally false to say that love leads to understanding—as everybody knows that it blinds more often than not. But something better is true: Love *is* understanding in a specific form. It is the direct communion and at-one-ment of two spirits, the final identity of what cannot really be united on earth. But for that very reason, there can be no spiritual love as opposed to earthly love, once man has reached the plane of complete as opposed to specialized spirituality. Spirit being related to matter, as meaning is to the letters of the alphabet, and representing, moreover, the ultimate creative principle, it can express itself by all earthly means. And it can realize itself only completely by pervading all, down to the last material atom, as the intended meaning of the poet pervades down to the punctuation of his verse. It is this kind of understanding which alone signifies true and complete understanding. Christianity started its career on too low a level of recognition to be able to express its profound insight in a way true to both meaning and fact. Hence its misunderstanding of the emotion of love as a value; hence the very un-love-like direction of development it soon took. Today, however, we *can* understand. Today, on the other hand, owing to the shift that has taken place in man's consciousness, the emphasis *has* to be laid on understanding. But again, this true understanding, which is today "the one thing needful," is anything rather than abstract understanding. It has nothing to do with either information or explanation. It has nothing whatever to do with science, nor even with philosophy in the current sense of the term. In this respect, the case is exactly analogous to that of the beginning of our era, when the "poor in spirit" were rightly thought more capable of attaining to truth than were the wise. *What is needed is a focussing of the vital centre of consciousness in Creative Understanding, so that man may henceforth understand as naturally and necessarily as he breathes.* This is the one adequate way of spiritualization in the geological Epoch of Man. Here lies the only escape from materialism and soul-draining intellectualism. And here lies the only salvation precisely for the United States, the country of all countries where soul and spirit are in mortal peril.

But how and in what way would spiritualization change the world? In the first instance, it would not change externals. It would shift man's centre within him. Growing aware of spiritual reality, modern man would again realize what all great and profound ages have known to be true: that facts are of vital significance and value only as far as they are directly experienced as symbols. That the true way of understanding them is to see through them, to live through them. That the belief in facts as ultimate things is really the grossest of all superstitions. And then, from within, in some mysterious way, a transfiguration would take place. Elijah expected to see the Lord as a great and strong wind; but He came as a still small voice. Even so, there would be no violent transformation. But it would be all the more radical. The animal ideal would die in due course a natural death. Environment, institutions, information, education would automatically lose importance. Material progress would cease to be considered as an end in itself. As a result, an inward spiritual Cosmos, which is man's only true home, would permeate and pervade and hold together the whole of the intricate structure of the modern world. But this would not mean the restoration of ancient spirituality. It would mean a spirituality of a new and deeper kind. It would be an expression of deeper understanding. And it is because of this deeper spiritual understanding alone that then man will be able to hold his own, as a spiritual being, in his new rôle of the Lord of material creation. Such as it is, life seems to have lost all meaning; hence the suicidal tendencies of this age. Only if the roots stretch down farther into the soil—to use the central image of *Creative Understanding*—can the crown of the tree send forth fresh leaves. But, then this giving of meaning, again, depends on man. As a spirit, he is free in his very essence. It is by virtue of freedom only, on this plane, that the same fulfilment can take place, which happens of natural necessity on that of nature. Thus deeper, ever deeper understanding is required. There is no other way, no other hope, no other salvation. A man possesses a woman exactly in proportion to the depth with which he understands her: even so it depends on the spiritual depth he attains to, whether man will ever possess the material world he has conquered externally, or be possessed by it, as is the case today. Nor is this all. The greater the possibilities, the greater the inherent dangers. The present state of America suffices to show what a terrible judgment awaits those who do not understand. Thus, if man cannot definitely transform the age in which he has conquered nature into one rung higher on the ladder that leads him up to the spiritual world, then that which appears to be progress will mean a fall—not the First Fall, this time, but the last. For if the earth be materially conquered, but spirit vanquished at the same time, what other issue or solution can there be? . . . The more all-important and full of significance matter appears to be, the more does spirit alone really count. A final material victory not permeated by spirit would mean death absolute. For, ultimately, man is nothing but spirit.

# ERRATA

Page xiii, line 7: should read "spirit and that of the passively receptive"
Page xix, line 10: omit the word "real"
Page 46, line 18: should read "And now let us survey"
Page 89, line 16: should read "and not its pragmatic value"
Page 96, line 26: a new paragraph should begin after "America's soul"
Page 115, line 6: there should be a semicolon after "significance"
Page 125, line 8: should read "Turkey" instead of "Russia"
Page 147, line 11: should read "or Prussian" instead of "of Prussian"
Page 159, line 2: should read "on the Territory of the United States"
Page 206, line 29: "becoming" should not be in italics
Page 212, line 3: should read "the right way" instead of "the rigid way"
Page 239, line 9: should read "to counteract within the soul"
Page 259, lines 11 and 12: should read "world-wide" instead of "worth-while"
Page 261, lines 31 and 32: should read "and being exclusive as such to a degree almost equal to that of"
Page 263, line 27: should read "highly" instead of "mighty"
Page 264, line 21: should read "will unto power"
Page 286, lines 10 and 11: the phrase "No political system has ever been so" should be part of the quotation
Page 285, line 20: should read "Appenzell" instead of "Appenfell"
Page 291, lines 14 and 15: the sentence should read "Only two hundred years ago a merchant was honest in no other sense than a conqueror is"
Page 308, line 9: should read "but it means"
Page 367, line 28: a new paragraph should begin after "subjective reality"
Page 390, footnote, line 3 of verse: should read "reigner partout"
Page 393, line 13: there should be a period after "years"
Page 409, line 16: should read "positive" instead of "passive"
Page 430, line 18: should read "mere financial power"
Page 436, line 2: should read "nation consciously does not belong"
Page 450, line 16: after the period following "whatsoever" there should be a dash
Page 454, line 29: should read "leads" instead of "lead"

Page 471, line 10: should read "joy" instead of "happiness"
Page 486, line 21: should read "all the less" instead of "all the more"
Page 489, line 25: should read "with moral outlooks"
Page 493, line 15: should read "blessed Queen Victoria"
Page 500, line 13: there should be a period after "follows"
Page 505, line 32 (second from bottom): should read "psychical" instead of "physical"
Page 509, line 20: should read "Romier" instead of "Rémier"
Page 520, line 22: omit the word "the" so that it reads "But then"
Page 524, line 3: should read "at the age of eighteen in a way which"
Page 529, line 8: there should be a period after "stimulation"
Page 531, line 4: should read "in the world" instead of "imaginable"
Page 543, line 13: should read "we reach the final solution"
Page 575, line 29: should read "for being" instead of "since it is a question here of"
Page 606, line 5, second column: should read "Romier" instead of "Rémier"

# Index

Y